Anomie

Ten Years of Independent Arts Publishing

KW-552-051

Anomie Publishing

Introduction

The idea for Anomie Publishing came, like a beautiful cliché, in a bathtub, in the village of Sandal in Wakefield, West Yorkshire, in the winter of 2012. Having worked in arts publishing since graduating from the MA in curating at the Royal College of Art at the turn of the millennium, I had recently been trying to work out how – and indeed if – it would be possible to set up a small independent arts publishing house to be able to produce, publish and distribute books for some of the artists and gallery clients I was working with and/or for. Knowing that most art titles sell in modest quantities, can take a lot of time to make and cost quite a bit of money, I couldn't figure out how it could be financially viable, from scratch, with no office, no staff, no storage facilities and, quite crucially, no budget to speak of. Underneath the coconut-scented bubble bath foam, I figured out a model, both logistical and financial, that I thought might work, and would involve a mixture of public, private and charitable funding and finance along with some revenue from sales. The model could not be loss making from the outset, though I knew its success (or perhaps more likely, failure) would only be determined by giving it a try.

Something I discovered to be important for many successful publishers is sales of backlist titles – often relatively small amounts of money coming in from selling copies of many older titles. If the backlist becomes large and strong enough, it can even generate more income in a year than new titles from that same year, as one grandee of British arts publishing recently confided to my new business partner Francis Atterbury. The question is, can an independent arts publisher without backers survive long enough to develop a backlist, especially in an era of late capitalism in which, after retailers, wholesalers and distributors have taken their share (plus customers conditioned not to expect to have to pay full price for a book if they order it online) publishers might only ever receive twenty-eight per cent of the cover price of a book, and that really doesn't leave a lot to pay writers, designers, editors, reprographers, printers, binders, shippers and so forth. With print runs of regularly just five hundred or a thousand copies, it's easy to do the maths. I'm often amazed there are so many small publishers out there, clearly all sharing Anomie's passion for art, writing and making books. In some ways it's still too early to say if it will work out in the long run for Anomie, but I'm delighted and proud to say Anomie is still here after ten years and in spring 2023 released its fiftieth published title. We thought this was worth celebrating.

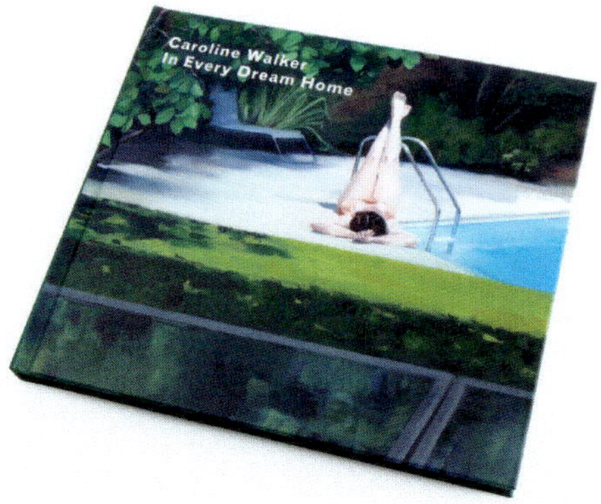

The impetus to get started on this print-based flight of fancy was an exhibition of works by Scottish-born and based painter Caroline Walker, which I was curating at Pitzhanger Manor and Gallery in Ealing, West London, in the late summer of 2013. It was to be Walker's first solo exhibition in a public institution, and we both thought it would be good opportunity to make a first publication to accompany the show. It was very much a test run for Anomie, and so I needed to rapidly figure out how to *become* a publisher and to get books out into the trade. I emailed a large fulfilment centre I knew of in Dorset and asked if they would be open to working with a new independent arts publisher. To my surprise, I got an email back the next day, from the company's director no less, asking if I'd like to meet for a coffee at Waterloo Station early one morning the following week. I enthusiastically put together a list of possible ideas for books in the hope of showing that I had some kind of business plan, or at least more than just the one book in development. The gentleman was very kind, listening to my journey through the world of arts publishing thus far, and my plans to establish a new publishing house. He then gently explained that while his company could offer fulfilment, i.e. the warehousing of my books and the physical management of orders to and from wholesalers and retailers, there would be little point if I didn't have any sales staff trying to solicit orders and manage the sales. Understanding that I was a one-man band, he offered to put me in touch with one of the numerous distributors that were his clients – one that he knew was looking to increase its arts publisher lists.

It was an Anglo-American company called Casemate, and I was delighted to get a swift response from CEO and founder David Farnsworth suggesting I speak with his then VP and Head of Development Simone Drinkwater. I met with Simone, who turned out to be a ray of sunshine; she was incredibly positive about my starting up as a publisher and, again, having patiently sat through my PowerPoint presentation, signed Anomie up on the spot. She then introduced me to the then Head Sales Rep (now Director of Sales) Jean-Marc Evans, who also turned out to be incredibly supportive. It soon became apparent that he had not only a vast knowledge and experience of selling art books, but a genuine passion for both art and books! Along with other key members of the team, Casemate really took me under their wing, helping me to get Anomie Publishing set up both in the UK and USA and guiding me through the various practical and administrative steps needed to run a distributed trade publishing house.

Apart from being an opportunity to thank those at Casemate who have supported Anomie over the past ten years, this is also a platform for me to say how happy I was that they took my proposal seriously. So often as a freelancer in the arts you propose things – exhibitions, books, articles etc – and people say no (though many of them often seem to do similar things later...). With just my planned book for Caroline Walker on the table, David, Simone and Jean-Marc all said, 'Yes, if you want to set up a publishing house, go for it.' I appreciate the opportunity they gave me and the time they put in to helping me get started on that journey. Just a few months later, we launched Caroline's exhibition and accompanying publication *In Every Dream Home* at Pitzhanger Manor, and the title entered the international book trade just a couple of weeks later. It's now long out of print, is occasionally touted for silly money on the Internet, and I still receive enquiries about it almost every month.

While living in Yorkshire, I had been introduced by my old friend and colleague, the curator, writer and art consultant Jane Neal, to a graphic designer by the name of Joe Gilmore who she knew was living not too far away from me in a suburb of Leeds. He ran an understated though decidedly cool design agency called Qubik and was also a senior lecturer in graphic design at the university there. We met up in a coffee house, showed each other books and catalogues we had worked on, and I told him of my plans to set up an independent

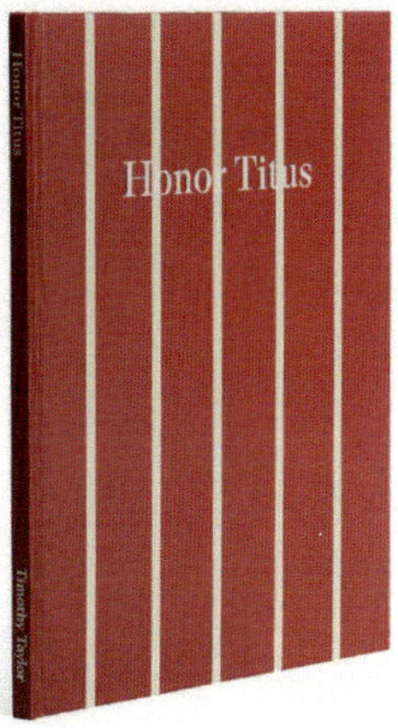

arts publishing house. He kindly agreed to work on Anomie's branding and website, and the design of the first publication. Of course, I had no idea at that moment that it was to be the start of a great ongoing collaboration and friendship. Indeed, my wife Coco and I were delighted to get to know Joe, his wife Rhiannon and daughter Edith, and to continue to be in touch long after we returned from Yorkshire to London. Joe, now based in York, has designed many of Anomie's titles over the past decade, most recently Honor Titus's debut publication for Timothy Taylor Gallery New York this past spring, and both Tom de Freston's *I Saw This* project and Jonathan Wateridge's *Uncertain Swimmer*, launched in autumn this year. So this is my moment to thank Joe for all of the time, work, care, expertise and beautiful design he has brought to Anomie and its identity. He's kind of in the DNA of Anomie, and I hope will remain so for many years to come.

Another person who is inextricably interwoven with Anomie, and has been since day one, is the sub-editor and proofreader William Lambie. We have a much longer history than Anomie, having met at secondary school in Birmingham sometime around 1989. We were both on a school trip to Italy to study classical antiquity, organised by William's father, Phil, who was a classics teacher at our school and taught me Latin. We realised we had a lot in common, including a shared sense of humour and a passion for learning, literature, history, music and art. And, of course, aged twelve, we both loved J.R.R. Tolkien, Games Workshop and heavy metal! William probably still does. We have worked on many books together for numerous clients over the years, and his name appears in the colophon of a high proportion of Anomie's titles. He always goes the extra mile, often working late into the night to help us meet a deadline

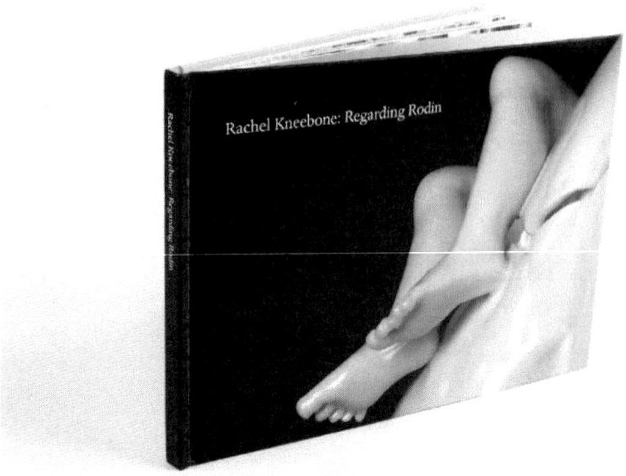

in the late stages of a project. He is a self-professed pedant, and that is precisely what is needed of a good proofreader. He is also a thoroughly decent fellow, and can often be found carrying bags of ice and opening bottles of Prosecco at Anomie's book launches – we tend to be an all-hands-on-deck kind of a publishing house! Again, this is an opportunity to publicly convey my gratitude to William for all that he has done for Anomie.

Anomie's network, or rather community, of arts and publishing professionals is one of the things of which I'm most proud – a lovely group of designers, writers, printers and so on with whom Anomie regularly works. Anomie likes to think it is open to newcomers to its network, often working on projects with people who have found their way to Anomie's virtual door from various directions or recommendations. Some of the remarkable designers we have worked with in various capacities include Modern Activity, A Practice for Everyday Life, Textbook Studio, Jo Deans/Identity, Melanie Mues/Mues Design, work-form, Peter B. Willberg, and Hyperkit. One of our regular design and production partners is the legendary duo Herman Lelie and Stefania Bonelli, to whom I owe a lot: I met them as a young editor and publishing manager while we were both working for the Serpentine Galleries around seventeen years ago, and they effectively trained me in book production – the nuts and bolts of the process of developing and producing a book, from preparing specifications and sourcing quotes to colour proofing and press passing. Already having several years of intense editing experience under my belt, this was the other side I needed to make the transition from magazines into catalogues, monographs and anthologies. In a most cosmopolitan fashion, Herman and Stefania work out of studios in both West London and central Italy, and are famous for their warm hospitality to anyone who ends up visiting. In fact, if you leave their studio without having had a bowl of pasta and a glass of wine, you've been very unlucky.

Titles on which we have worked together range from Rachel Kneebone's *Regarding Rodin*, which documented her 2012 exhibition at Brooklyn Museum and was released to coincide with her 2014 exhibition 399 Days at White Cube Bermondsey, to Gideon Rubin's *Look Again*, which was on press at the time of writing this introduction ahead of its launch at his exhibition *Living Memory* at All Saints Chapel in Fitzrovia during Frieze Week 2023, in which a new series of his paintings will be on display alongside sculptures by Louise Bourgeois and a soundscape by Nicolas Godin. Their support in the early days of Anomie was crucial for getting the ball rolling, which encouraged others to sign up with their book projects.

Indeed, I am grateful to all those who took the plunge in the early days, before Anomie had much to show, who put their trust in us to make or publish and distribute their titles, among them Meekyoung Shin, Robert Fry and Kamrooz Aram. Paul Simonon, the artist and former bassist with The Clash, opted to publish his distinctive book of paintings, *Wot No Bike*, with Anomie, which we launched at Waterstones in Piccadilly. When I arrived for the event, there was already a queue of people outside that snaked around inside – fans waiting to get their copies signed. We launched the book alongside Paul's exhibition of the featured body of works at the ICA in early 2015, and you could hardly move for all the celebrities in there, from Kate Moss to Bob Geldolf and Damon Albarn. We headed on to a rickety old pub on the edge of Soho for the after party, which was a memorable night. Needless to say, Paul's book sold out in just a few months.

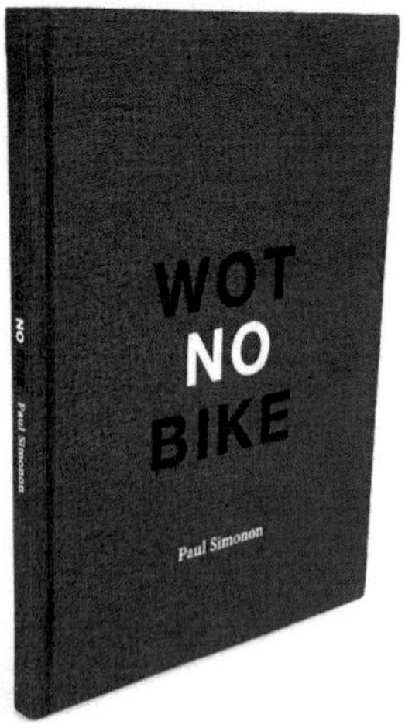

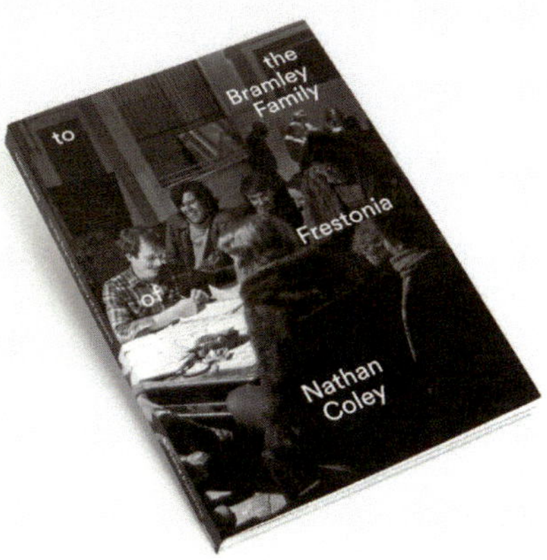

Later that year – introduced via the book's designer, Peter Willberg, another legendary designer whom I had first met while I was a student at the Royal College of Art – I received a call from Lord Cholmondeley (which, when he rang, I discovered is pronounced 'Chumley'), asking if Anomie would be interested in partnering to publish a book about James Turrell's forthcoming exhibition and new site-specific work *LightScape* at Houghton Hall. I didn't need much persuading, and again it was a great boost to Anomie to have such a high-profile international artist on its lists in the early years. Today, some eight years later, we continue to sell copies of the book most months, with stock now almost depleted.

There are often nice or serendipitous connections spanning decades that spring up and result in Anomie publishing a title. When I was living back in my home city of Birmingham as a recent graduate in the early 2000s, I spent a lot of time at Ikon Gallery, and one of my favourite projects from that period was by Scottish artist Nathan Coley, as part of the exhibition *As It Is*, called *The Lamp of Sacrifice*, in which, for the duration of the exhibition, he worked in the gallery making beautiful cardboard models of the 161 places of worship listed in the Birmingham Yellow Pages. As an intercultural theologian who had published a book specifically about interfaith encounter and dialogue in Birmingham, I thought my mother Lynne would be interested in the project, so invited her to see the exhibition with me. Nathan was there working away on his models, now starting to fill the gallery space, and he and my mother began a conversation which was to be continued one evening over a balti (as so many cultural exchanges in Birmingham are). Nigel Prince was there too, and the conversation resulted in my mother giving a presentation to members of Selly Oak Methodist Church about Coley's practice. She would follow his career and projects with great interest for many years to come. I was delighted, therefore, when Nathan got in touch to ask if Anomie would be open to publishing a book he was working on, entitled *to the Bramley Family of Frestonia*, about a major public sculptural commission he was creating for a new residential complex in West London on the site where the somewhat radical commune The People's Republic of Frestonia had developed in the 1970s when houses that had been due for demolition were left unoccupied for several years. Through Coley's project, I thoroughly enjoyed discovering all about this commune, enriched by the photography of Tony Sleep who lived and documented life within it. Some seven years later, I had a magical frisson when I was invited by the charming Rollo Campbell and Matt Incledon of Frestonian Gallery to collaborate with them to produce a publication for the amazing Anna Freeman Bentley's exhibition *make believe*. Frestonian Gallery is located in what was once the town hall of the People's Republic of Frestonia, and I enjoy regularly attending exhibitions there.

Anomie's projects often involve working in partnership with charities, trusts and public interest companies, and one of the highest profile to date has been with the Daphne Oram Trust to make a new edition of the electronic music pioneer Daphne Oram's 1972 book *An Individual Note of Music, Sound and Electronics*. Again born from a relationship spanning decades, and, in fact, also originating via a chance encounter at Ikon Gallery early in the new millennium, in 2015 I was approached by Richard Whitelaw, then Director of Programmes at the Sonic Arts Network (now Sound and Music), in his capacity as one of the board members of the Daphne Oram Trust. He was looking for some advice about publishing the new edition, and when I heard about their plans, I asked if I could make a pitch to produce and publish it with the trust. A couple of weeks later I

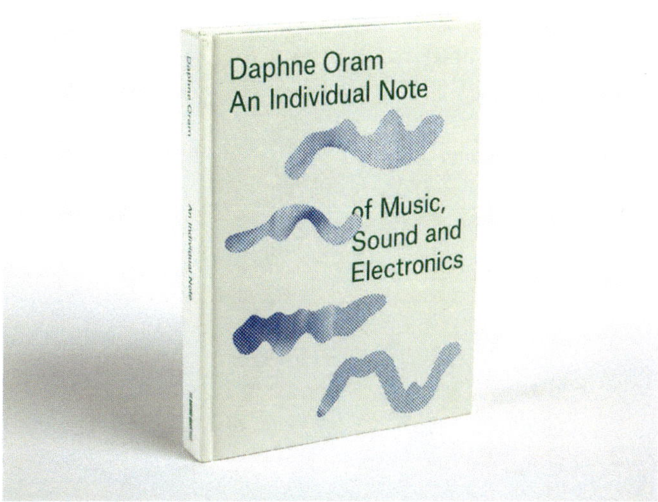

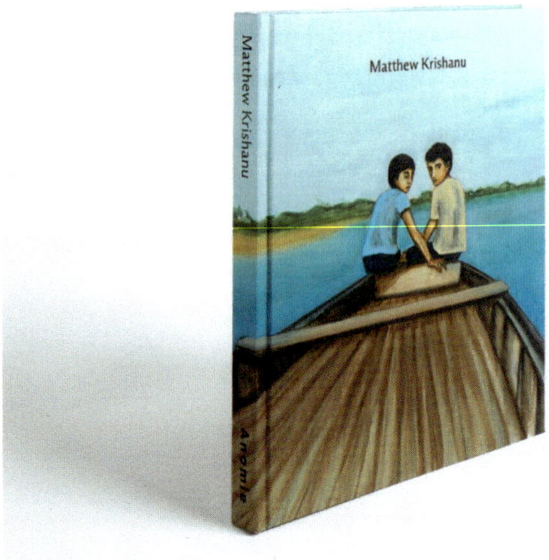

attended a board meeting and was able to do just that, and around a year later, in November 2016, we released a beautiful hardback book designed by Joe Gilmore and featuring a newly commissioned introduction by composer, musician and roboticist Sarah Angliss. With the help of a Kickstarter campaign, we also raised some not inconsiderable cash to support the project and to be able to make it such a high-spec book. It is now in its third reprint and has been selling in bookshops all around the world. Naturally, having titles such as this that can sell several thousand copies is vital for the success of a small publishing house such as Anomie.

Contemporary painting, especially contemporary British painting, has become a particular specialism for Anomie, as I had always hoped it would. With new and forthcoming titles on Anomie's lists this autumn for Gideon Rubin, Andrew Cranston, Jonathan Wateridge and Nick Goss, you'd be forgiven for thinking contemporary British painting has been taking front and centre stage at Anomie. As well as publishing titles for internationally recognised figures with careers spanning several decades, such as Richard Patterson and Ian McKeever, Anomie has become known for working with artists at early and pivotal moments in their careers, including the aforementioned Caroline Walker and Anna Freeman Bentley, Louise Giovanelli, Jadé Fadojutimi and, earlier this year, first major monographs for Matthew Krishanu and Alastair Gordon, and a first solo publication on Kathryn Maple to accompany her solo exhibition at the Walker Art Gallery, Liverpool – part of her reward for winning the John Moores Painting Prize. In 2017 there was so much exciting new contemporary British painting around that I thought it would be a good moment to launch a new series of anthologies focusing on the medium, and a year later Anomie published the first *Anomie Review of Contemporary British Painting*, documenting solo exhibitions in public, commercial and independent gallery spaces in Britain and abroad by forty artists born or living in Britain. It proved popular and so in September 2021 we published the second volume, increasing the scope to sixty artists. A third is in the pipeline for spring 2024, and promises to be the most ambitious yet.

But it's certainly not all about painting. Anomie is also passionate about other mediums, demonstrated by our commitment to contemporary sculpture, with recent titles on Bill Woodrow and Richard Deacon, Mariele Neudecker, David Batchelor and Manolo Valdés, all of whom are doing their bit for three dimensions. Valdés' imposing and impressive publication, designed by Peter Willberg, was the most recent title from Anomie to be shortlisted for the British Book Design and Production Awards, in 2022. Anomie has also developed a close relationship with British sculptor Nick Hornby, having not only produced a publication to accompany his major solo exhibition curated by Alfredo Cramerotti at MOSTYN, Wales in 2020–21 (to this day I have no idea how Nick and Alfredo managed to make this happen during a pandemic), but also the first major trade monograph on Hornby's remarkable career and oeuvre to date, featuring contributions from Dr Helen Pheby, Associate Director, Programme, at Yorkshire Sculpture Park, Dr Hannah Higham, then Senior Curator of Collections and Research at the Henry Moore Foundation (now Senior Curator of Collections at the Royal Academy), and Luke Syson, Director of the Fitzwilliam Museum, Cambridge. The publication was launched at Hatchards Piccadilly in winter 2021, in the middle of a public transport strike. (Again, I have no idea how he managed to fill the venue when nobody could get around town.) Since then Nick has produced a number of major permanent public sculptures across London, so I'm expecting to get a call about making a third book any day now...

One of the greatest pleasures of making books about art is working with artists, many of whom Anomie develops ongoing relationships with. In October 2020, for instance, Caroline Walker published her third title with Anomie, *Janet*, produced by her representatives in Scotland, Ingleby Gallery. It has been a delight to see Caroline's career blossom over the past decade, and to have been part of her remarkable journey. The same is true for Anna Freeman Bentley, who has also published three titles to date with Anomie. Sometimes an artist has been part of Anomie's community for a long time before an opportunity presents itself for us

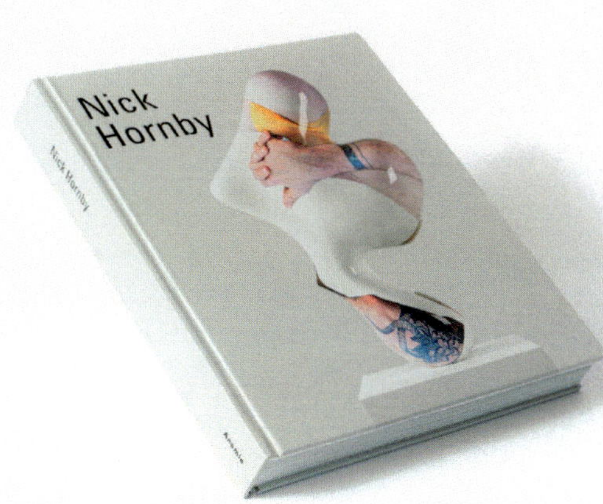

to work together on a publication – this is certainly true for Justin Mortimer (whose artwork graces the cover of this special anniversary catalogue); we met back in 2008 but it was not until 2018 that we would make his *Hoax* publication of extraordinary paintings of dead and dying flowers, beautifully designed by Matt Appleton from Modern Activity. It is a similar story with Matthew Krishanu, whom I met for the first time at Caroline Walker's exhibition at Pitzhanger Manor back in 2013. How lovely it is to think that ten years later we would be working together on his first major trade monograph, supported by his gallery representatives around the world.

Anomie regularly works in dialogue with public and private galleries to develop and/or publish titles. Among the public institutions connected to Anomie's programmes to date are the Grundy Art Gallery, Blackpool; MOSTYN, Llandudno; Ikon, Birmingham; the Walker Art Gallery, Liverpool, and Compton Verney, Warwickshire. Some of the private galleries with which Anomie has collaborated include Timothy Taylor, Niru Ratnam, Houldsworth Gallery, Karsten Greve Gallery, Ingleby, GRIMM and Tiwani Contemporary. Add to this the other numerous and diverse organisations, charities and foundations and it becomes clear how much a part of the fabric of the national and international art world Anomie has become over the past decade. Needless to say, I am very grateful for the faith these partners have put in Anomie and for the support they have given to Anomie's programmes, and I'm proud that we have produced so many memorable and significant publications together. When Anomie started up I could not have imagined that we would be working with so many incredible artists, galleries and institutions working at the forefront of contemporary art today.

The same is true for the impressive roll-call of writers who have provided texts that have been commissioned or published by Anomie, from Ali Smith to Ekow Eshun, Richard Dyer to Habda Rashid. There are too many to mention, but some who have written on more than one occasion include Jennifer Higgie, Hettie Judah, Marco Livingstone, Jane Neal, Michele Robecchi and Jon Wood. From early-career writers such as the brilliant Dr Matthew Holman to stalwarts of art criticism from the past half-century such as Edward Lucie-Smith, the ever-growing list of remarkable contributors and collaborators is also something of which Anomie can rightly be proud.

As this introduction has also doubled up as an extensive list of thanks, I'd like to take the opportunity to thank my family for their support for Anomie from the outset. My wonderful wife Coco has lived every step of the Anomie journey with me, sometimes through challenging periods and often through long phases of late nights and weekends with me glued to my computer screen. My father Richard has helped a huge amount with behind-the-scenes administration and accounting, going far beyond the call of duty. There are so many people to thank: sales reps, book handlers, printers, reprographers, photographers – not to mention that most legendary of men, Richard Bucht, who manages the arts department at Hatchards Piccadilly and has supported so many of Anomie's book launches over the years. I am grateful to Anomie's recently acquired partners, Hurtwood – a publishing house I have known and admired for over fifteen years – who are helping to take Anomie forward into its next chapters. And, of course, a huge thank you to all of Anomie's customers and to everyone who has read any of Anomie's titles. It is a real source of happiness when I find one of Anomie's titles on a bookshelf when entering someone's studio, home, office or a library or bookshop. And it is deeply satisfying to feel that Anomie has been playing an active role in supporting the creative industries, and the lives and careers of so many amazing creative people.

Matt Price
August 2023

Jonathan Wateridge
Uncertain Swimmer

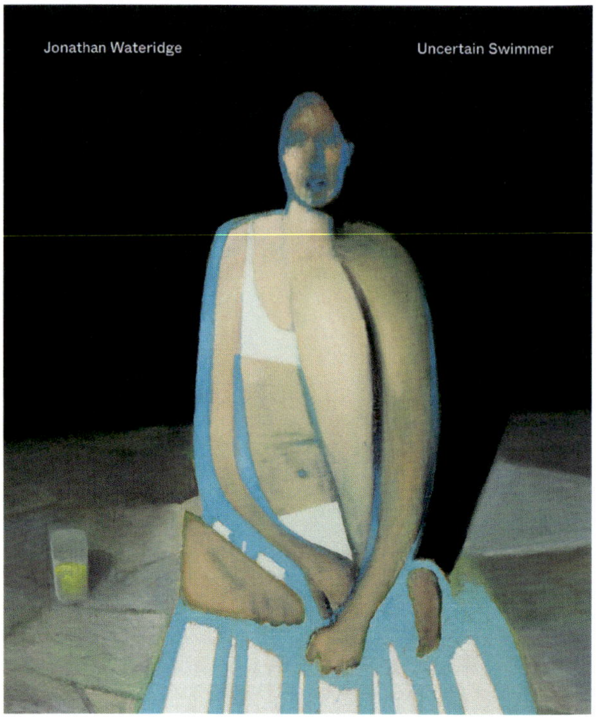

Contributors:
Marco Livingstone
Caroline Walker

208pp
Hardback
290 × 245 mm
c. 150 images
ISBN: 978-1-910221-51-8
RRP: £50
UK Release: 12 October 2023
Edited by Matt Price
Designed by Joe Gilmore
Print management by Hurtwood
Published by Anomie Publishing, London

Uncertain Swimmer is the second monograph on the work of British artist Jonathan Wateridge (b. 1972, Lusaka, Zambia), presenting eighty paintings and works on paper made between 2019 and 2022. Following on from the bodies of work *Enclave* and *Expatria* (2016–18), *Uncertain Swimmer* develops the artist's interest in modes of representation and the legacies of twentieth-century modernist painting through a visual and social exploration of the motif of the pool, depicting swimmers and sunbathers, often by night. Far from being an escapist environment of aspiration and privilege, Wateridge imbues the pool with a disquieting atmosphere, creating a cumulative feeling of unease and ennui among those present, now seemingly unsure of their world.

The publication charts a marked evolution in the artist's style from the realism of his earlier paintings with multi-figure compositions to more solitary, gestural and expressive works. His masterly application of paint takes new forms in the beautiful, curious and often haunting paintings and works on paper showcased here. Art historian and curator Marco Livingstone's essay considers the change from Wateridge's naturalistic paintings to the flattened, reduced shapes, forms and lines of the modernism- and abstraction-infused pieces he is making today. Francis Bacon, Edvard Munch and Paul Cézanne are among numerous art historical influences cited by Livingstone, who ruminates on the identity of the people in Wateridge's portraits and the mercurial spaces they occupy, examining how Wateridge's current critical preoccupations have transitioned from the autobiographical to more formal concerns.

In the featured conversation between Wateridge and fellow painter Caroline Walker, the two artists discuss their overlapping experiences studying painting at Glasgow, as well as Wateridge's fourteen-year break from painting until 2005. He eventually returned to the medium when he realised it excited him more than anything else. Wateridge elaborates on his fascinating painting process, staging shoots in studios with hired actors and using elements from the photographs in the paintings, often over a period of years. For Wateridge, a painting works when it stops failing, and he embraces unforeseen conclusions.

Wateridge has recently exhibited with the Hayward Gallery, London; TJ Boulting, London; Galerie Haas, Zurich; Pace Gallery and HENI, London. His art is in the collections of institutions worldwide, including Aïshti Foundation, Lebanon; Pinault Foundation, Venice; the Saatchi Collection, London; the Rennie Collection, Vancouver; and Simmons & Simmons, London. He has been featured in publications such as *The Sunday Times*, *The Independent*, *Fad Magazine*, *Artforum* and *Artnet*.

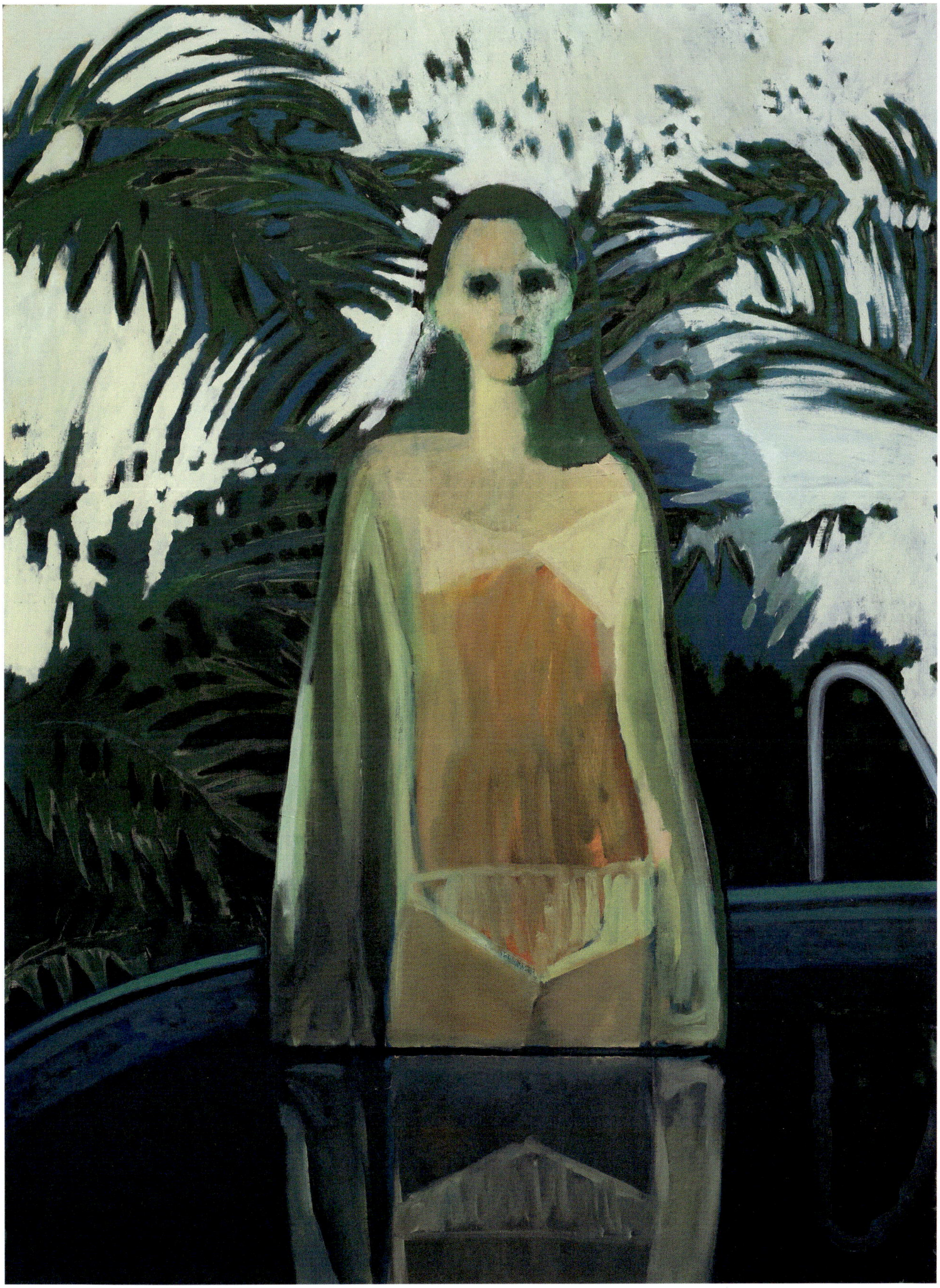

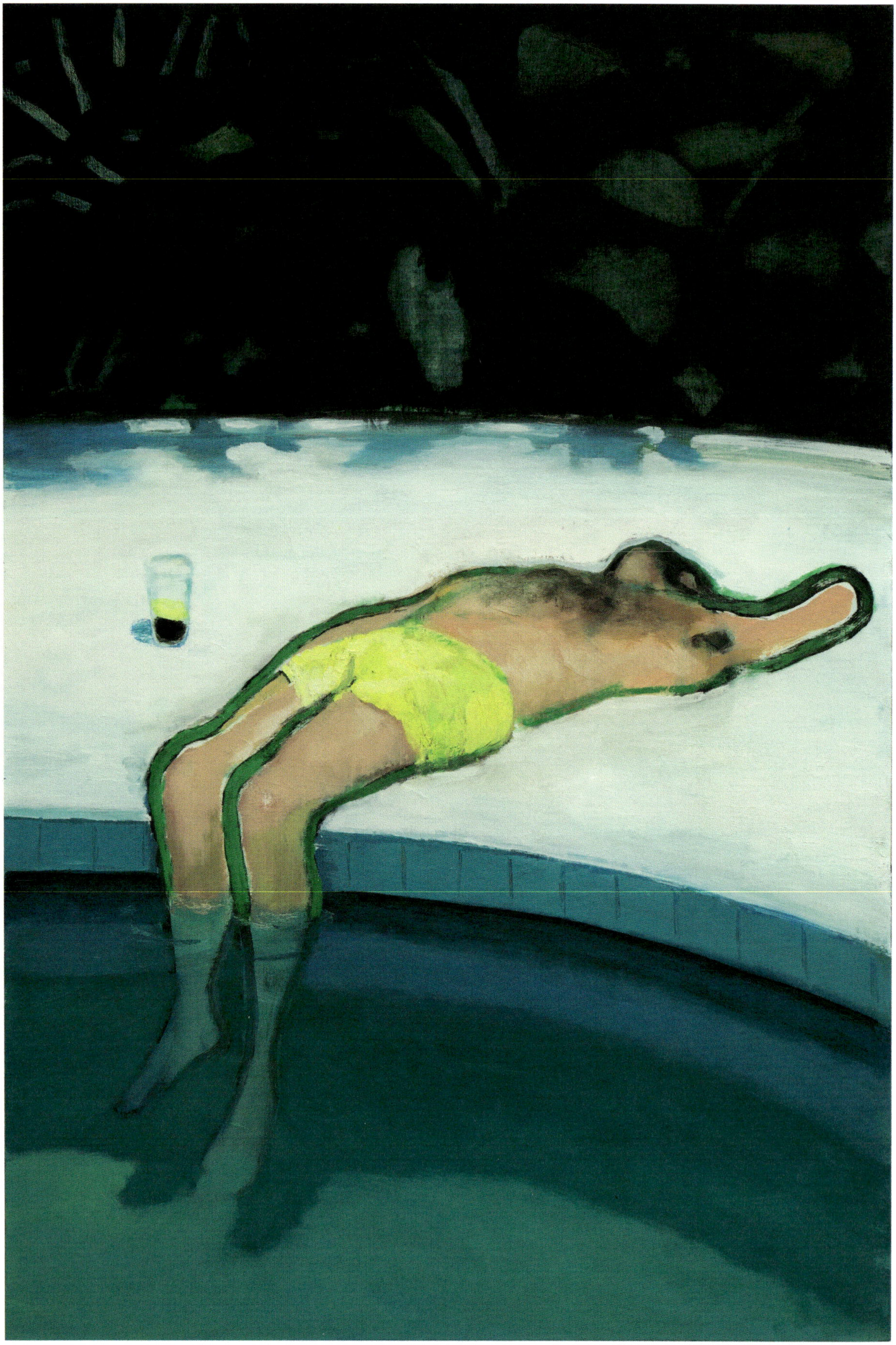

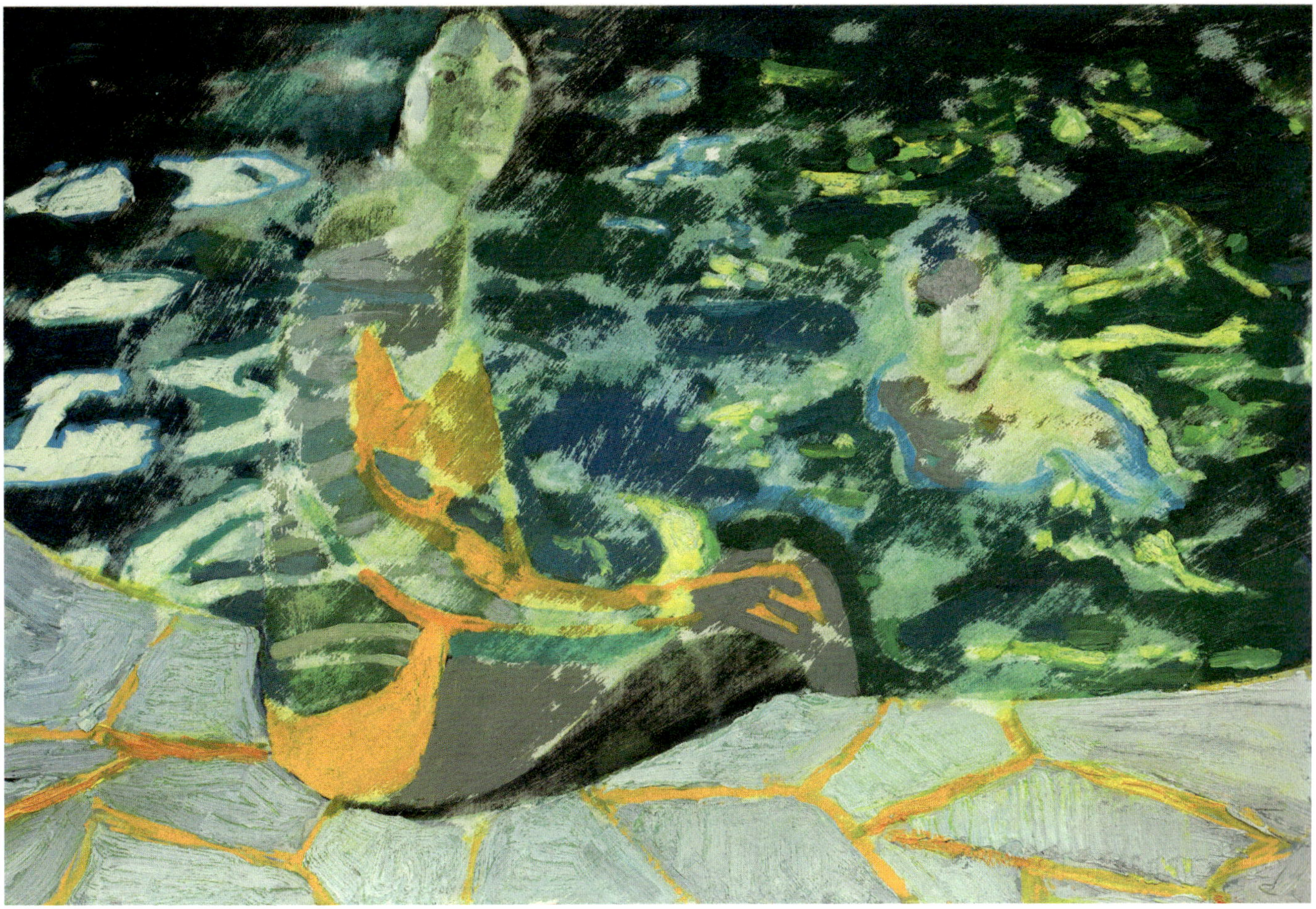

p. 11
Jonathan Wateridge
Garden Pool, 2022
Oil on linen
200 × 150 cm

Jonathan Wateridge
(His) Long Day in the Sun, 2020
Oil on linen
110 x 75 cm

Jonathan Wateridge
Couple, 2021
Oil on paper
24 × 36.5 cm

All © Jonathan Wateridge
Photos: Jonathan Wateridge Studio

Andrew Cranston
Never a Joiner

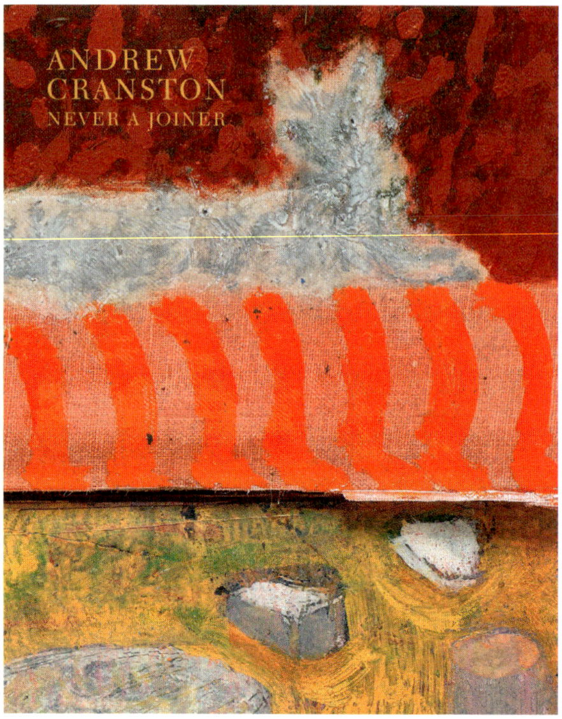

Contributors:
Andrew Cranston

184pp
Hardback
240 × 190 mm
c. 87 images
ISBN: 978-1-910221-53-2
RRP: £35
UK Release: 6 October 2023
Edited by Richard and Florence Ingleby
Designed by Jo Deans, Identity
Printed by Albe De Coker, Antwerp
Co-published by Ingleby, Edinburgh, and
Anomie Publishing, London

Andrew Cranston is a painter-storyteller whose way of working is enhanced by his often painting on the linen-bound covers of old books. His stories coalesce in the process of making – the paintings emerging through the manipulation of his materials: layering, lacquering, bleaching, collaging and constantly reworking his way into images that seem to shift backwards and forwards in time. They are resolutely contemporary in spirit yet connected by a strong thread to painters of the past, especially perhaps to the intimism of Vuillard and Bonnard, or to Matisse or Munch. These are narrative paintings, drawn from the artist's memory and observations of life, liberally sprinkled with references to cinema, literature and art history.

This publication presents a selection of the book cover paintings for which Cranston has become well known in recent years. The cover image is a detail of *Cat and cheeseboard* (2018) in which a cat sits on the upholstered arm of a sofa surveying what the artist describes as 'a selection of bries and camemberts, as mousetraps'. Other animals pop up from time to time – a horse, some fish, a leopard; the skeleton of an elk. There are still lifes with fruit, flowers and pottery, and landscapes, from the bleak to the fantastical. There are peopled and unpeopled interiors, portraits of family members and celebrities (occasionally curious hybrids thereof), and childhood memories from classical music-filled assemblies to Granny's flat. And there are quite a few watering cans too.

Each featured painting is accompanied by a text based on notes made by the artist before, during or after making a work. Mostly private thoughts, memories and anecdotes, these fragments jotted down on scraps of paper or tapped into his mobile phone were never intended to be published, but the resulting texts offer personal observations and reflections that Cranston considers 'something like album sleeve notes where a musical artist might give some background to each song'. The texts are at times amusing, at others melancholic and moving, offering illuminating insights into the mind and life of the artist and the subjects, references and influences that feed into his painting practice.

Andrew Cranston – Never a Joiner was published to coincide with an exhibition of the same name at Ingleby, Edinburgh, and launched as part of the Edinburgh Art Festival 2023.

Cranston was born in Hawick in the Scottish Borders in 1969 and currently lives and works in Glasgow. He studied at Gray's School of Art in Aberdeen and at the Royal College of Art in London. Cranston has exhibited widely in the UK and USA and his work is housed in many museums and institutions across the world.

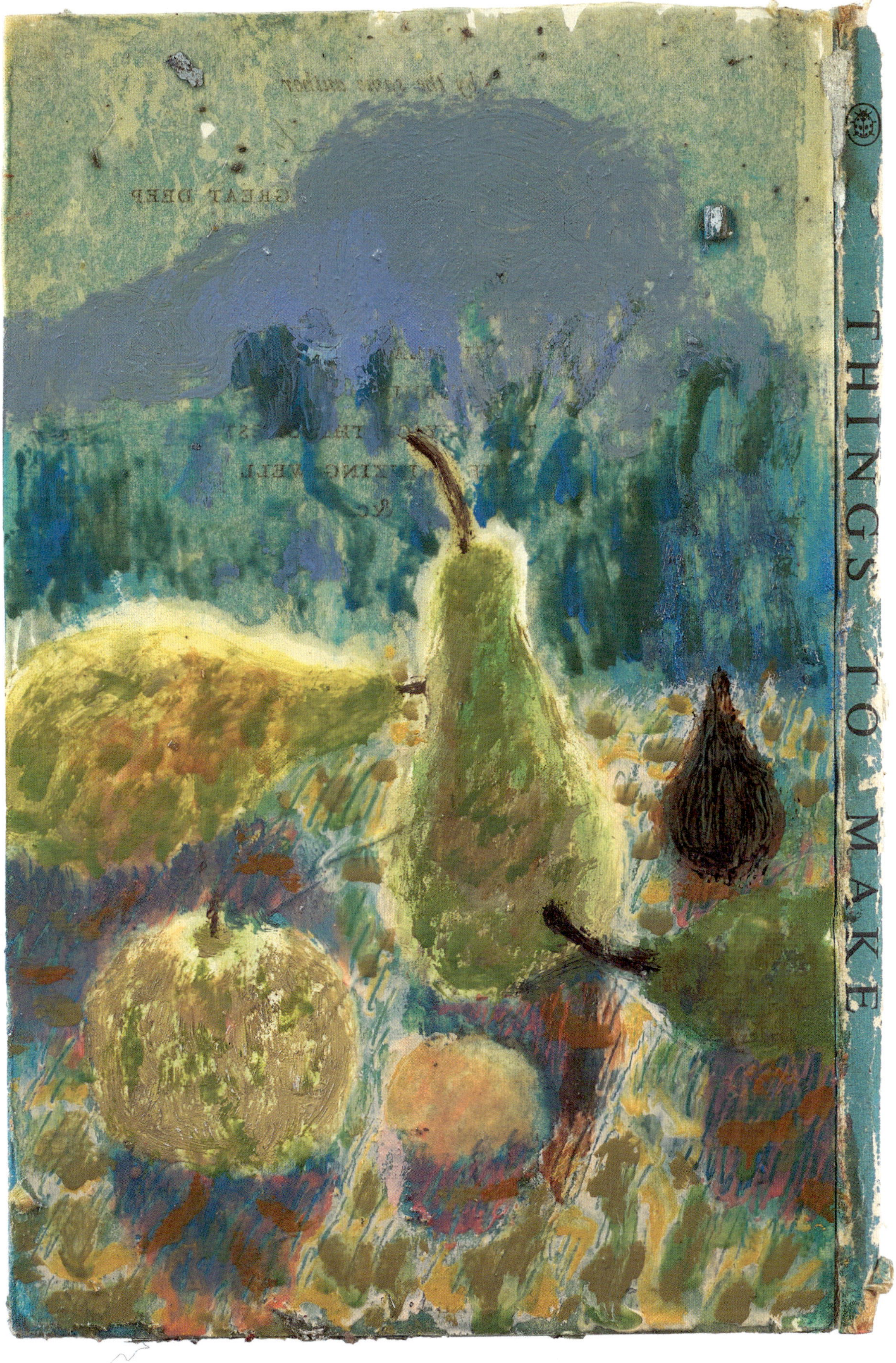
THINGS TO MAKE

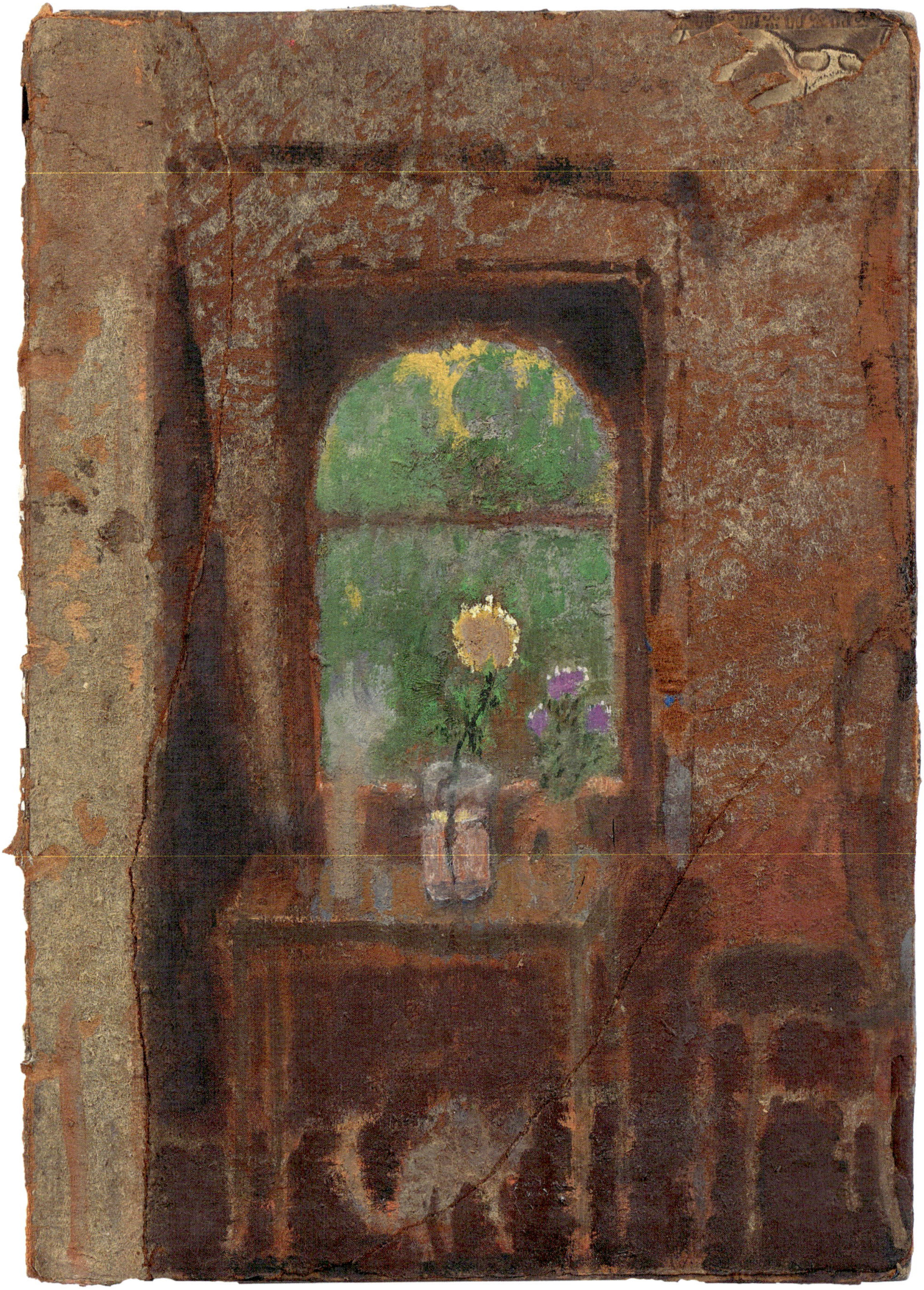

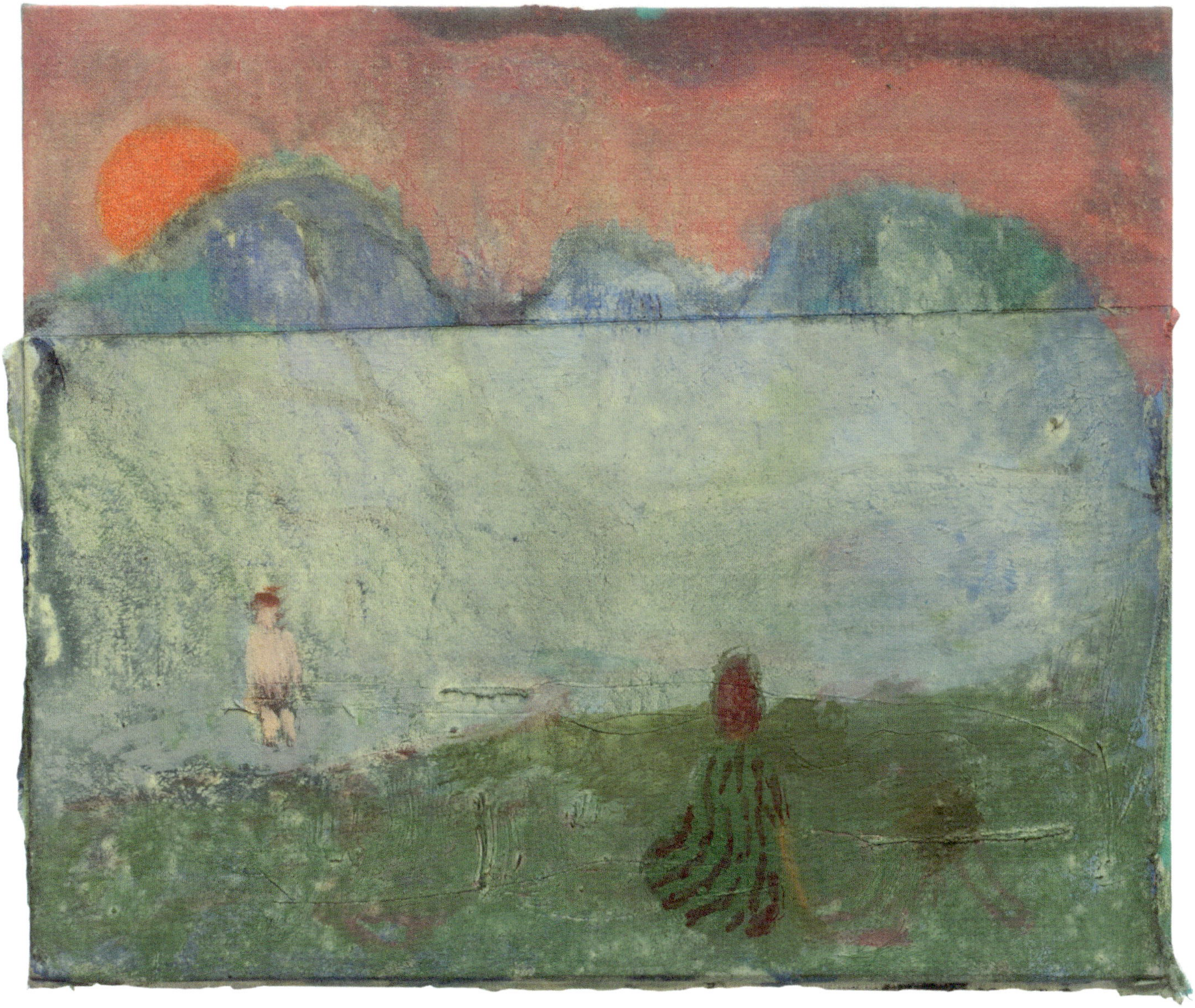

p. 15
Andrew Cranston
(in Scotland) how means why, 2022
Oil and varnish on hardback book
17.8 × 10 cm

Andrew Cranston
All the world is green, 2023
Oil on hardback book cover
34.5 × 24.9 cm

Andrew Cranston
Scene from a marriage, 2021
Oil on hardback book cover
22 × 26 cm

All courtesy of the artist and Ingleby, Edinburgh
Photos: John McKenzie

Tom de Freston
I Saw This

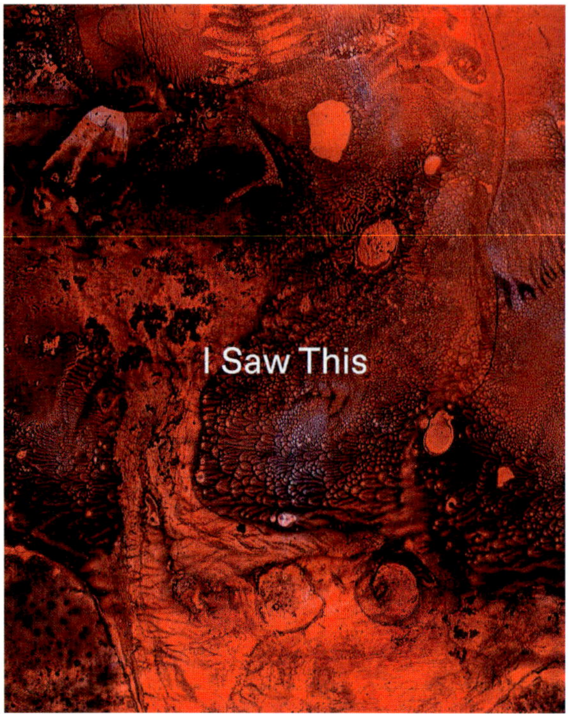

A collaboration with Ali Souleman and
Mark Jones

Contributors:
Habda Rashid
Yasmina Floyer
Matt Price
Mark Jones
Tom de Freston
Ali Souleman

192pp
Softback
265 × 215 mm
c. 200 images
ISBN: 978-1-910221-50-1
RRP: £30
UK Release: 5 October 2023
Edited by Matt Price
Designed by Joe Gilmore
Produced by Hurtwood
Published by Anomie Publishing, London

Tom de Freston (b. 1983) is a British artist and writer, living and working in Oxford. He graduated from Cambridge University in 2007. De Freston's multimedia art tackles themes of trauma, humanity and intimacy across paintings, films and performance. A prolific author, Granta published de Freston's debut non-fiction book, *Wreck*, in 2022 and his second will be released in 2024. De Freston was chosen to illustrate the twenty-fifth-anniversary edition of David Almond's *Skellig*, published in 2023.

I Saw This was born out of a collaboration between de Freston, filmmaker Mark Jones and Dr Ali Souleman after de Freston was introduced to the academic in 2017. The paintings and mixed-media works that resulted from the project are an exploration into Souleman's experiences of terrorism, displacement and war in Syria, and ruminate on how art can attempt to represent suffering and terror. In 1996, a bomb explosion in Damascus on New Year's Eve nearly killed Souleman and left him blind. A sensitive and highly charged topic, Souleman explained to de Freston the importance of engaging with what is happening in Syria. Disembodied mouths, hands and feet appear frequently in the works. Circles recur as a motif, which bear an uncomfortable resemblance to eyes and eye sockets. In the *Mirror* paintings which stand upright in black boxes, de Freston embeds ash, screws, thick glue, dirt and bits of wood into the canvas. They are corporeal and volcanic, visceral and abstract. The sense of molten heat in the paintings was compounded by a fire in de Freston's studio in 2020, which was simultaneously destructive while giving the artist and the collaboration new momentum. The collaborative process involves de Freston describing the paintings to Souleman through words and touch. Souleman brings fresh meaning to the works, grounding them in his psychological landscape. Mark Jones captures these interactions in striking photographs and film footage.

Habda Rashid, Senior Curator of Modern and Contemporary Art at Kettle's Yard and the Fitzwilliam Museum, introduces *I Saw This* and considers the challenges of incorporating elements from real life. Journalist Yasmina Floyer's contribution describes her reaction to de Freston's work at his 2022 exhibition *From Darkness* at No 20 Arts, London, where she found aspects that resonated with her own experience of child loss. The moving text shows how de Freston's art carries both specific and universal meanings. Editor Matt Price focuses on de Freston's paintings, structuring his essay with fascinating quotes from Abu al-Ala al-Ma'arri, the eleventh-century blind Arab philosopher. Crucially, de Freston, Jones and Souleman's voices are present in the book, with each shedding light on their part in the project. De Freston's art is rooted in empathy and *I Saw This* is a culmination of this, translating Souleman's world of memory and metaphor.

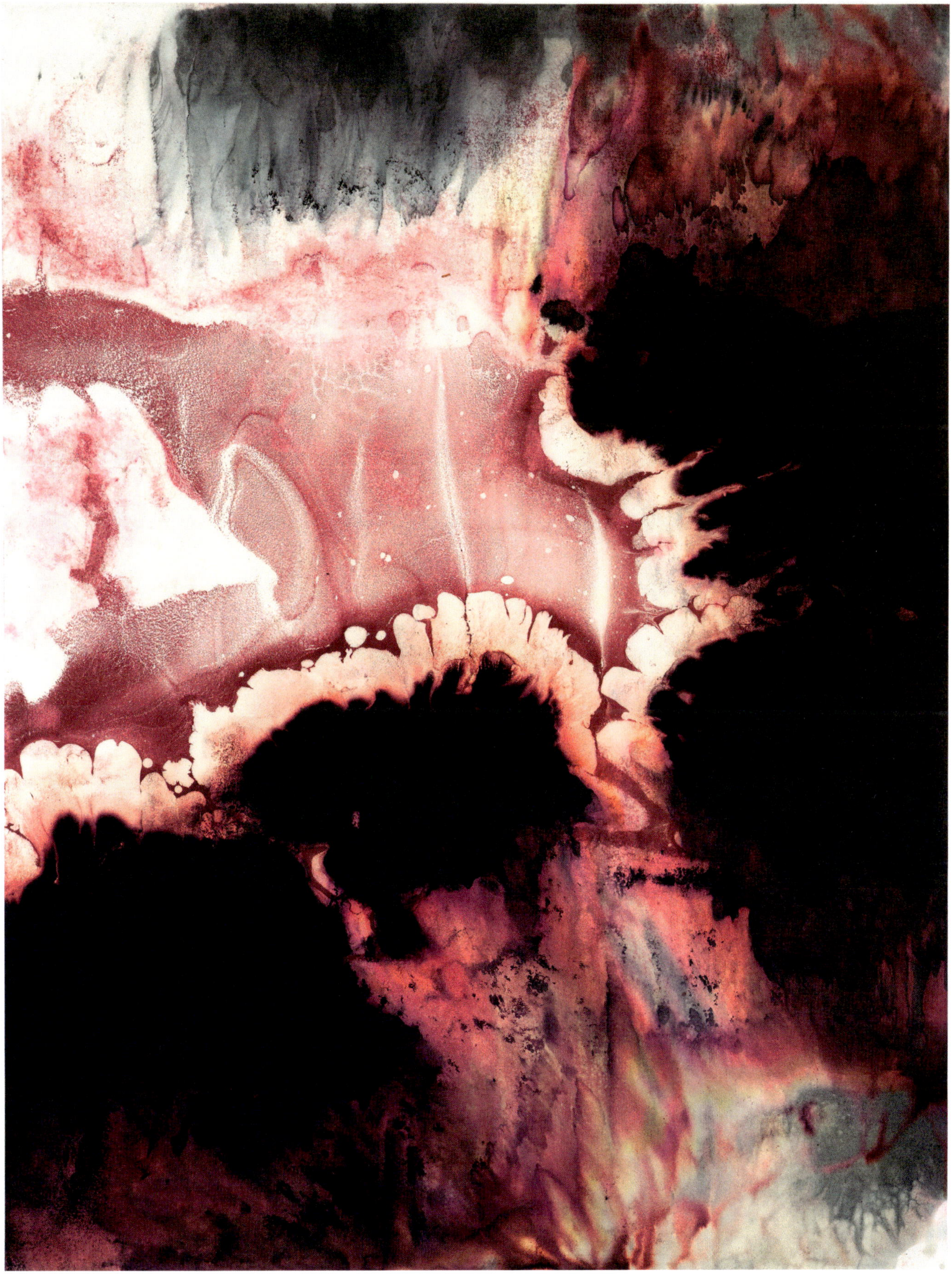

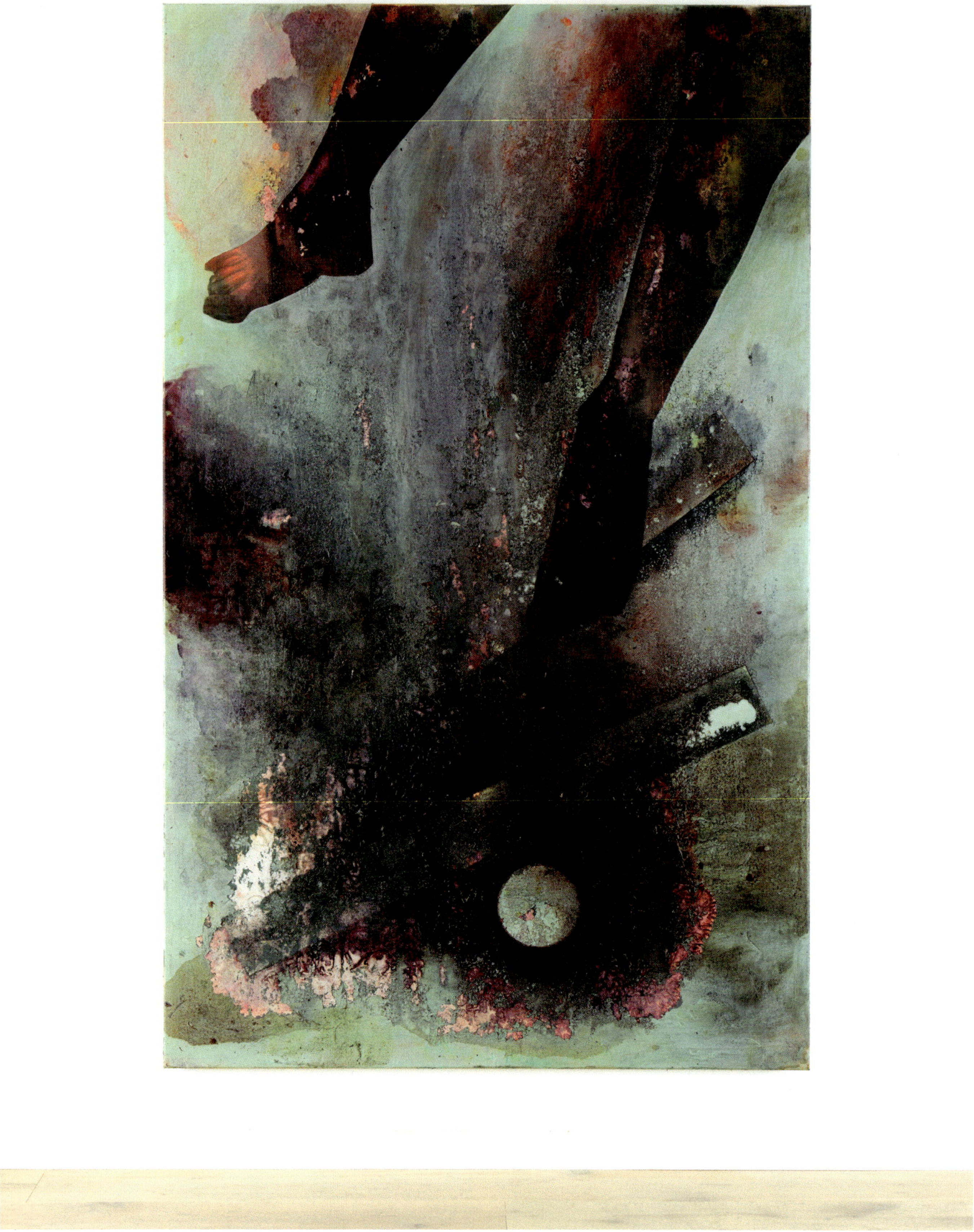

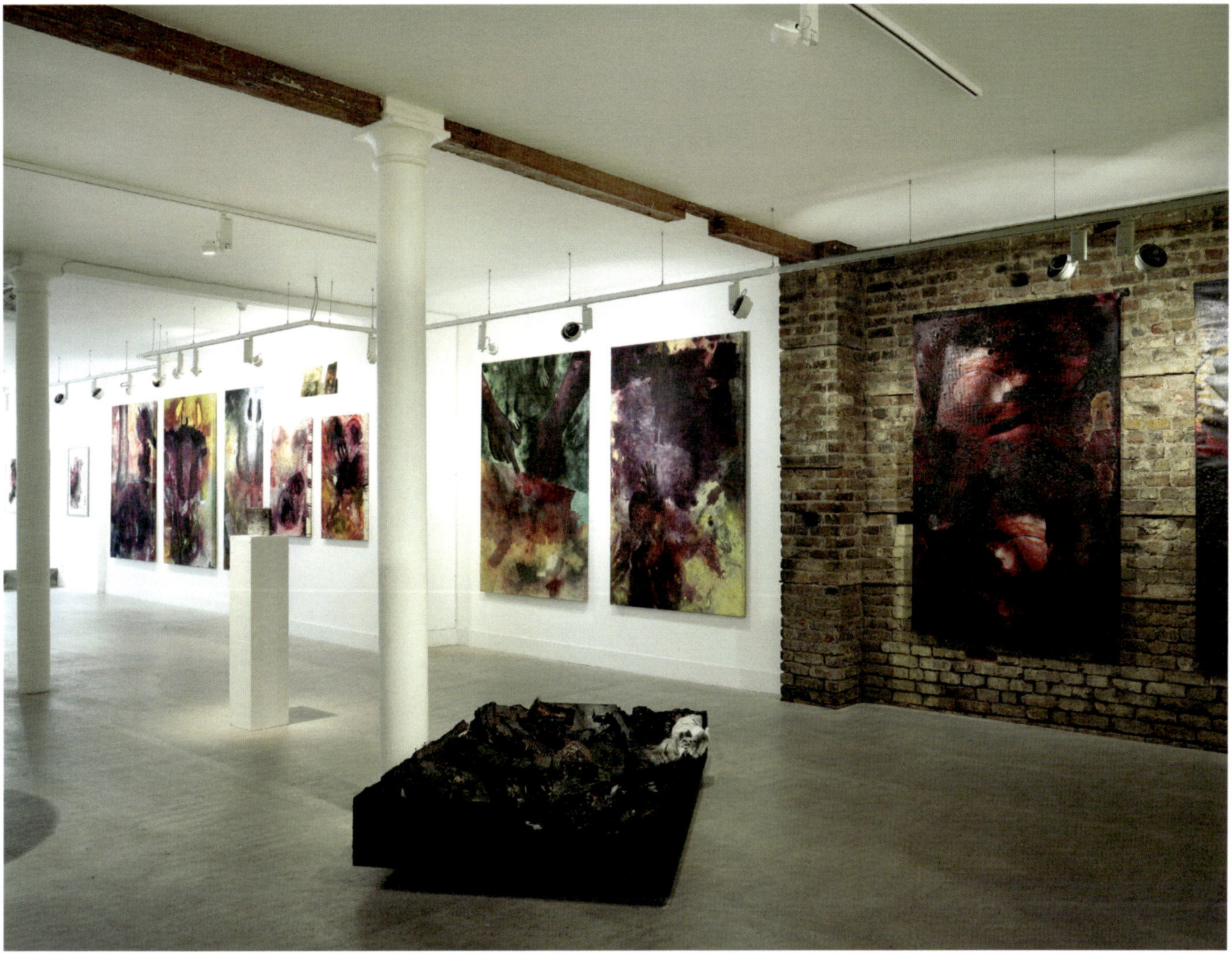

p. 19
Tom de Freston
Pulse, 2023
Mixed media on paper
76 × 55.7 cm

Tom de Freston
Submergence, 2021
Oil on canvas
200 × 125 cm

Tom de Freston
Exhibition view of *From Darkness*, No 20 Arts, London, 2022
Courtesy the artist and No 20 Arts, London

All © Tom de Freston
Photos: Peter Mallet

Q&A with... Tom de Freston

Can you tell us about a book that had a particular impact on you as a child?

Where the Wild Things Are by Maurice Sendak. I instantly connected with Max, with the idea of escaping to other worlds. It's so obviously a model of everything I have tried to do since: attempting to picture the wild landscapes and lives of internal, psychological worlds.

What about your teenage years – was there a book or exhibition catalogue that was significant in terms of your decision to become an artist?

The Complete Poems and *Selected Letters* of John Keats. I remember reading 'Ode to a Nightingale' for the first time, and thinking that is it, that's what I want to paint, to feel.

Similarly, when you were at art school, were there specific books you can remember that influenced how you think or work?

Thomas Puttfarken's *Titian and Tragic Painting*. It was in part what made me return to image-making over pure abstraction, and to a desire to explore the translations between word and image.

Rosalind Krauss's *The Optical Unconscious*, which shifted how I thought about viewing and making art.

Susan Sontag's *Regarding the Pain of Others* and Guy Debord's *The Society of the Spectacle* both introduced me to new methods of thinking and probing at how we consume images of suffering.

Roland Barthes' *A Lover's Discourse* tapped into feelings about the manifestation of desire.

What kinds of books do you enjoy reading now – do you have a favourite genre?

Recently I have enjoyed *Matrescence: On the Metamorphosis of Pregnancy, Childbirth and Motherhood* by Lucy Jones, *Bright Fear* by Mary Jean Chan, *Keats's Odes: A Lover's Discourse* by Anahid Nersessian, *The Skull* by Jon Klassen, *Notes Made While Falling* by Jenn Ashworth and *Shy* by Max Porter. Also, anything by Rebecca Solnit, Maggie Nelson, Daisy Johnson and Sarvat Hasin. My collection of art books is slightly out of hand and includes nearly everything from the Anomie list.

What proportion of the books you read are fiction?

It's a fairly even split between fiction, non-fiction, art books and poetry.

What book helped you through a difficult time?

Notes on Suicide by Simon Critchley and *In the Presence of Absence* by Mahmoud Darwish.

Has a book ever made you laugh out loud?

The Golden Mole by Katherine Rundell. I don't think there is a writer better able to mix wonder, deep intellect and astounding wit.

What are some of your favourite art books?

I have a collection of a few thousand books, so it is hard to pick favourites. I love everything by Anomie, truly, but *Jesture*, the book on painter Jadé Fadojutimi (co-published by Houldsworth Gallery), is such an amazing mixture of design, production and wonderful writing. It feels like more than just an exhibition catalogue – a work of art in its own right.

I also think Thames & Hudson and Phaidon continue to make brilliant survey books on painting.

Has being the subject of a book changed how you view other artist monographs?

I have been lucky enough to work on books across various genres in the last decade. Working on the *I Saw This* book with Anomie was further proof of how books are a collective effort, labours of love. The book feels like more than a documentation of the project, and something closer to an expansion, with the writing, editing and design work becoming integral players.

What aspect of making a book did you most enjoy?

The first read of the essays and view of the layout – both felt like the work had been opened up in new ways.

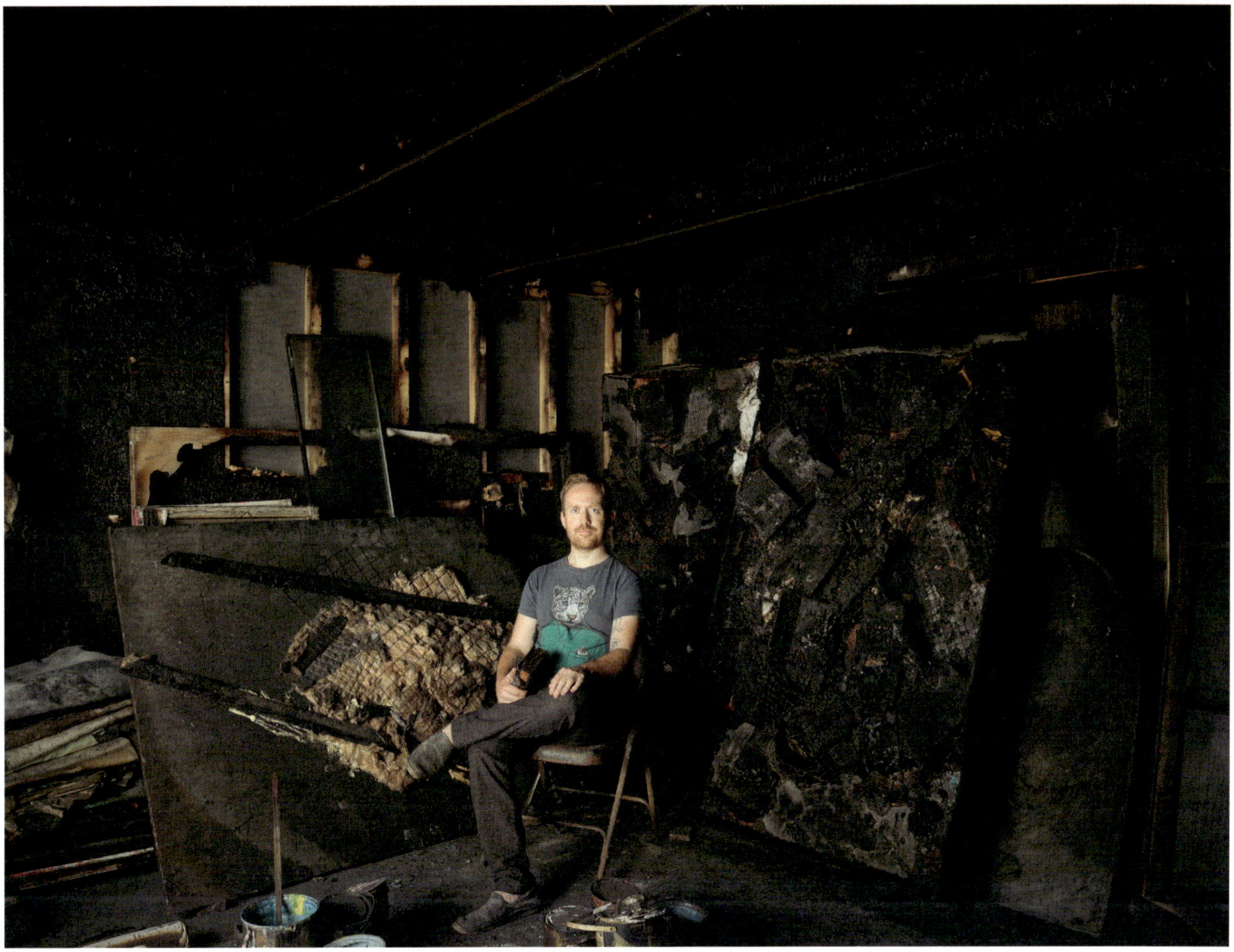

Tom de Freston in his studio following the fire in 2020. Portrait by and courtesy of Peter Mallet.

Honor Titus

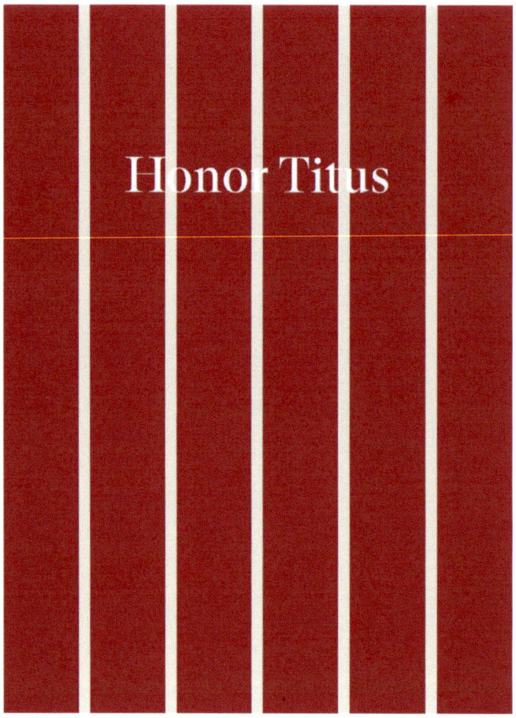

Contributors:
Henry Taylor
Durga Chew-Bose
Klaus Ottmann

68pp
Hardback
300 × 220 mm
c. 35 images
ISBN: 978-1-910221-44-0
RRP: £26
UK Release: 25 May 2023
Edited by Chloe Waddington
Designed by Joe Gilmore
Print management by Roy Killen, London
Co-published by Timothy Taylor, New York, and
Anomie Publishing, London

Honor Titus is an American artist who lives and works in Los Angeles. A self-taught painter, Titus is deeply influenced by his creative past as a musician and poet. Titus's paintings, often suffused with a sense of romance, are embedded with nostalgic references to a simpler time and feature dark, luminous jewel tones. His works often depict faceless figures in minimal urban landscapes, reflecting the isolation that stems from metropolitan anonymity. Titus's simplified compositions and striking patches of colour are inspired by Les Nabis, while his flat, decorative surfaces echo the graphic hyperrealism of artists inspired by American advertising, such as Alex Katz.

This, the artist's first trade monograph, presents new and recent works, including a body of work presented in his 2022–23 solo exhibition at Timothy Taylor, London, *Bourgeoisie in Bloom*. Here Titus expands on the themes of ritual, class and nostalgia that have characterised previous work, incorporating debutante balls in which young adults are presented to society. Favouring bright panels of colour, Titus evokes traditions of cultural formality, using precise brushwork to delineate details of old-world glamour such as the tilt of a bow-tie and the line of a ballgown.

A foreword by artist Henry Taylor considers his first encounters with Titus's work and their continuing friendship. A text by Durga Chew-Bose brings the themes of nostalgia and memory into the field of discussion. The artist's own words illuminate filmic, musical, photographic and romantic influences on the paintings, while dwelling, lastly, upon his studio space. Klaus Ottmann's text reflects philosophically and sociologically on Titus's oeuvre, bringing key art historical reference points into the discussion. Ottmann's contribution draws connections to key works of literature and criticism that contextualise his work.

Honor Titus (b. 1989, Brooklyn, NY) lives and works in Los Angeles, California. Recent solo exhibitions include *Honor Titus: Bourgeoisie in Bloom*, Timothy Taylor, London (2022–23); *Spotlight: Honor Titus*, The FLAG Art Foundation, New York (2022); *Honor Titus: For Heaven's Sake*, Timothy Taylor, New York (2021) and *Honor Titus: Goodness Gracious*, Studio Henry Taylor, Los Angeles (2020). Group exhibitions include *IRL (In Real Life)*, Timothy Taylor, London (2021); *Parallel Worlds*, Nassima Landau, Tel Aviv, Israel (2021); *and I will wear you in my heart of heart*, The FLAG Art Foundation (2021) and *(Nothing but) Flowers*, Karma, New York (2020), among others. His work is represented in the collections of the Dallas Museum of Art, Dallas, Texas; Nasher Museum of Art, Durham, North Carolina; Rennie Collection, Vancouver, Canada; The Bunker Artspace, Palm Beach, Florida; and the Longlati Foundation, Shanghai, China.

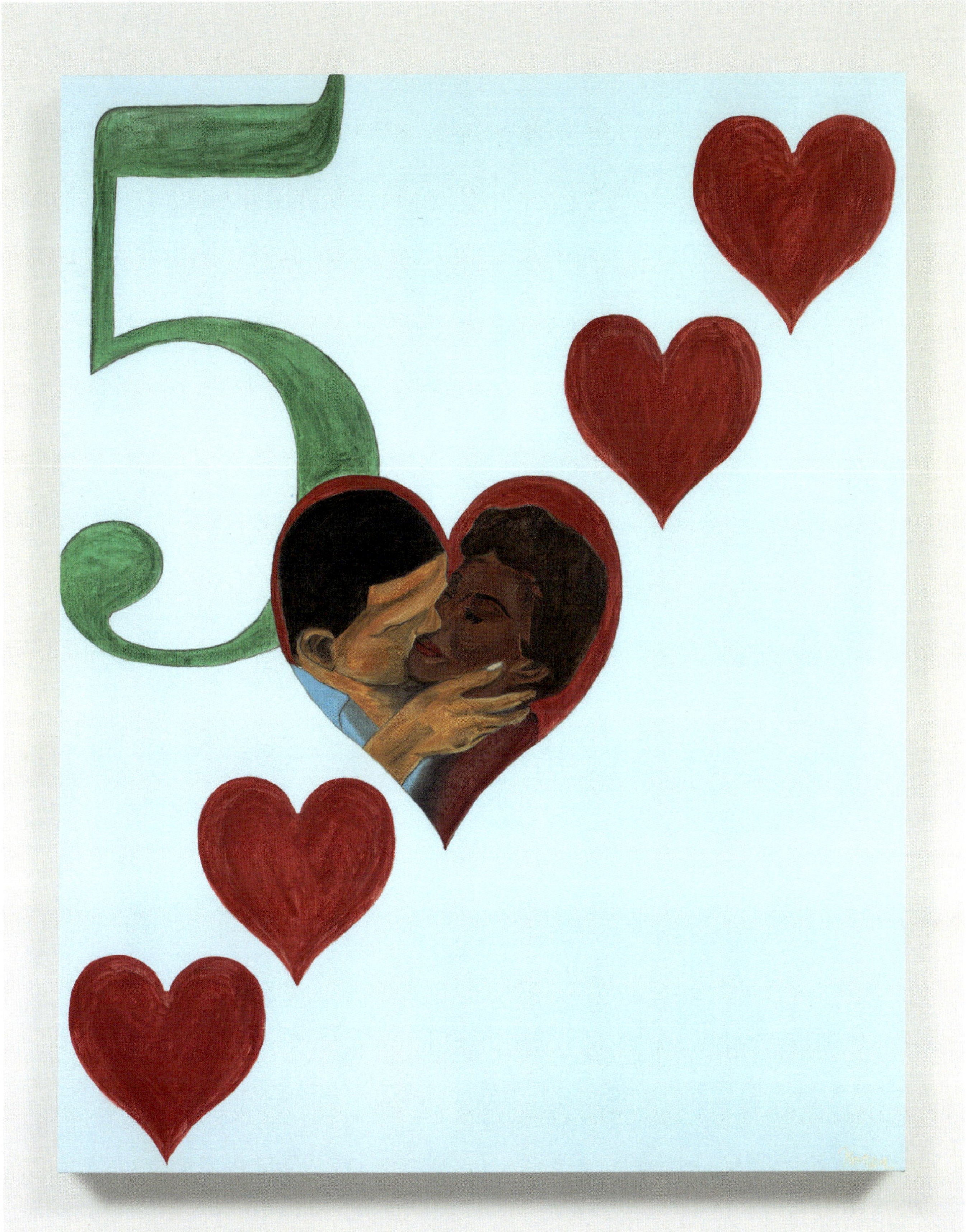

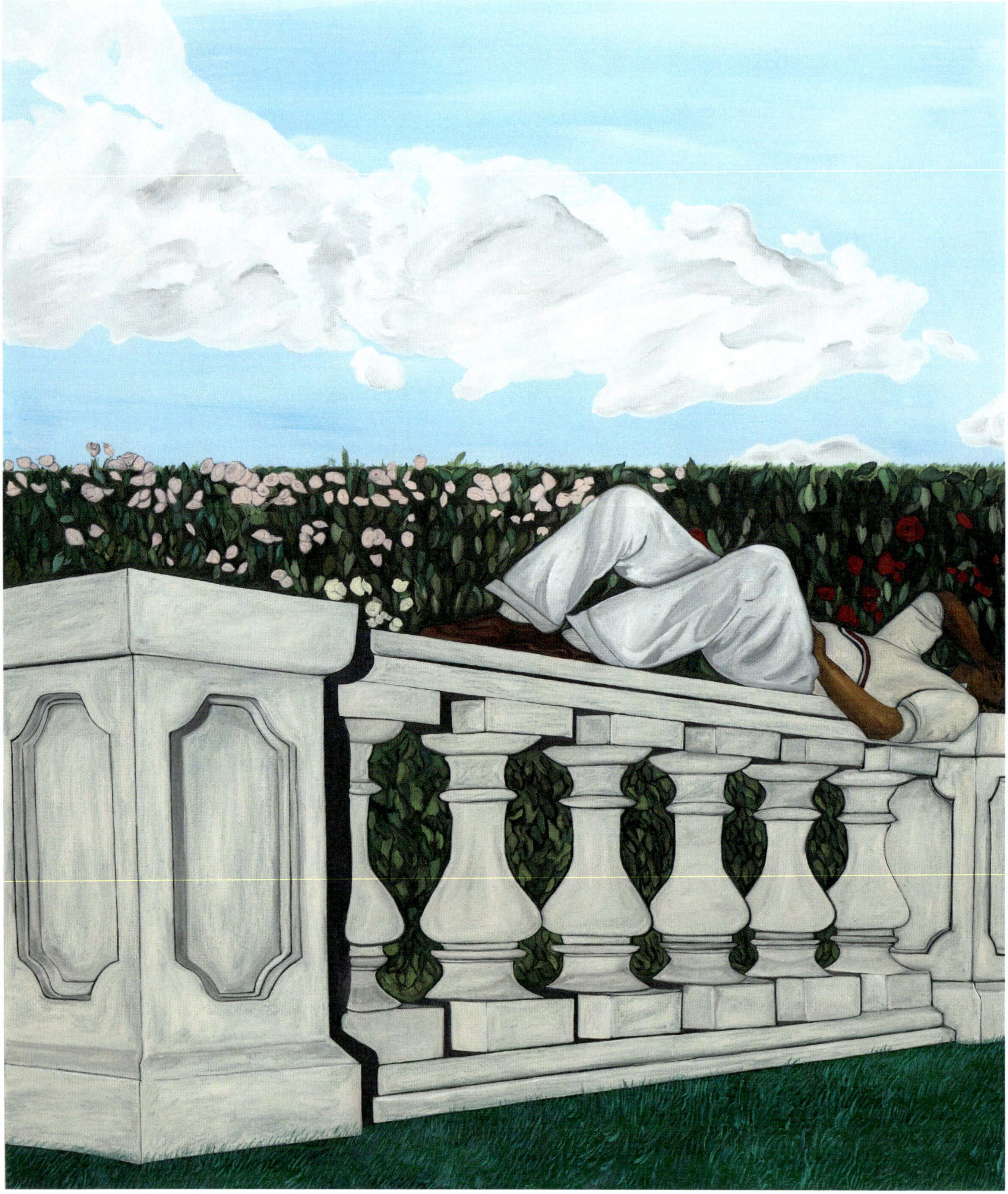

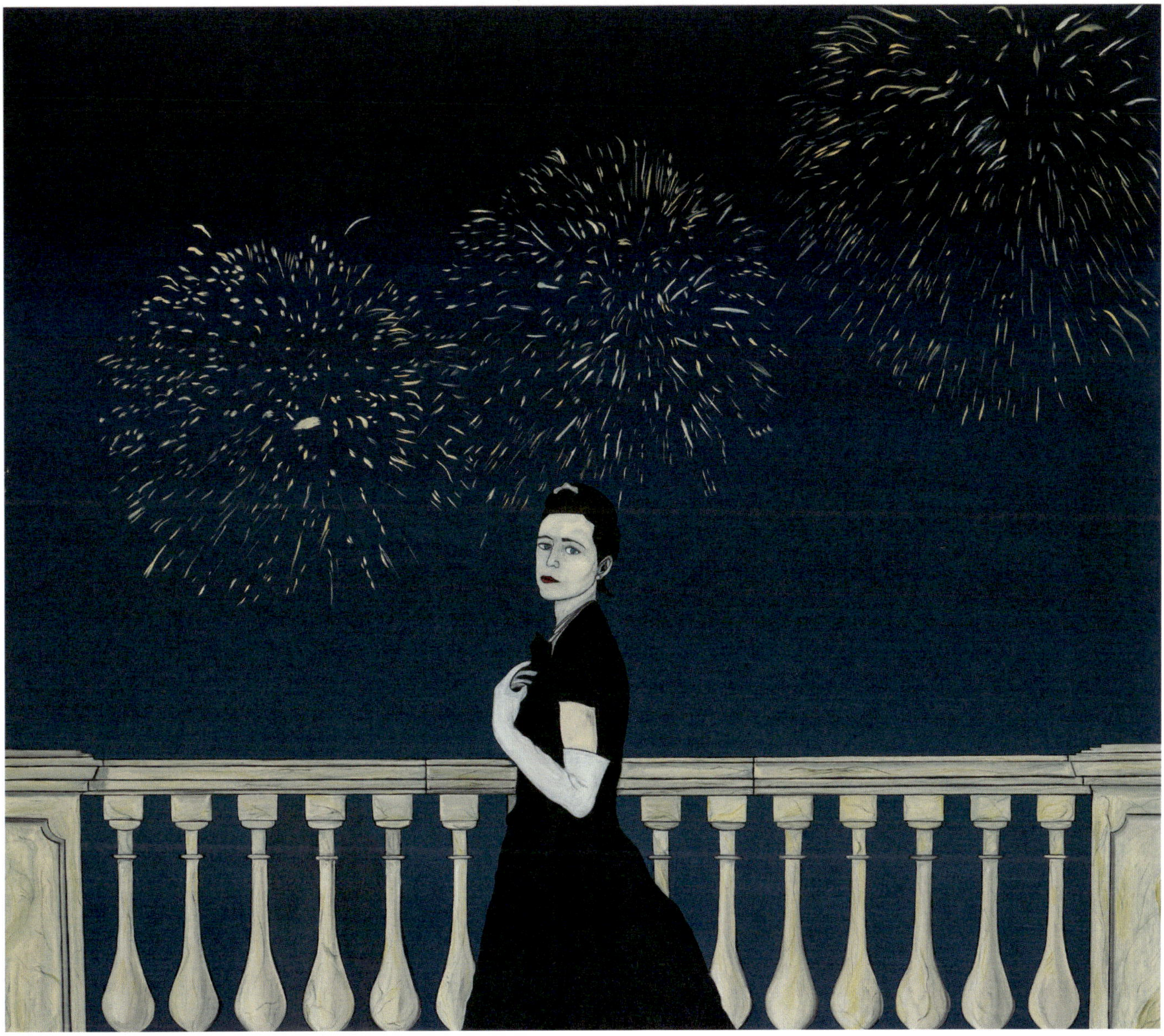

p. 25
Honor Titus
5 of Hearts, 2020
Oil on canvas
152.4 × 121.9 cm
Photo: Lance Brewer

Honor Titus
A Long Beautiful Year, 2022
Oil on canvas
213.4 × 182.9 cm
Photo: Ed Mumford

Honor Titus
Shimmering Jubilee, 2022
Oil on canvas
182.9 × 213.4 cm
Photo: Lance Brewer

All © Honor Titus
Courtesy of Timothy Taylor, London/New York

Alastair Gordon
Quodlibet

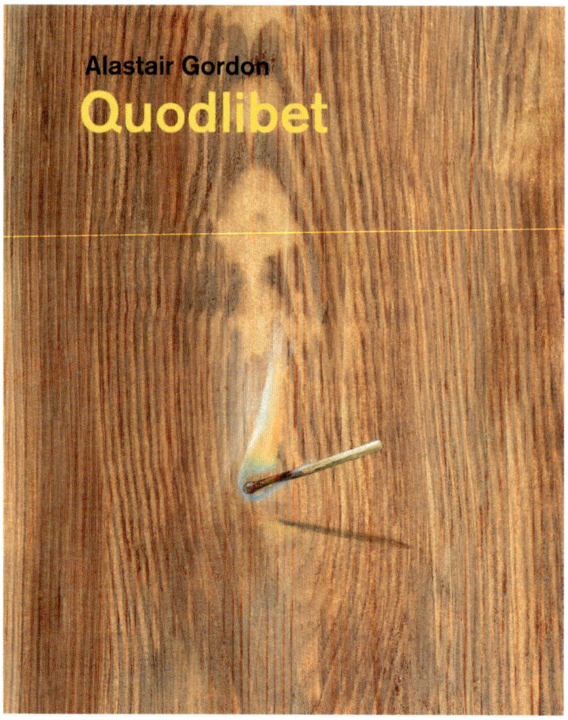

Contributors:
Julia Lucero
Jorella Andrews
Alastair Gordon

168pp
Hardback
260 × 210 mm
c. 180 images
ISBN: 978-1-910221-48-8
RRP: £30
UK Release: 23 May 2023
Edited by Alastair Gordon Studio
Designed by Herman Lelie
Layouts by Stefania Bonelli
Printed by EBS, Verona
Published by Anomie Publishing, London

Alastair Gordon is an artist based in London. This, the first major monograph of his career, includes more than 160 paintings, drawings and documentational photographs, along with notes by Gordon himself. The book introduces this accomplished and engaging new voice in British painting.

Gordon's paintings bring the historic languages of genre painting and the quodlibet into a contemporary discourse that pushes the boundaries of realism, figuration and illusionism to focus on everyday moments. His work often elevates seemingly ordinary objects – feathers, matchsticks, postcards – allowing them to speak to wider concerns of beauty, truth, life and death.

An introduction by Julia Lucero, Associate Director of Nahmad Projects, London, emphasises the importance of nature and of meditation within Gordon's practice. Specifically, Lucero brings out the idea of the 'axis mundi, that metaphysical and mystical connecting point where heaven meets Earth'. She explores the significance of quodlibet, a seventeenth-century trompe-l'oeil painting technique that Gordon favours, rendering brushstrokes invisible and affording everyday objects new significance, even 'profound value'. Humble objects such as a matchstick or paper aeroplane might be elevated to the realms of the divine.

An essay by Jorella Andrews, Professor of Visual Cultures at Goldsmiths, University of London, describes the influence of Gordon's time on a residency in the studio of Paul Cézanne at Les Lauves on the outskirts of Aix-en-Provence. His experiences there proved pivotal to the direction of his practice, in which both the 'visual misdirection' of quodlibet and the qualities of wood have become central. Andrews brings art history into relation with Gordon's paintings, making comparisons between subject, form and approach. Andrews' text further details the recent synthesis of two sides of Gordon's work: precise illusionism combined with looser observations made in the natural landscape.

Designed by Herman Lelie, printed by EBS Verona and published in 2023 by Anomie Publishing, London, the publication has been generously supported by Howard and Roberta Ahmanson through Fieldstead and Company.

Alastair Gordon (b. 1978, Edinburgh) is an artist whose works span painting, drawing and installation. He received his BA from Glasgow School of Art and his MA from Wimbledon School of Art, London. His work has been shown in recent solo exhibitions at Ahmanson Gallery in Irvine, California (2017), Aleph Contemporary, London (2020 and 2021) and in the group exhibition *Unpacking Gainsborough* (2021) at Cynthia Corbett Gallery, London.

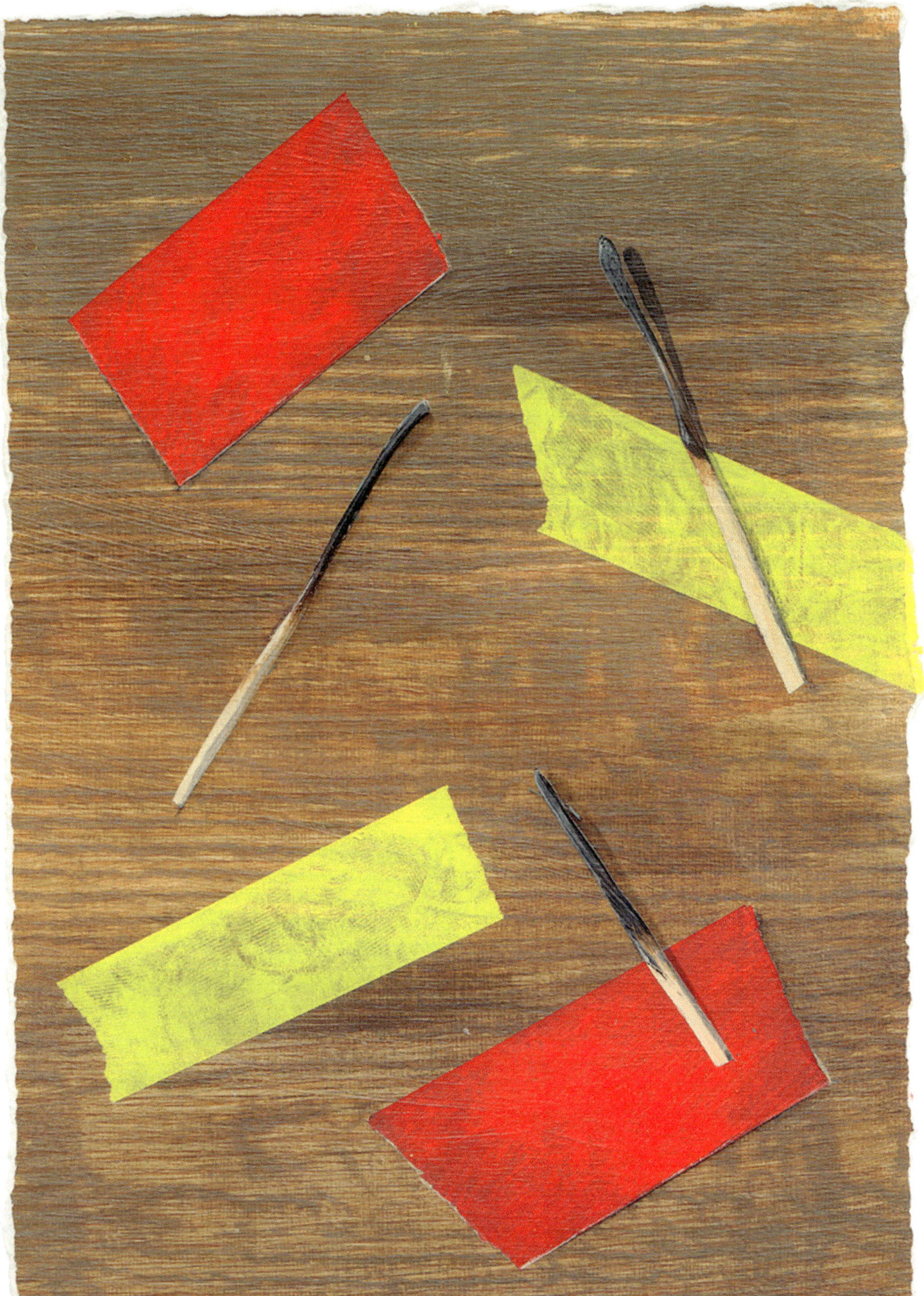

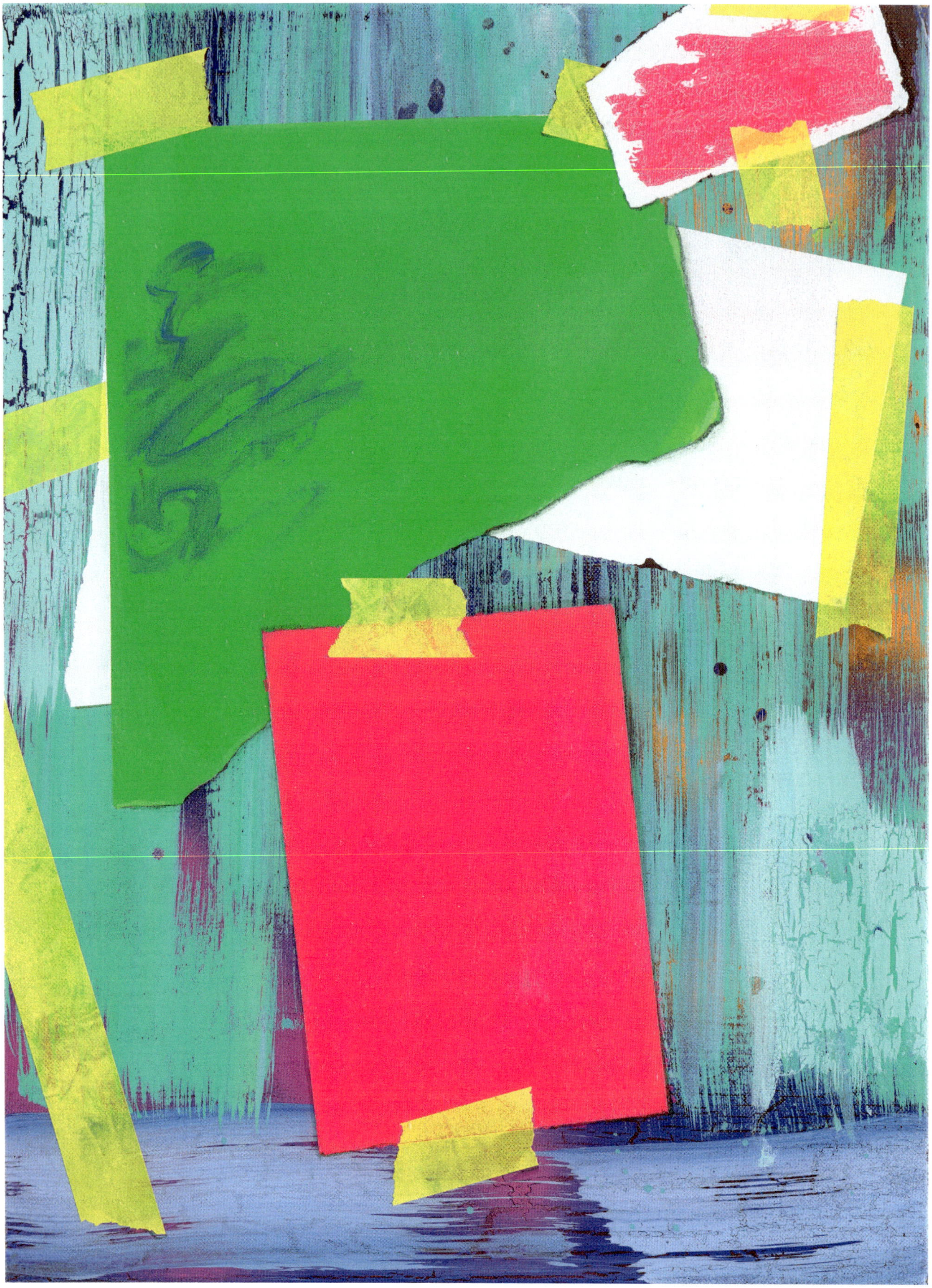

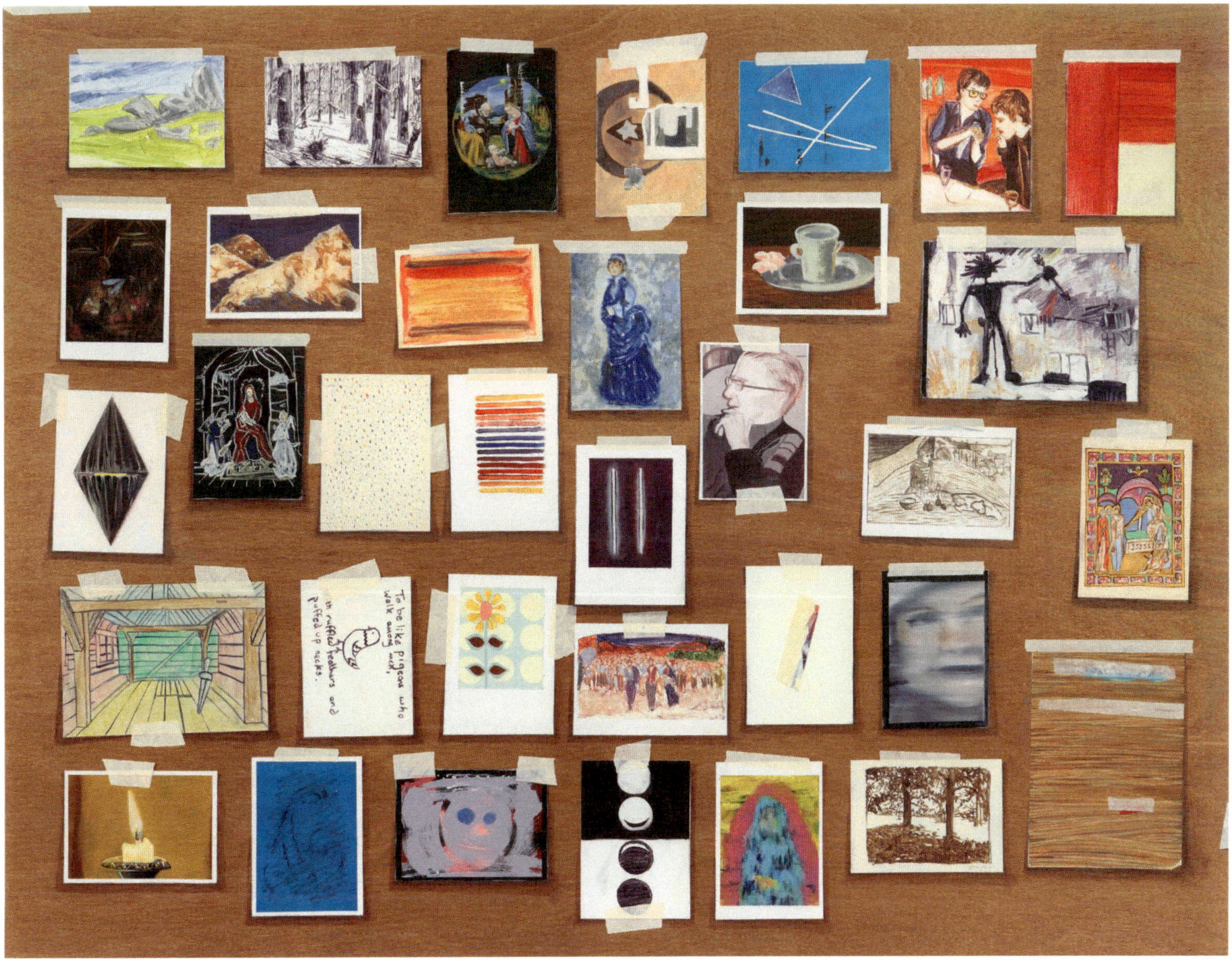

p. 29
Alastair Gordon
Study (Three Graces) from the *Prayer Match* series, 2020
Oil and acrylic on linen
20 × 14 cm
Photo: Alastair Gordon Studio

Alastair Gordon
I Could Be the Walrus, 2018
Oil and acrylic on linen
40 × 30 cm
Photo: Anna Arca

Alastair Gordon
All the Postcards Sent to My Studio (01.12.14 to 25.12.14), 2015
Oil and acrylic on wood
90 × 120 cm
Photo: Anna Arca

All © Alastair Gordon

Anomie Collections 1

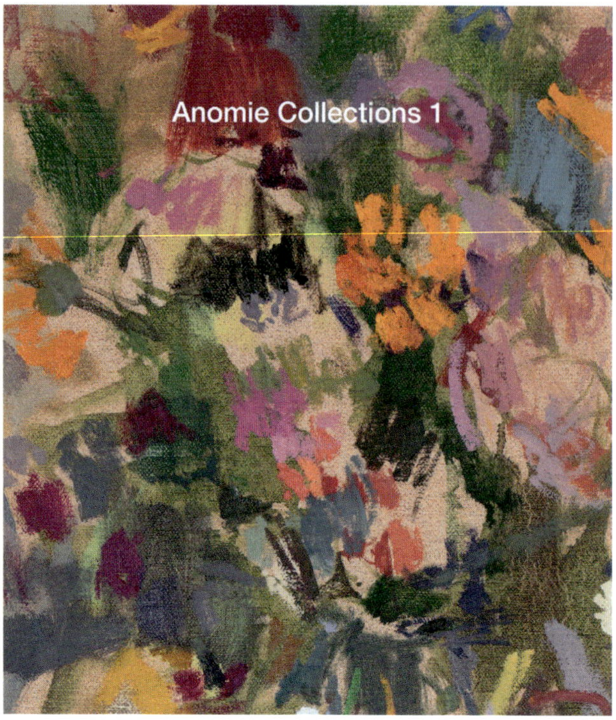

Contributors:
Matt Price
Anneka French

104pp
Softback
240 × 210 mm
c. 60 images
ISBN: 978-1-910221-45-7
RRP: £20
UK Release: 18 May 2023
Edited by Matt Price
Designed by Anomie Studio
Printed by Mixam, Watford
Published by Anomie Publishing, London

Anomie Collections 1 is a publication accompanying the first edition of Anomie Collections – a London-based initiative that supports the work of contemporary British painters by acquiring works on behalf of a group of private collectors.

This first edition of the scheme resulted in the purchase of fifty-six paintings and works on paper by eight artists, documented and presented here along with newly commissioned texts by Anneka French and an introduction by Matt Price, Publisher at Anomie Publishing and curator of the edition. The works span a variety of genres, from landscapes and urban scenes to still lifes, portraits and abstractions.

The artists featured in *Anomie Collections 1* are:

Jasmir Creed
Marguerite Horner
Cathy Lomax
Kathryn Maple
Kate Mary
Daniel Shadbolt
Caroline Thomson
Jim Threapleton

Anomie Publishing is an international publishing house for the arts based in London, UK, dedicated to enabling quality arts books – especially small and medium print-run titles – to reach the book trade. Anomie works in partnership with public and commercial galleries, museums, arts organisations, agencies, academic institutions, charities, collectors, established artist studios and private clients to publish or co-publish books. Anomie Collections is an initiative started in 2022 to encourage and support the private acquisition of works by British painters.

Matt Price is a London-based arts publisher, editor and writer. He has published over fifty books and catalogues under his Anomie imprints, and edited publications for other publishers including Phaidon, Rizzoli, Thames & Hudson and Hatje Cantz. He has compiled and written two volumes of *The Anomie Review of Contemporary British Painting*.

Anneka French is a curator and critic who writes for *Art Quarterly*, *Burlington Contemporary* and *Photomonitor*. She has been commissioned by the Turner Prize, worked at Tate Modern, Ikon, The New Art Gallery Walsall and Wolverhampton Art Gallery, and curated exhibitions at Grand Union, Birmingham; KH7 ArtSpace, Denmark and Coventry Biennial.

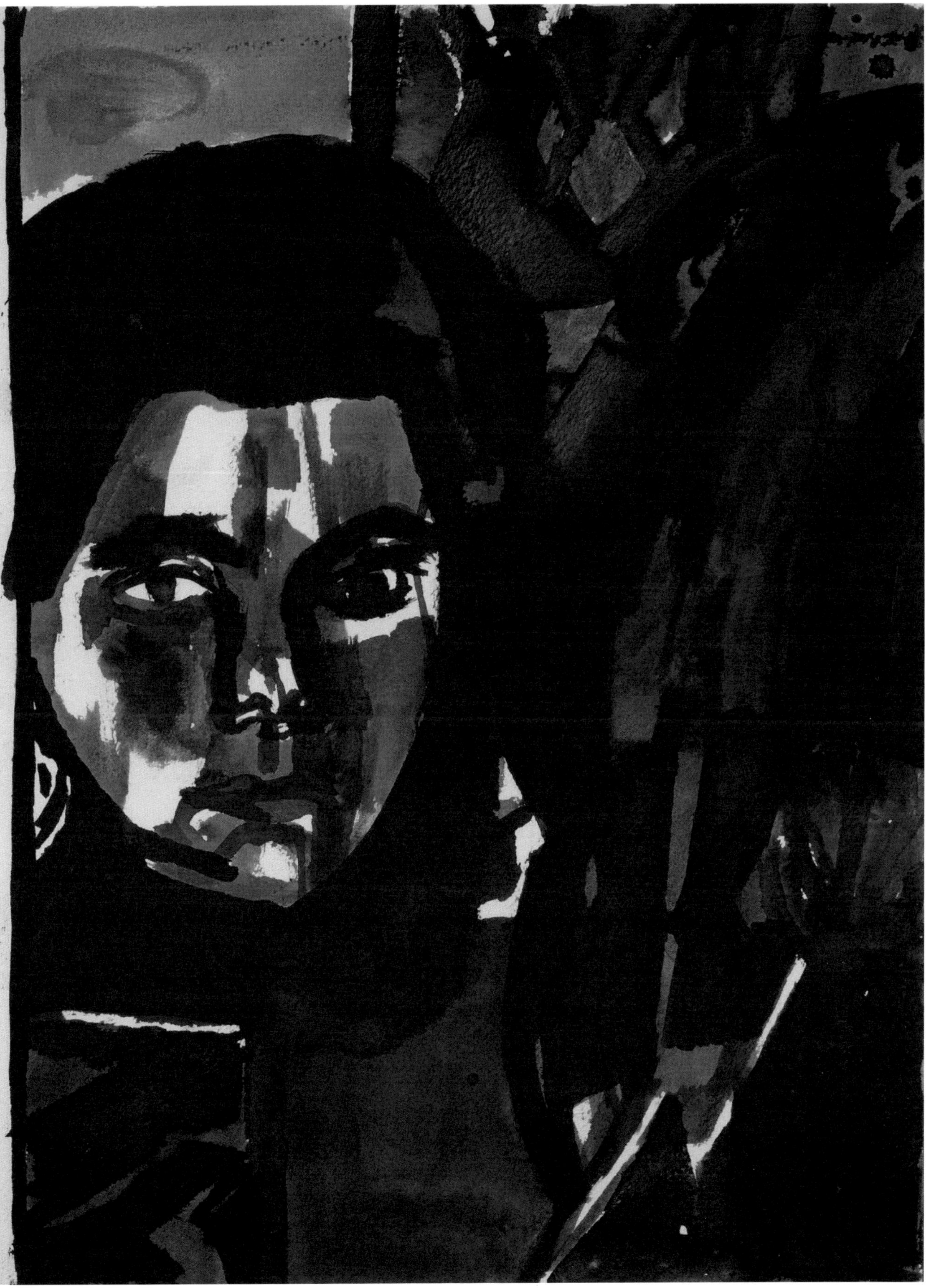

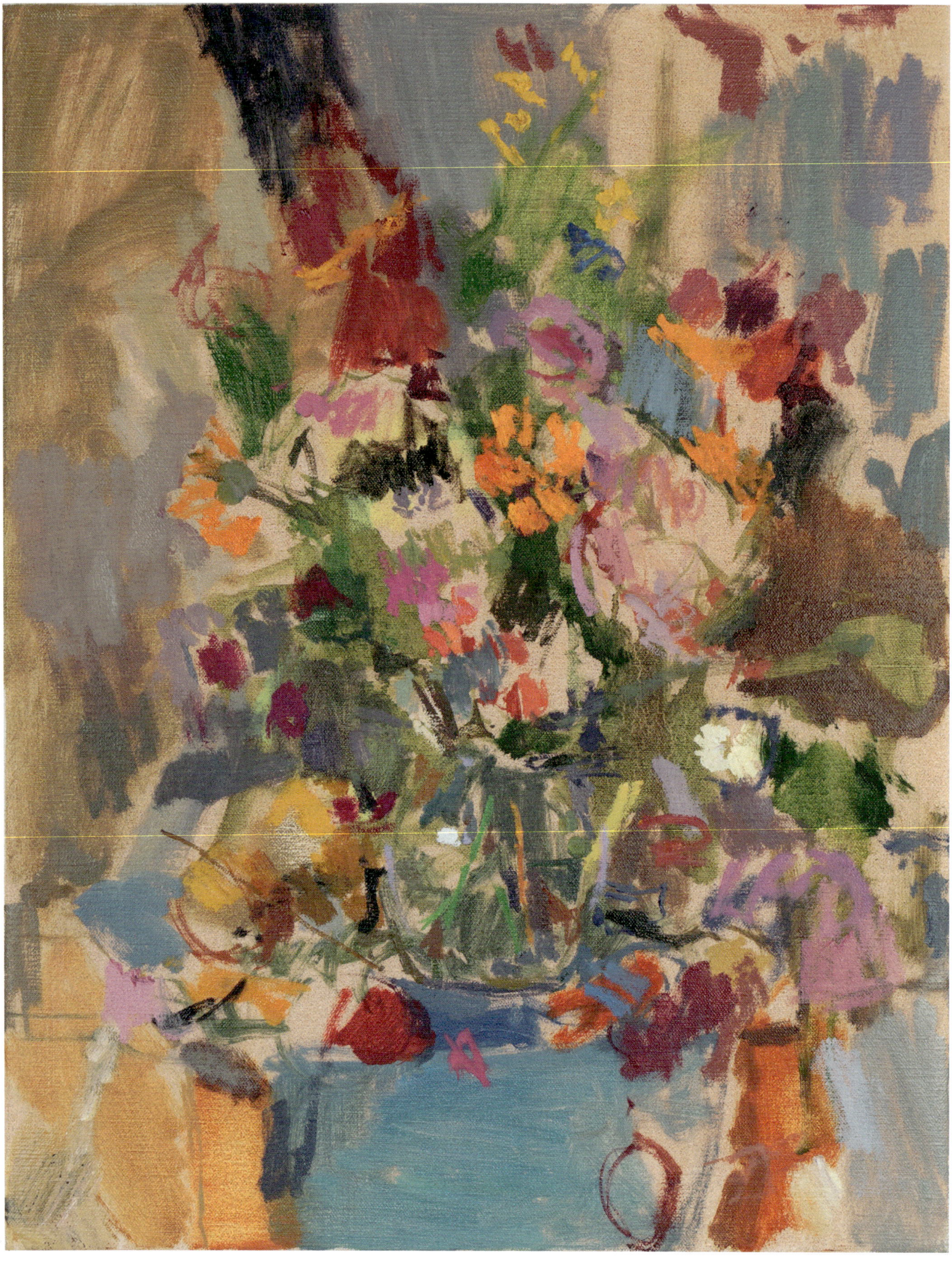

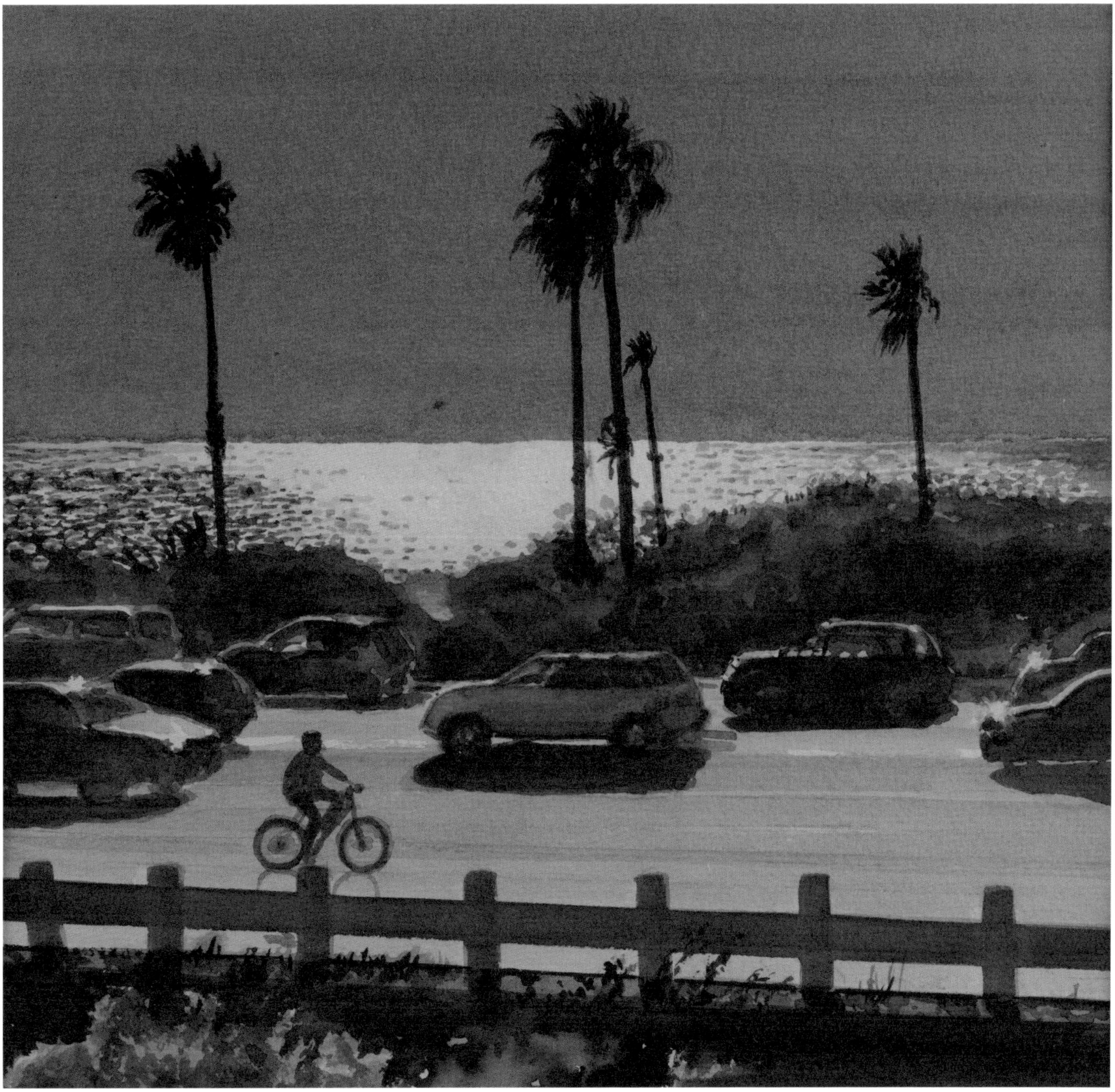

p. 33
Jasmir Creed
Her Gaze, 2021
Ink on paper
42 × 29 cm
© Jasmir Creed

Daniel Shadbolt
Mixed Flowers III, 2022
Oil on linen
61 × 45.5 cm
© Daniel Shadbolt

Marguerite Horner
Get there in the end, 2022
Watercolour on paper
19.5 × 19.5 cm
© Marguerite Horner

All images courtesy of Anomie
Photos: John Howard Davies

Kathryn Maple
A Year of Drawings

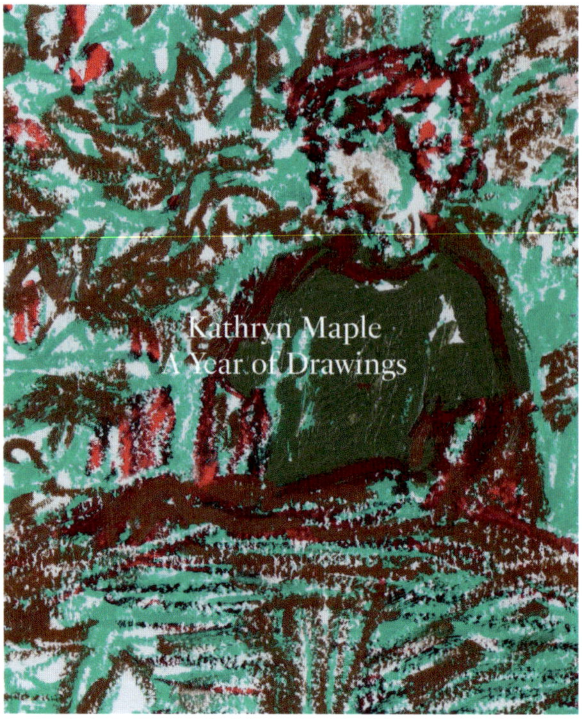

Contributors:
Kathryn Lloyd
Anneka French
Matt Price

348pp
Softback
235 × 215 mm
c. 375 images
ISBN: 978-1-910221-47-1
RRP: £24
UK Release: 6 April 2023
Edited by Matt Price
Designed by Anomie Studio
Printed by Mixam, Watford
Published by Anomie Publishing, London

Kathryn Maple is an artist specialising in drawing and painting. Her large-scale paintings feature urban, suburban and rural landscapes, frequently populated by human figures. Her work is distinctive for its intensely layered mark-making, lending the work both urgency and intimacy. The places and people depicted are afforded a sense of wildness or mystery by dint of the colour palette, collage-like compositions and recurring motifs such as wind-blown trees and winding pathways. This, her first monograph, features 379 images, many of which are reproduced for the first time. These include the presentation of her recent major series of oil pastel on paper works *A Year of Drawings*, alongside reproductions of her mixed-media works on paper, as well as large oils on canvas.

An essay by Kathryn Lloyd, writer, artist and Contemporary Art Editor at *The Burlington Magazine*, offers insight into Maple's impulse to explore the world around her through her work. Large-scale paintings are constructed by means of personal encounter, memory and imagination. Details of man-made objects, tree bark and human skin, for instance, become composite, crucial in capturing fleeting experiences of place and of people. Lloyd brings out the symbolism of Maple's work, making art historical comparisons while connecting these to the specific local characteristics of Maple's familiar South London landscapes and the importance of walking to the artist's practice.

An interview with curator and critic Anneka French is focused on *A Year of Drawings*, a series of 365 drawings made daily since 1 January 2022. They discuss the process, materials and art historical and literary influences, with a focus on how her drawing and painting strands impact on each other. Their conversation provides an insight into Maple's thinking at a crucial stage in her career. Editor Matt Price's essay 'Into the Trees' offers an introduction to *A Year of Drawings*, discussing examples of the works and considering aspects of the series ranging from art historical precedents to themes, recurring motifs and interpretation.

Kathryn Maple (b. 1989, Canterbury) lives in South London. She graduated in 2011 with a degree in Fine Art Printmaking from the University of Brighton, before undertaking a postgraduate programme at the Royal Drawing School in 2012–13. Maple has featured in exhibitions at venues including Barber & Lopes at the British Art Fair, London; The Royal Academy, London; Beers London; Messums Wiltshire; Flowers Gallery, London; Frestonian Gallery, London; Christies New York; Kristin Hjellegjerde Gallery, London and Drawing Room, London. She was the winner of the *Times* Watercolour Competition 2014 and 2016 and the John Moores Painting Prize 2020. Her exhibition *Under the Hot Sun* at the Walker Art Gallery, Liverpool, 2023, was awarded to Maple for winning the latter.

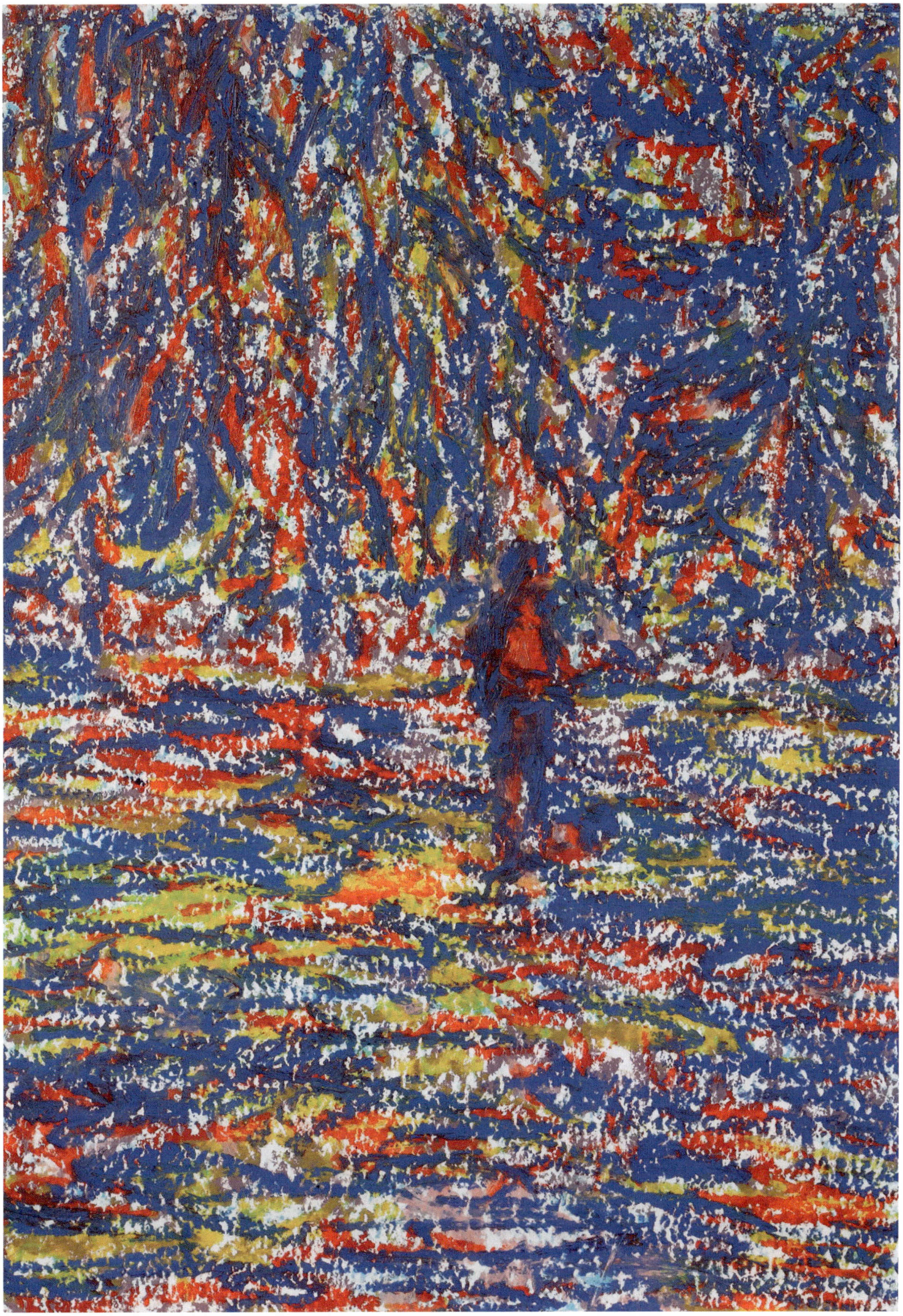

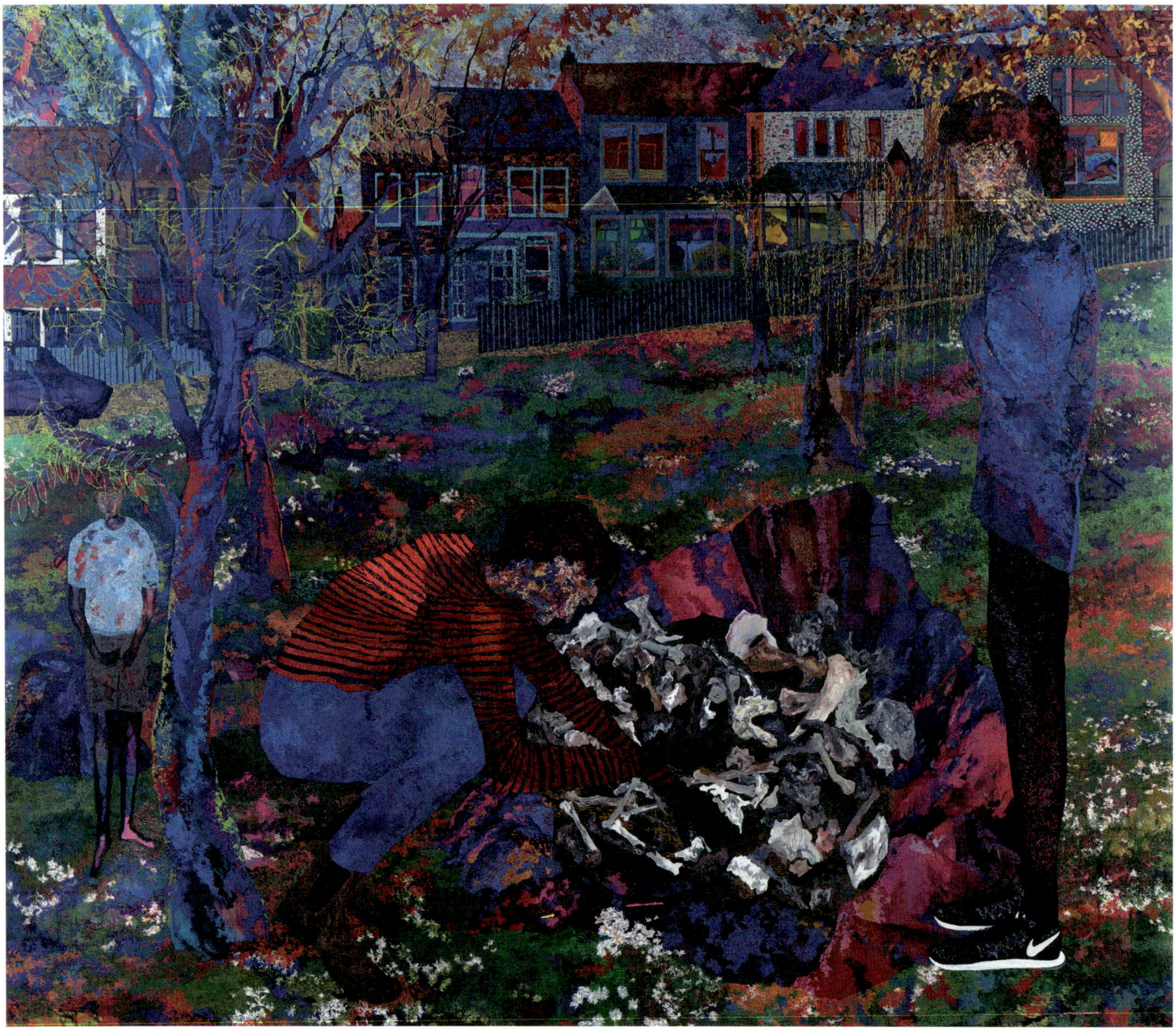

p. 37
Kathryn Maple
A Year of Drawings (10 June), 2022
Oil pastel on paper
21 × 14.8 cm

Kathryn Maple
Old Bones, 2022
Oil on canvas
170 × 220 cm

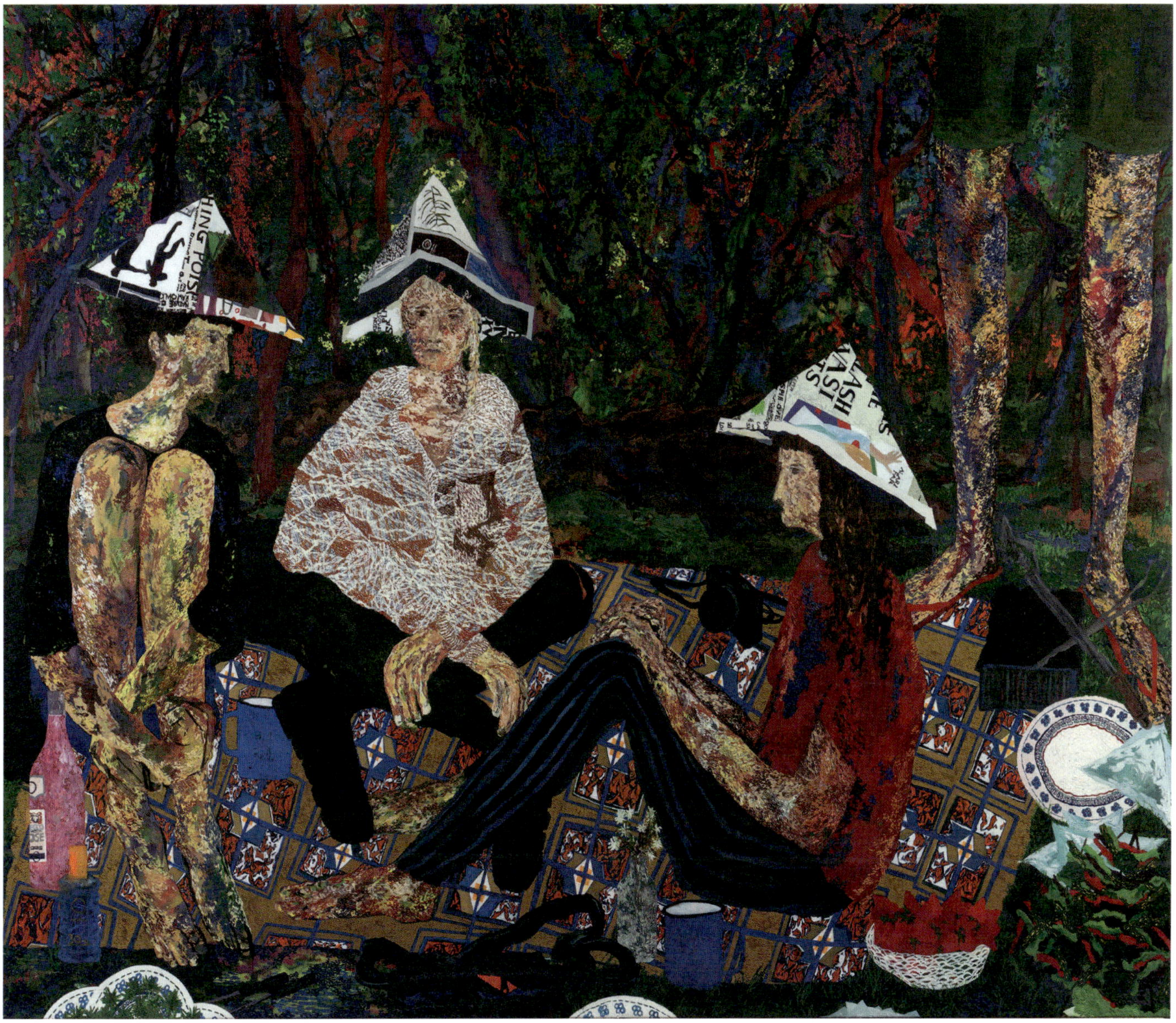

Kathryn Maple
Paper Hats, 2022
Oil on canvas
124 × 166 cm

All © Kathryn Maple
Photos: John Howard Davies

Q&A with... Kathryn Maple

Can you tell us about a book that had a particular impact on you as a child?

As a child I really enjoyed *Cockatoos* by Quentin Blake. My mother would use a different voice for each of the birds and then adapt them to pheasants we saw en route to school. Active participation was required to keep me engaged!

What about your teenage years – was there a book or exhibition catalogue that was significant in terms of your decision to become an artist?

The art school bookshelf never seemed to change too much, but all the books were regularly looked at, which made looking through them very easy as I remember the paper being very soft by the time I was in the sixth form. There were all the obvious favourites: Matisse, van Gogh and Cézanne. I do remember a book on Friedrich Stowasser [Friedensreich Hundertwasser] turning up once, which at the time was a refreshing change! Paul Klee has always been in the background, as someone noticed even in non-arty households. I have always enjoyed the playful nature of his works and how the colours are orchestrated, keeping the eye dancing around the composition.

What kinds of books do you enjoy reading now?

It takes me an awfully long time to get through any book – and be still for that matter. I find any Martin Gayford books a real conversation and can get through several chapters.

What are some of your favourite art books?

Hannah Ryggen: Weaving the World [Walther König] and *Vincent van Gogh: The Drawings* [Metropolitan Museum of Art]. My Partner Alison always has a sharp eye in any charity shop's book section and once found *Dead Souls* by Nikolai Gogol, illustrated by Marc Chagall. This is a favourite of ours.

Has being the subject of a book changed how you view other artist monographs?

I tend not to flick through but to appreciate how each page has been put together through many different eyes and visions. I think the balance between the amount of text and imagery is very important. Allowing pages for details of paintings helps give moments of pause.

What aspects of making a book did you most enjoy?

The days spent working towards the publication were, in a strange way, meditative – maybe not the word Matt would use?! Working with a photographer to make sure my work would be put into print with the most clarity and definition was vital and something I will carry forward. I came to understand that making a book is an art form, not just an extension of an exhibition or review. I enjoyed processing everyone's input and decision-making, as predominantly my work is done on my own. Ahead of my show it helped me think about curation and how the works may look together in the exhibition. Visiting the repro house – something I had to google! – was a very interesting experience, and being able to make colour adjustments, as well as holding a copy in my hands, gave me a sense of being one step closer.

What books have inspired you in recent years?

A bit of local history. I have discovered the work of Evelyn Dunbar. Her mural paintings inside the Prendergast school in Brockley contain so much drawing, and I enjoy walking around the area thinking of her panoramic paintings of hilly fields.

What are you reading at the moment?

Olivia Laing's *To the River: A Journey Beneath the Surface*, and I am looking at a catalogue of Egon Schiele's landscapes from an exhibition at the Leopold Museum in Vienna in 2004–05.

Is there a book you are looking forward to reading that you have not yet had chance to?

The catalogue *Joseph E. Yoakum: What I Saw*. I bought it in 2021 and have used it a number of times when I am teaching, but I really need to sit down with it properly.

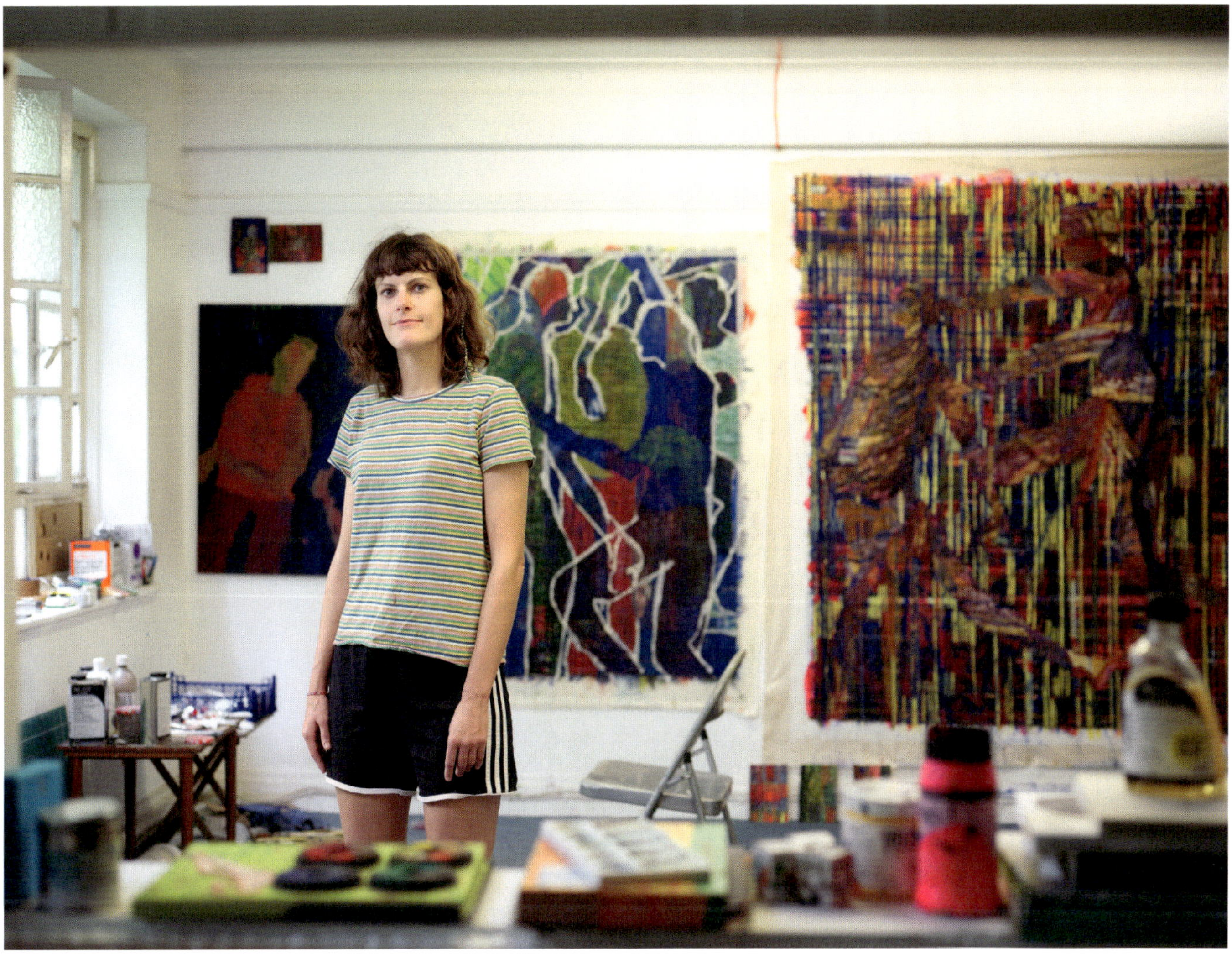

Portrait by and courtesy of Peter Mallet.

Matthew Krishanu

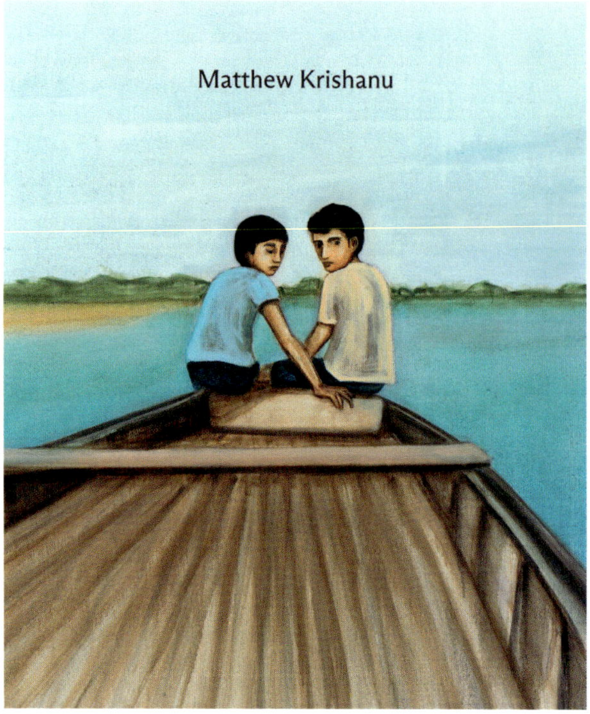

Contributors:
Mark Rappolt
Ben Luke
Dorothy Price

192pp
Hardback
290 × 245 mm
c. 125 images
ISBN: 978-1-910221-33-4
RRP: £30
UK Release: 23 March 2023
Edited by Georgia Griffiths and
Matt Price
Designed by Joe Gilmore
Printed by EBS, Verona
Published by Anomie Publishing, London

Matthew Krishanu's paintings explore childhood, race, religion, art history, family, grief and love. His subjects – frequently Brown people – are realised with a shallow pictorial depth, delicate washes of colour and a sense of interior life. Krishanu questions the positions of his painterly subjects and depictions of landscapes in relation to the legacy of European colonialism and the art historical canon. His practice is heavily informed by his early childhood spent in Dhaka where his parents moved in order to work for the Church of Bangladesh.

This, his first trade monograph, presents a number of series of Krishanu's works: *Another Country*, *Expatriates*, *Mission*, *House of God*, *Religious Workers* and *In Sickness and In Health*. A section of the publication is devoted to exhibition views, providing a sense of scale between artworks and their connections to each other. The publication features essays by Mark Rappolt and Dorothy Price, alongside an interview with the artist by Ben Luke. Rappolt, Editor-in-Chief at *ArtReview* magazine, details the various worlds present within Krishanu's paintings and draws out key themes within Krishanu's oeuvre such as power, religion, identity and memory, while highlighting its distance from didacticism and carefully constructed ambivalence. Price, Professor of Modern and Contemporary Art and Visual Culture at The Courtauld, writes sensitively about solitude, memory and emotion which are palpable within Krishanu's work, in particular in the series *In Sickness and In Health*, which traces a life path of Uschi Gatward, the artist's late wife, over sixteen years to her death from cancer in late 2021. In an interview with Luke, a critic and editor at *The Art Newspaper*, Krishanu discusses his practice in relation to ideas of religion, race, global art history, photography, health and personal experiences. His work explores, Krishanu says, 'the puzzle of painting'. The publication has been supported by Guy Halamish; Jhaveri Contemporary, Mumbai; Niru Ratnam, London; Taimur Hassan and Tanya Leighton, Berlin and Los Angeles.

Matthew Krishanu was born in 1980 in Bradford and is based in London. He completed an MA in Fine Art at Central Saint Martins in 2009. Recent solo exhibitions include *Playground*, Niru Ratnam, London (2022); *Undercurrents*, LGDR, New York (2022); *Picture Plane*, Niru Ratnam, London (2020); *Arrow and Pulpit*, Tanya Leighton, Berlin (2021) and *Corvus*, Iniva, London (2019). He has recently been in the group exhibitions *The Kingfisher's Wing*, GRIMM, New York (2022); *Prophecy*, Mead Gallery, Warwick Arts Centre (2022); *Mixing It Up: Painting Today*, Hayward Gallery, London (2021); the Coventry Biennial, Leamington Spa Art Gallery & Museum and Herbert Art Gallery & Museum (2021); John Moores Painting Prize, Walker Art Gallery, Liverpool (2021) and *A Rich Tapestry*, Lahore Biennale (2020).

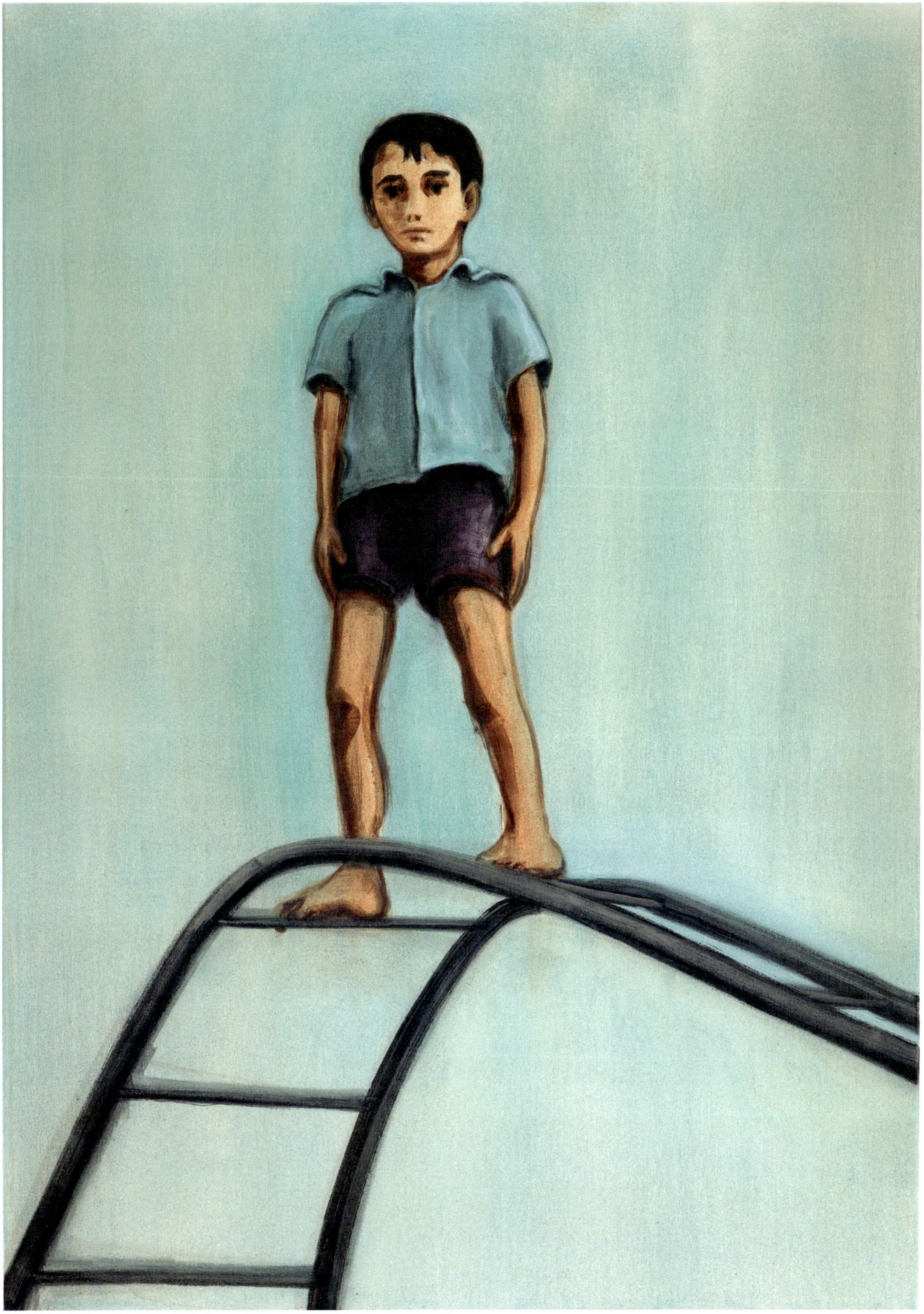

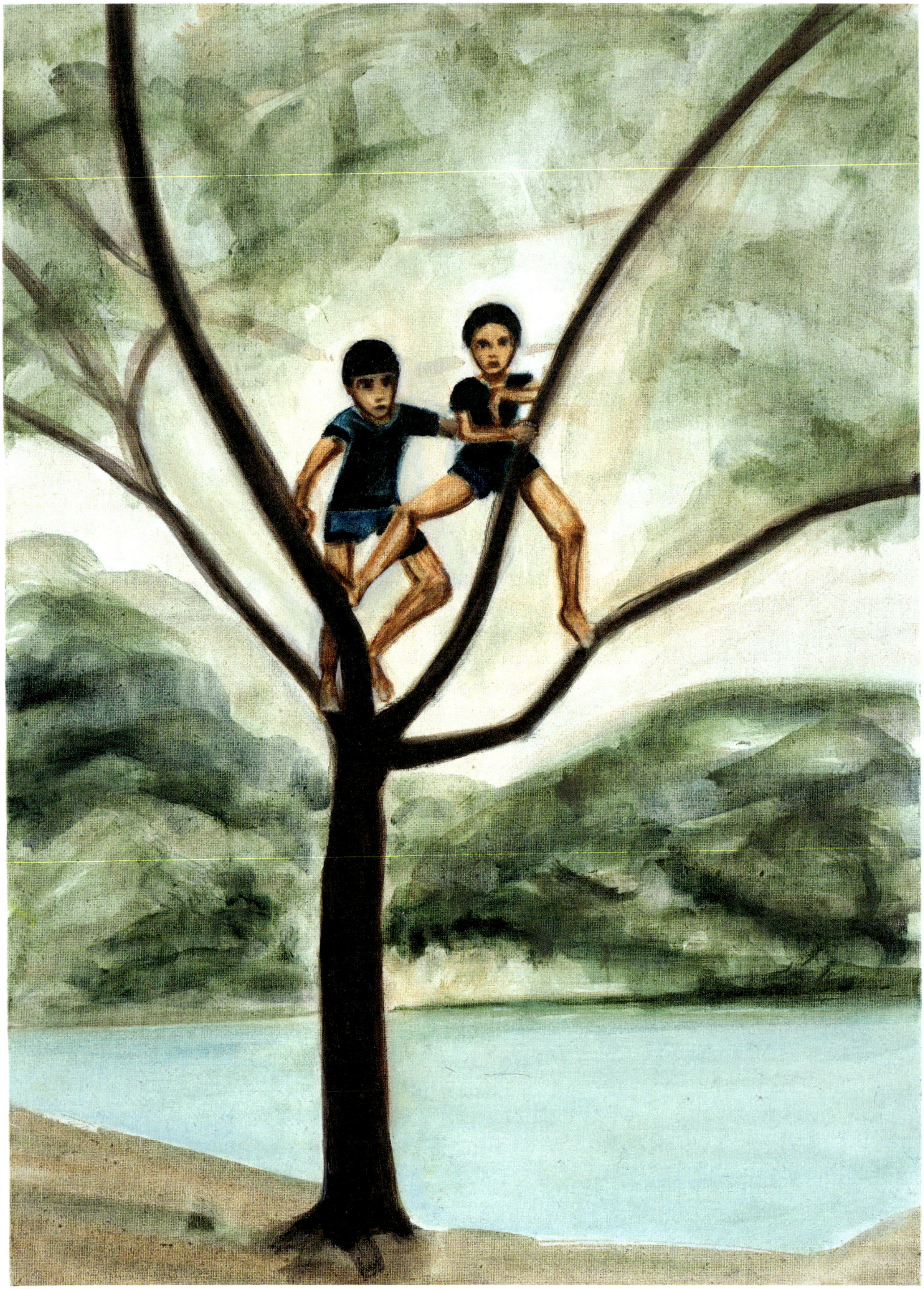

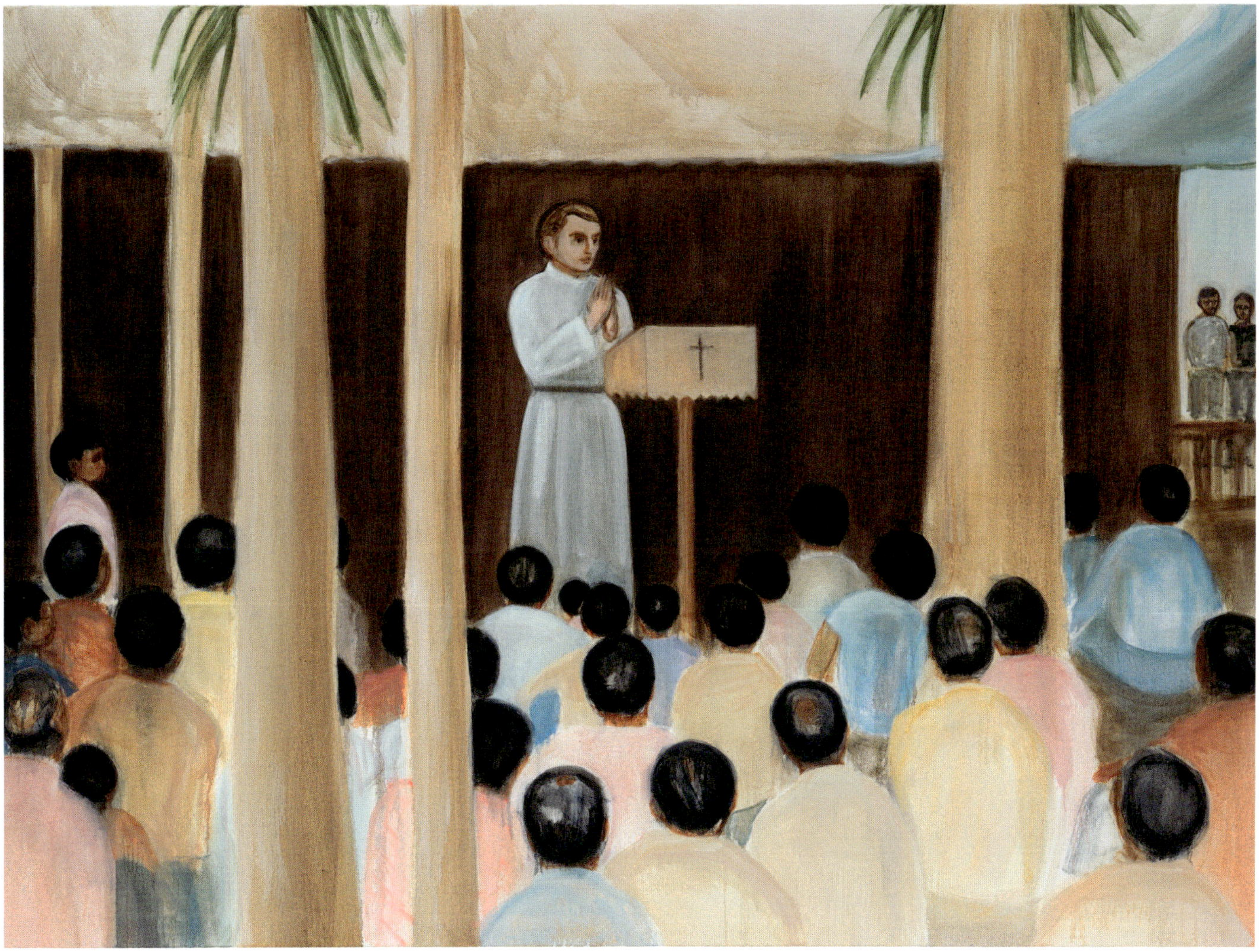

p. 43
Matthew Krishanu
Boy on a Climbing Frame, 2022
Oil on canvas
160 × 120 cm

Matthew Krishanu
Two Boys in a Tree, 2019
Oil on board
61 × 46 cm
Government Art Collection, UK

Matthew Krishanu
Mission, 2020
Oil on canvas
180 × 240 cm

All © Matthew Krishanu
Courtesy of the artist and Jhaveri Contemporary, Mumbai; Niru Ratnam, London and Tanya Leighton, Berlin and Los Angeles
Photos: Peter Mallet

Q&A with... Matthew Krishanu

Can you tell us about a book that had a particular impact on you as a child?

The *Earthsea* trilogy has always stayed with me. I read it several times as a child and soaked in the atmosphere. I have returned to it over the years, and I love the lyrical beauty of Ursula K. Le Guin's prose and the sense of world-building and character in these books.

What about your teenage years – was there a book or exhibition catalogue that was significant in terms of your decision to become an artist?

I remember borrowing a large catalogue of Alberto Giacometti's work from the library and holding on to it for months. I found the crossover between his drawings, sculptures and paintings fascinating and inspiring.

Similarly, when you were at art school, did any specific book influence how you thought or worked?

During my BA I was first introduced to Basquiat's paintings through the Whitney Museum catalogue [1993] of his first major retrospective – it played a large part in my move to painting from sculpture. Rasheed Araeen's *The Other Story* catalogue was also hugely important to me – allowing me to orientate myself within an international art historical perspective.

What kinds of books do you enjoy reading now?

I tend to alternate between art historical books and fiction. I end up having several books on the go at any one time. Re-reading Chinua Achebe's *Things Fall Apart* trilogy recently very much resonated with me. I also enjoy reading graphic novels.

Do you have a favourite character from a book or one that you most relate to?

I've always loved Ged in the *Earthsea* trilogy. The fact that he was brown-skinned in a genre – fantasy – so dominated by whiteness also felt significant to me.

What book helped you through a difficult time?

Poems from Rabindranath Tagore's *Shesh Lekha (Last Writings)* – in translation – came back to me during the terrible period of my late wife's terminal cancer.

Has a book ever made you laugh out loud?

Asterix makes me laugh out loud.

What are some of your favourite art books?

Hurvin Anderson [Rizzoli]; *El Greco* [Thames & Hudson}; *Gwen John* [Yale] and *Peter Doig: No Foreign Lands* [Hatje Cantz].

Has being the subject of a book changed how you view other artist monographs?

I looked at artist monographs more carefully during the process of making my book – how large images were, how works were captioned, and if there were details of paintings.

What aspect of making a book did you most enjoy?

I was pleased with the days spent in repro – getting the colours as close to the original paintings as possible.

What books have inspired you in recent years?

English Magic – a collection of short stories by Uschi Gatward. It's an incredible work. *Maus* by Art Spiegelman. *The Fire Next Time* by James Baldwin, which I re-read this year, having first read it in my late teens. And Raymond Carver's short story collections.

What are you reading at the moment?

The Mirror and the Palette by Jennifer Higgie; *Creation* by John-Paul Stonard and *Ivanhoe* by Sir Walter Scott.

Is there a book you are looking forward to reading that you have not yet had chance to?

There are too many to count. *Alice Neel: People Come First* and Donna Tartt's *The Goldfinch* are high up on my list.

Which one book do you think everyone should read?

English Magic by Uschi Gatward.

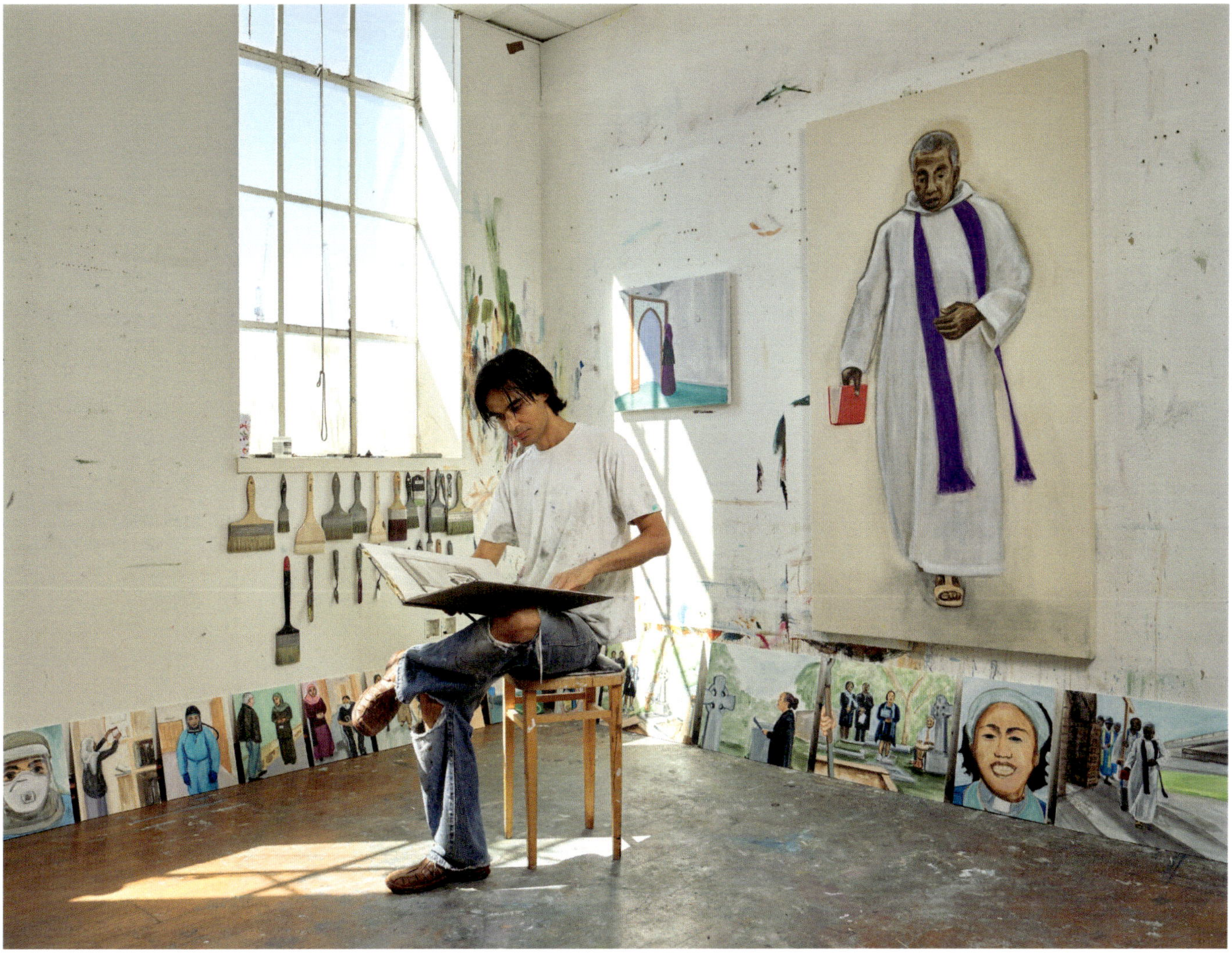

Portrait by and courtesy of Peter Mallet.

Chibụike Ụzọma
To Kick a Stone

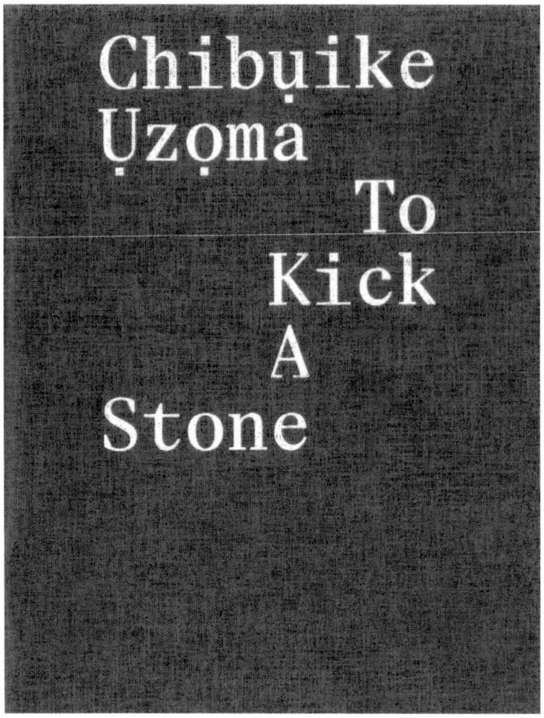

Contributors:
Ekow Eshun
Bishupal Limbu
Kat Sapera
Chibụike Ụzọma
Carlos Valladares

72pp
Softback
235 × 175 mm
c. 22 images
ISBN: 978-1-910221-46-4
RRP: £20
UK Release: 16 March 2023
Edited by Kat Sapera
Designed by Joe Gilmore
Printed by Pression, Leeds, UK
Co-published by Simon Lee Gallery and Anomie Publishing, London

Chibụike Ụzọma is a multidisciplinary artist working with painting, photography, drawing, text and video, based in New Haven, Connecticut.

Documented here are sixteen of the artist's large paintings rendered in oil and acrylic or acrylic spray-paint on canvas made in 2022. Accompanying an exhibition of the same name at Simon Lee Gallery, London, the first solo exhibition of his work in the UK, this publication is the fourth pillar of a collaborative project by the artist, setting his paintings in relation to video and audio works by Edward Owens and João Orecchia respectively. Ụzọma works with non-linear narratives, using a mix of languages that dodges and weaves the liminal spaces between representation and meaning. Fragments of stencilled letters jolt against textured pools of paint, and diaphanous figures are cropped by cinematic horizons. Comprising colourful, abstruse portraiture against stark black-and-white backgrounds, the paintings in *To Kick a Stone* are deeply suggestive, but ultimately formalist explorations of shape and composition.

An introduction to the monograph, written by Kat Sapera, Director of Simon Lee Gallery, details the influence of philosophy and the act of looking. Sapera brings the collaboration with Orecchia and Owens to the forefront of her discussion while touching on Ụzọma's making processes.

In his own essay, Ụzọma writes lyrically upon subjects including poetry, religion, good and evil.

Essays by Bishupal Limbu, Associate Professor of English at Portland State University, and Carlos Valladares, writer and critic, help amass a portrait of an artist whose enquiry is informed by film, philosophy and pictorial language – with the layering, unravelling and opening-up of narrative as a core focus. Lastly, the artist appears in conversation with writer and curator Ekow Eshun. This frank and illuminating conversation provides insight into the artist's painting practice, previous series of works and intentions, while also discussing issues of identity and Blackness. Their interview further reflects on past exhibitions, connections with other key artists and Ụzọma's recent MFA studies at Yale.

Chibụike Ụzọma (b. 1992, Port Harcourt, Nigeria) received his BFA from the University of Benin, an MFA from Yale University School of Art and was awarded the Francis Greenburger Fellowship in 2018. His work is included in the public collections of Kistefos Museum, Jevnaker, Norway; Didi Museum, Lagos, Nigeria and Fotohof Salzburg, Austria. Recent exhibitions include Pace, New York (2021); Lyles & King, New York (2021); Everard Read, Cape Town, South Africa (2019); Florida Museum of Photographic Arts, Florida (2019); Circa Gallery, Cape Town, South Africa (2017) and D-Contemporary Gallery, London, UK (2017).

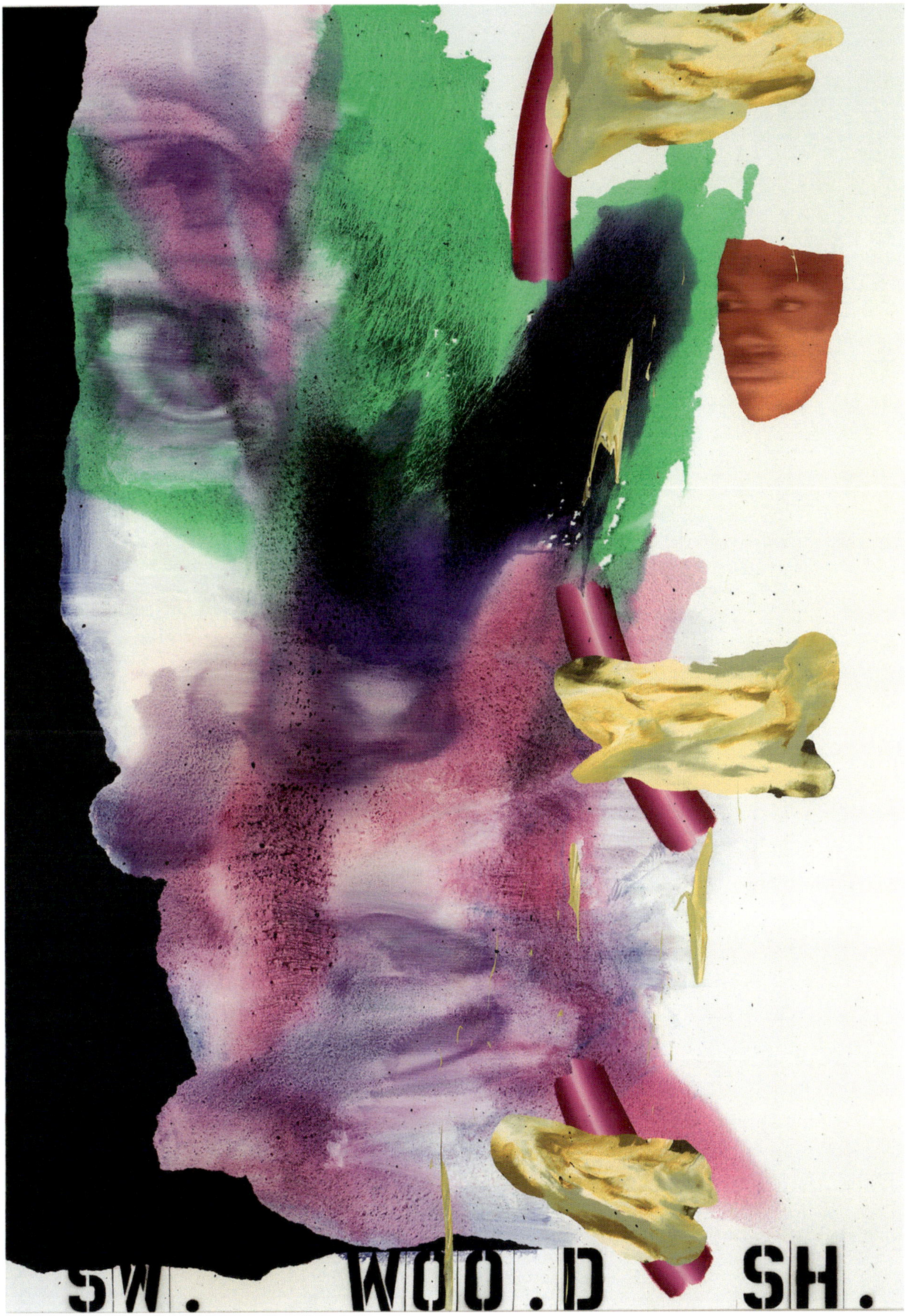
SW. WOO.D SH.

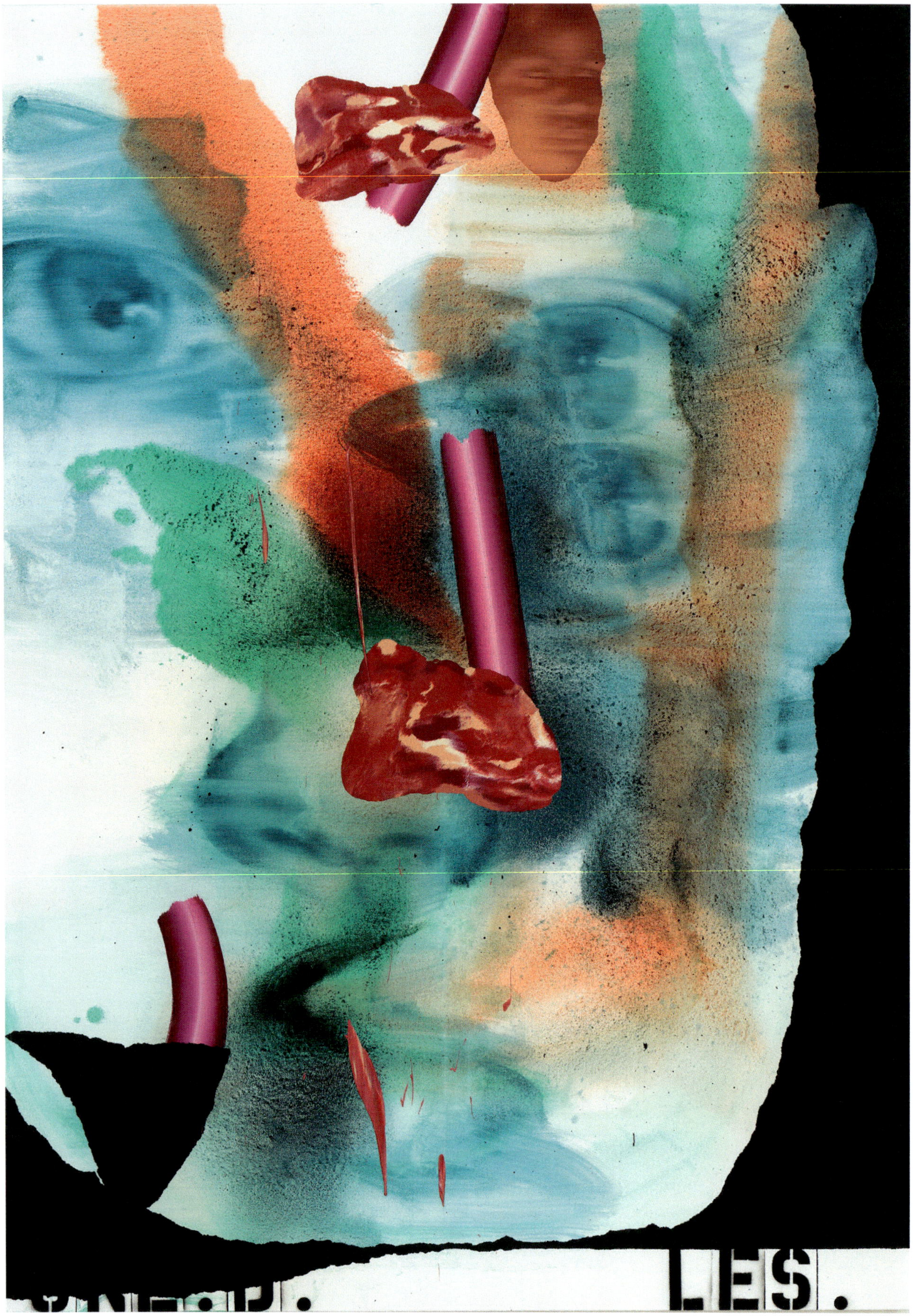
LES.

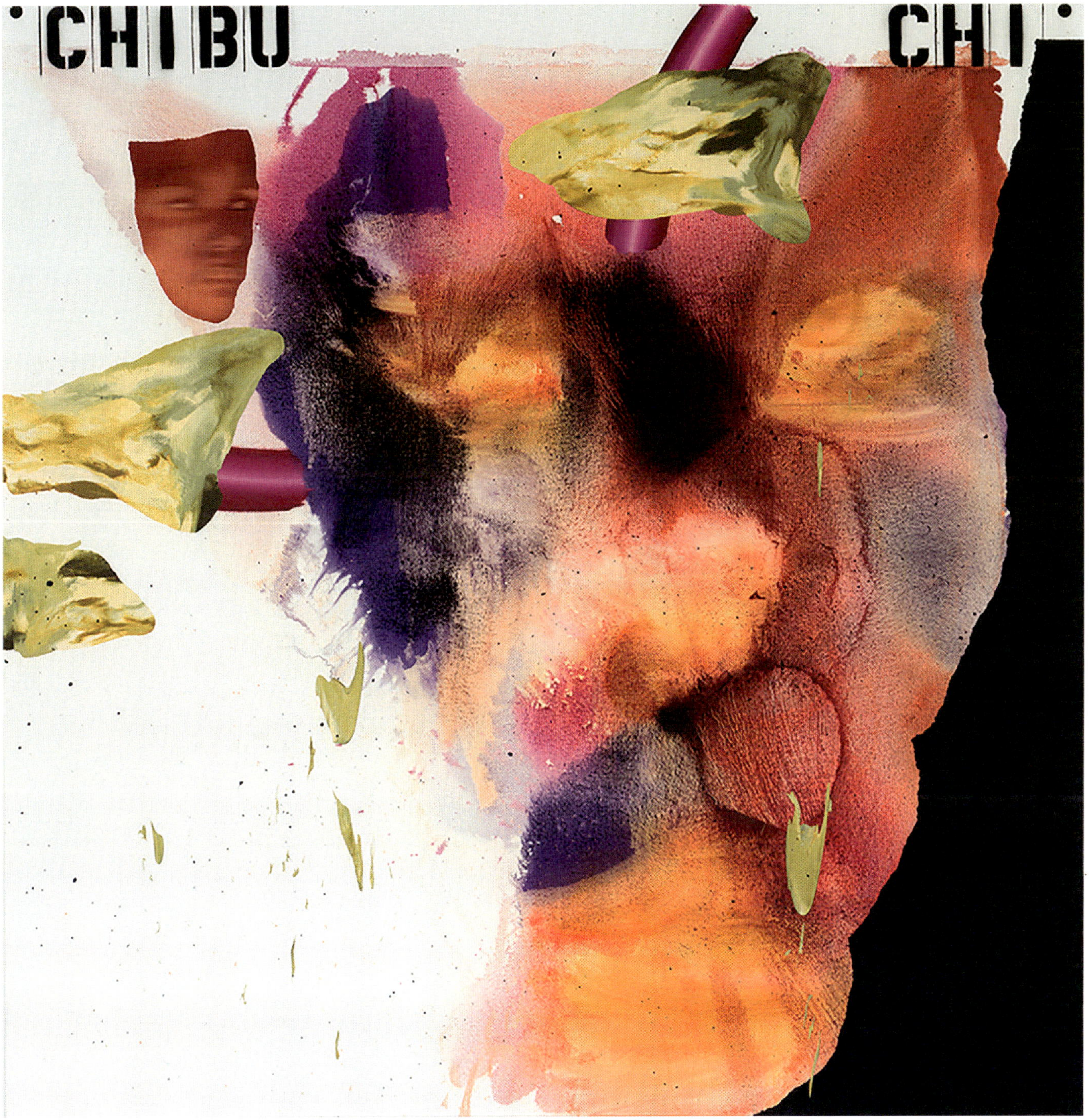

p. 49
Chibụike Ụzọma
Mother, Mother..., Times Have Changed, 2022
Oil and acrylic on canvas
213.4 x 152.4 cm

Chibụike Ụzọma
Mother, Mother..., Times Have Changed, 2022
Oil and acrylic on canvas
213.4 x 152.4 cm

Chibụike Ụzọma
Mother, Mother..., Times Have Changed, 2022
Oil and acrylic on canvas
182.9 x 182.9 cm

All © Chibụike Ụzọma
Courtesy of Simon Lee Gallery, London
Photos: Adam Reich

Nick Hornby

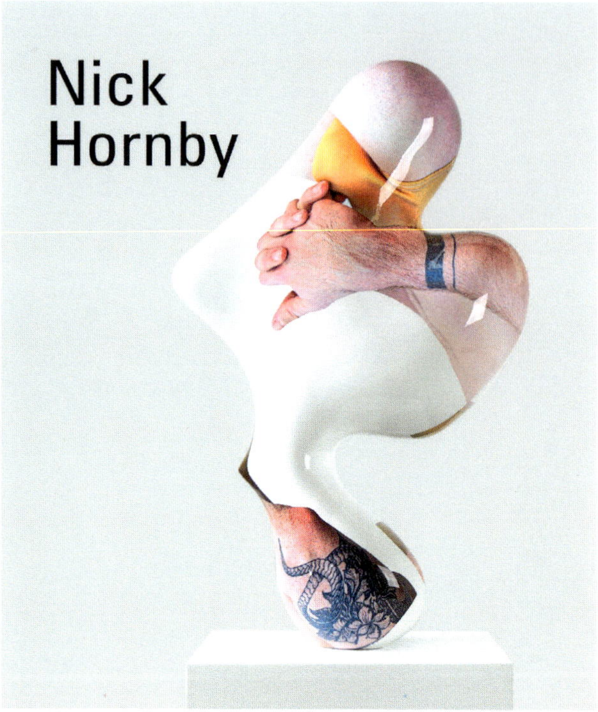

Contributors:
Hannah Higham
Helen Pheby
Matt Price
Luke Syson

256pp
Hardback
280 × 245 mm
c. 175 images
ISBN: 978-1-910221-24-2
RRP: £35
UK Release: 8 December 2022
Edited by Matt Price
Designed by Herman Lelie
Layouts by Stefania Bonelli
Printed by EBS, Verona
Published by Anomie Publishing, London

Nick Hornby (b. 1980, London) is one of the leading sculptors of his generation in Britain today, creating works on both intimate and monumental scales, and at the intersection of art history and contemporary technology. Hornby's practice uses software that allows him to extract, alter and hybridise sculptures from art history into new works made from marble, steel, bronze, resin, wood and composite materials. It could be said that Hornby has opened up a new sculptural language for the twenty-first century.

This, his first major monograph, features approximately 175 images, many of which are reproduced here for the first time or have been commissioned for the publication. Alongside documentation of works presented in galleries and outdoor spaces are production images taken in the studio and fabrication workshops. Hornby's practice is here divided into four categories: Intersections, Extrusions, Hydrographics and Collaborations.

A foreword by Luke Syson, Director of the Fitzwilliam Museum, Cambridge, offers insight into Hornby's internal and external relationship with sculpture, considering the links between two and three dimensions, abstraction and representation, the 'real' and the digital. Editor Matt Price's introduction takes readers on a whistle-stop tour of the artist's oeuvre, from his early family life and studies at Chelsea and the Slade in London, to his latest major exhibitions and commissions. An essay by Dr Hannah Higham, Senior Curator of Collections and Research at the Henry Moore Foundation, provides the most substantial piece of critical writing on Hornby's work to date, drawing out specific touchstones in the history of art and discussing the relationship between the work and time. Higham further explores the ways that the motion and position of the viewer alter the experience of the sculptures, with new angles revealing fresh artistic inspirations from Hans Arp to Elizabeth Frink. An interview with Dr Helen Pheby, Associate Director, Programme, at Yorkshire Sculpture Park, probes the artist about his cultural and theoretical inspirations, methods, materials and ideologies, including his views on collaboration, the public nature of art and its accessibility. Their conversation provides an insight into the thinking of the artist at a crucial stage in his career.

Nick Hornby is a British artist living and working in London. In the UK he has exhibited at Tate Britain, Southbank Centre, Leighton House (all London); Cass Sculpture Foundation and Glyndebourne (both Sussex); MOSTYN, Wales and the Fitzwilliam Museum, Cambridge. International exhibitions have been held at the Museum of Arts and Design, New York and Poznań Biennale, Poland, along with residencies with Outset, Israel, and Eyebeam, New York. In 2014 Hornby was made a fellow of the Royal Society of Sculptors.

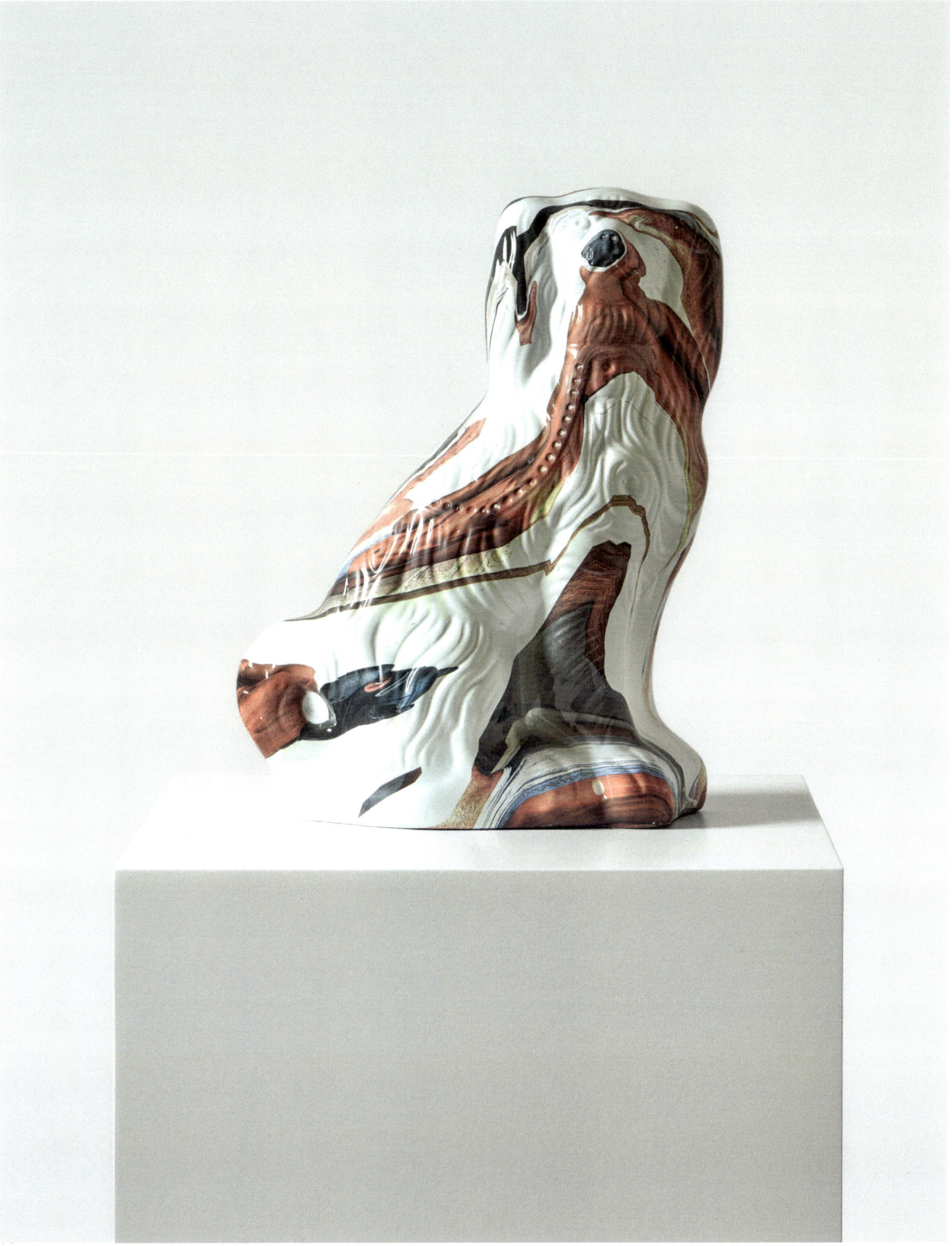

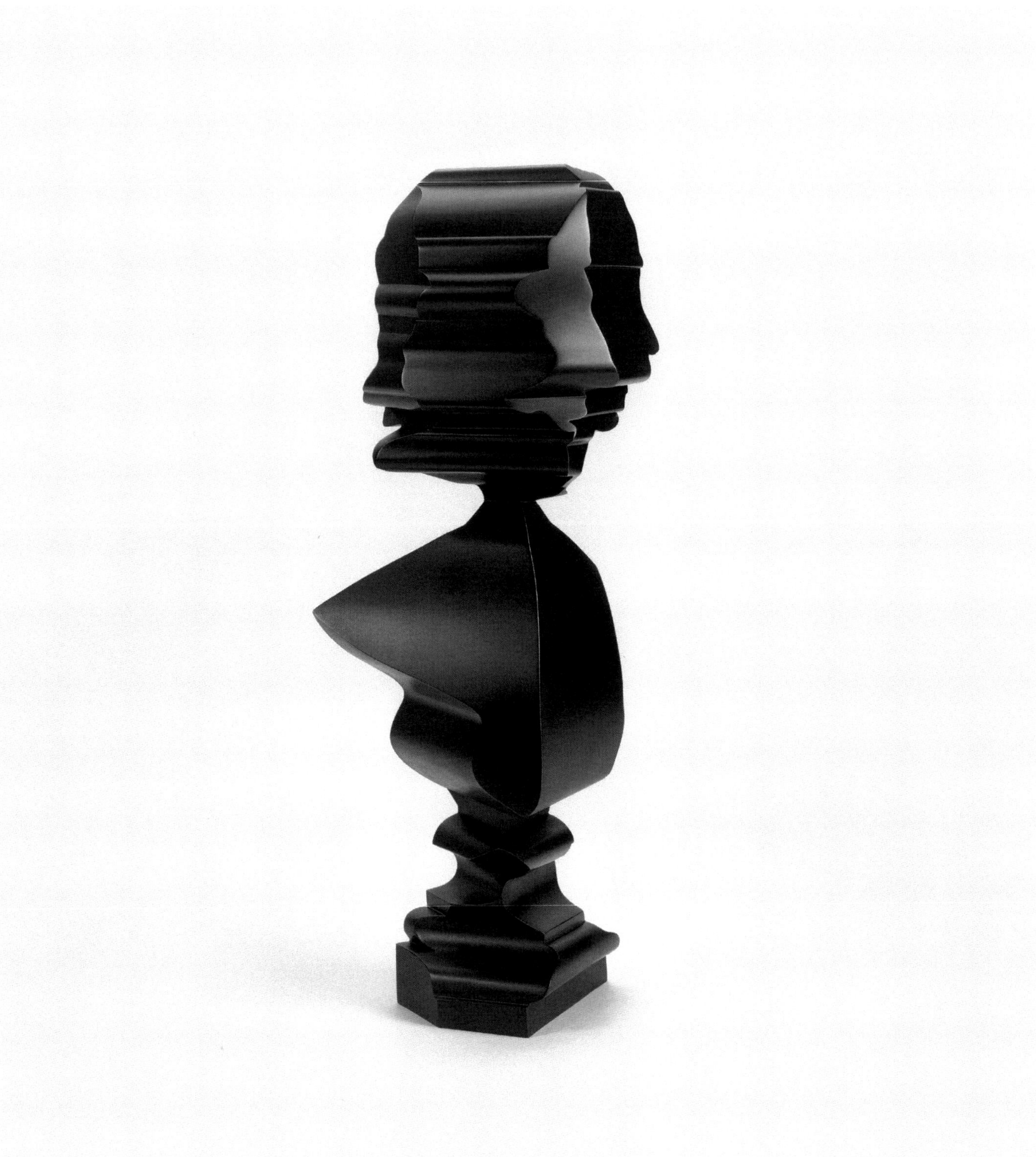

p. 53
Nick Hornby
Dear Dashy Dash, 2020
Resin, ink, lacquer
36 × 28 × 15 cm
Photo: Ben Westoby

Nick Hornby
I found my friends, they're in my head (Kurt Cobain), 2014
Bronze
60 × 30 × 30 cm
Photo: Studio Nick Hornby

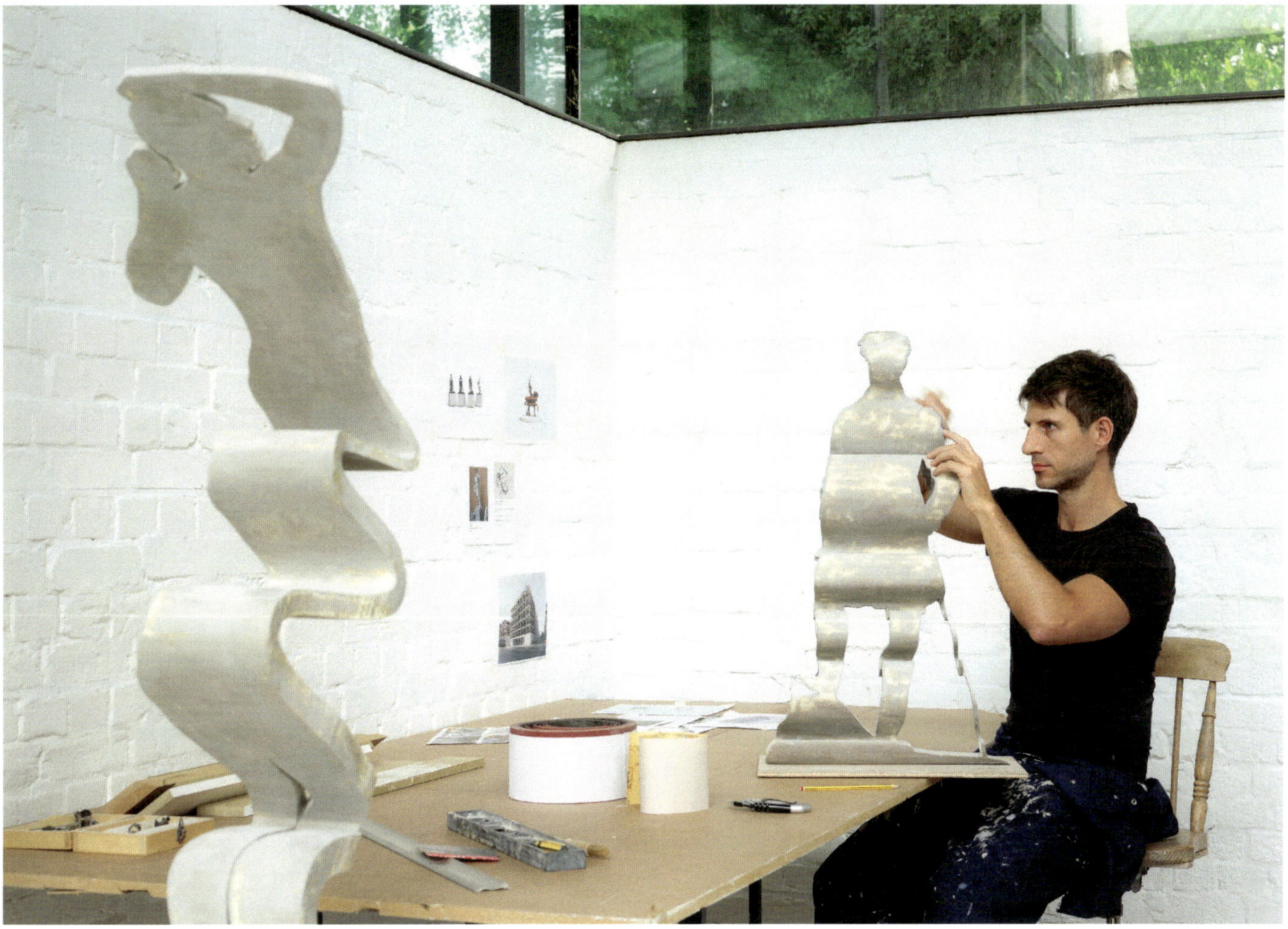

Nick Hornby in his studio, London, 2022
Photo: Peter Mallet

All courtesy of the artist

Q&A with... Nick Hornby

Can you tell us about a book that had a particular impact on you as a child?

The Tree That Sat Down by Beverley Nichols, which is about a magical world inside a tree. As a sculptural proposition – inverting things – it was wonderful. Also Jonathan Swift's *Gulliver's Travels* – again, this is all about shifting scales and therefore very sculptural (think model vs monument à la Rosalind Krauss).

What about your teenage years – was there a book or exhibition catalogue that was significant in terms of your decision to become an artist?

No. I was very dyslexic, and I only learnt to read for pleasure in my mid-twenties. It was Roland Barthes's *Mythologies* and Jacques Derrida's *The Truth in Painting* which set off the dominoes.

And when you were at art school? Were there specific books you can remember that influenced how you thought or worked?

Sadly, the dyslexia was quite severe, but I always loved poetry, because it is bitesize and non-linear. I recall passages from Christopher Marlowe's *Doctor Faustus* and poems by Elizabeth Bishop, which, looking back, were both queer texts.

What kinds of books do you enjoy reading now – do you have a favourite genre?

I have just finished *Tiepolo Blue* by James Cahill. My favourite genre now is probably queer fiction.

What proportion of the books you read are fiction?

Ten per cent.

Do you have a favourite character from a book or one that you most relate to?

Mole from Kenneth Grahame's *The Wind in the Willows*, Reepicheep from C.S. Lewis's *The Voyage of the Dawn Treader [The Chronicles of Narnia]*, Doctor Faustus and Mister Magnolia [Quentin Blake]. Oh, and sometimes Mr Twit from Roald Dahl's *The Twits* – I love a prank.

What book helped you through a difficult time?

The Velvet Rage by Alan Downs changed my life.

Has a book ever made you laugh out loud?

Nope. But, cry, yes. Philippe Besson's *Lie with Me* and Jonathan Safran Foer's *Extremely Loud & Incredibly Close*.

What aspect of making a book did you most enjoy?

The long, messy and amusing meetings with Matt, which he somehow consolidated into a coherent, finished, beautiful product.

What books have inspired you in recent years?

I have re-read Rainer Maria Rilke's *Letters to a Young Poet*, which irritates me – a form of inspiration.

What are you reading at the moment?

Nothing. I'm back at work. Doomscrolling.

Is there a book or catalogue that you are looking forward to reading that you have not yet had chance to?

Henry Moore: Friendships and Legacies by Tania Moore, published by the Sainsbury Centre for Visual Arts.

Which one book do you think everyone should read?

At the first signs of spring, the first twenty pages of *The Wind in the Willows* – up until the picnic on the river bank. And the first fifteen pages of *Restitutions of the Truth in Pointing [Pointure]* by Derrida, where he analyses van Gogh's old boots.

Is there anything else you'd like to tell us here about your life, work and books that we've not already covered?

I'm sorry – I have some library books at home which I've not returned.

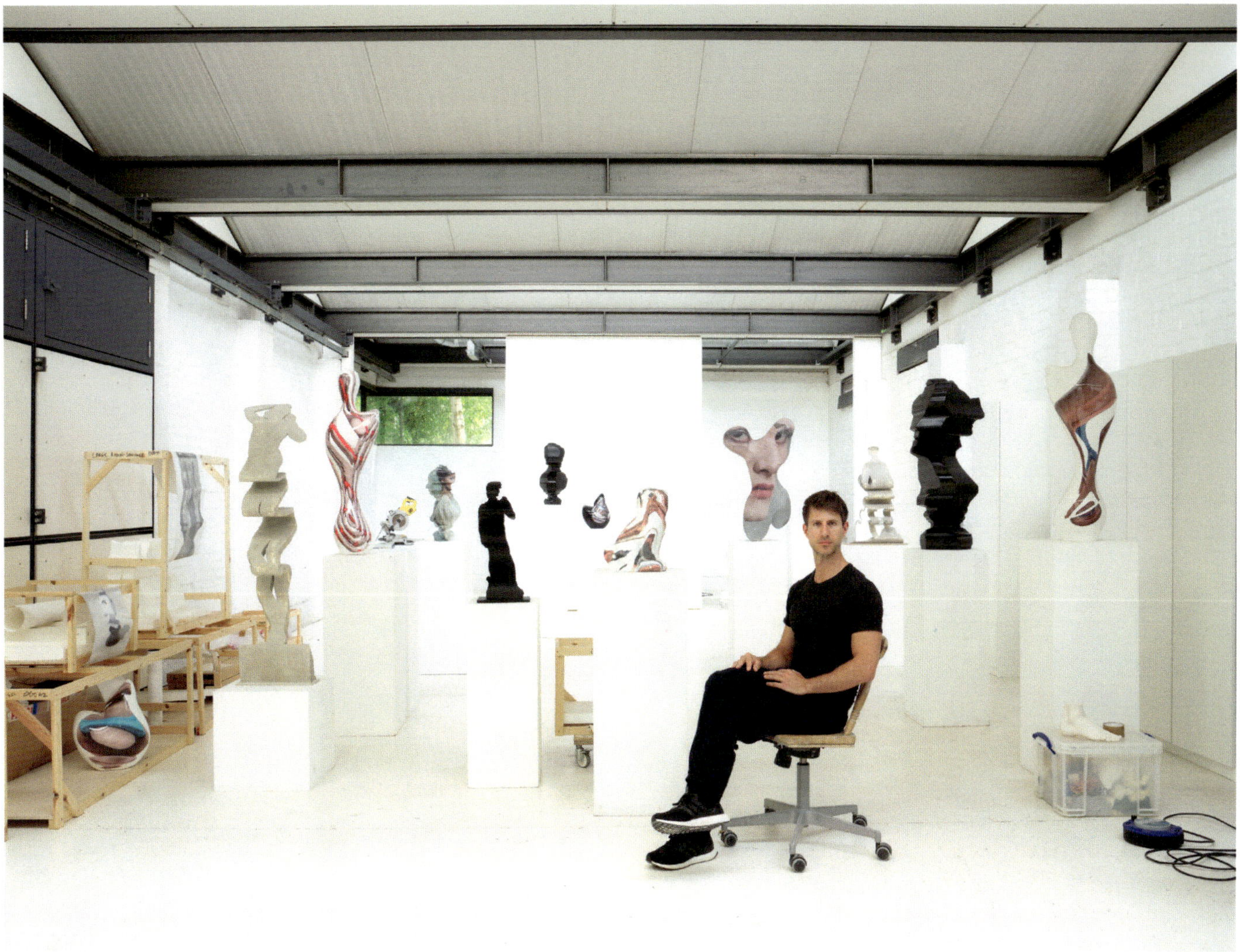

Portrait by and courtesy of Peter Mallet.

Anna Freeman Bentley
make believe

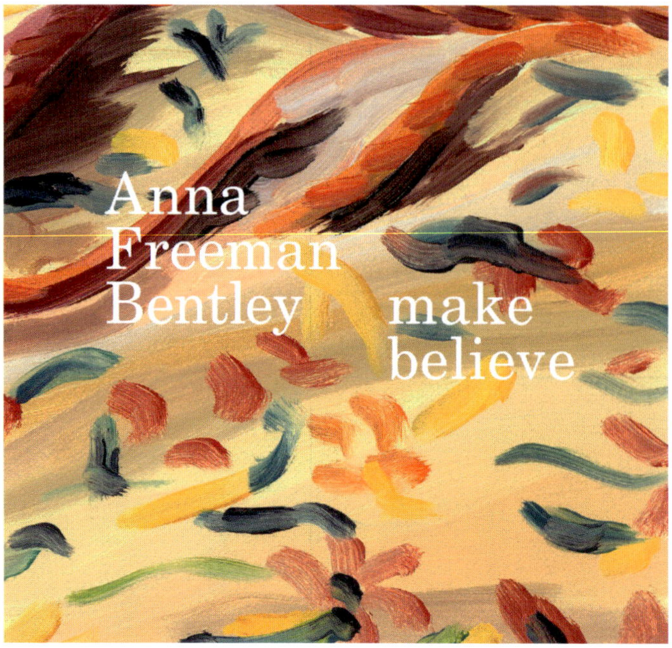

Contributors:
Thomas Marks
Georgie Paget
Rollo Campbell
Matt Incledon

84pp
Hardback
240 × 260 mm
c. 50 images
ISBN: 978-1-910221-43-3
RRP: £25
UK Release: 22 September 2022
Edited by Matt Incledon and Matt Price
Designed by Joe Gilmore
Printed by Gomer, Wales
Co-published by Frestonian Gallery and
Anomie Publishing, London

Anna Freeman Bentley's paintings use architectural imagery to explore the emotive potential of space and its associations with longing. Grounded in an interest in the baroque, her source material includes junk shops, restaurants, private members clubs, flea markets and designed interiors. Central to her work is an investigation into surface, tension and the atmosphere evoked by these different interior surroundings. The spaces she depicts are empty, yet visual signifiers point to evidence of people and social happenings.

This, Freeman Bentley's third publication to date, is centred on the relationship between painting and cinema and is divided into sections dedicated to major paintings on canvas and panel, and a number of works on paper (all works 2021–22). Freeman Bentley's work here is focused on sets from *The Colour Room* (2021), a film that tells the story of the early career of celebrated British ceramicist Clarice Cliff (1899–1972). Many of the titles of the paintings are taken from lines of the film's script.

The foreword is by Rollo Campbell and Matt Incledon of Frestonian Gallery. An essay by writer and critic Thomas Marks draws out the importance to her work of historic and contemporary cinema and temporary architecture. Marks notes a change in palette in these new paintings, with Freeman Bentley embracing pastels and tracing parallels between the artist herself and Cliff. An interview with Georgie Paget, co-founder of Caspian Films, production company for *The Colour Room*, meanwhile, provides insight into the artist's particular interest in the artifice of film props and of the film set as a layered space 'steeped in meaning, purpose and potential'. The two discuss the reciprocity of painting and cinema in detail, recounting Freeman Bentley's experiences on the film's sets and discussing her working processes, beginning with taking photographs on set, through to oil sketches and the later development of large-scale canvases.

Anna Freeman Bentley studied Painting at Chelsea College of Art, Kunsthochschule Berlin Weissensee and the Royal College of Art. Awards and residencies include Palazzo Monti Residency, Brescia, Italy (2019); The Elizabeth Greenshields Foundation Grant (2019 and 2017) and Artist in Restaurant residency at Michelin-starred restaurant Pied à Terre, London (2012). Selected exhibitions (* denotes solo) include DENK Gallery, Los Angeles, 2019*; Ahmanson Gallery, Irvine (2018)*; Space K, Seoul, 2017; 68projects, Berlin (2017); the East London Painting Prize (2014 and 2015); Workshop Gallery, Venice (2012)*; MAC Birmingham (2011); Prague Biennale (2011) and the Bloomberg New Contemporaries (2009).

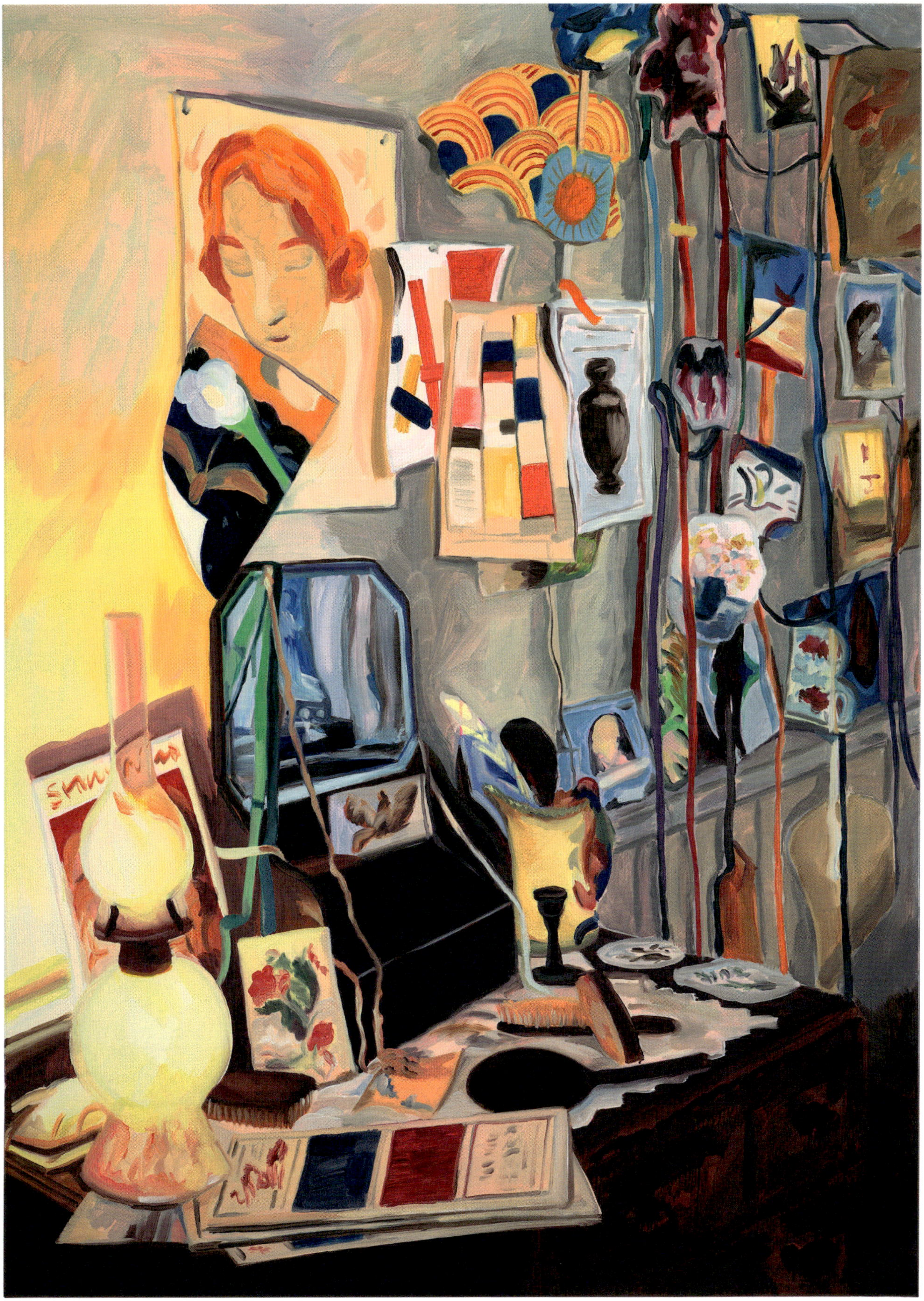

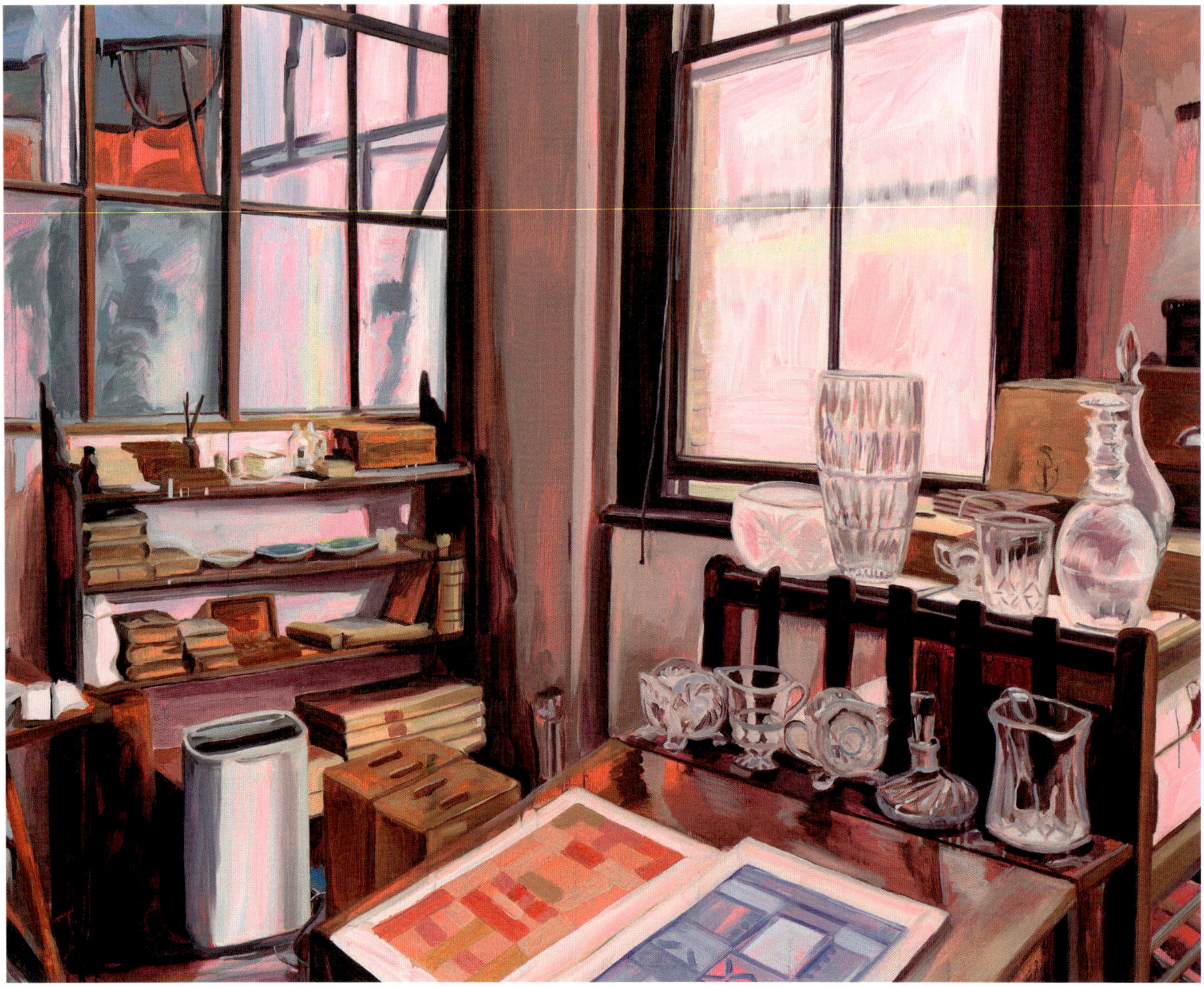

p. 59
Anna Freeman Bentley
Placeholders, 2022
Oil on canvas
109 × 80 cm
Photo: Peter Mallet

Anna Freeman Bentley
The door to the office is open, 2022
Oil on canvas
135 × 205 cm
Photo: Anna Arca

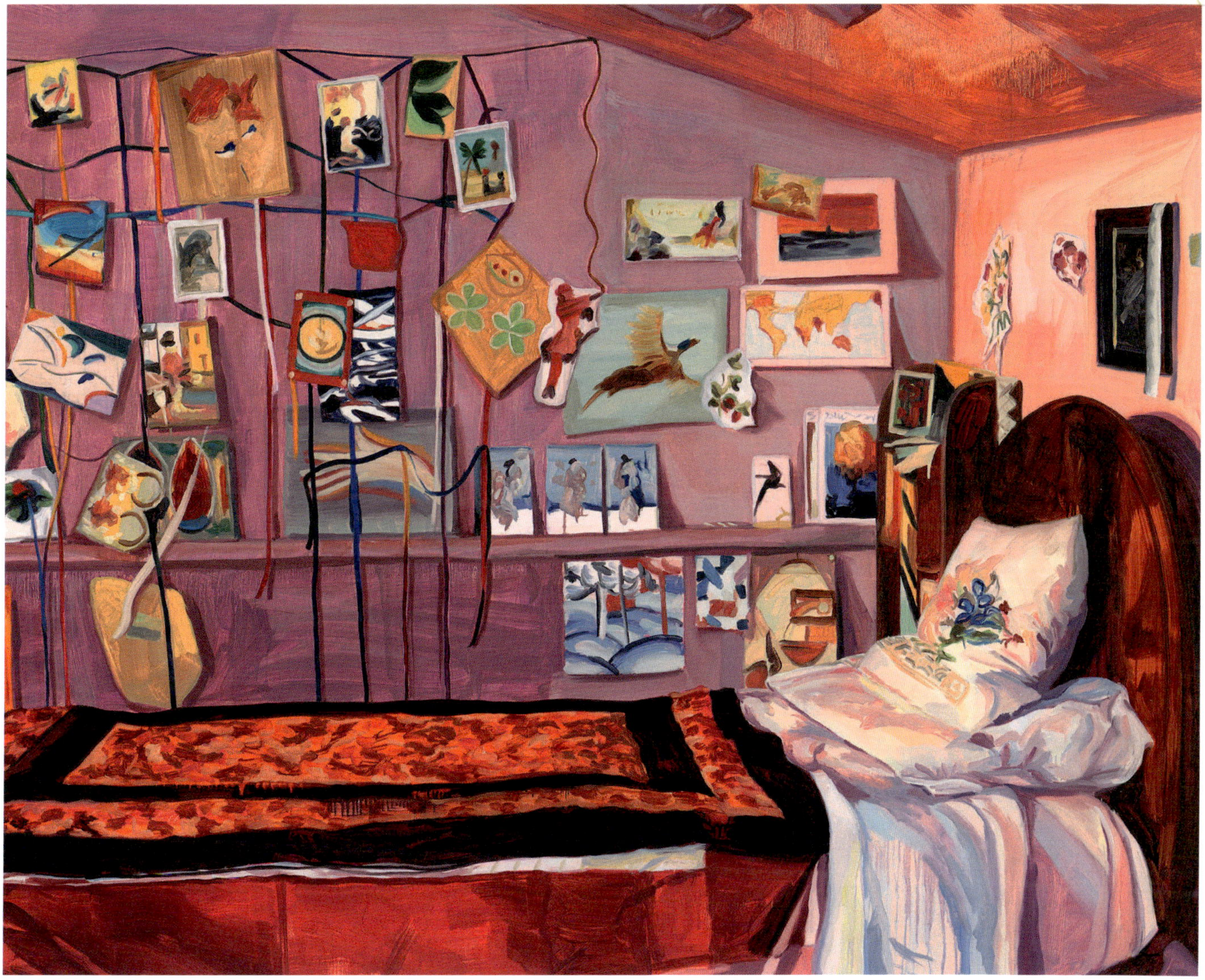

Anna Freeman Bentley
Ribbons, wrappers, designs, 2022
Oil on canvas
135 × 203 cm
Photo: Peter Mallet

All courtesy of the artist and
Frestonian Gallery, London

Q&A with... Anna Freeman Bentley

Can you tell us about a book that had a particular impact on you as a child?

I have strong memories of my dad reading the *Just So Stories* by Rudyard Kipling when I was a child. 'The Elephant's Child' was my personal favourite. Now that I have a kid of my own, I can see the relation to the elephant's child and his 'satiable curtiosity'! I'm not sure about all the spanking though – that hasn't aged well.

Similarly, when you were at art school, did any specific book influence how you thought or worked?

I often feel like I fell into art school, driven mostly by the desire and ambition to make my own work, rather than being inspired by others, or even by the idea of being an artist. It was a slow awakening for me. There was an exhibition that had a profound effect on me, though. I saw it in Frankfurt in 2003 while on an Erasmus exchange in Berlin. It was at the Schirn Kunsthalle and was called *Dear Painter, Paint Me*. I bought the catalogue and devoured it. I still enjoy looking at it every now and then. It's funny, really, as it is all about painting the figure, which is something I specifically don't do, but so many of the artists in that exhibition have become points of reference at different stages in my career. The varied materiality of mark-making in works by Luc Tuymans, Elizabeth Peyton, Sophie von Hellermann and Neo Rauch has fed into the work I make. I would say that was one of the first exhibitions that really made me want to be an artist, to make works that would become part of a conversation about painting as a way of expressing some sort of current or lasting moment.

What proportion of the books you read are fiction?

I enjoy reading novels, but I rarely allow myself that luxury. I only read fiction on holiday. The rest of the time I feel there are so many books that I should be reading: books about art, about artists, about faith, about parenting, etc. But I'm always seeking a really good page-turner.

Do you have a favourite character from a book or one that you most relate to?

Hmm, I've not really thought in those terms for a long time, so I guess my characters will be pretty classic. Jane Eyre (Charlotte Brontë), Anne Shirley (from *Anne of Green Gables* by L.M. Montgomery), and Elizabeth Bennet (from *Pride and Prejudice* by Jane Austen).

Has a book ever made you laugh out loud?

I loved *Zona* by Geoff Dyer, a book reflecting on Andrei Tarkovsky's film *Stalker*. I remember laughing out loud when he talks about the writer character being stuck for inspiration and so embarking on this journey in the hope of finding ideas. Dyer steps out of his description of the film (in a sort of breaking-the-fourth-wall moment) and exclaims understanding and exasperation at the sentiment, as here he is writing a book about a film that has stayed with him, because he too is stuck for inspiration. I can relate to that. I spend a lot of time questioning myself, my motives and my ideas. It can be overwhelming sometimes, but reading that other people feel the same is a comfort. The idea of using someone else's work as a starting point for discovering new ideas of my own is also familiar. I've been thinking recently about musicians who cover songs by other artists. They use the fact that they have not composed the music to connect with it on a more emotional level.

What are some of your favourite art books?

As well as being a big fan of her work and the writings in this book, Clare Woods' monograph *Strange Meetings* is a playful way of presenting an art book. How the book itself becomes a physical representation of a painting is great, with the sides of the book looking like the sides of one of her paintings.

What are you reading at the moment?

I just read *Maame* by Jessica George as I was on holiday. It was a very enjoyable, if at times sad, read. I also recently read *The Hare with Amber Eyes* by Edmund de Waal. I found that book so profoundly moving and relevant, tracing such significance through objects and using them as a way to investigate his family history as well as a wider European history.

Which one book do you think everyone should read?

I honestly think there is no other book as profound, poetic, hard to read, inspiring, misunderstood, comforting and all-encompassing as the Bible.

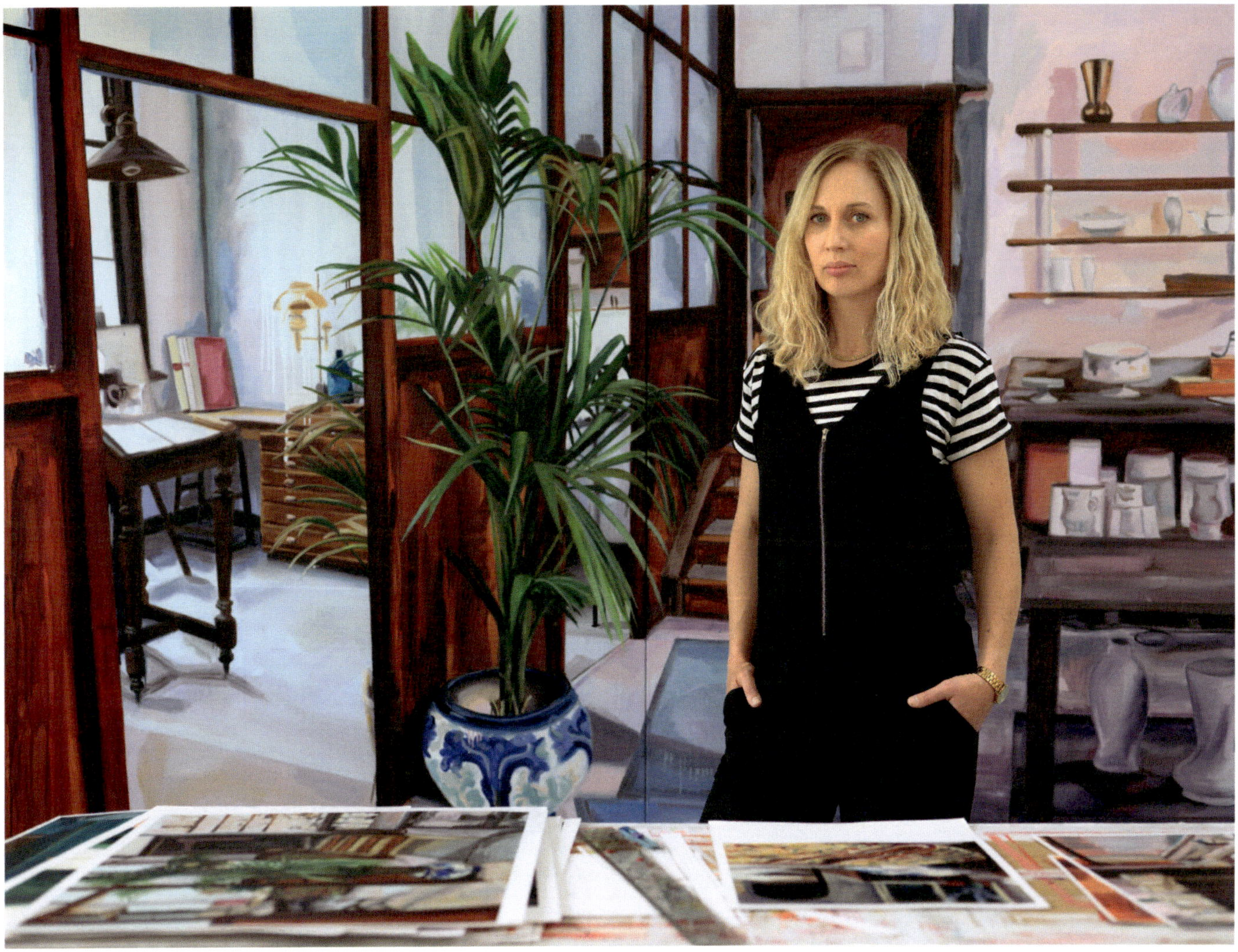

Portrait by and courtesy of Peter Mallet.

Lorna Robertson
thoughts, meals, days

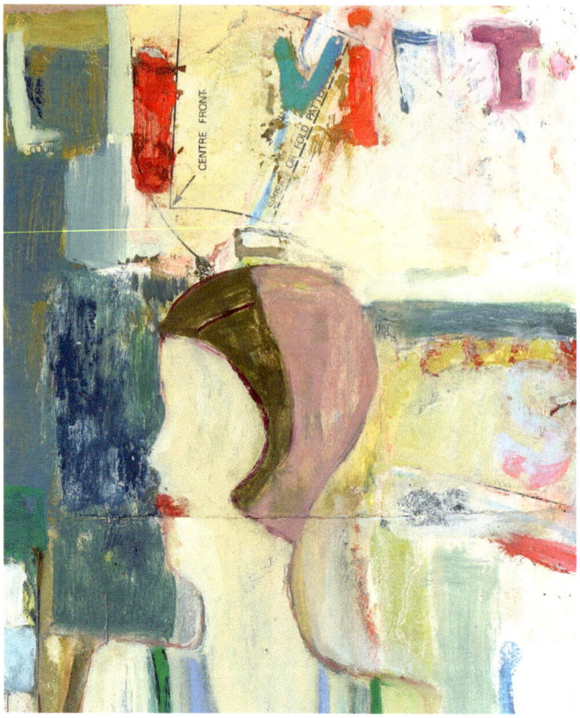

Contributors:
Hettie Judah
Mikey Cuddihy

160pp
Hardback
260 × 210 mm
c. 100 images
ISBN: 978-1-910221-42-6
RRP: £28
UK Release: 8 September 2022
Edited by Ingleby, Edinburgh
Designed by Joanna Deans, Identity
Printed by Albe de Coker, Antwerp
Co-published by Ingleby, Edinburgh, and
Anomie Publishing, London

Lorna Robertson's colourful paintings, often made with a combination of oil paint and collage, have a distinctly nostalgic tone. Shimmering female forms with swinging skirts from the 1950s or bonneted bathers from the 1920s jostle with richly described interiors and crowded tabletops. Hints and glimpses of tangible forms – a fashion model, for example, or a vase – appear and then fragment into patterns and explosions of colour. 'My paintings,' Robertson says, 'sit somewhere between abstraction and figuration, a tangled game of hide-and-seek that plays with the visibility and readability of an image. I often paint to find out what to paint, creating harmonies and tensions through placement of shape, specificity of colour – the process itself becoming an act of revealing.'

This publication is divided into sections that feature collections of recent large paintings by the artist (2015–22), small paintings (all 2022) and works on paper (2016–22), all of which demonstrate Robertson's characteristic layered interpretations of the female form alongside recurring motifs such as hats, long dresses and flowers. Her drawings (2018–20) offer fluid forms in ink, pencil and watercolour. These reproductions are accompanied by photographs of Robertson's busy studio walls and painting tools which provide an intimate picture of her working environment and processes.

An essay by art critic Hettie Judah explores Robertson's work in terms of pattern, costume and architecture, drawing out key inspirations including tapestry, advertising and magazine design through abstracted forms. The influence of contemporary female painters and those from art history is further considered. Robertson's paintings 'are often composed like sound works, punctuated by returning motifs, balanced between harmony and discord, built up in many layers of different elements.' But, warns Judah, 'Don't be fooled by the cool abstraction, there's feeling here too – memory floods in waves of colour and rhythm through these.' In a further text, Robertson is in conversation with artist and writer Mikey Cuddihy. This frank interview reveals much about Robertson's intuitive working processes: from starting points, colour decisions, the rhythms of brushwork and considerations of scale, to the wider relationship between text, music, drawing and painting.

Lorna Robertson was born in Ayr on the west coast of Scotland in 1967. She studied at Duncan of Jordanstone College of Art in Dundee and currently lives and works in Glasgow. The artist is represented by Ingleby Gallery. Her first solo exhibition *thoughts, meals, days* was held at Ingleby Gallery, Edinburgh, in 2022.

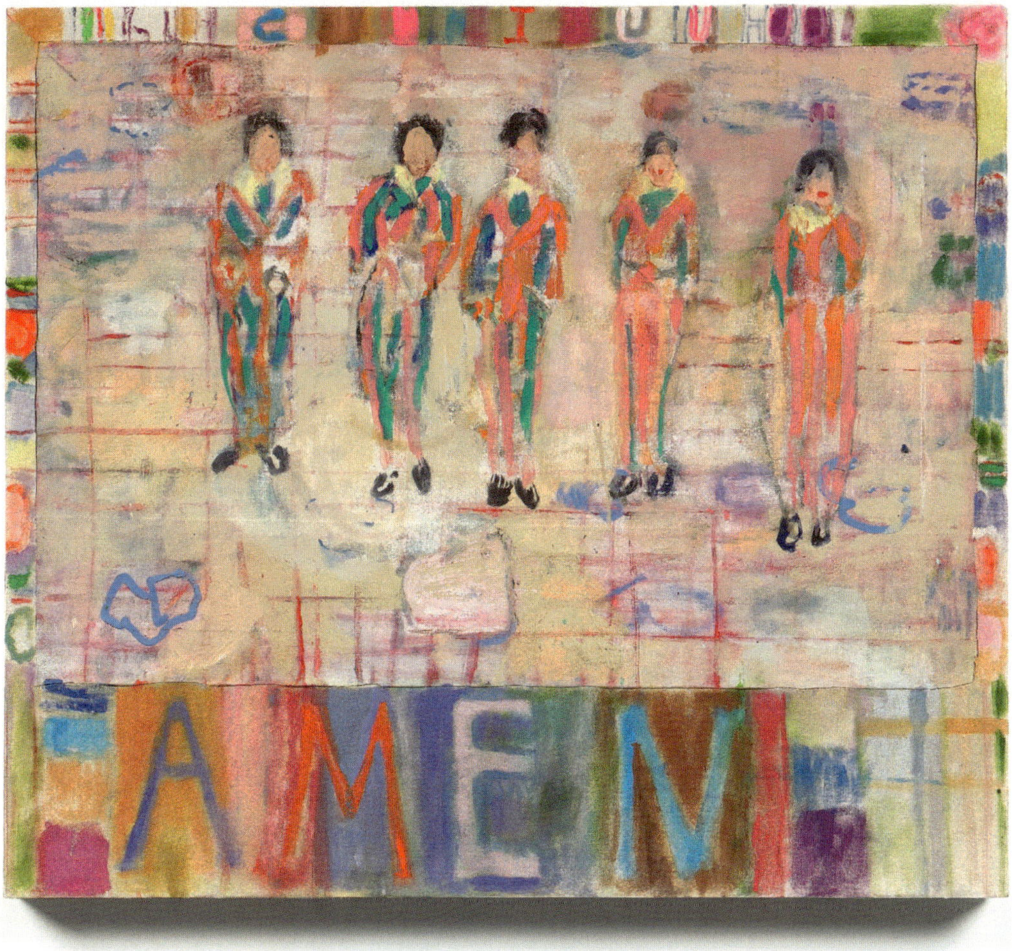

Lorna Robertson
Benedictus, 2022
Oil on canvas
82 × 95 × 4 cm
Courtesy of the artist and Ingleby, Edinburgh
Photo: John McKenzie

David Batchelor
Concretos

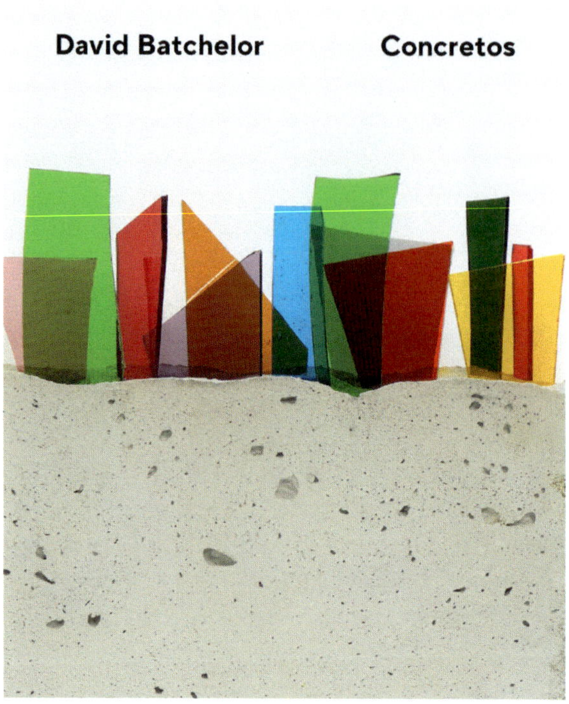

Contributors:
David Batchelor
Adrian Forty
Eleanor Nairne

144pp
Softback
265 × 215 mm
c. 100 images
ISBN: 978-1-910221-38-9
RRP: £20
UK Release: 28 July 2022
Edited by David Batchelor and Matt Price
Designed by Hyperkit, London
Printed by Park, London
Published by Anomie Publishing, London

Throughout his international career spanning more than thirty years, artist and writer David Batchelor has long been preoccupied with colour. 'Colour is not just a feature of [my] sculpture or painting,' he notes, 'but its central and overriding subject.' This new publication is devoted to an ongoing series of sculptures titled *Concretos*. First made in 2011, *Concretos* combine concrete with a variety of brightly coloured – and often found – materials.

The publication features a text by Batchelor charting the development of *Concretos*, revealing that the first *Concreto* was made after encountering coloured glass shards embedded in a concrete wall in the back streets of Palermo. Over time these *Concretos*, their title a nod to the Latin American art movement to which Batchelor's work is much indebted, have become more complex adventures in layering, pattern and process. Elements such as acrylic plastic, spray and household gloss paint, steel, fabric and found objects all find themselves set in a concrete base.

In an essay commissioned for the publication, curator Eleanor Nairne considers *Concretos* in light of their material possibilities. Nairne's vivid text draws connections between the sculptures and a wide range of art historical and literary references. Some of the playful and sensual characteristics of Batchelor's artistic vocabulary are considered in relation to floral bouquets, sewing-machines, ice cream and poetry. Architectural historian Adrian Forty's essay discusses concrete's relationship with modernity. He notes that the imperfect nature and apparent neutrality of the material are key to its enduring place within architecture, design and, in Batchelor's case, contemporary sculpture. 'In the *Concretos*,' asserts Forty, 'concrete plays a necessary part in allowing colour to be itself. Present, but at the same time part of the barely noticed, half-invisible infrastructure of the city, concrete's very neutrality performs an unexpectedly active part in these works.'

The publication has been supported by Goldsmiths' College, University of London, and Arts Council England.

David Batchelor was born in Dundee in 1955 and lives in London. In 2013, a major solo exhibition of Batchelor's two-dimensional work, *Flatlands*, was held at Fruitmarket Gallery, Edinburgh and toured to Spike Island, Bristol. The solo exhibition *My Own Private Bauhaus* was presented by Ingleby Gallery during the Edinburgh Art Festival, 2019. Between 2017 and 2020 a large-scale work was displayed at Tate Modern. He is represented by Ingleby Gallery, Edinburgh, and Galeria Leme, São Paulo. Batchelor's portfolio also features major artworks in the public realm including *Sixty Minute Spectrum* – a chromatic clock installed in the roof of the Hayward Gallery, London.

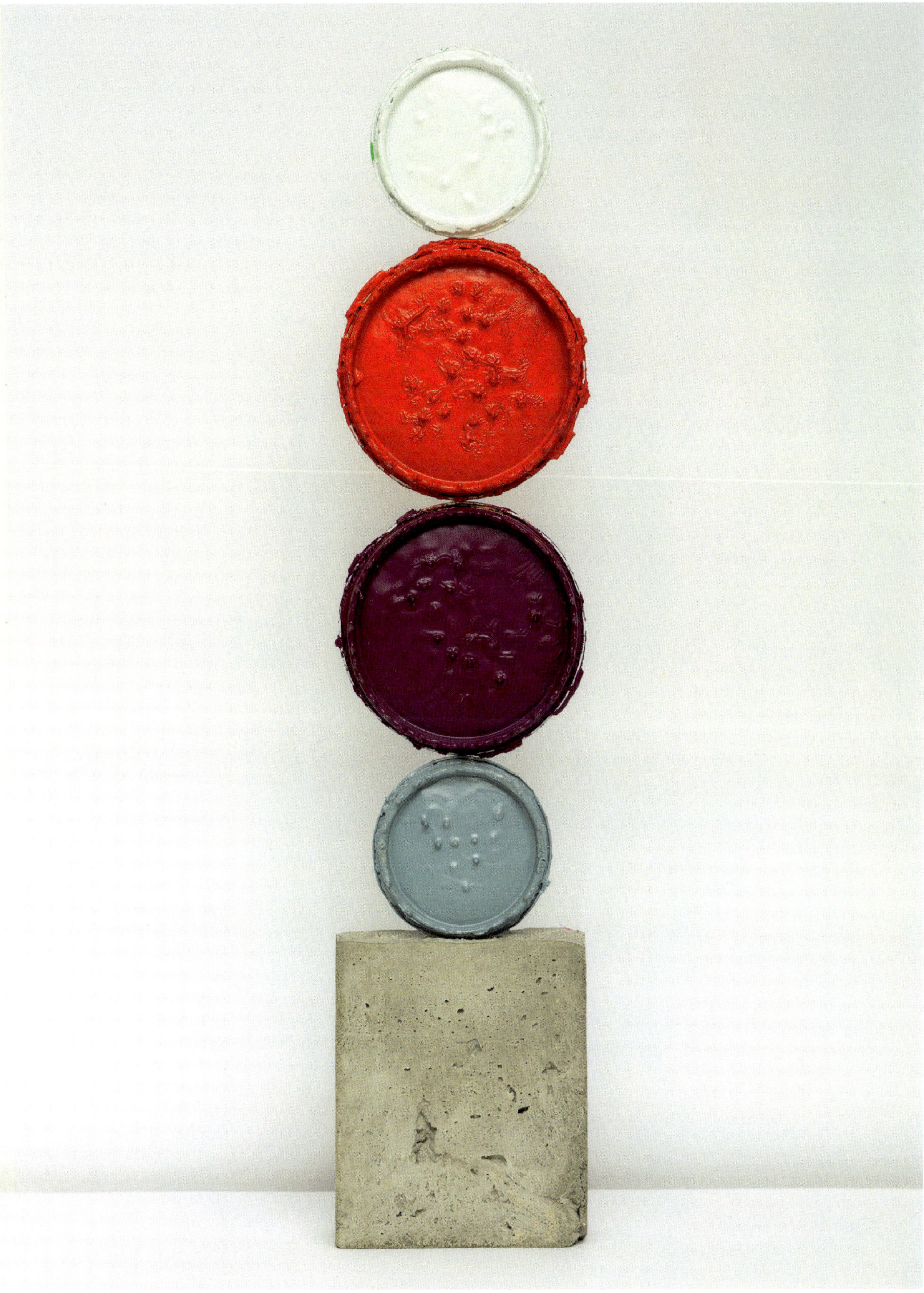

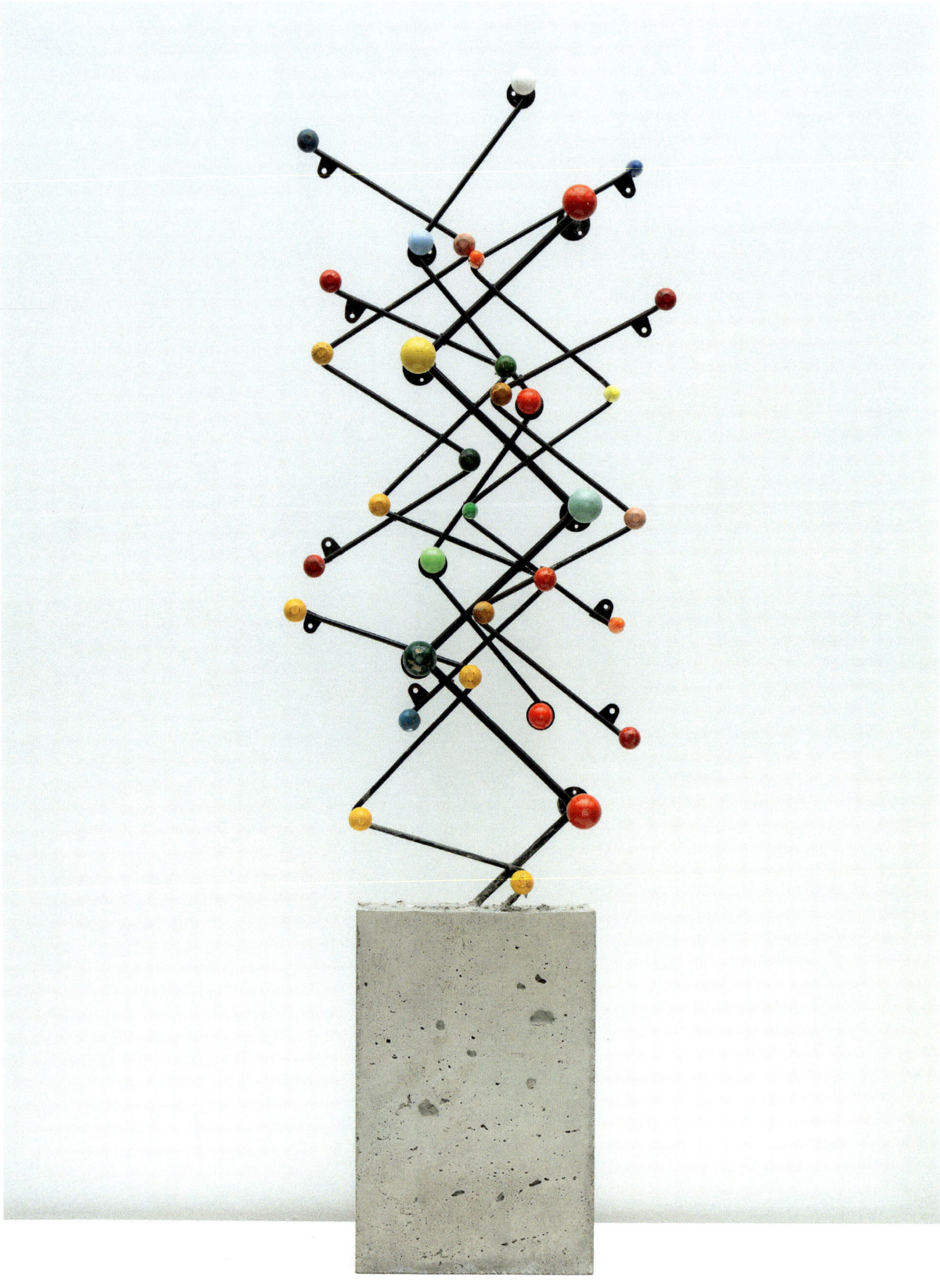

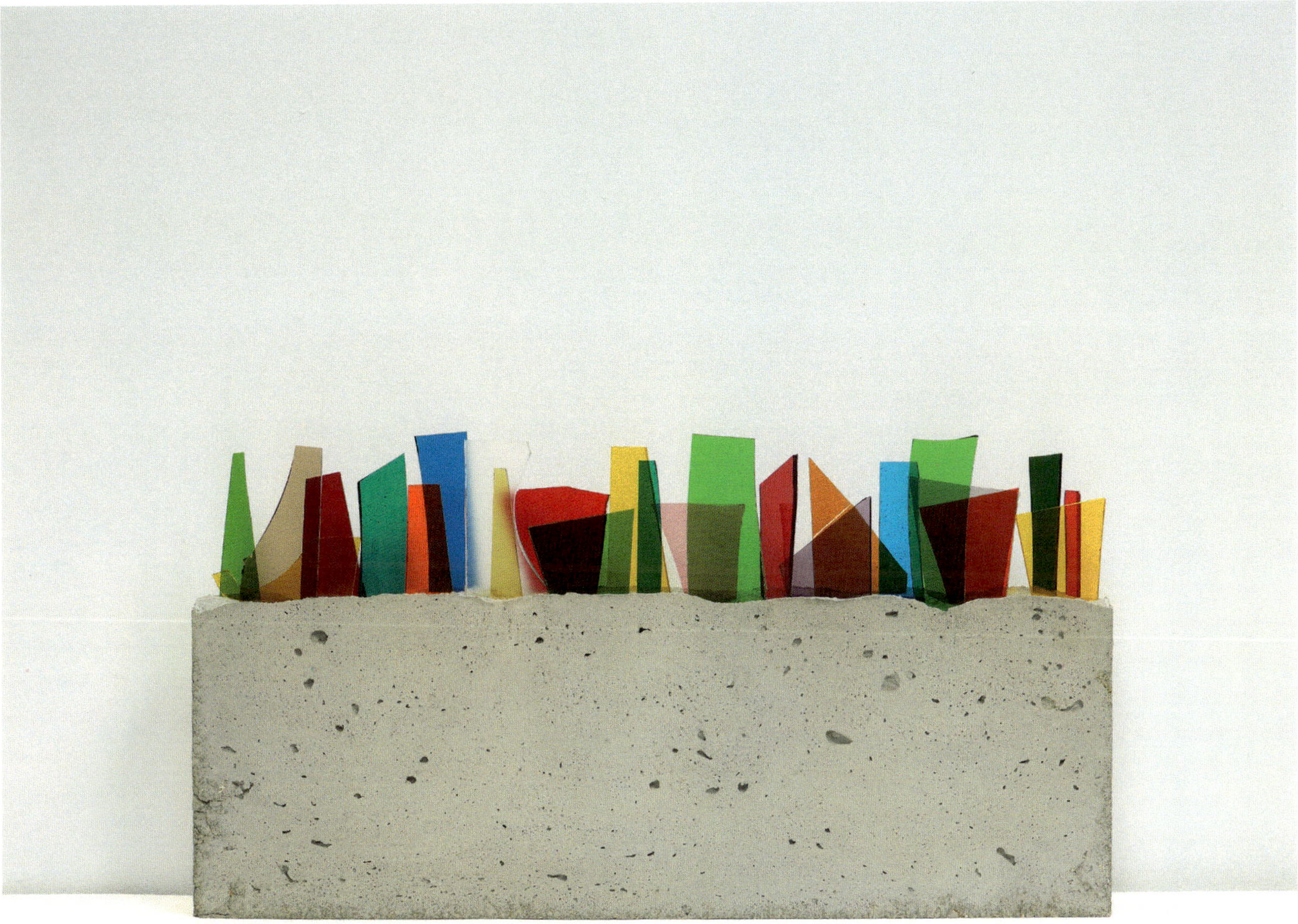

p. 67
David Batchelor
Geo-Concreto 12, 2018
Tin lids, gloss paint, concrete
70 × 15 × 5 cm
Photo: Lucy Dawkins

David Batchelor
Inter-Concreto 10, 2019
Steel coat hangers, paint, wood, plastic, concrete
125.5 × 43 × 11 cm
Photo: Angus Mill

David Batchelor
Concreto 6.0/01, 2019
Glass, concrete
30.5 × 60 × 6 cm
Photo: Lucy Dawkins

All © David Batchelor

Ian McKeever
Henge Paintings

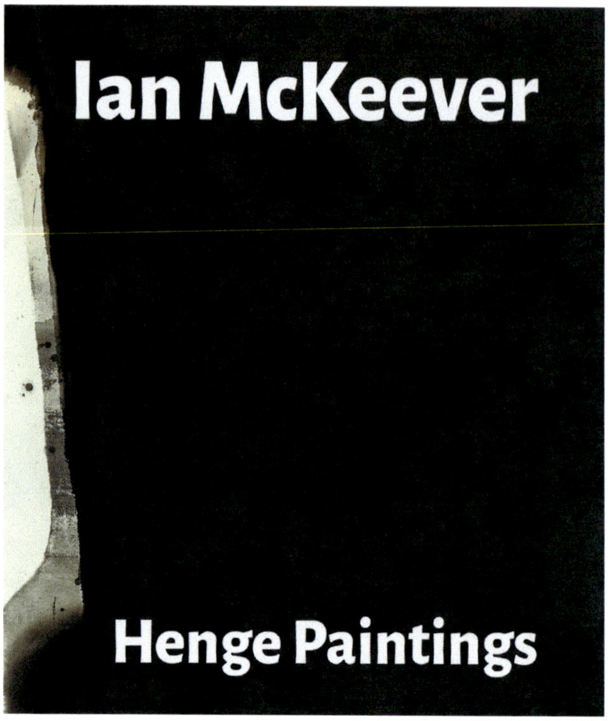

Contributors:
Ian McKeever
Paul Moorhouse
Jon Wood

96pp
Softback
285 × 244 mm
c. 43 images
ISBN: 978-1-910221-41-9
RRP: £25
UK Release: 9 June 2022
Co-ordinated by Gerlinde Gabriel
Designed by Tim Harvey
Printed by Narayana Press, Denmark
Published by Anomie Publishing, London

With a career spanning more than five decades, Ian McKeever is one of Britain's most senior artists working on the international stage. This, his latest publication, documents the *Henge* paintings – a series started in 2017 and completed over the course of five years, inspired by prehistoric standing stones in the county of Wiltshire, England, and continuing the artist's long-standing investigation into the languages and possibilities of abstract painting.

Comprising thirty paintings, along with numerous works on paper, the genesis of the series was a visit by McKeever to the world-famous neolithic site in the village of Avebury in 2016, where he took black-and-white photographs of the large stones that form three discrete circles: two smaller ones contained within the largest. Art historian and curator Paul Moorhouse, in his essay commissioned for the publication, describes how McKeever 'framed each megalith in close-up, their edges visible at the extremity of the resulting images', explaining how 'the experience of moving around Avebury and responding to the huge stones' monumental presence made an abiding impression that resonated with deep-seated preoccupations.' McKeever's resulting body of work is a considered exploration into how paint can convey universal forces and properties such as mass, gravity and time, and how colour, texture and abstraction can converse with three-dimensional space, form and materiality.

The relationship between painting and sculpture in McKeever's work is discussed by means of an in-conversation between the artist and Dr Jon Wood. 'My interest in alluding to early megalithic sites in titling the group of paintings *Henge* paintings,' says McKeever, 'was in touching that deeper sense of time, time's weight, so to speak. How to imbue a painting with its own weight of time, forsake the immediacy of the here and now.'

The publication has been supported by Galleri Susanne Ottesen, Copenhagen, and Heather Gaudio Fine Art, New Canaan, Connecticut.

Ian McKeever was born 1946, Withernsea, Yorkshire, UK. He lives and works in Hartgrove, Dorset. Recent public solo exhibitions include *Ian McKeever/Tony Cragg – Painting and Sculpture*, Skulpturenpark Waldfrieden, Wuppertal, Germany (2020); *Paintings 1992–2018*, Ferens Art Gallery, Hull, UK (2018); *Hours of Darkness, Hours of Light*, Kunstmuseet i Tønder, Denmark (2015); *Between Darkness and Light*, National Gallery of the Faroe Islands, Tórshavn, Faroe Islands (2015); *Hours of Darkness, Hours of Light*, Kunst-Station Sankt Peter Köln, Cologne, Germany (2014); and *Hartgrove. Malerei und Fotografie*, Josef Albers Museum, Bottrop, Germany (2012).

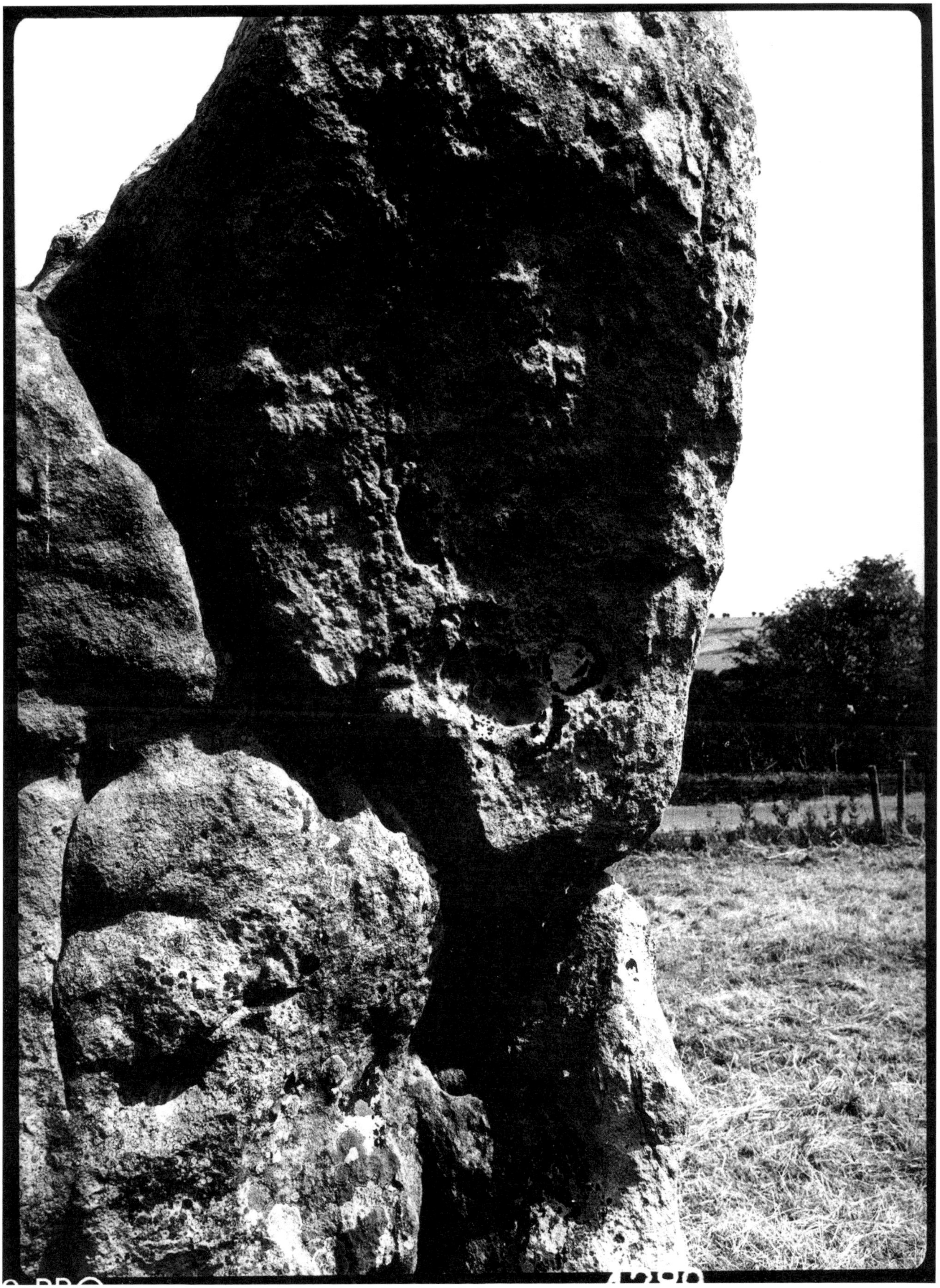

p. 71
Ian McKeever
Black and white analogue
photograph taken at
the Neolithic Henge
Monument, Avebury, 2017

Ian McKeever
Henge XI, 2019
Acrylic and oil on canvas
240 × 285 cm
Photo: Jonathan Bassett

Ian McKeever
Henge No.7, 2021
Watercolour, gouache and pencil on
handmade paper
38 × 43 cm
Photo: Jonathan Bassett

All © DACS/Ian McKeever

Manolo Valdés
In Glass

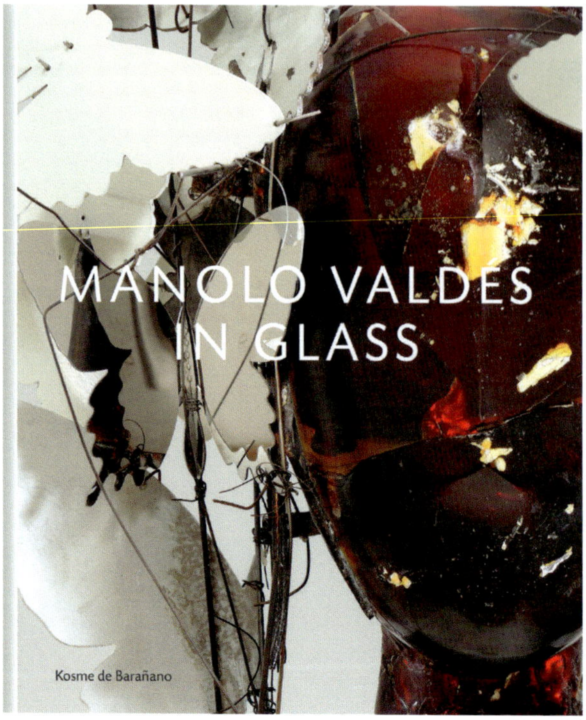

Contributors:
Kosme de Barañano

112pp
Hardback with a transparent dust jacket
340 × 270 mm
c. 65 images
ISBN: 978-1-910221-37-2
RRP: £35
UK Release: 12 May 2022
Edited by Kosme de Barañano
Designed and produced by Peter B. Willberg
Printed by Printer Trento, Italy
Published by Anomie Publishing, London

For over half a century, Manolo Valdés has been a prominent international figure in the arena of contemporary art, known for his work in the mediums of sculpture, painting, drawing and collage. In this striking and imposing publication, designed in close dialogue with the artist by Peter B. Willberg, Valdés presents a body of thirty-five sculptures created in 2020 and 2021. Along with wood, alabaster, aluminium, steel and resin, the primary medium is glass, following a significant and intense period of research and experimentation.

The resulting works are engaging contemporary portrait busts that make reference to the history of modernist painting and sculpture, taking inspiration from imagery and objects by twentieth-century masters such as Pablo Picasso, Henri Matisse and Constantin Brâncuşi. Developing his 'recipes' for their fabrication – materials, processes, conditions and timings – with care and flair, Valdés has created glass busts in amber oranges, ruby reds, emerald greens, sapphire blues, and onyx blacks, all of which seem to glow with what Dr Kosme de Barañano, the author, describes as 'an inner light'.

Barañano's comprehensive and illuminating essay not only investigates aspects of the history of glass-making and its use as a material by artists past and present, but also traces the evolution of the language and forms of Valdés' glass and mixed-media works across a number of key exhibitions and bodies of work over the course of the past two decades. These include his monumental sculptures at the New York Botanical Garden in 2012 and his dramatic solo presentation in the Place Vendôme in Paris in 2016, both of which offered opportunities to see the artist's large-scale sculptural works in outdoor settings.

This large-format publication, with commissioned photography by Tom Powel, documents many of the sculptures from different angles and by means of details, revealing not only the subtleties and qualities of the surfaces of the abstracted, humanlike glass heads, but also the curious and eclectic appendages that appear to burst forth from them like unorthodox fascinators or eccentric jewellery, from nails and steel rods to glass or metal butterflies and wooden geometric forms. With a timelessness that speaks of civilisations long gone and a modernity that simultaneously seems to look to the future, Valdés has created a body of sculpture in glass that transcends time, touching on the metaphysical nature of the human mind and its outward manifestation in the physical world.

Manolo Valdés (b. 1942, Valencia) is one of the most significant post-war Spanish artists. A key member of the Equipo Crónica until 1981, in 1989 he moved to New York. Major solo exhibitions include the Guggenheim Bilbao, the Reina Sofía, Madrid, the New York Botanical Garden and the Château Royalede Chambord, France.

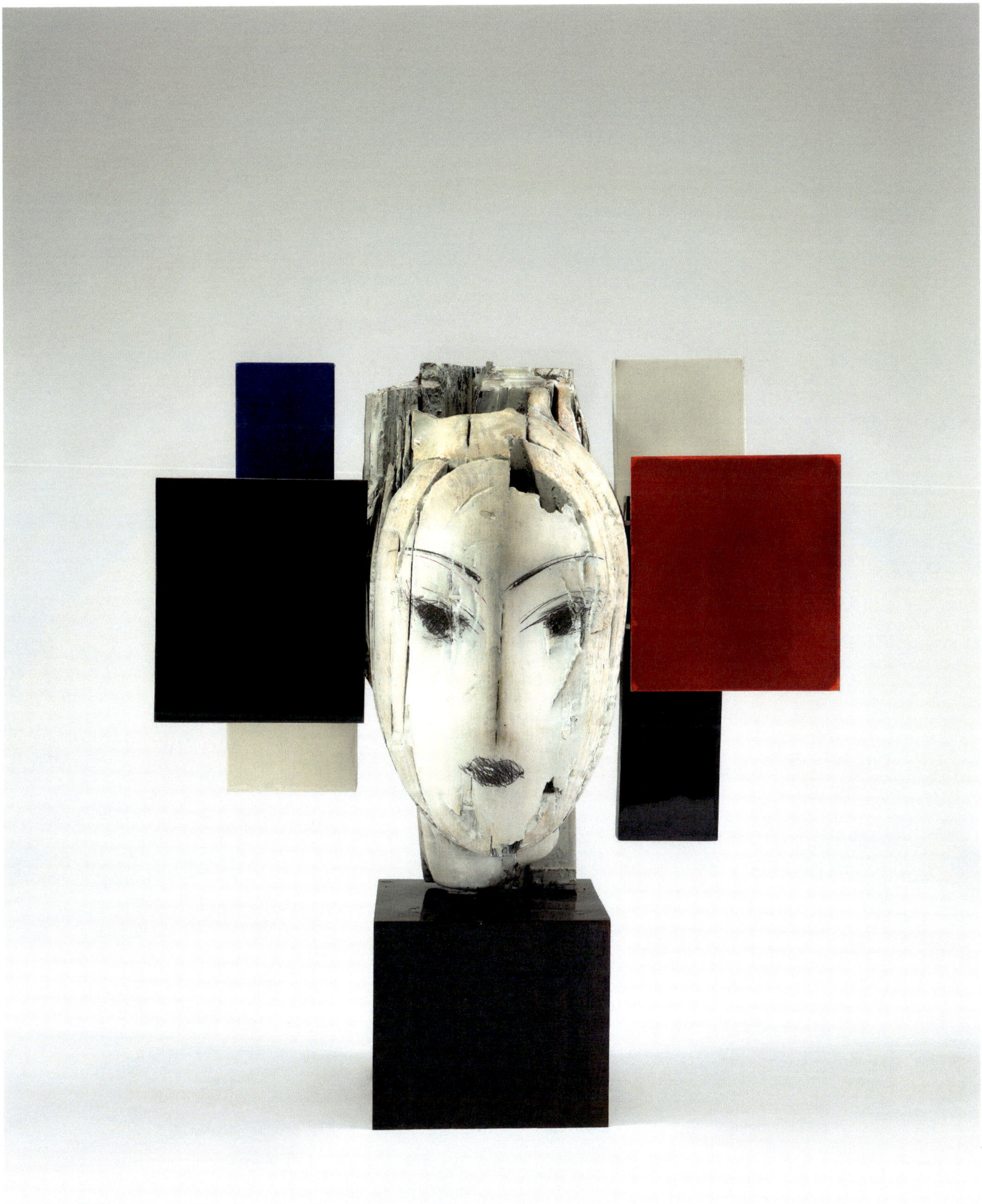

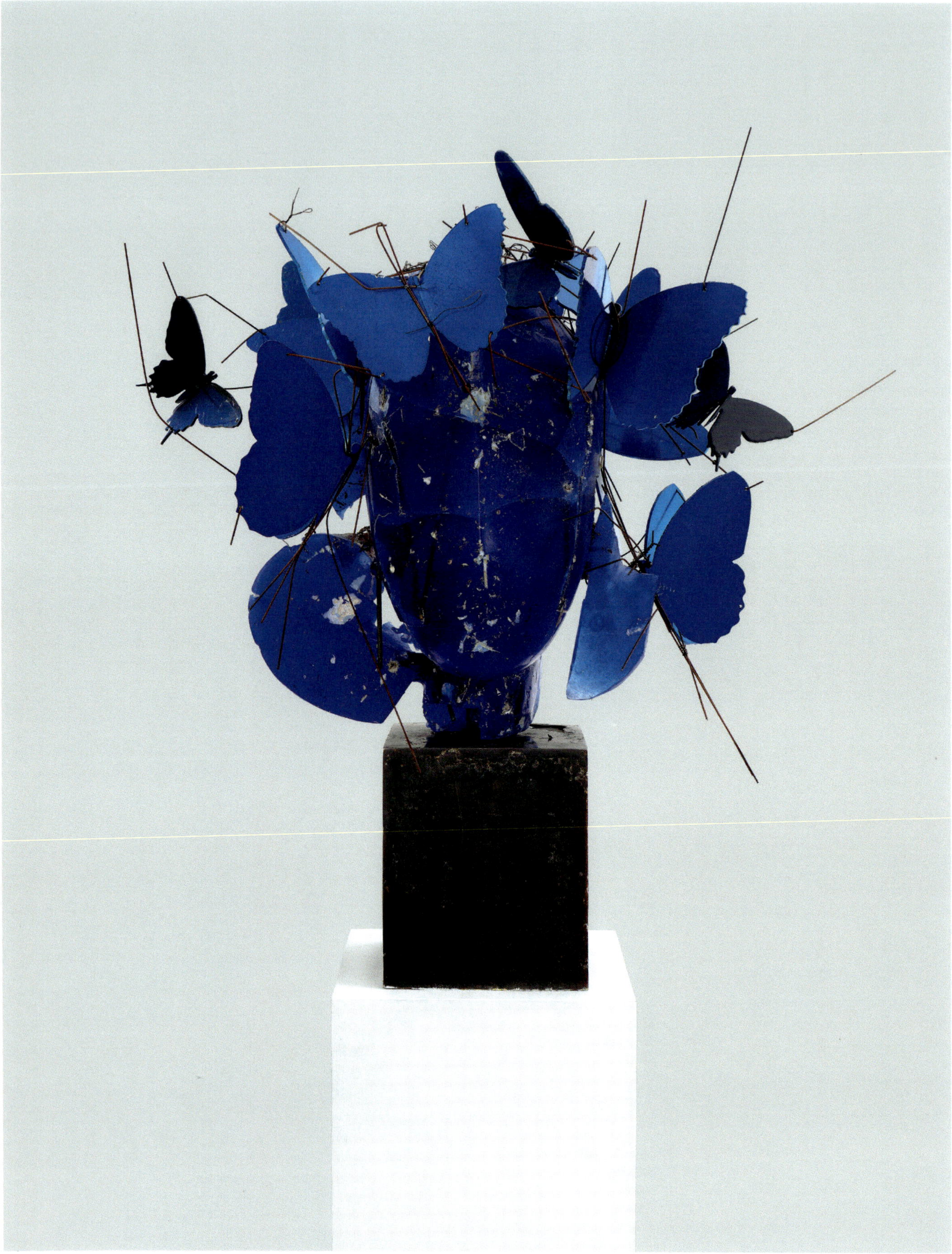

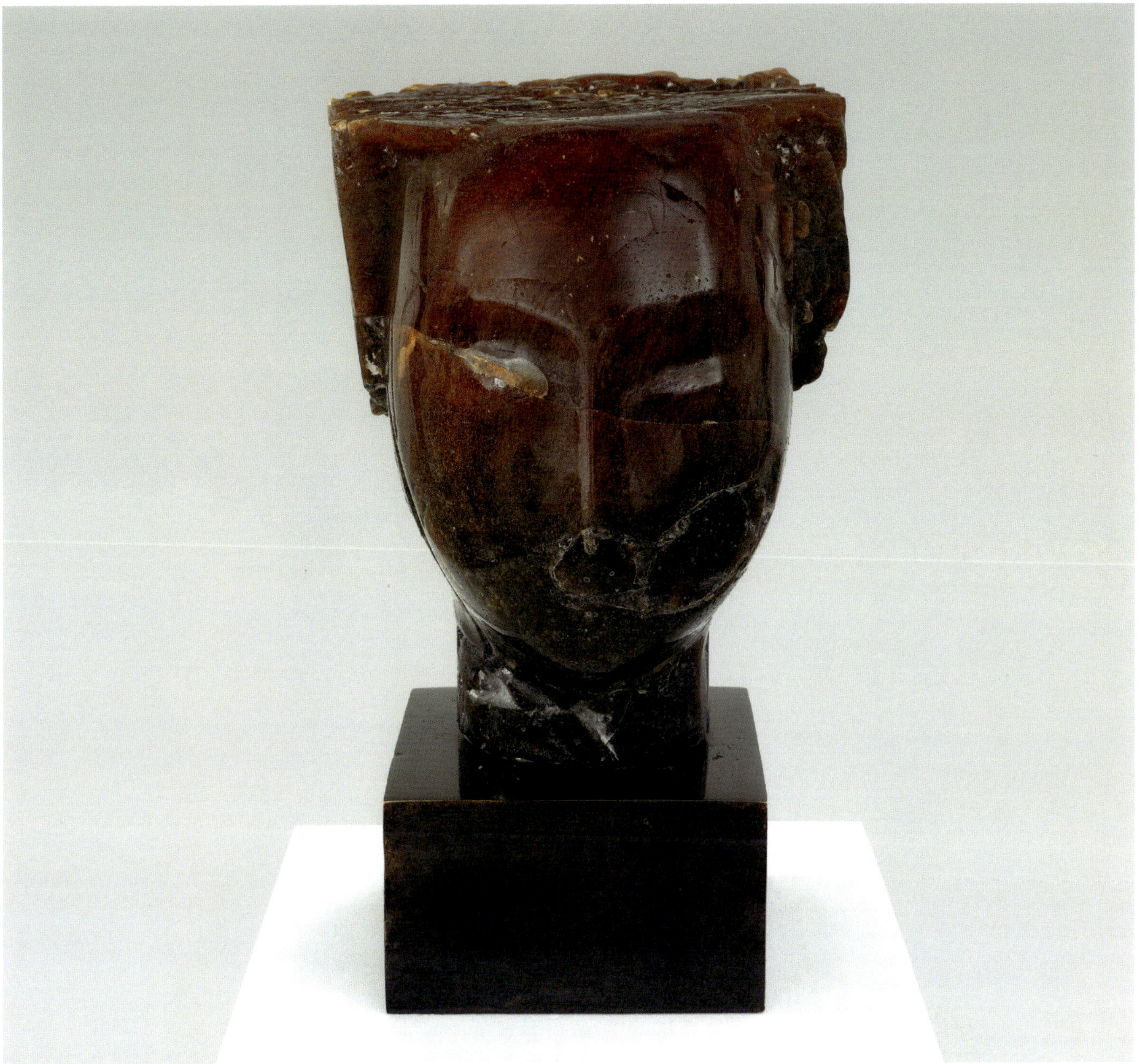

p. 75
Manolo Valdés
Constructivismo como Pretexto II, 2021
Polychromated wood
110.5 × 97.8 × 50.8 cm

Manolo Valdés
Cabeza con Mariposas Azules, 2021
Glass and steel
100 × 70 × 61 cm

Manolo Valdés
Cabeza de Cristal III, 2021
Glass
28 × 23 × 26 cm

All © Manolo Valdés
Photos: Tom Powel Imaging

Sarah Medway
The River Series

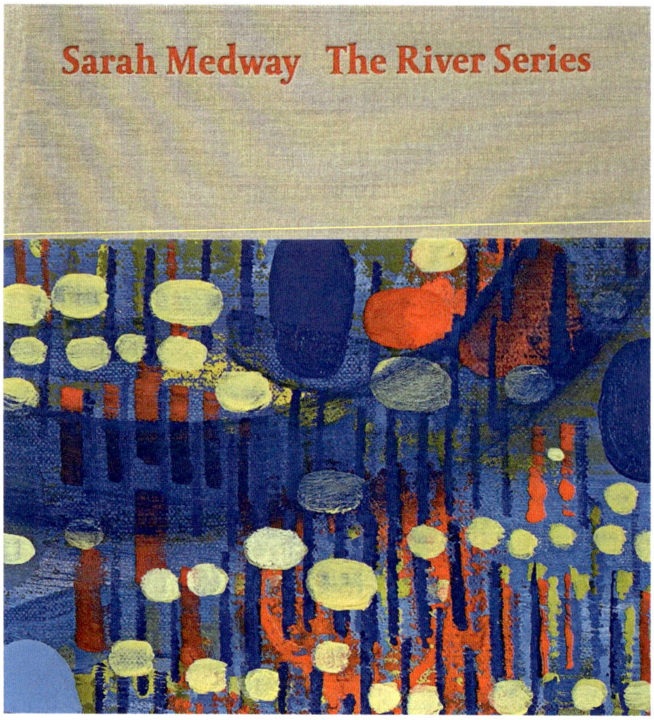

Contributors:
Sue Hubbard
Anna McNay
Sarah Medway

88pp
Hardback
260 × 245 mm
c. 58 images
ISBN: 978-1-910221-30-3
RRP: £28
UK Release: 28 April 2022
Designed and produced by Peter B. Willberg
Printed by Esperia Srl, Trento
Published by Anomie Publishing, London

This, London-based painter Sarah Medway's second publication from Anomie, is devoted to the subject of the River Thames. It presents a series of twenty-eight oil paintings created in Medway's canal-side studio in central London during the Covid-19 lockdowns of 2020–21. An introductory text by critic and writer Sue Hubbard takes readers through the series, exploring how the paintings engage with the qualities of the river to represent all manner of concepts, experiences and emotions, from a yearning for lost freedoms to roam the city to evocations of the subterranean waterways that form part of the city's mythology. Like a *flâneuse*, Medway follows the river across the city, spanning the seasons, in various weather, light and atmospheric conditions, at different times.

The Thames is beautiful, terrifying, powerful, alluring and dangerous. Medway captures the river's eclectic dynamics, rhythms and energy through the language of abstract painting, the ripples, bubbles, eddies and currents, the reflections and refractions denoted through sinuous lines, ellipses and spots, dots and loops, flecks and swirls. Referencing twentieth-century modernist movements such as De Stijl, Tachisme and post-war American Abstract Expressionism, Medway's own lyrical, often graphic approach to painting the Thames results in a vivid interplay between pattern and colour. The paintings have overt musical resonances – tempo, rhythm and dynamics as might be encountered in an orchestral score. Like the river, the paintings are at times joyous and playful, at others brooding and menacing, yet always moving, in flux, travelling onwards towards the sea.

An in-conversation between Medway and writer, editor and curator Anna McNay provides insight into the artist's life and work, discussing the processes by which Medway makes her paintings and the thinking behind them. Speaking to McNay, Medway asserts: 'Water has always flooded the abstract language in my work. Not just the sea, but lakes, ponds, canals, dykes and rivers. The myriad and multiple reflections on water, during daylight or at night, have always been present in my paintings.' Designed and produced by Peter B. Willberg, this foil-blocked, clothbound hardback publication with a special dust jacket also features an illustrated chronology documenting Medway's life and career.

Sarah Medway (b. 1955, Seaton Carew, UK) is a painter based in London. As well as group exhibitions at institutions such as Tate Britain, the Whitechapel, the Royal Academy, the World Trade Center and Austin Museum of Art, Medway's solo shows include Flowers East, London; Chelsea Hotel, New York; Kienbaum Gallery, Frankfurt; The Mandalai, Thailand and Atelier Gallery, Spain. She has works in public, private and corporate collections in the UK, US, Germany, Italy, Spain, Belgium, Hong Kong and Thailand.

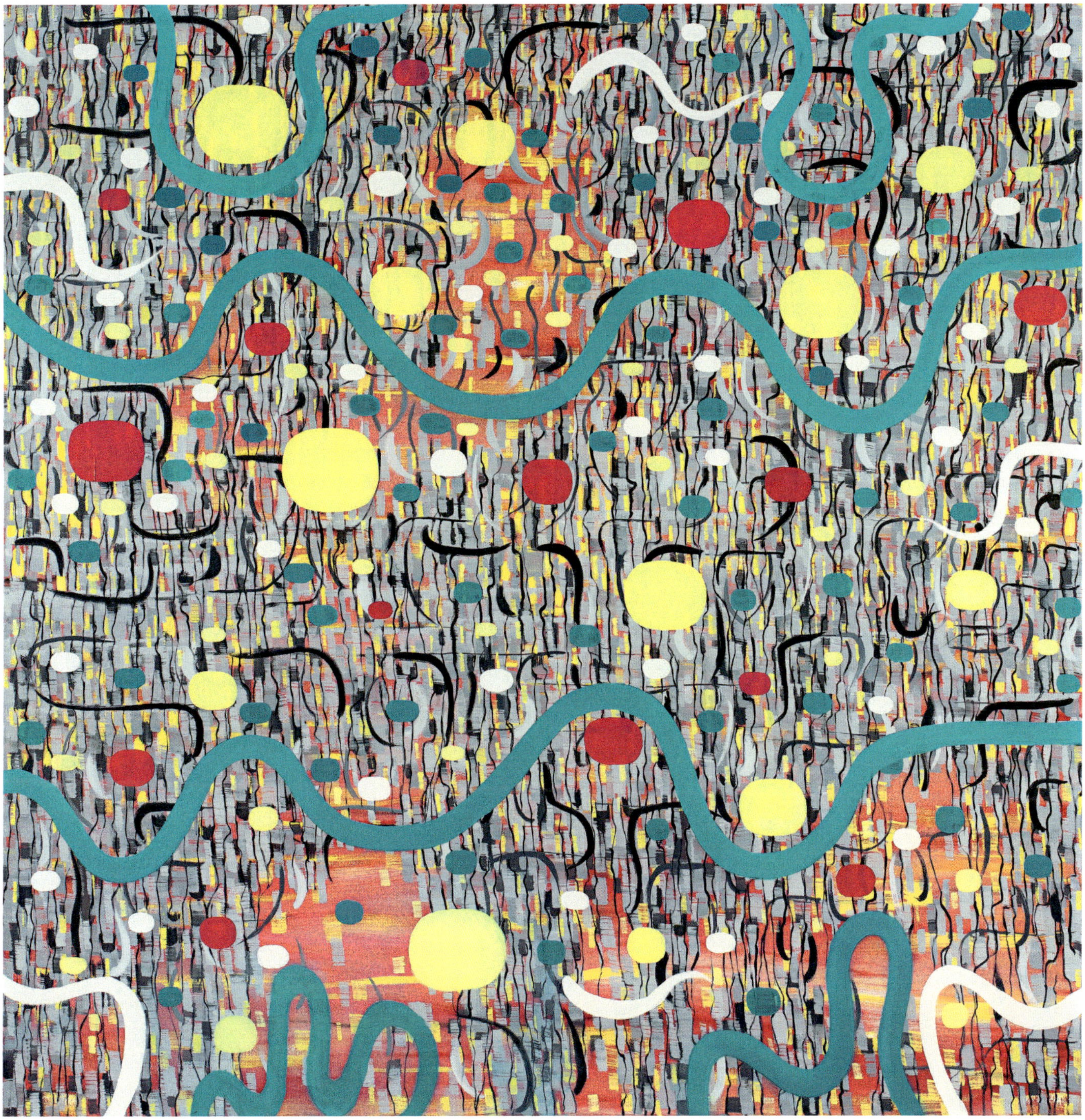

Sarah Medway
Watershed, 2020
Oil on linen
152.4 × 152.4 cm

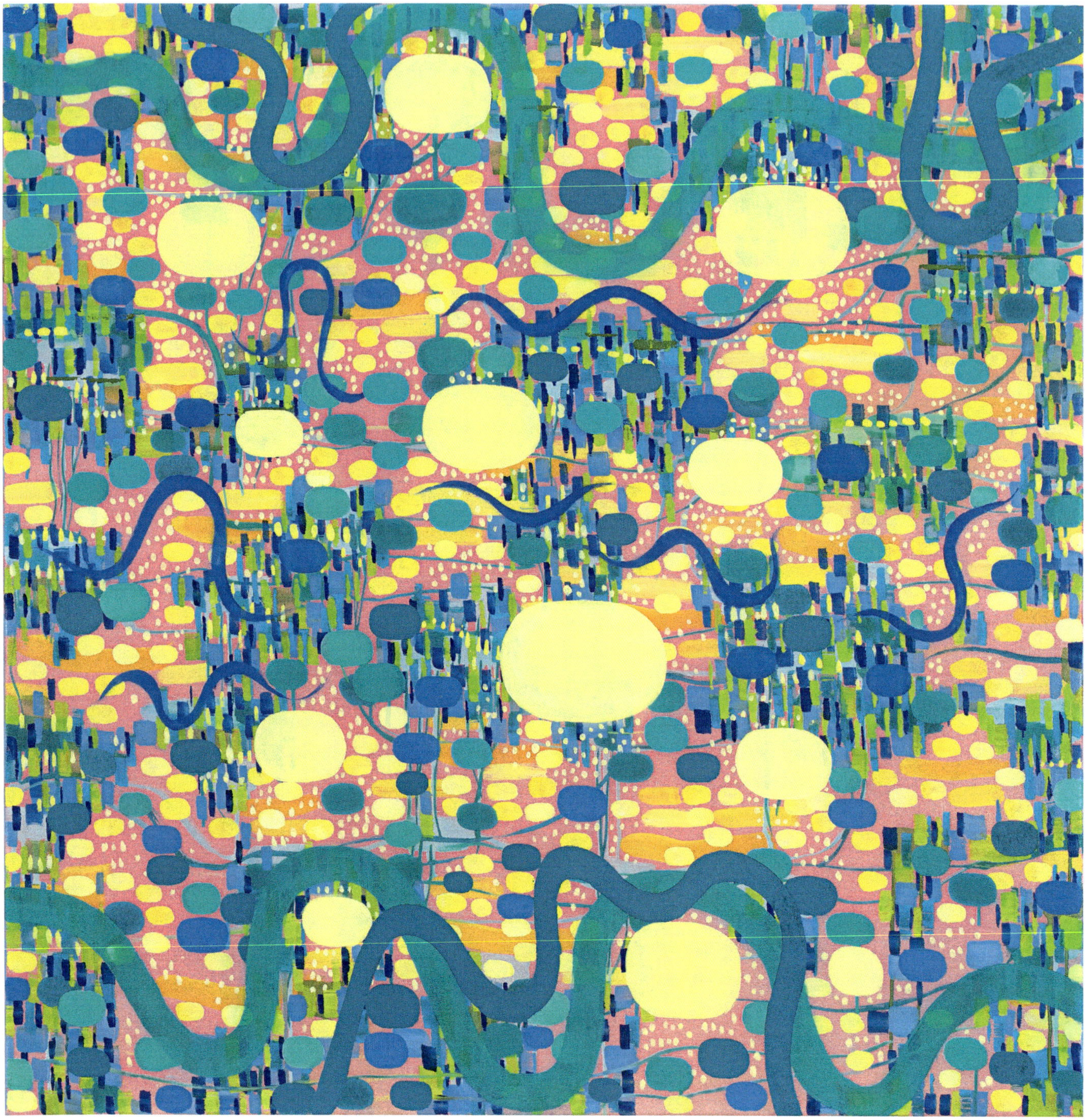

Sarah Medway
Limpid Pool, 2021
Oil on linen
91.4 × 91.4 cm

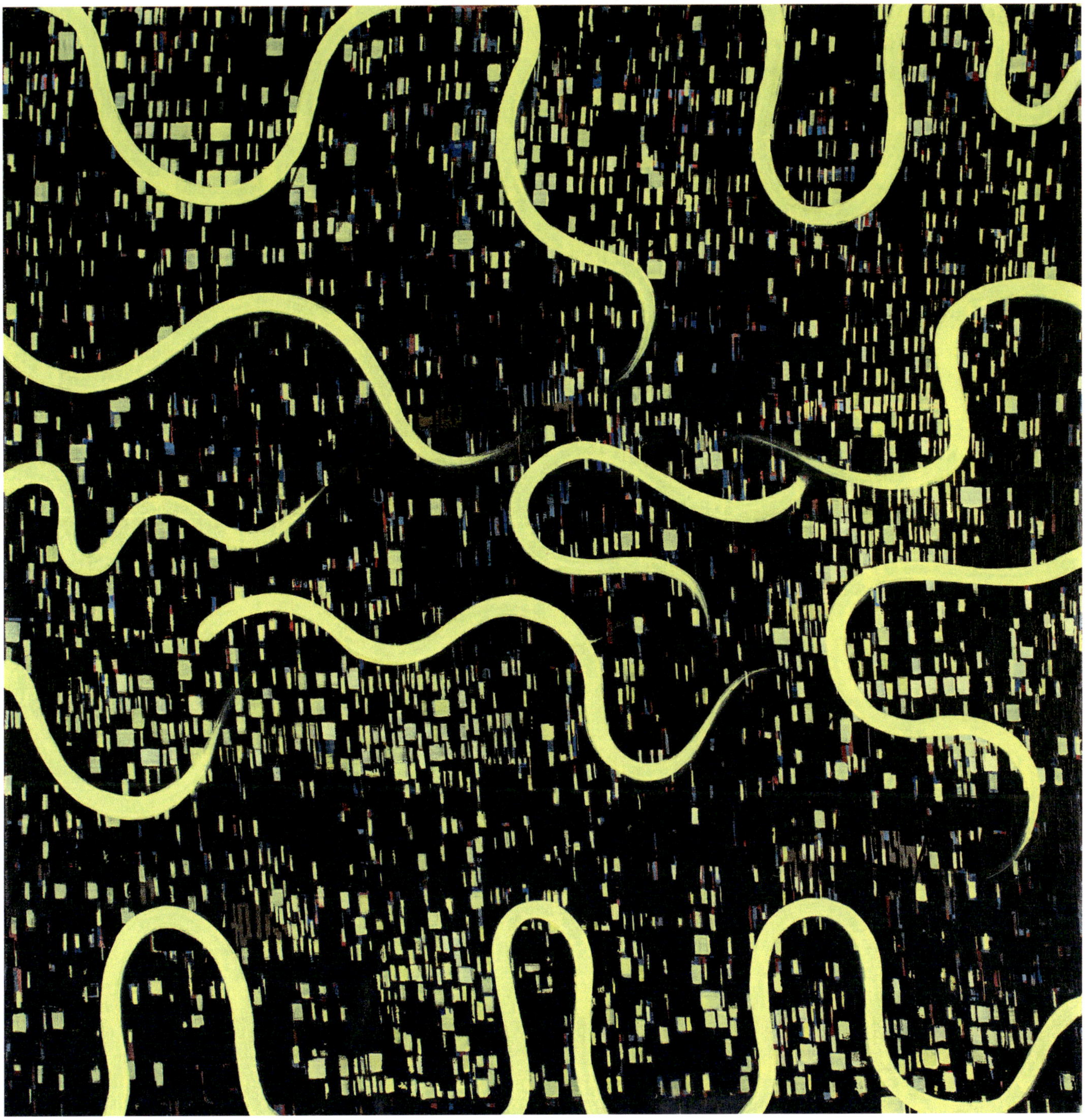

Sarah Medway
Hidden Rivers, 2020
Oil and silver leaf on linen
91.4 × 91.4 cm

All courtesy of the artist
Photos: James Tye

Journey of the Mind

Contributors:
Koi
Kanwar Singh

144pp
Hardback, clothbound
220 × 220 mm
c. 40 images
ISBN: 978-1-910221-35-8
RRP: £30
UK Release: 11 November 2021
Developed by GMGG, Slough
Designed by Herman Lelie and Stefania Bonelli
Printed by EBS, Verona
Co-published by Without Shape Without Form, Slough, and Anomie Special Projects, London

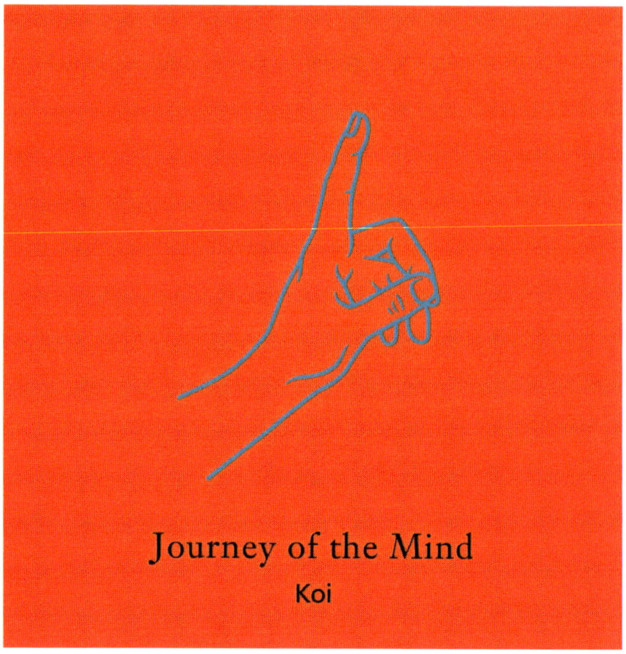

Journey of the Mind is the first publication from Without Shape Without Form (WSWF), an arts organisation and arts space established in 2017 by volunteers from the Guru Maneyo Granth Gurdwara (GMGG) in Slough, England. WSWF is the UK's first, and currently only, permanent Sikh art gallery.

The publication has been created as an illustrated introduction to the history, stories, and teachings of Sikhism. The Gurus – the teachers of the Sikh faith – shared a message of kindness, equality and inclusivity, helping all humanity find peace in troubled times and connect with truth through the journey of the mind.

We live in difficult times. Many people struggle with hectic schedules and constant pressure from a busy world in which we are always connected through digital media but are somehow less connected to each other in real life. The impact of Covid-19, and the constant worry and isolation that many of us experienced, have left their mark on our mental health. On top of this, concern for the health of our planet and social injustice have left some feeling hopeless.

The mission of the Gurus was supported by brave and inspiring warriors who, following the teaching of the Gurus, devoted their minds to Waheguru (the Creator) and found peace in the face of adversity. The last Guru, Sri Guru Granth Sahib Ji, is not a person, but a collection of texts embodying the teachings of Sikhism, accessible to everyone, for all time. *Journey of the Mind* shares the wisdom of these texts, including excerpts in the original Gurmukhi, Punjabi.

Digital paintings by world-renowned Sikh artist Kanwar Singh illustrate the stories. In today's frenetic, turbulent world, the message of the Gurus is more relevant than ever – we have everything we need within us to achieve peace. It is the ambition and hope of WSWF that people will be inspired by these words to embark on their own journey of the mind.

Journey of the Mind is a publication and travelling exhibition by Without Shape Without Form.

Kanwar Singh
Defying all odds, 2013
Digital painting
Dimensions variable
© Kanwar Singh, Art of Punjab
Courtesy of Kanwar Singh and Without Shape Without Form

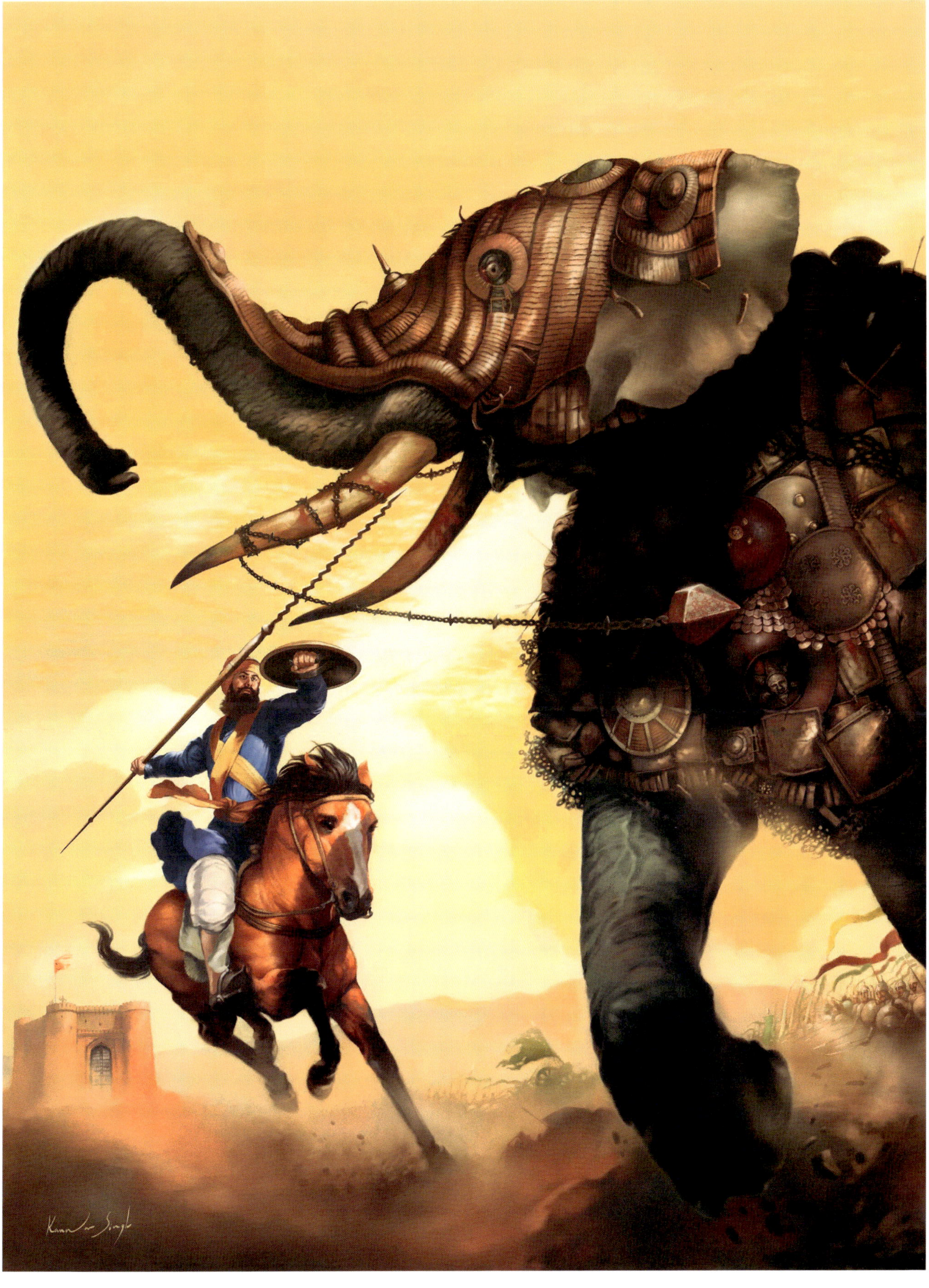

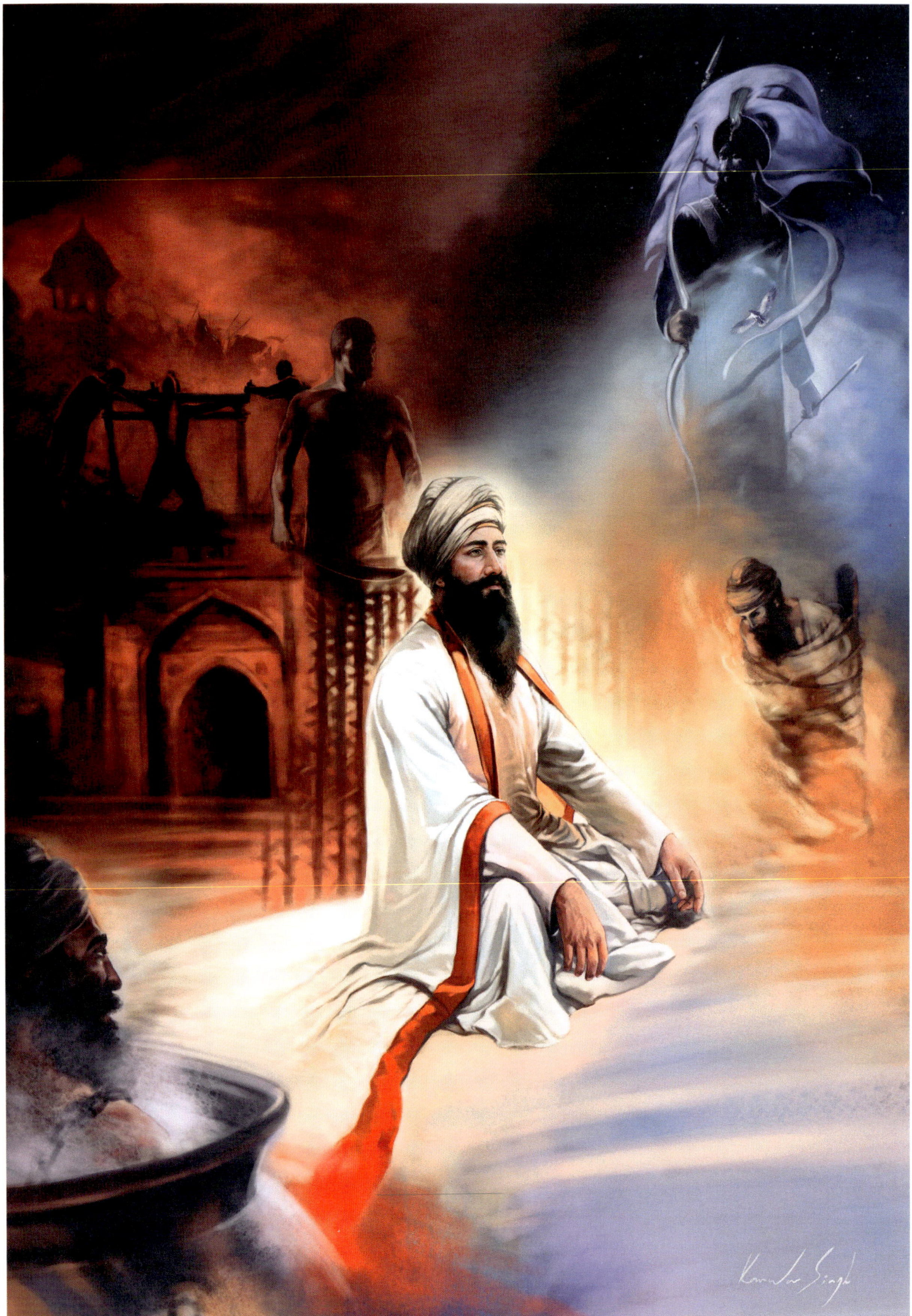
Kanwar Singh

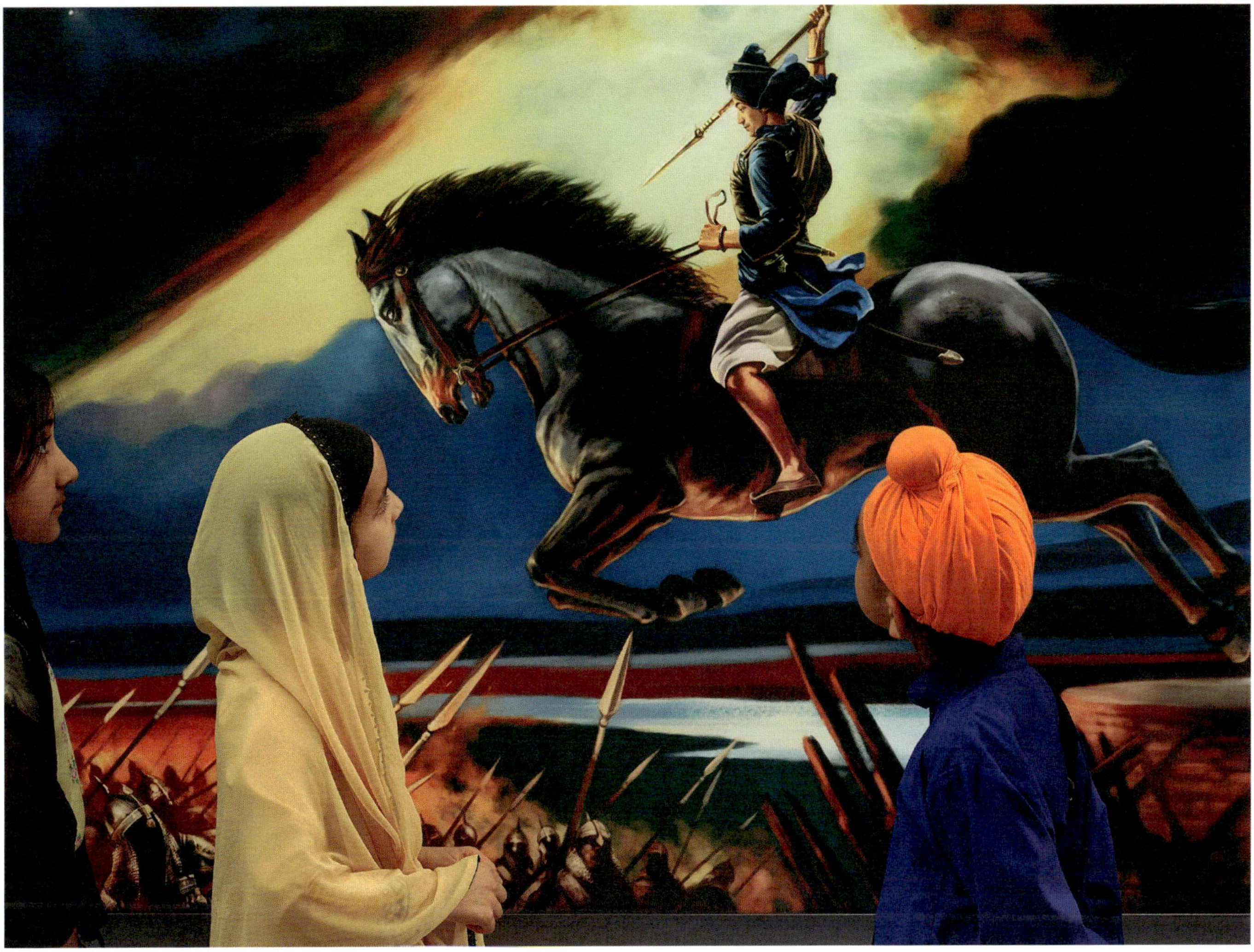

Kanwar Singh
The ninth Guru and Gurmukhs endure torture, 2017
Digital painting
Dimensions variable
© Kanwar Singh, Art of Punjab
Courtesy of Kanwar Singh and Without Shape Without Form

Visitors looking at Kanwar Singh's *Fearless against persecution*, 2017, Without Shape Without Form, GMGG, Slough, 2021
© / courtesy of Without Shape Without Form
Photo: Peter Mallet

Mariele Neudecker
SEDIMENT

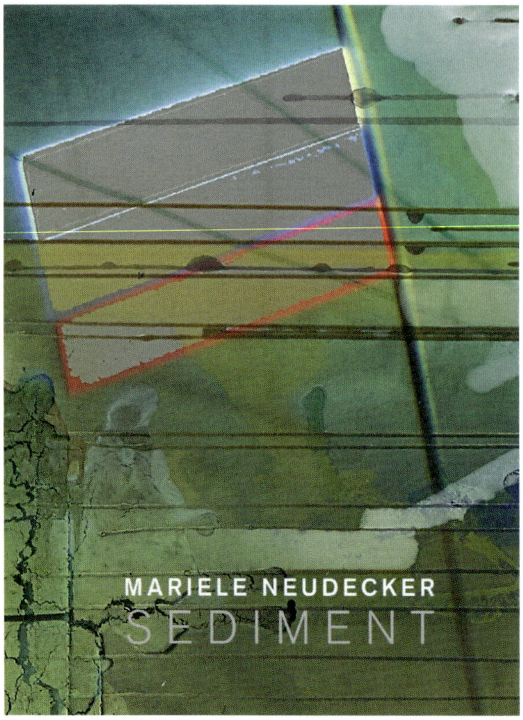

Contributors:
Greer Crawley / Klaus Dodds / Dominic Gray /
Ariane Koek / Pontus Kyander / Úna McCarthy /
Kerstin Mey / Mariele Neudecker / James Peto /
Alice Sharp

224pp
Softback
220 × 165 mm
c. 190 images
ISBN: 978-1-910221-32-7
RRP: £28
UK Release: 7 October 2021
Edited by Greer Crawley
Designed by Herman Lelie
Layouts by Stefania Bonelli
Printed by EBS, Verona
Published by Anomie Publishing, London

Mariele Neudecker's multimedia practice, which incorporates sculpture, video, painting and sound, explores the processes and effects of perception, the complexities and contradictions of landscapes and visuality, and the politics of representation and territorialisation. The influence of the nineteenth-century German romantic sublime is interwoven alongside inspiration from Neudecker's work with scientists, as a guest artist on the Arts at CERN programme, her trips to the Arctic and travel elsewhere. This major monograph, published following an exhibition of the same name at Limerick City Gallery of Art – Neudecker's first comprehensive solo exhibition in Ireland – presents more than two hundred works from a thirty-five-year-long career. In addition to a foreword by Úna McCarthy, the gallery's Director and Curator, essays by academics and curators from across the fields of art and science address diverse areas of Neudecker's practice. A 'timeline' by Neudecker concludes the publication.

Greer Crawley, an Honorary Research Fellow in the Department of Drama, Theatre and Dance at Royal Holloway, University of London, considers Neudecker's archive, studio and working processes, while Ariane Koek, an expert in the field of arts, science and technology, suggests that the contemporary sublime, for Neudecker, is the very process of perception itself. Her comprehensive introduction to Neudecker's practice also discusses the tank works, for which the artist is best known, in which fibreglass landscapes are suspended in chemical solutions. James Peto, from the Wellcome Collection, London, focuses on issues of representation, post-colonialism and 'time', while Alice Sharp, Artistic Director of Invisible Dust, looks at Neudecker's work and collaborations concerning the deep sea. Klaus Dodds, Professor of Geopolitics at Royal Holloway, returns to questions of territorialisation in and around the Arctic, and Professor Kerstin Mey, Interim President of the University of Limerick, considers the genre of still life in Neudecker's photographic series *Plastic Vanitas* (2015). Dominic Gray, Projects Director at Opera North, offers insight into Neudecker's work with sound and music, while writer and curator Pontus Kyander returns to the motif of the forest, considering how Neudecker's work addresses contemporary ecological questions. Finally, Crawley's second offering returns to Neudecker's use of sound, and the use of the window as a device, considering how each creates 'an entanglement of materiality, space, form and position'.

Mariele Neudecker (b. 1965, Germany) undertook a BA at Goldsmiths' College, London (1987–90), and an MA in Sculpture at Chelsea College of Art and Design, London (1990–91). She has shown widely in international exhibitions. Neudecker is Professor of Fine Art at Bath School of Art, where she runs the research cluster Making | Art | Science | Environment. She is on the European Commission's JRC SciArt advisory panel.

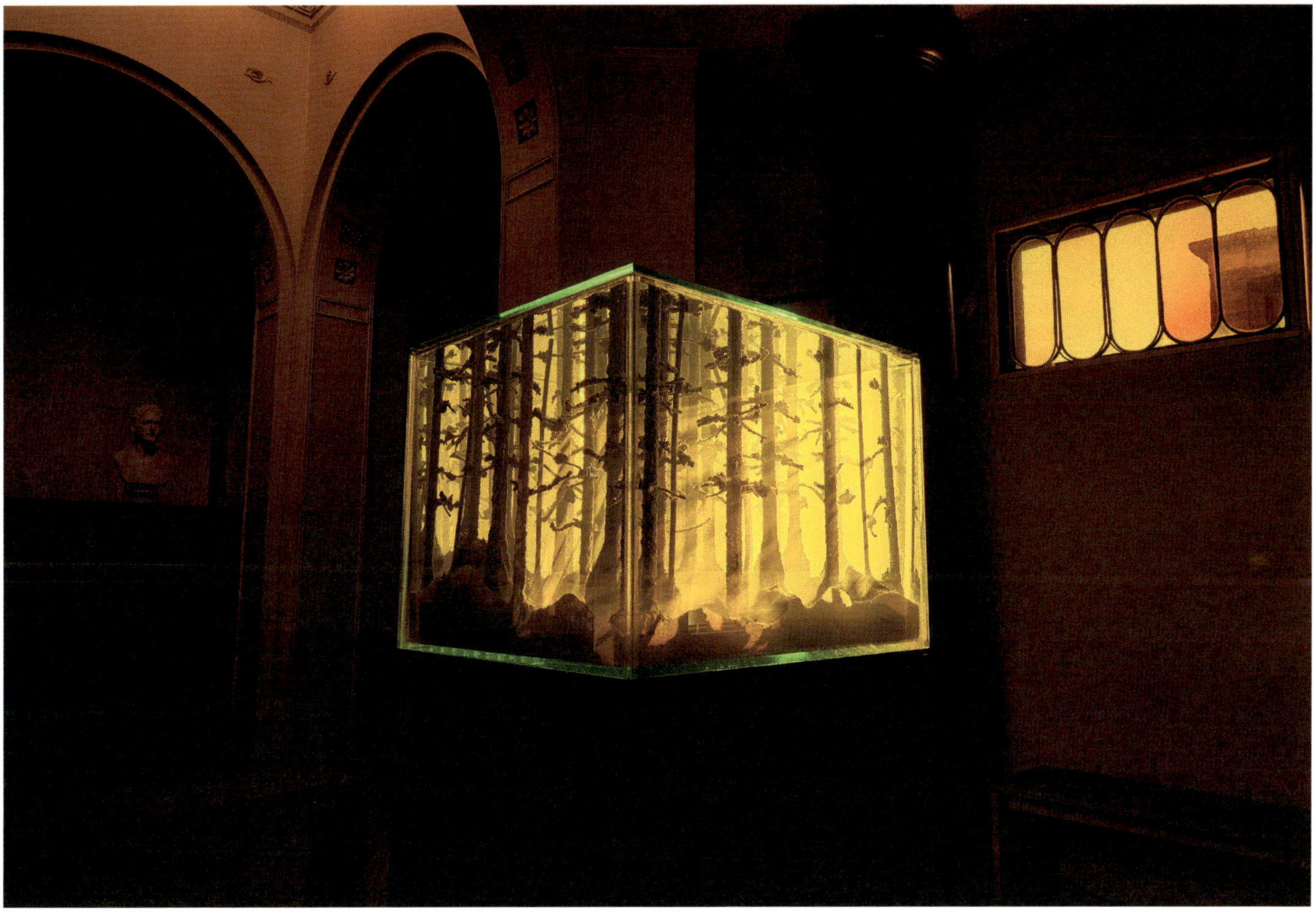

Mariele Neudecker
Then the World Changed Colour: Breathing Yellow, 2019
Giclée print on archive paper
58 × 42 × 3 cm (framed)
Edition of 24 plus 3 A/Ps
Installed in SEDIMENT, LCGA, Limerick, 2019
With thanks to Arts Council England
Courtesy of Pedro Cera, Lisbon
Photo: Benjamin Jones

Bill Woodrow & Richard Deacon A Democratic Process: Shared Sculptures and Drawings

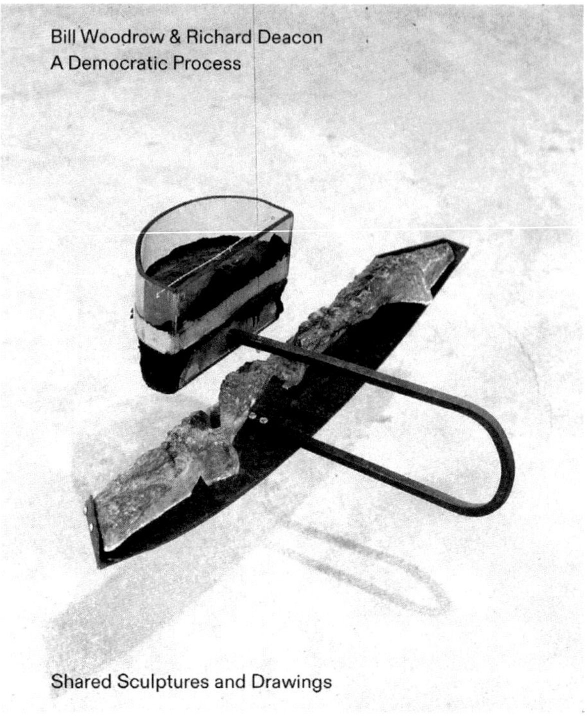

Contributors:
Jon Wood

120pp
Softback
230 × 190 mm
c. 120 images
ISBN: 978-1-910221-31-0
RRP: £24
UK Release: 16 September 2021
Edited by Jon Wood
Designed by Joe Gilmore
Printed by EBS, Verona
Published by Anomie Publishing, London

Bill Woodrow and Richard Deacon have been making sculpture together since 1990. This new book is the first to showcase the work made over this thirty-year period. They have created over sixty works altogether which they call 'shared sculptures', highlighting the important equality of authorship and responsibility at stake for both these artists.

They became friends while studying at St Martin's School of Art in London and as they both became known in the early 1980s as part of the 'New British Sculpture' group. The first sculpture they made was titled *Democratic Process* (1990), which is indicative of the mood of their endeavours. Woodrow and Deacon's shared sculptures have continued in this vein, taking them both into new artistic terrains, outside the logic of the individual artist's oeuvre and off the beaten track of their own artistic branding.

Their shared sculptures exist as five main bodies of work, which have been variously shown in exhibitions in Britain and abroad: *Only the Lonely* (1993), *monuments* (1999), *Lead Astray* (2004), *On the Rocks* (2008) and *Don't Start* (2016). Their recent body of work, *We Thought About It A Lot* (2021), has seen them working on paper to explore their ideas together.

This new book provides a rich visual account of these works, showing new and original photographs of them individually and in their exhibition contexts. It also includes images of the preview cards that they have designed for exhibitions over the years and reproduces one of their earlier fax exchanges. The publication features an introductory essay by the art historian and curator Jon Wood and was released to coincide with the artists' joint exhibition, *We Thought About It A Lot, and other shared drawings* at Ikon, Birmingham, in autumn 2021.

Bill Woodrow (b. 1948) has exhibited internationally, representing Britain at biennales in Sydney (1982), Paris (1982, 1985) and São Paulo (1983). He was shortlisted for the Turner Prize in 1986 and participated in Documenta 8 in 1987. He was elected a Royal Academician in 2002 and had a major retrospective at the Royal Academy of Arts in 2013. Richard Deacon (b. 1949) has exhibited internationally throughout his career. He was awarded the Turner Prize in 1987, elected to the Royal Academy in 1998 and to the Akademie der Künste in Berlin in 2010. A large exhibition of his work was shown at Tate Britain in 2014, the same year as a collected edition of his writings was published. Dr Jon Wood (b. 1970) is a writer and curator, specialising in modern and contemporary sculpture. Recent publications and exhibitions include: *Sean Scully* (2020), *Contemporary Sculpture: Artists' Writings and Interviews* (2020), *Tony Cragg at the Boboli Gardens* (2019) and *Sculpture and Film* (2018). He is a trustee of the Gabo Trust.

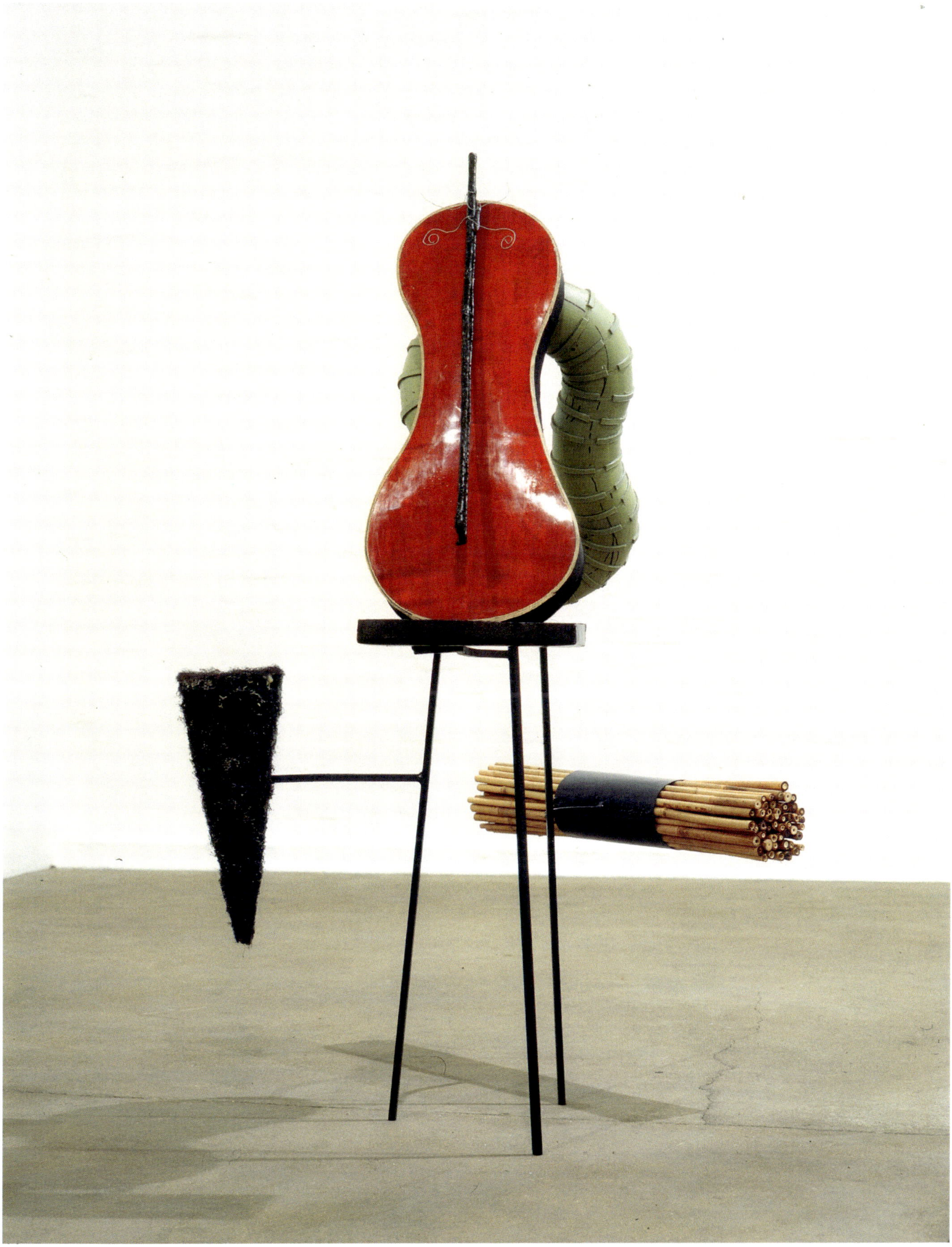

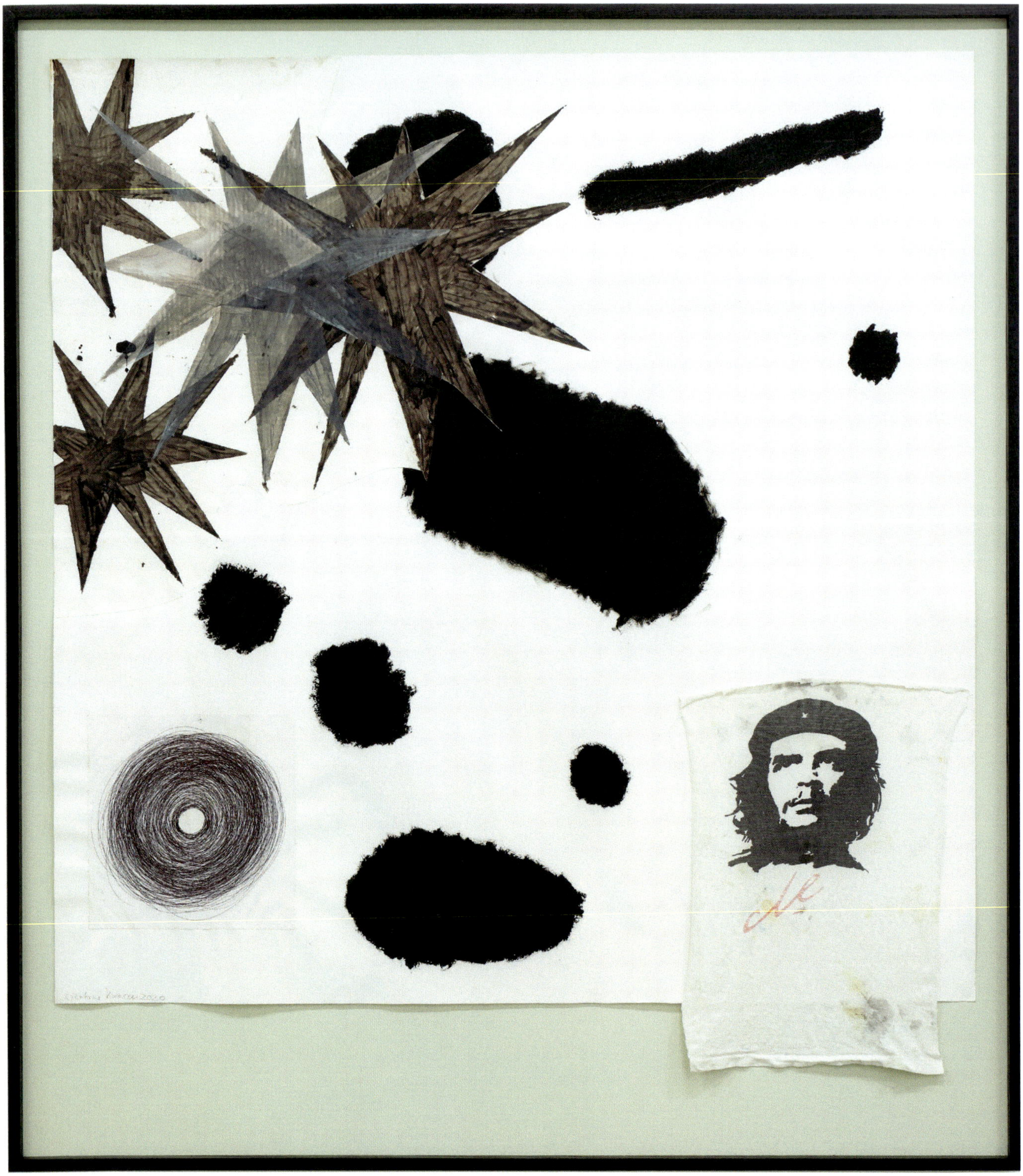

p. 89
Bill Woodrow and Richard Deacon
Wooly Bully, 1993
Steel, plastic, wood, card, wax, bamboo, nylon fibre
155 × 110 × 100 cm

Bill Woodrow and Richard Deacon
Shroud, 2020
Paint, oil stick, graphite, fabric, collage, paper
160 × 150 cm
Photo: Stuart Whipps

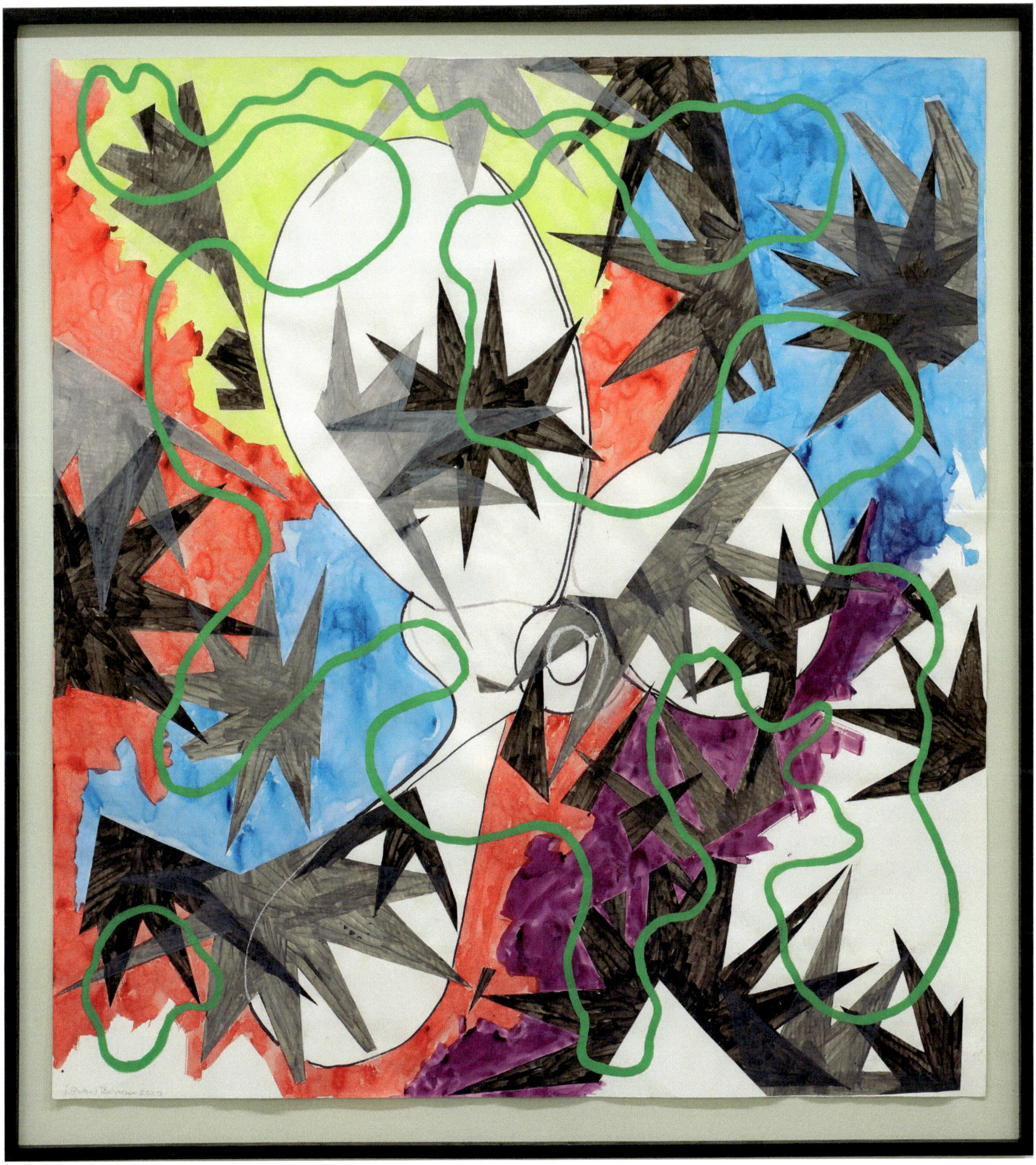

Bill Woodrow and Richard Deacon
Shaft, 2020
Paint, collage, ink, paper
150 × 150 cm
Photo: Stuart Whipps

All © and courtesy of the artists

Frank Walter
Music of the Spheres

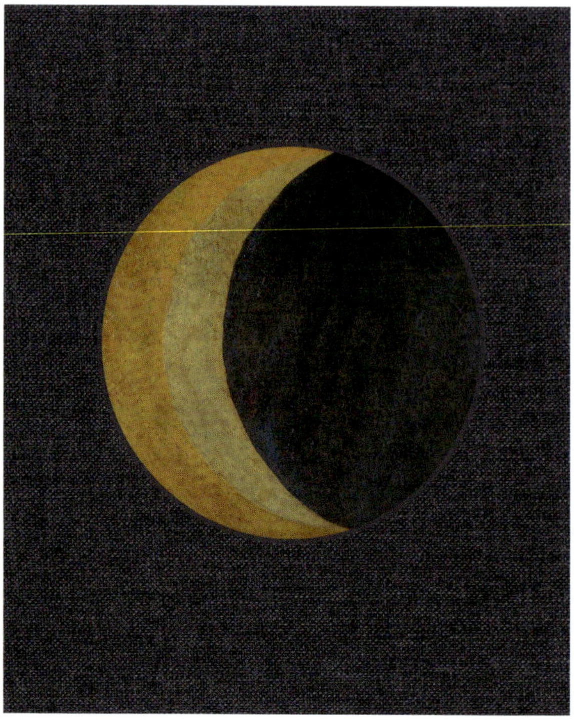

Contributors:
Barbara Paca
Prof. Paget Henry
Kenneth M. Milton
Mary-Elisabeth Moore
Frank Walter

256pp
Hardback, cloth-bound
260 × 215 mm
c. 150 images
ISBN: 978-1-910221-34-1
RRP: £30
UK Release: 9 September 2021
Produced by Ingleby, Edinburgh
Designed by Joanna Deans / Identity
Printed by Graphius, Ghent
Co-published by Ingleby, Edinburgh, and
Anomie Publishing, London

This publication was produced to accompany an exhibition staged by Ingleby Gallery, Edinburgh, for the 2021 Edinburgh Art Festival. The exhibition was the first devoted to Frank Walter's 'Spools' – small circular paintings which, in their consistency of scale and form, provide a lens through which to witness the workings of Walter's inner eye. Walter's work was unknown during his lifetime, but in the decade since his death he has emerged as one of the most distinctive and intriguing Caribbean voices of the last fifty years. Painted with directness and immediacy on whatever material came most readily to hand, his works describe a visionary artist – romantically and spiritually inclined in the manner of William Blake or Hilma af Klint – but rooted in the landscape of Antigua, the island of his birth.

His work was the subject of Antigua and Barbuda's inaugural appearance at the Venice Biennale in 2017, and Hans-Ulrich Obrist described him as 'the Leonardo da Vinci of Antigua'. A retrospective at MMK Museum of Modern Art Frankfurt in 2020 was accompanied by a monograph in which Barbara Paca, the chronicler of Walter's life, notes: 'The *Spool* series brings together all the elements of Walter's universe, with each painting fitting together in dynamic groupings to provide an investigation into the workings of Walter's mind...'

This publication, co-published by Ingleby, Edinburgh, and Anomie Publishing, London, features contributions by Barbara Paca, Professor Paget Henry, Kenneth M. Milton and Mary-Elisabeth Moore.

Frank Walter (1926–2009) was born Francis Archibald Wentworth Walter on Horsford Hill, Antigua. He spent much of the 1950s travelling in Scotland, England and West Germany. While in Europe, Walter pursued various creative activities including drawing, painting and creative writing. He returned to the Caribbean in 1961, where he began a prolific output of painting, drawing, writing, sculptural work, photography and sound art.

Walter's work was first exhibited alongside paintings by Alfred Wallis and Forrest Bess in the exhibition *Songs of Innocence and Experience* at Ingleby Gallery in spring 2013. A solo exhibition of his work was presented by The Douglas Hyde Gallery, Trinity College, Dublin, in summer 2013, and later that year Ingleby Gallery presented a solo display of Walter's paintings at Art Basel Miami Beach. A major solo exhibition followed at Ingleby Gallery in 2015. In 2017, Walter represented Antigua and Barbuda at the Venice Biennale in a show called *Frank Walter: The Last Universal Man 1926–2009*. A solo presentation of Walter's work also took place at Harewood House, Leeds, UK, in 2017. A retrospective of the artist's work was held at MMK Museum of Modern Art Frankfurt in 2020 and David Zwirner, London, in 2021.

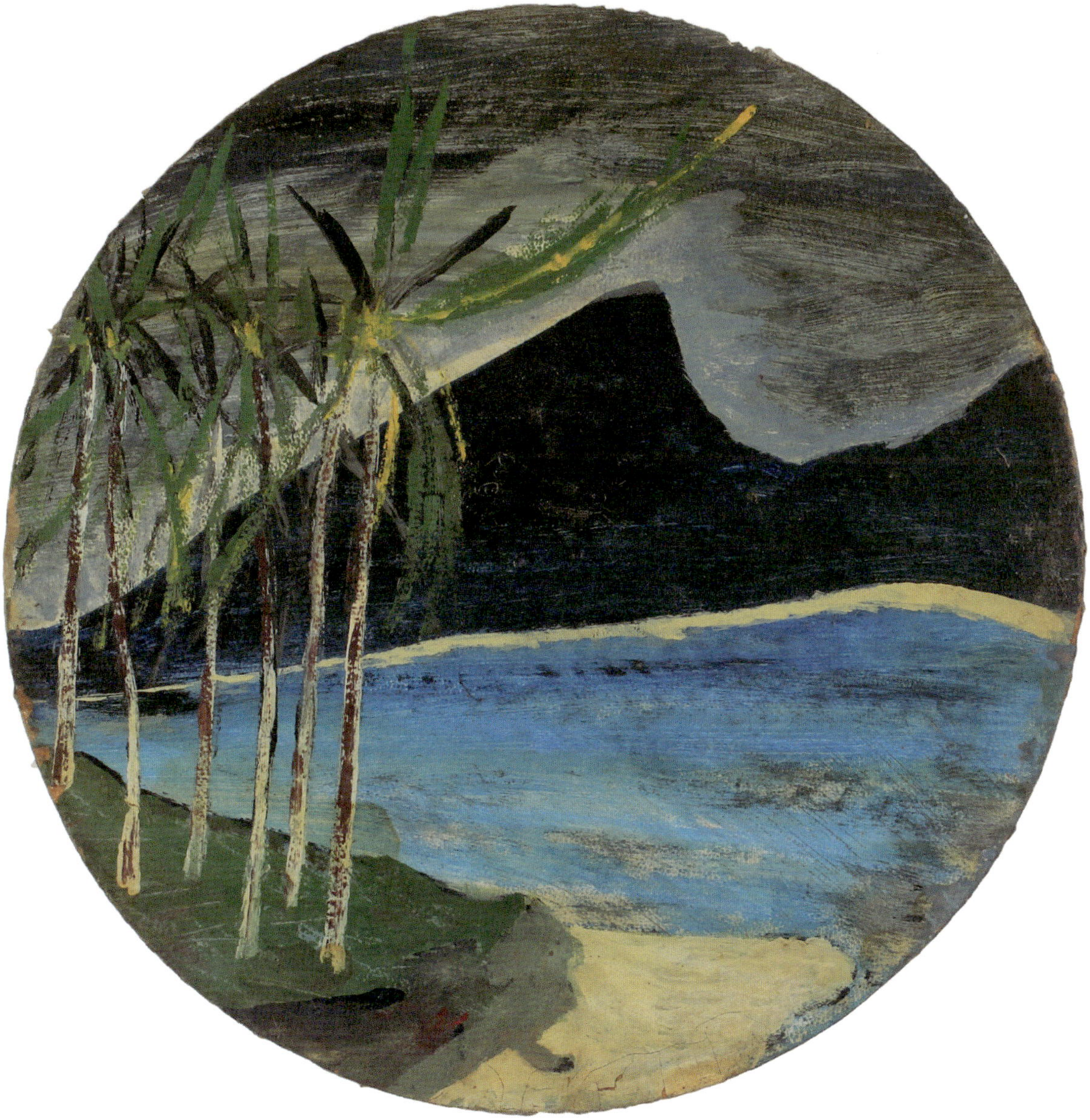

Frank Walter
Untitled (Black peaks, coconut palms, beach and bay)
Oil on pressed fibre with Masonite backing
21.7 cm diameter

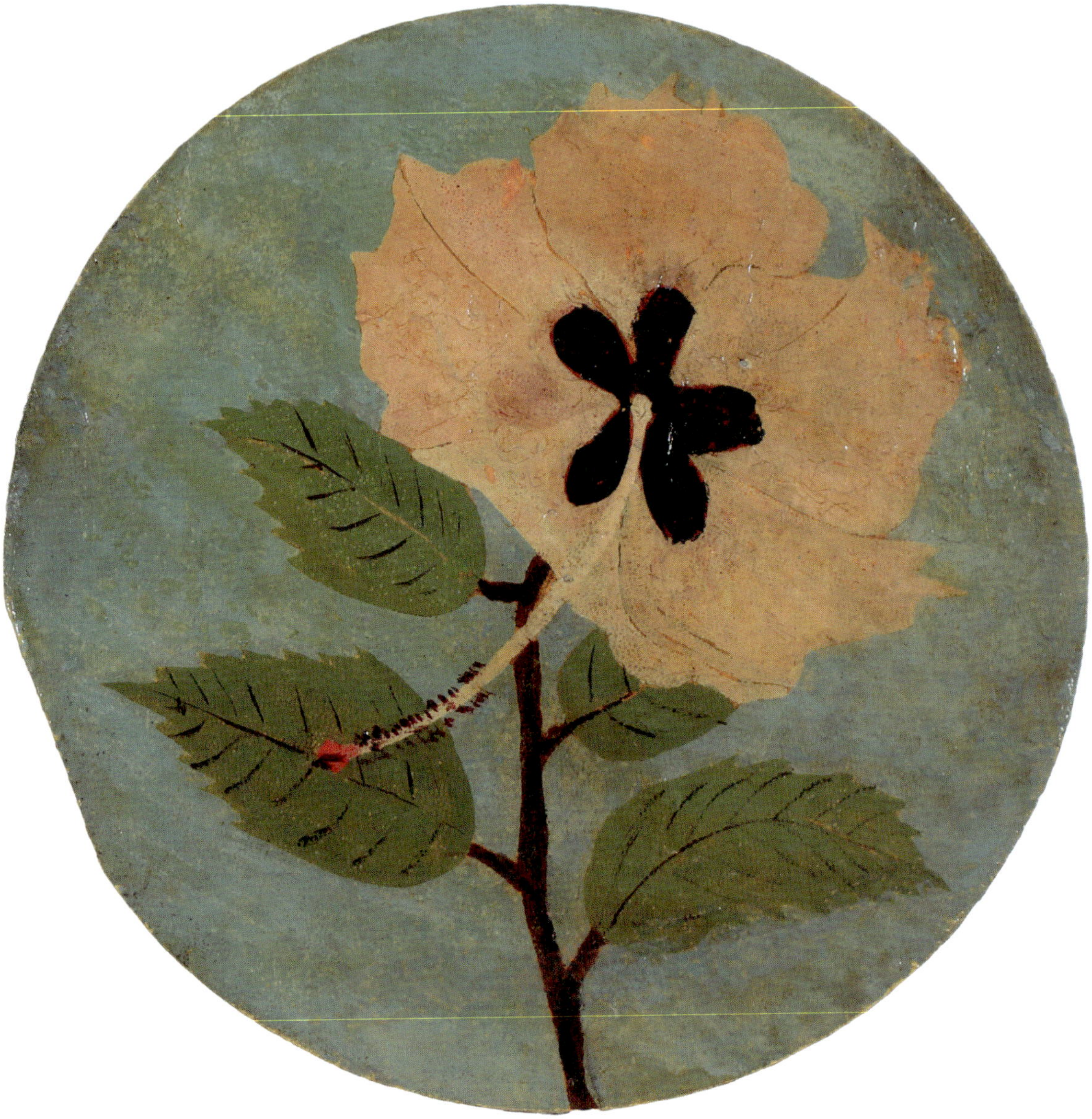

Frank Walter
Untitled (Pale hibiscus)
Oil on pressed fibre with Masonite backing
19.5 cm diameter

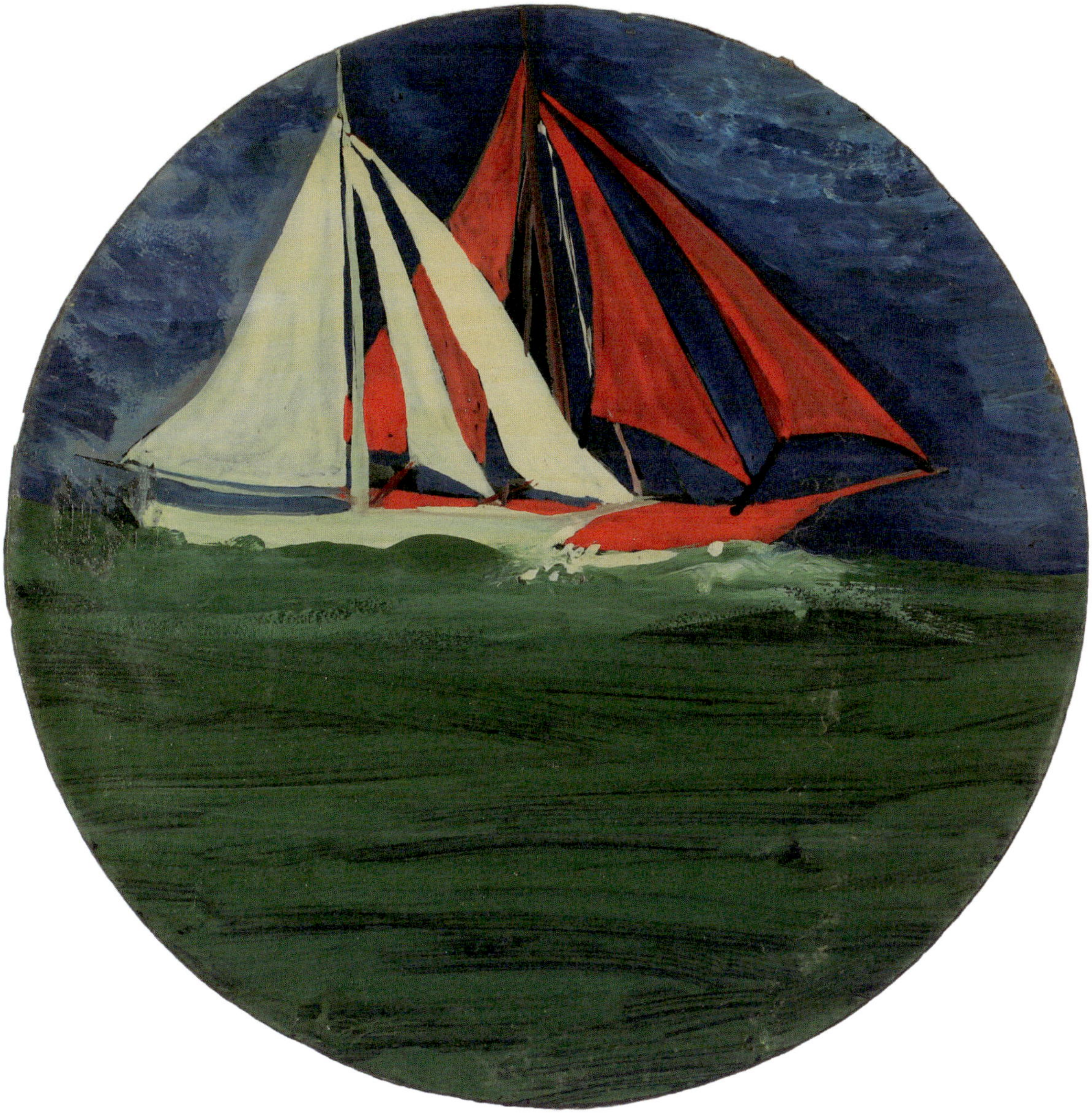

Frank Walter
Untitled (White sailboat, red sailboat)
Oil on asphalt roofing material with
Masonite backing
21.8 cm diameter

All courtesy of the artist’s family and Ingleby,
Edinburgh
Photos: Kenneth Milton

The Anomie Review of Contemporary British Painting 2

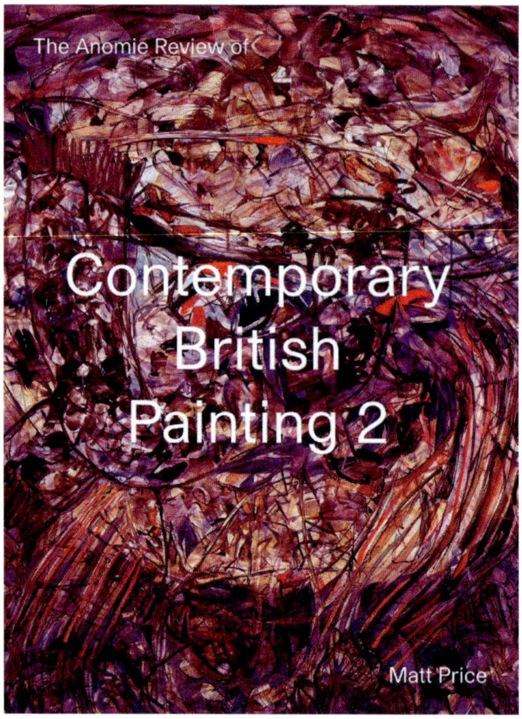

Contributors:
Matt Price

240pp
Softback
280 × 210 mm
c. 200 images
ISBN: 978-1-910221-27-3
RRP: £30
UK Release: 9 September 2021
Designed by Joe Gilmore
Copy editor: William Lambie
Assistant editor: Anna McNay
Printed by S&G, Merthyr Tydfil
Published by Anomie Publishing, London

Following the success of *The Anomie Review of Contemporary British Painting* in 2018, a second volume has been created to showcase solo exhibitions that have defined contemporary painting in Britain since the first volume. This new, larger anthology presents the work of sixty artists born or living here through documentation and discussion of solo exhibitions of their work in museums and galleries around the UK and internationally. Featuring artists at different stages of their careers, from senior figures exhibiting at major museums to emerging artists presenting some of their first commercial gallery exhibitions, *The Anomie Review of Contemporary British Painting 2* offers an overview of recent activity in the medium of painting in this country.

Artists and venues featured in this new volume include Hurvin Anderson at Rat Hole Gallery, Tokyo; Frank Bowling at Tate Britain, London; Lisa Brice at Stephen Friedman Gallery, London; Gareth Cadwallader at Josh Lilley, London; Denzil Forrester at Nottingham Contemporary; Sophie von Hellermann at Pilar Corrias, London; Matthew Krishanu at MAC, Birmingham; Joy Labinjo at BALTIC, Gateshead; France-Lise McGurn at Simon Lee, London; Anj Smith at MOSTYN, Llandudno; Tim Stoner at Modern Art, London; and Phoebe Unwin at Towner Eastbourne.

The anthology, which features cover artwork by Jadé Fadojutimi from her spring 2019 exhibition at PEER, London, has been compiled and written by London-based editor and writer Matt Price, who in addition to editing more than fifty catalogues, monographs and books including Phaidon's international anthologies of painting and drawing *Vitamin P2* and *Vitamin D2*, has written for magazines such as *Art Monthly*, *Art Quarterly*, *ArtReview* and *Frieze*.

Endorsements for the first volume of *The Anomie Review of Contemporary British Painting*:

> 'It is hard to believe that nobody has thought to publish an anthology of this sort before, so valuable is it to current and future curators, artists and scholars, as well as audiences interested in the medium. A highly enjoyable read.'
> – Charlotte Keenan McDonald, Curator of British Art, Walker Art Gallery / National Museums Liverpool

> 'This insightful, richly illustrated anthology is a celebration of an artistic medium that is not only surviving but positively thriving. In discussing the work of [...] diverse painters, author Matt Price proves a passionate and engaging artworld guide to British painting today.'
> – Helen Sumpter, Editor, *Art Quarterly*, Art Fund

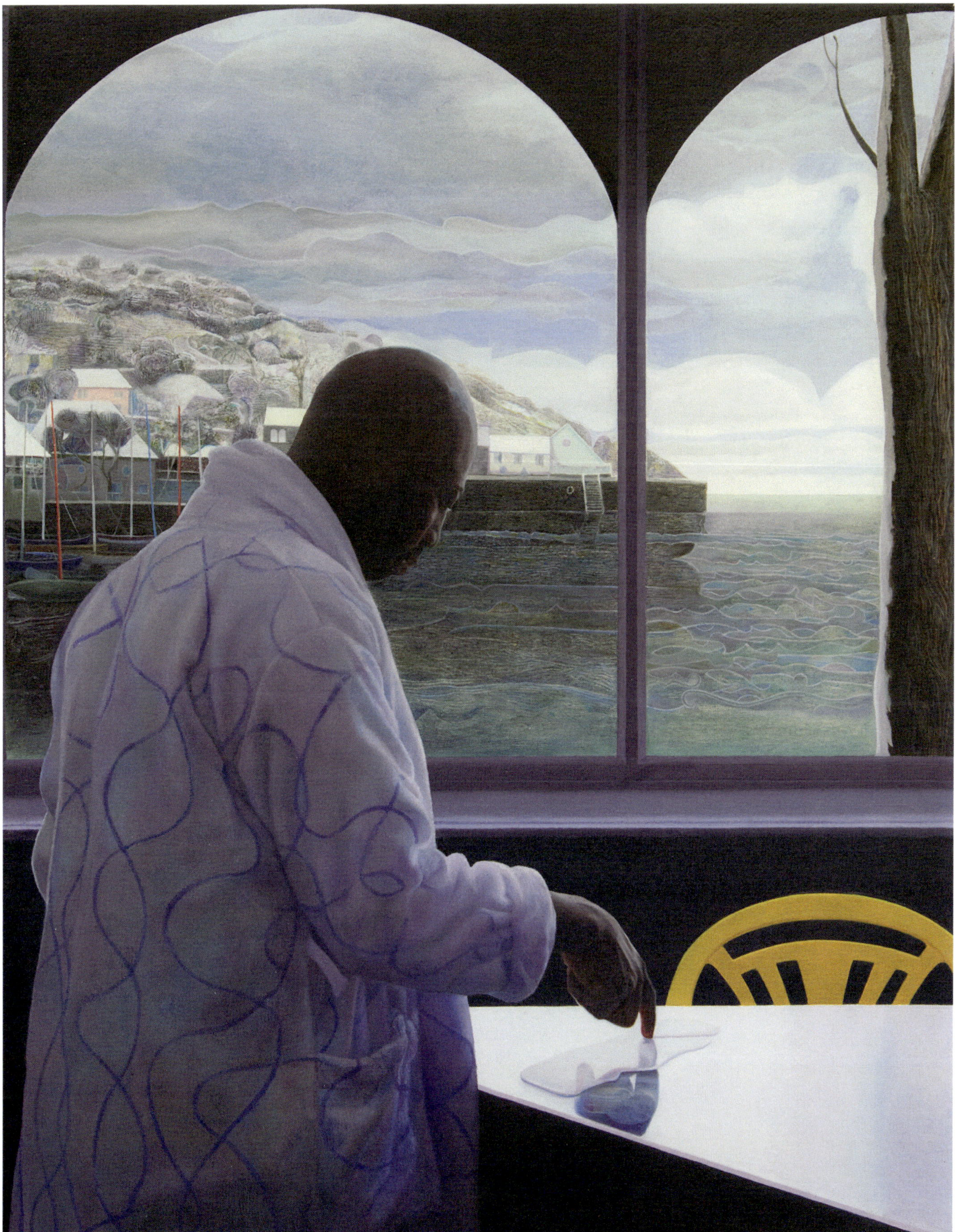

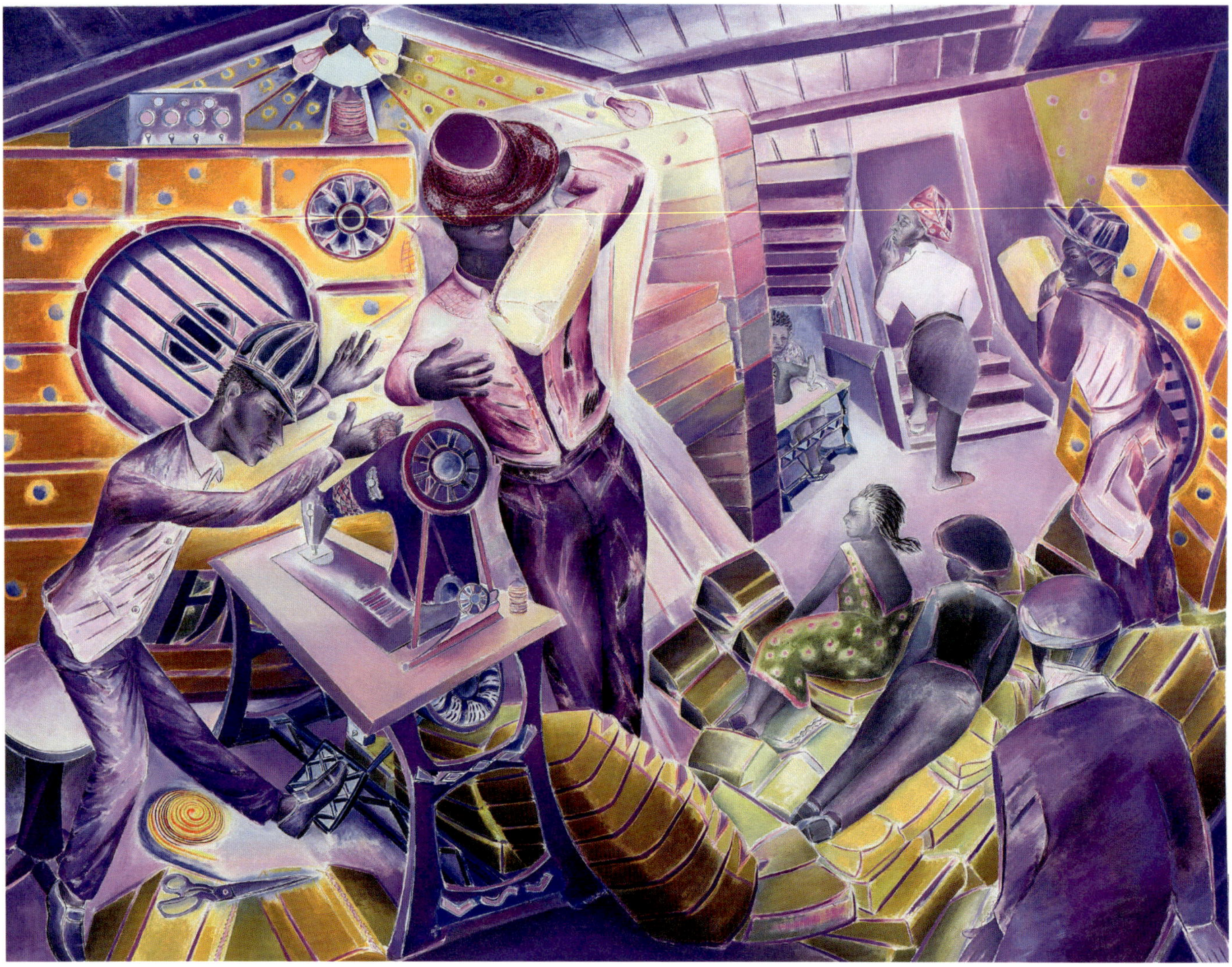

p. 97
Gareth Cadwallader
Milk, 2017
Oil on canvas
27 × 22 cm
© Gareth Cadwallader
Courtesy of the artist and Josh Lilley, London
Photo: Ben Westoby

Denzil Forrester
Stitch Up, 2017
Oil on canvas
202 × 245.5 cm
© Denzil Forrester
Courtesy of the artist and Stephen Friedman Gallery, London
Photo: Stephen White & Co.

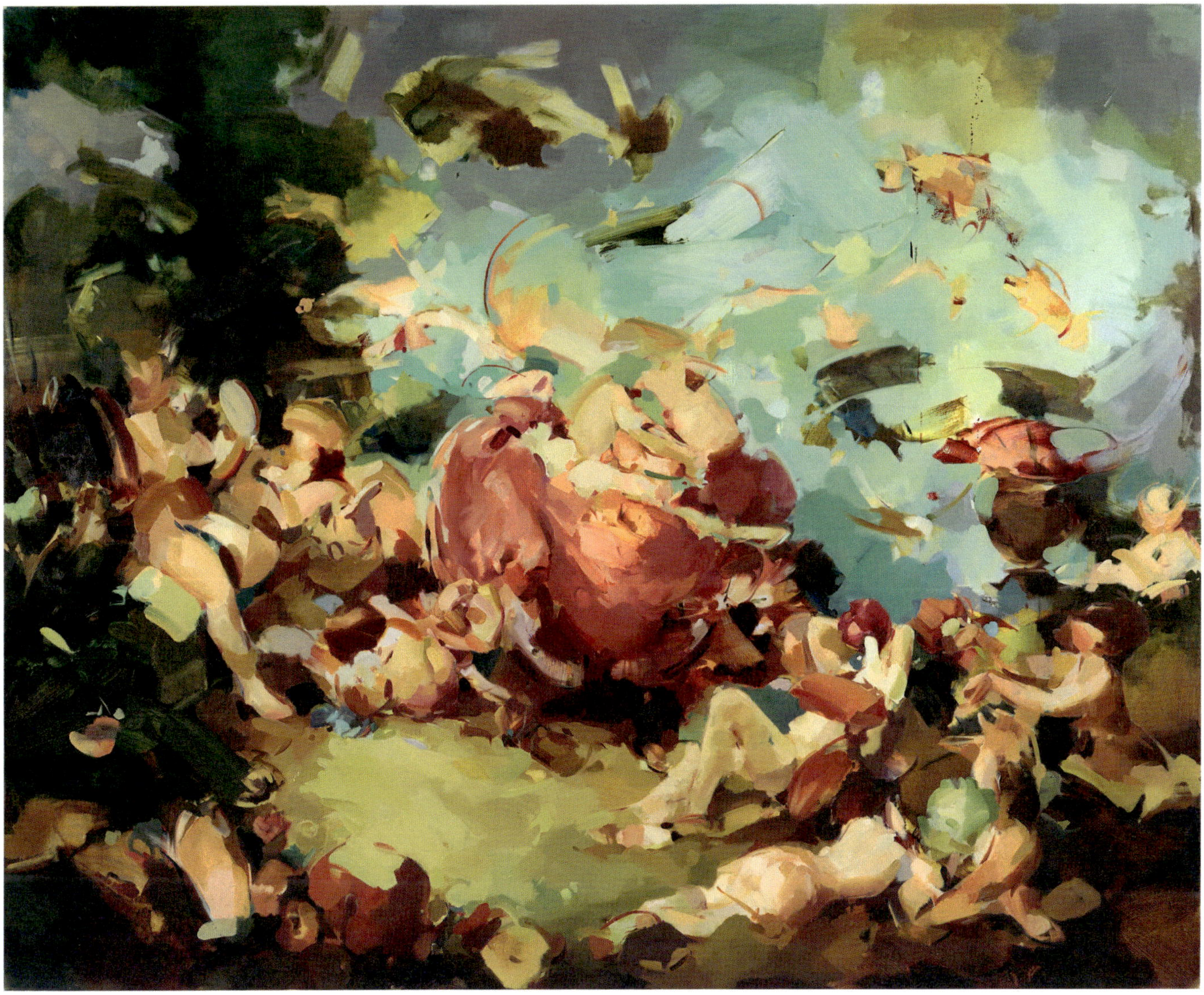

Flora Yukhnovich
I'll Have What She's Having, 2020
Oil on linen
170 × 220 cm
© Flora Yukhnovich
Courtesy of Victoria Miro, London
Photo: Peter Mallet

Kate McCGwire

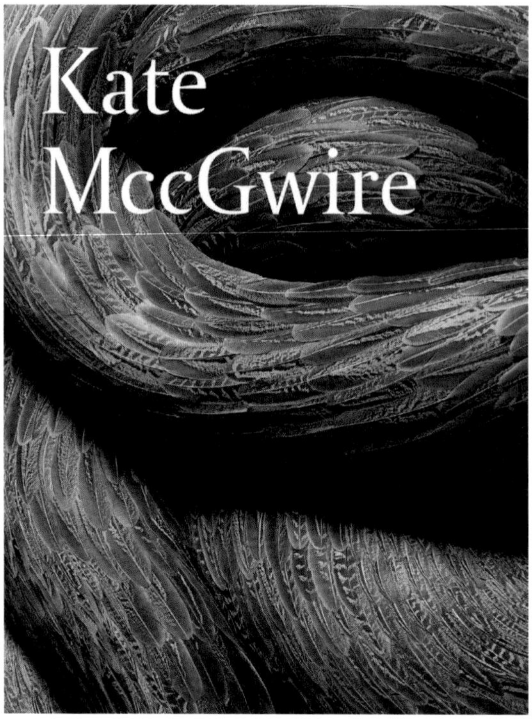

Contributors:
Jane Neal
Dr Catriona McAra

200pp
Hardback
310 × 240 mm
c. 140 images
ISBN: 978-1-910221-25-9
RRP: £45
UK Release: 8 April 2021
Edited by Mark Sanders
Designed and produced by Peter B. Willberg
Printed by SiZ, Verona
Published by Anomie Publishing, London

Kate MccGwire is an internationally renowned British sculptor whose practice probes the beauty of the uncanny. In creating arresting, sensuous, otherworldly sculptures, she explores ideas relating to Sigmund Freud's notion of the '*unheimlich*' or 'unhomely', rendering the familiar strange and disturbing, often triggering a visceral response in the viewer.

Growing up on the Norfolk Broads, MccGwire was fascinated by birds and the natural world from an early age, with avian subjects becoming a recurring theme in her artwork. Employing natural materials and, in particular, feathers, MccGwire creates freestanding sculptures and site-specific works, her forms evolving intuitively and subconsciously based on subtle patterns or details within her chosen materials.

This major monograph features works spanning her career, from the unsettling fabric and clothing works of the turn of the millennium through to the fantastical site-specific installation and interventions of her solo exhibition in 2020 at Harewood House. In the first essay commissioned for the publication, independent curator and writer Jane Neal explores themes of childhood and family, nature and the body, physics and metaphysics, opening up connections between MccGwire's works and myths, legends and belief systems across time and cultures. The second essay, by Dr Catriona McAra, an art historian and Curator at Leeds Arts University, explores MccGwire's oeuvre in relation to the history of soft sculpture, abstraction and surrealism, especially with regard to feminist histories and to notions of counter-modernism. She asserts: 'The grotesque and the uncanny have sustained a significant hold over MccGwire's creative imagination, with interlocking thought-forms and otherworldly beings dominating her oeuvre.'

Kate MccGwire (b. 1964) undertook a BA in Fine Art at University College for the Creative Arts, Farnham, before completing an MA in Sculpture at the Royal College of Art, London. Solo exhibitions include *Menagerie*, Harewood House, Leeds (2020); *Dichotomy*, The Harley Gallery, Welbeck, UK (2018); *Sasse/Sluice*, Aldeburgh Festival, UK (2018); *Secrete*, Galerie Huit, Hong Kong (2016); *Scissure*, La Galerie Particulière, Paris (2016) and *Covert*, Musée de la Chasse et de la Nature, Paris (2014). She has featured in group exhibitions at venues including the Fondazione Berengo, Murano, Italy; Gewerbemuseum Winterthur, Switzerland; Guerlain House, Paris; Centre of Contemporary Art, Torun, Poland; Anton Ulrich Museum, Braunschweig, Germany; the Museum of Arts and Design, New York and the Contemporary Art Society, London. In 2018 she was the winner of the Royal Academy of Arts' Jack Goldhill Award for Sculpture.

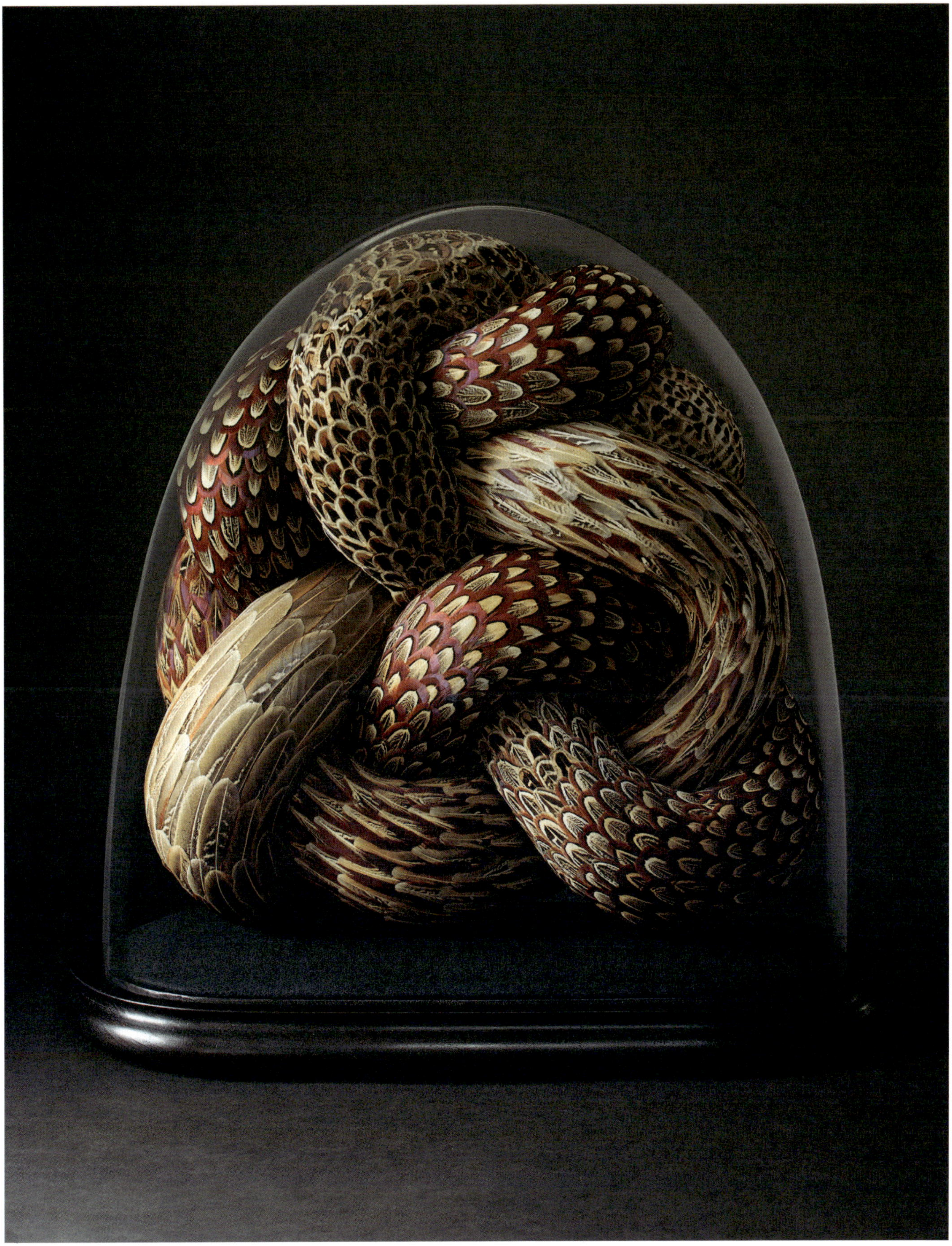

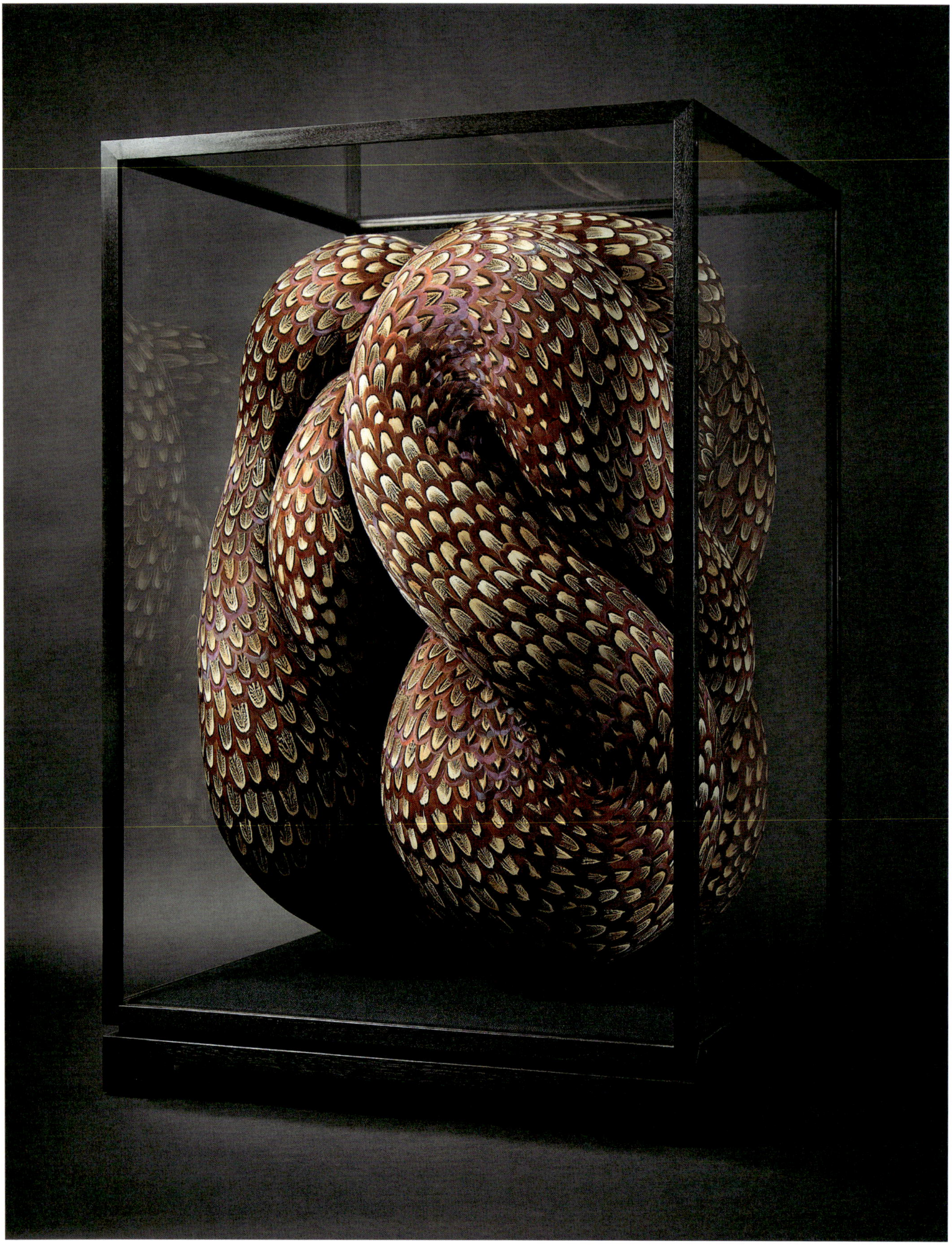

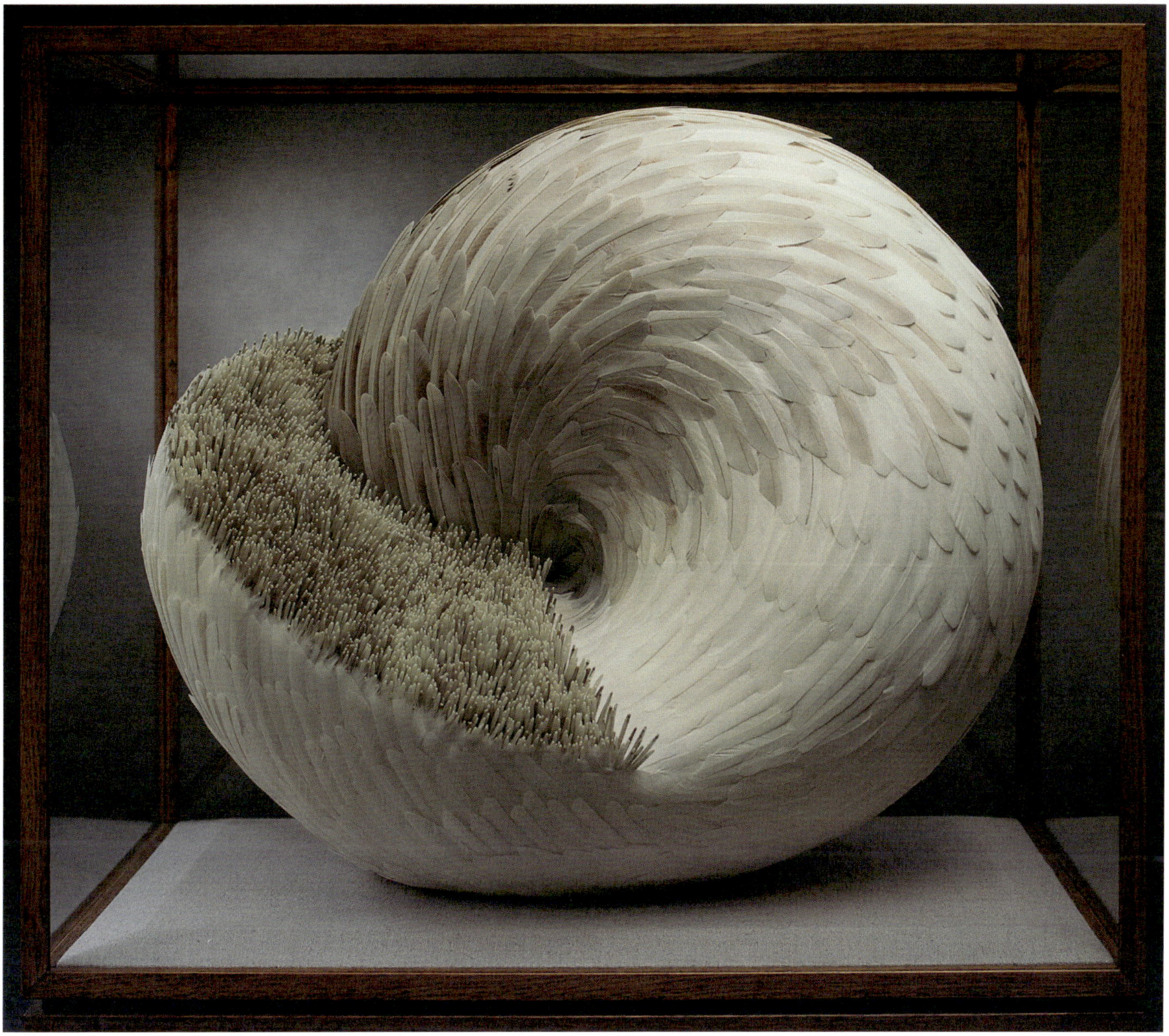

p. 103
Kate MccGwire
Turmoil, 2016
Mixed media with pheasant feathers in antique dome
58 × 43 × 60 cm

Kate MccGwire
Quandary, 2019
Mixed media with pheasant feathers in bespoke cabinet
80 × 50.5 × 50.5 cm

Kate MccGwire
Sominal, 2019
Mixed media with pigeon feathers in oak cabinet
63 × 68 × 48 cm

All courtesy of the artist
Photos: J P Bland

Jacqui Hallum
Workings and Showings

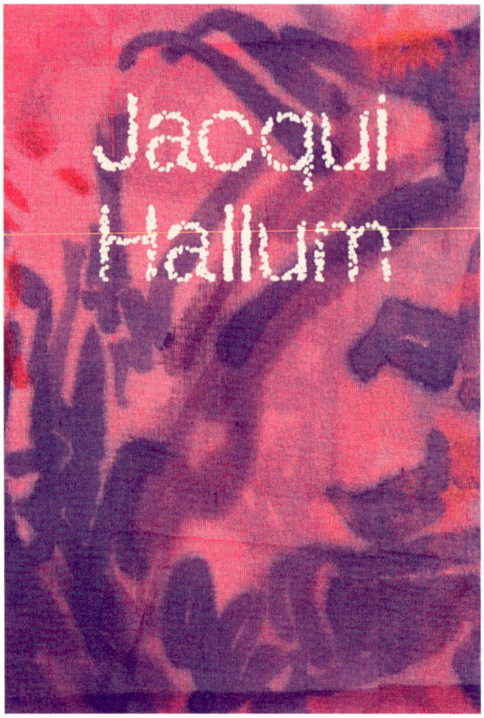

Contributors:
Dan Howard-Birt
Andrew Hunt
Hettie Judah
Caroline Wilkinson

128pp
Softback
245 × 170 mm
c. 158 images
ISBN: 978-1-910221-23-5
RRP: £25
UK Release: 25 March 2021
Edited by Susan Taylor
Designed by work-form
Printed by Gomer, Llandysul, Wales
Co-published by Kingsgate Project Space
and Anomie Publishing, London

This is the first monograph on the London-born, Devon-based artist Jacqui Hallum. The publication documents Hallum's solo exhibition at The Walker Art Gallery, Liverpool (10 October 2019 – 1 March 2020), along with a series of solo, two-person and group exhibitions held between 2014 and 2020.

Hallum is best-known for her mixed-media paintings on textiles, using techniques she has developed over the course of twenty years since completing her studies. Incorporating imagery and visual languages from medieval woodcuts and stained-glass windows to Art Nouveau, children's illustrations, tarot cards and Berber rugs, Hallum employs ink staining, painting, drawing and printing to create layers of pattern, abstraction and passages of figurative imagery. As part of her process, Hallum often leaves the fabrics in the open air, exposed to the elements, to introduce weathering into the works. History, religion, mysticism and the beliefs and creativity of past civilisations are among the themes that overlap – often in a literal sense of pieces of fabrics layered, pinned, draped and hung together – to form painterly palimpsests that carry a sense of the past with them into the present. Referencing modern visual cultures and movements such as punk, hippy, psychedelia, grunge, acid-house, traveller, folk, indie, goth and new-age, Hallum's approach to painting embraces alternative visual languages in dialogue with the history of art.

Along with a foreword by Professor Caroline Wilkinson, Director of the School of Art and Design at Liverpool John Moores University, and an introductory essay by artist, curator and director of Kingsgate Workshops and Project Space in London, Dan Howard-Birt, the publication features newly commissioned essays by arts journalist and critic Hettie Judah and by Andrew Hunt, Professor of Fine Art and Curating at the University of Manchester. Also featured is the edited transcript of a conversation between Hallum and Howard-Birt held at The Walker Art Gallery, Liverpool.

Jacqui Hallum (b. 1977) graduated with a BA in Fine Art from Coventry School of Art & Design, Coventry University, in 1999, and an MFA in Painting from the Slade School of Fine Art, University of London, in 2002. Hallum's solo exhibition at The Walker Art Gallery followed a three-month fellowship at Liverpool John Moores University, which resulted from winning the prestigious John Moores Painting Prize in 2018.

Jacqui Hallum
Red coats vs Blue jackets (compassionating), 2019
Mixed media on fabric
Installation view from *The View from the Top of a Pyramid*, The Walker Art Gallery, Liverpool, 2019
Courtesy of the artist and The Walker Art Gallery, Liverpool. Photo: Harry Meadley

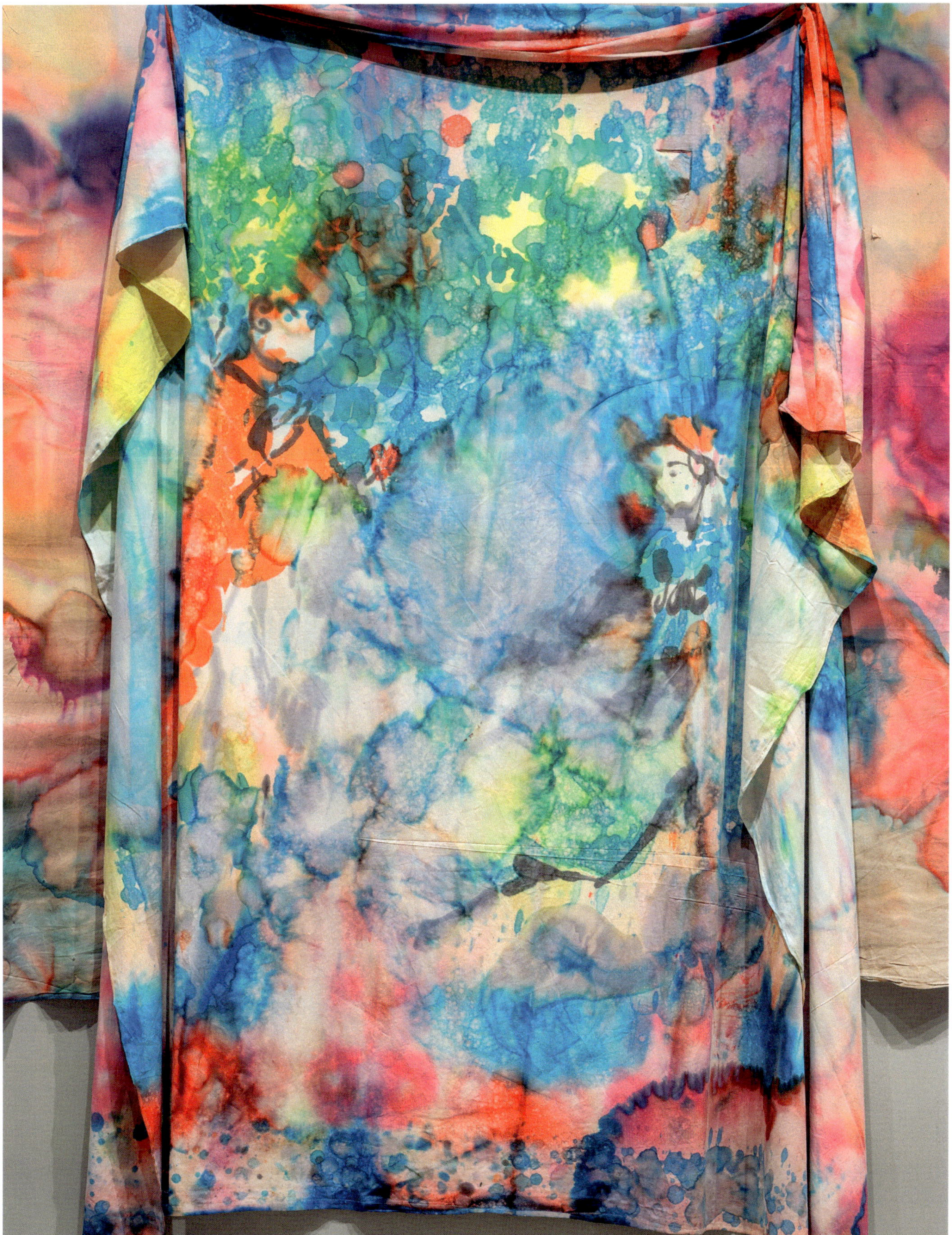

Jadé Fadojutimi
Jesture

Contributors:
Jennifer Higgie

76pp
Softback
280 × 240 mm
c. 30 images
ISBN: 978-1-910221-29-7
RRP: £30
UK Release: 21 January 2021
Designed by A Practice for Everyday Life
Photography by Mark Blower, Eva Herzog, and
Todd White Art Photography
Produced by Pippy Houldsworth Gallery, London
Printed by PUSH, London
Co-published by Pippy Houldsworth Gallery and
Anomie Publishing, London

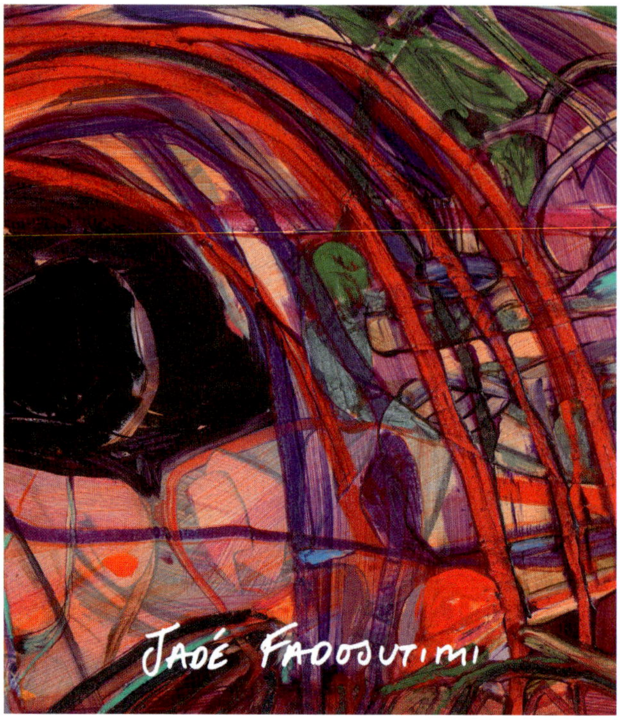

The word 'Jesture' in the title of this publication evokes a sense of the absurd, responding to the disruption of daily rhythms arising from forced isolation during lockdown. Central to Jadé Fadojutimi's practice is a repeated questioning of identity, its fluid nature and how the understanding of notions of pleasure, desire and choice are integral to a sense of self. Powerful memories, experienced whilst listening to film, animation and video game soundtracks, transport Fadojutimi to the first time she encountered them, eliciting a response that is experienced through intense colour. The synthesis of these various influences, through which Fadojutimi understands her sense of self, is transformed into large-scale gestural paintings charged with energy and emotion.

Described by Fadojutimi as 'environments', these complex compositions, neither wholly abstract nor figurative, are built up with layers of oil paint, interrupted by the more linear mark-making made possible by her recent adoption of oil pastels. The introduction of new materials into her painting has enabled Fadojutimi to think more broadly about palette, composition and depth, while translating the spontaneity of her drawing on to the canvas.

In her essay for the publication, *From Life – Thoughts on the paintings of Jadé Fadojutimi*, writer and editor-at-large of *Frieze* magazine Jennifer Higgie writes:

> 'In these paintings, the world, in all of its chaotic glory, exists as an intimation. Art is not an explanation: it's a shot of energy, a flash of colour; a shimmer, a reaction, a line thrown out to see who might pick it up. Pictures are made by people and, like people, their tone can switch direction in the blink of an eye.'

Jadé Fadojutimi (b. 1993) lives and works in London. She earned a BA from The Slade School of Fine Art, London, in 2015 and an MA from the Royal College of Art, London, in 2017. After Pippy Houldsworth Gallery took on representation of the artist and presented her first solo exhibition in 2017-18, she had her first one-person institutional show at PEER UK, London, in 2019. Acquisitions by Baltimore Museum of Art, ICA Miami, Tate and a promised gift to Dallas Museum of Art soon followed. She had her first solo exhibition in Germany with Galerie Gisela Capitain, Cologne, in 2019 and her first solo exhibition in Japan with Taka Ishii Gallery, Tokyo, in spring 2021. Fadojutimi was selected to participate in Liverpool Biennial 2021. Her first solo US museum exhibition was at ICA Miami, in November 2021. She also had a solo exhibition at The Hepworth Wakefield in 2021.

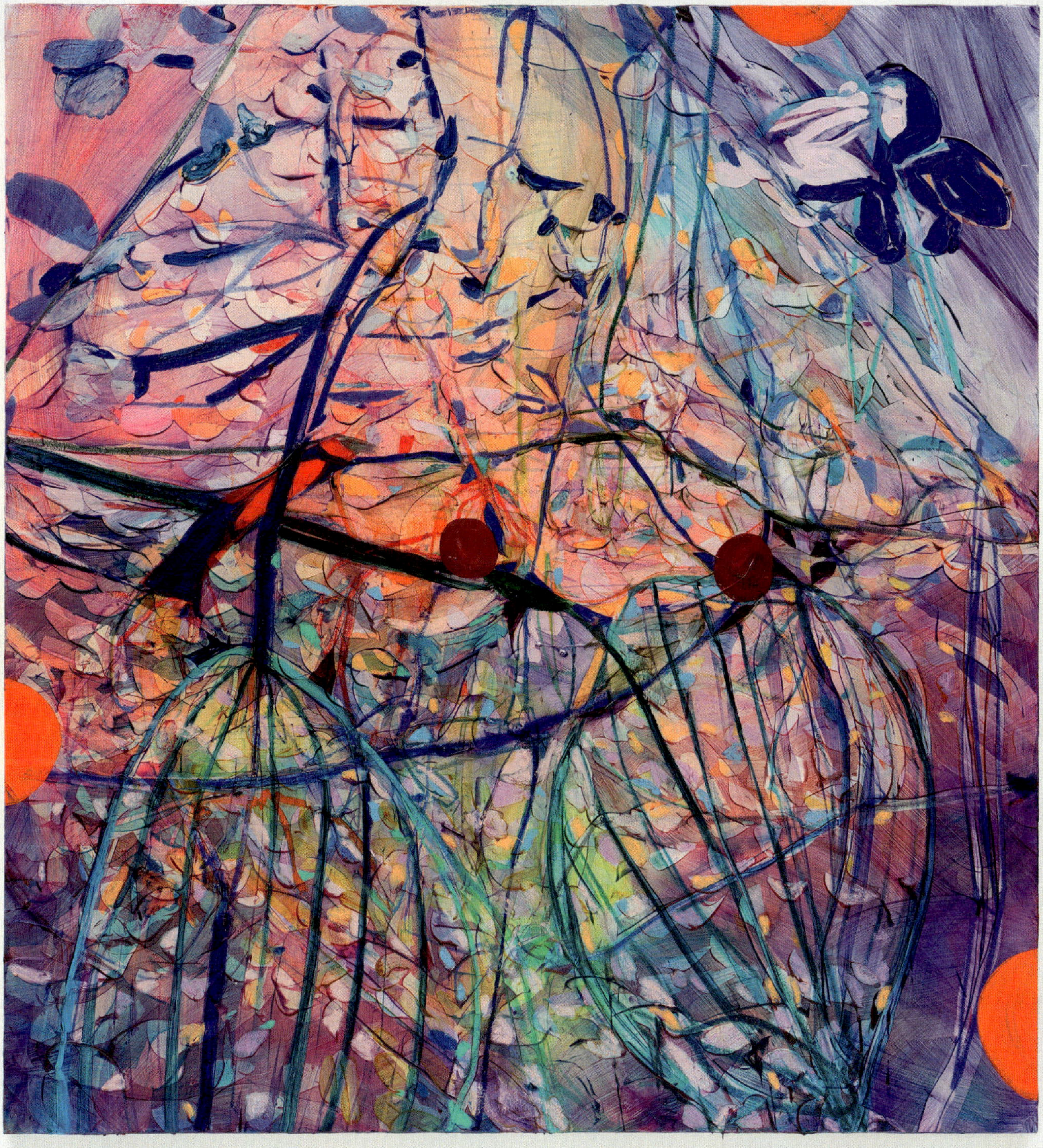

Jadé Fadojutimi
Ob-sess(h)-ion, 2020
Oil, acrylic and oil stick on canvas
180 × 170 cm
Photo: Mark Blower

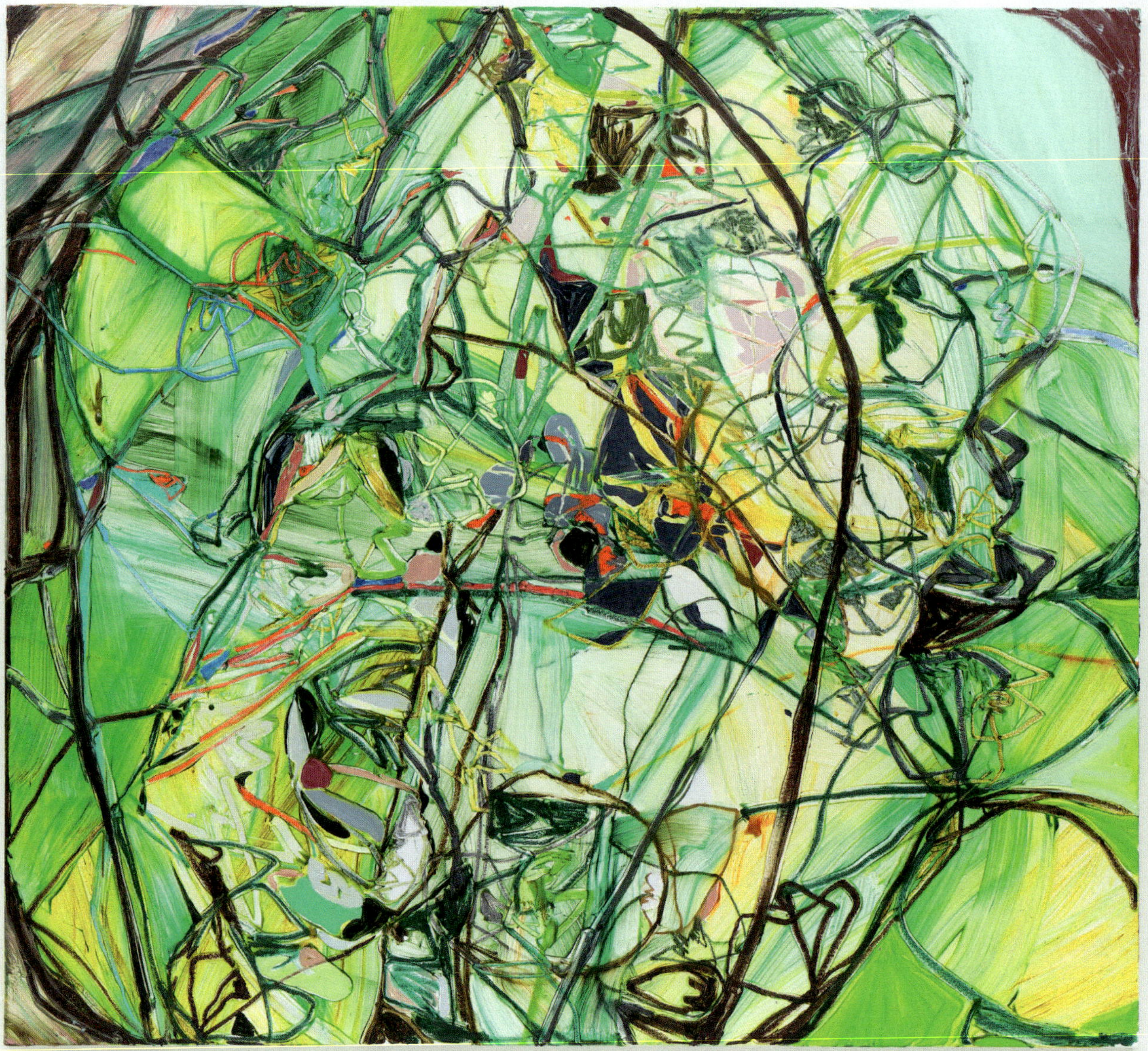

Jadé Fadojutimi
Mosaicked Utterance, 2020
Oil, acrylic and oil stick on canvas
160 × 180 cm
Photo: Mark Blower

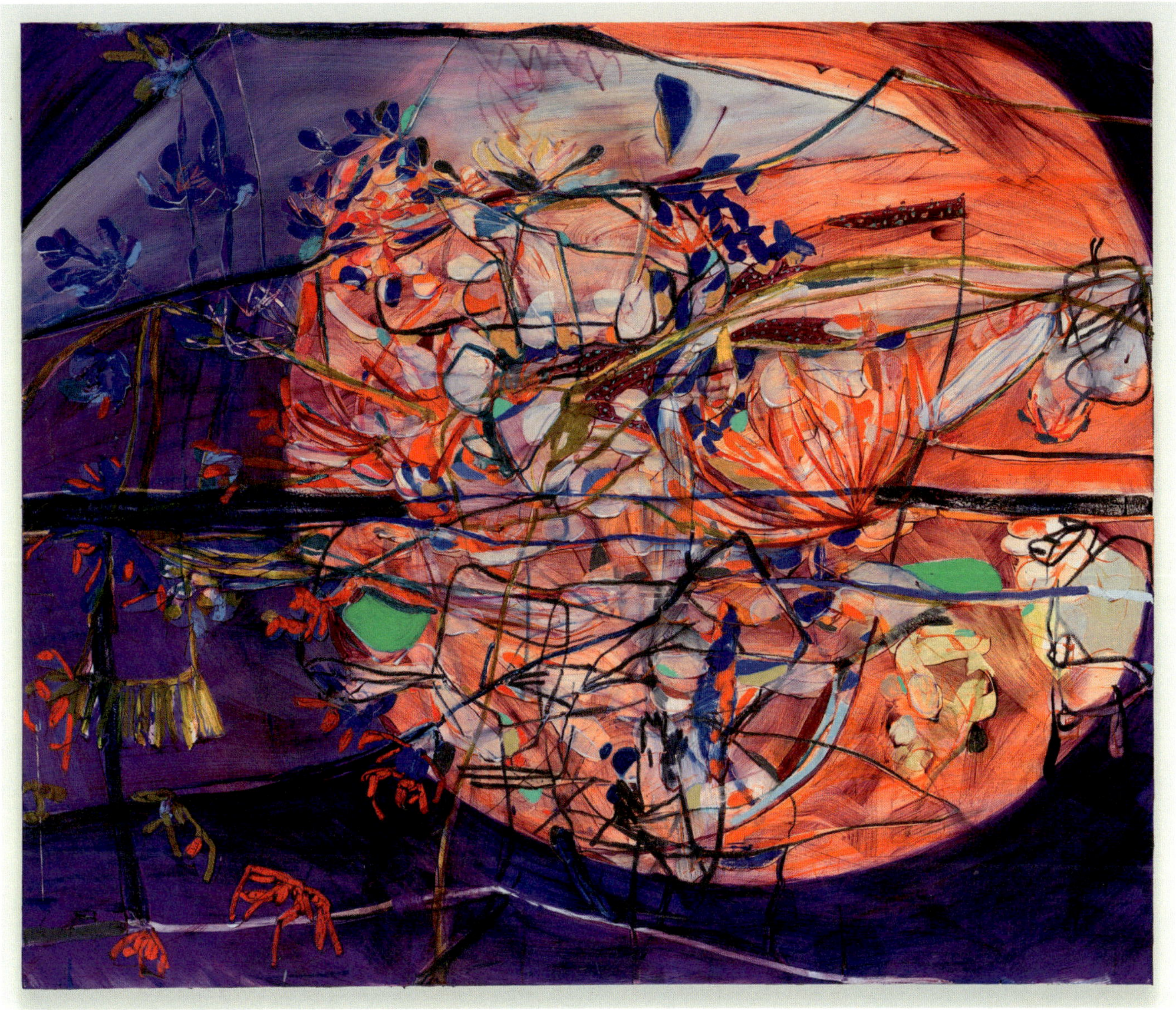

Jadé Fadojutimi
There exists a glorious world. Its name?
The Land of Sustainable Burdens, 2020
Oil, acrylic and oil stick on canvas
190 × 230 cm
Photo: Eva Herzog

All © Jadé Fadojutimi, 2020
Courtesy of the artist and Pippy Houldsworth
Gallery, London

Nick Hornby
Zygotes and Confessions

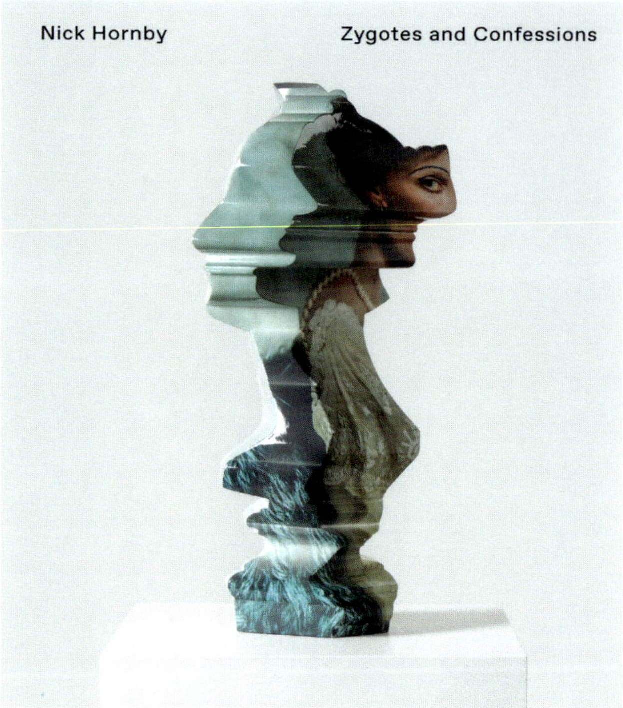

Contributors:
Helen Boyd
Alfredo Cramerotti
Matt Price

80pp
Softback
230 × 190 mm
c. 38 images
ISBN: 978-1-910221-28-0
RRP: £18
UK Release: 28 January 2021
Dual language – English and Welsh
Designed by Joe Gilmore
Photography by Ben Westoby and Mark Blower
Co-published by MOSTYN, Wales, and
Anomie Publishing, London

Zygotes and Confessions is a new publication devoted to the work of artist Nick Hornby, and was produced to accompany his first solo exhibition in a public gallery, presented at MOSTYN, Wales, from November 2020 to April 2021.

Hornby is known for his monumental site-specific works that combine digital software with traditional materials such as bronze, steel, granite and marble. In this publication he presents a substantial new body of smaller, more intimate work comprising three discrete yet interrelated series inspired by the history of sculptural busts, modernist abstractions and mantelpiece ceramic dogs. United by glossy photographic surfaces created by means of an industrial process in which his marble and resin composite sculptures are dipped into liquid photographs, these new works explore themes of portraiture, the body, identity, sexuality and intimacy in the digital era. A number of the works have been made in collaboration with fashion photographer Louie Banks.

Along with a foreword by Helen Boyd, Head of Marketing and Publisher Relations at the Casemate Group, the publication features a text by MOSTYN director Alfredo Cramerotti and an essay by London-based publisher, editor and writer Matt Price. Price writes: 'With one eye on the sculpture of the past and the other on that of tomorrow, technology is at the heart of London-based Nick Hornby's practice and is central to the production of his often imposing, mind-bending and futuristic-looking sculptures. Using materials such as bronze and marble, his work points back towards the Renaissance or the nineteenth century, yet his use of resin and digital technology positions him very much in the present, exploring languages both figurative and abstract, often simultaneously.'

The texts are presented in both English and Welsh. Newly commissioned studio photography of the works by Ben Westoby, along with installation views of the exhibition commissioned by MOSTYN from Mark Blower, illustrate the publication..

Nick Hornby (b. 1980) studied at the Slade School of Art and Chelsea College of Art. His work has been exhibited at Tate Britain, London; Southbank Centre, London; Leighton House, London; CASS Sculpture Foundation; Glyndebourne; Fitzwilliam Museum, Cambridge; Museum of Arts and Design, New York and Poznan Biennale, Poland. Residencies include Outset (Israel) and Eyebeam (USA), and awards include the UAL Sculpture Prize.

Nick Hornby
Little Sphinx (Jazzelle), 2020
Resin, ink, lacquer
80 × 36 × 15 cm

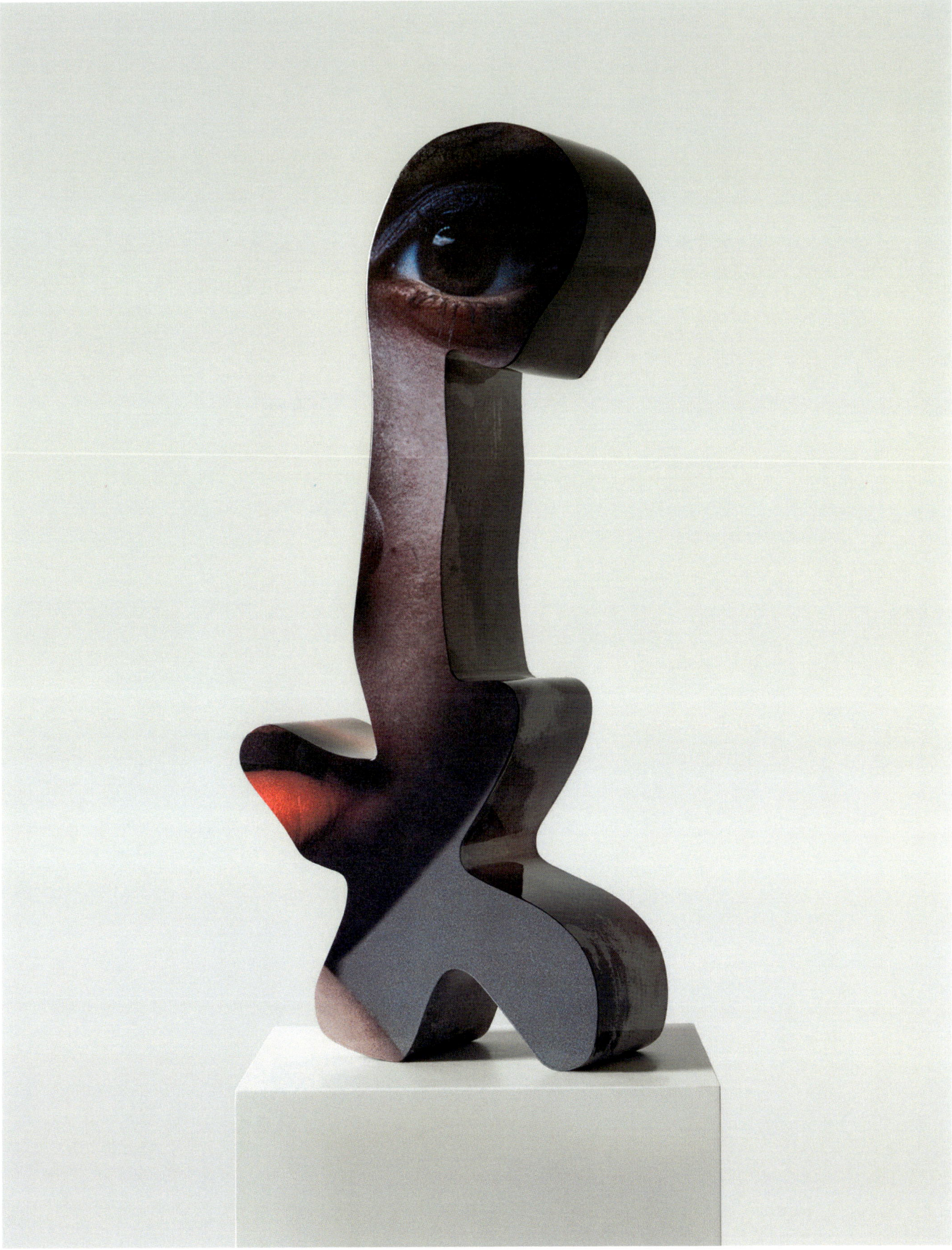

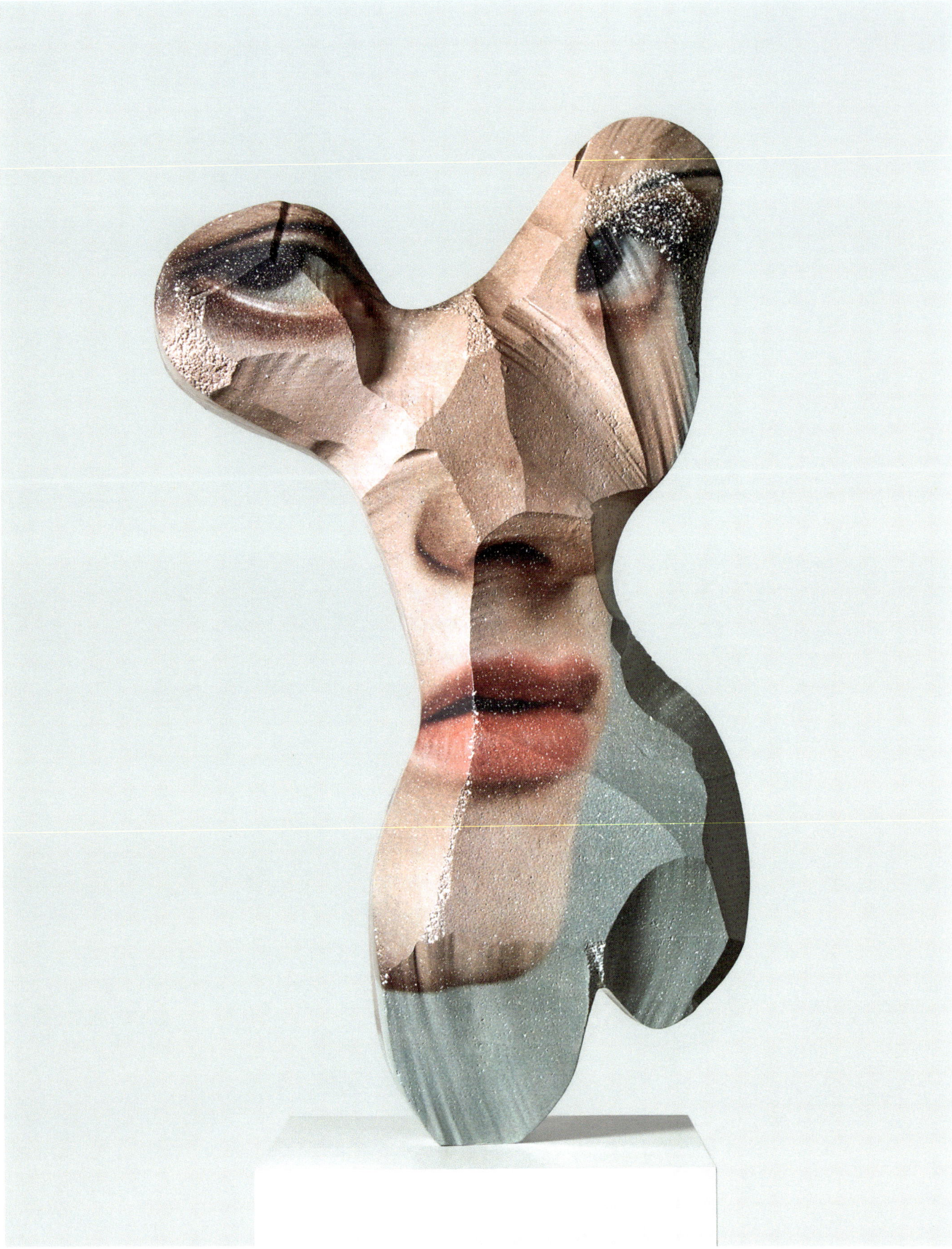

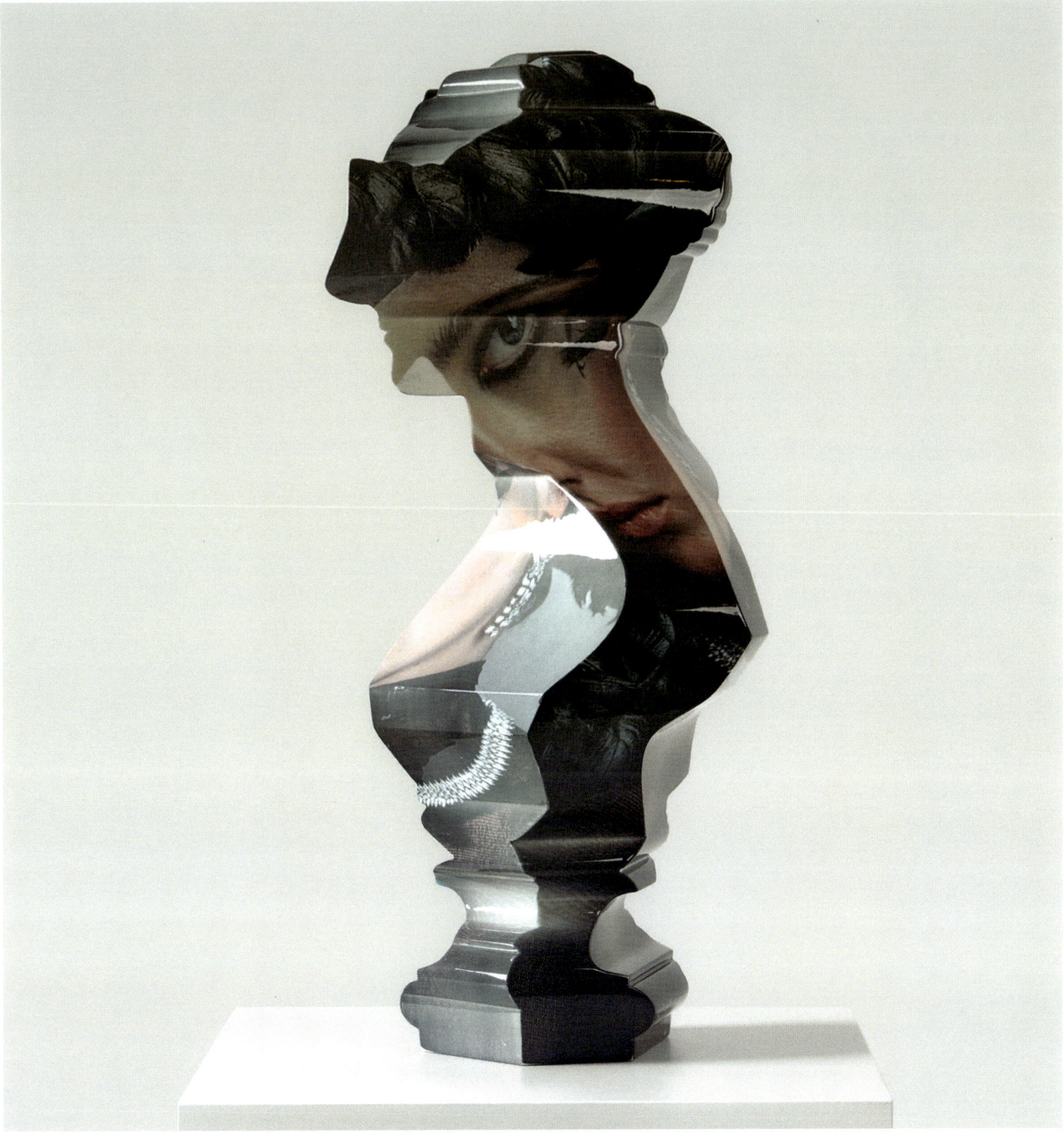

Nick Hornby
Torso (Lady James), 2020
Resin, ink, lacquer
90 × 55 × 20 cm

Nick Hornby
Muse I (Lady Eliza), 2020
Marble resin composite, ink, lacquer
59 × 27 × 28 cm

All made in collaboration with Louie Banks
© Nick Hornby
Photos: Ben Westoby

Caroline Walker
Janet

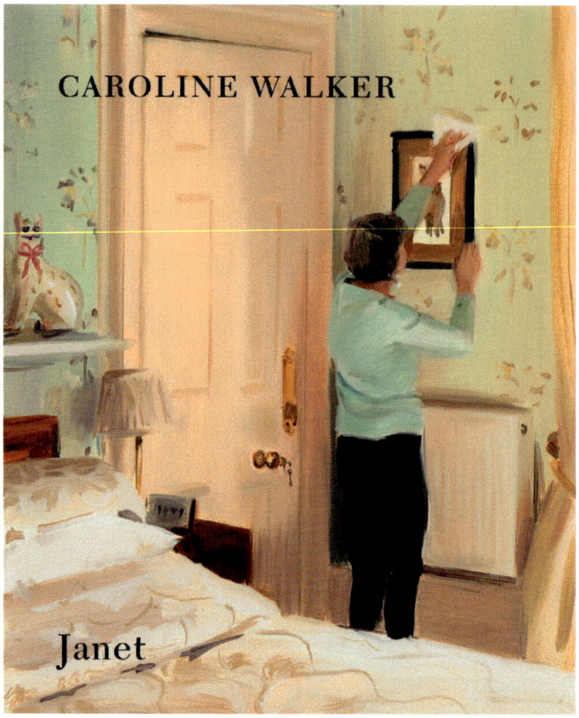

Contributors:
Hettie Judah

152pp
Hardback with dust jacket
260 × 215 mm
c. 80 images
ISBN: 978-1-910221-26-6
RRP: £28
UK Release: 15 October 2020
Designed by Joanna Deans / Identity
Photography by Peter Mallet
Produced by Ingleby Gallery, Edinburgh
Printed by Die Keure, Bruges
Co-published by Ingleby, Edinburgh, and
Anomie Publishing, London

Scotland-born, London-based artist Caroline Walker is celebrated for her paintings exploring the lives of women, from those living luxury lifestyles to those fleeing oppression. In this publication, which was produced to accompany Walker's first exhibition with Ingleby Gallery, Edinburgh, in autumn 2020, the artist turns her attention closer to home, presenting a series of paintings in which the focus is the artist's own mother, Janet, as she goes about her daily tasks: cooking, cleaning, tidying and tending the garden of the Fife home where the artist spent her childhood.

The publication features a newly commissioned essay and an interview with the artist by critic and author Hettie Judah. The essay opens by comparing Walker's works to the Dutch Golden Age, encouraging consideration of everyday domestic scenes. Judah then leads the reader through Walker's latest series of works, exploring the daily routines and household chores that have filled Walker's mother's days for the past forty years, along with the artist's treatment of these activities. Judah deftly locates this latest body of work within Walker's wider practice, opening up discussion of women at work in different capacities. She asserts: 'While *Janet* extends Walker's long-held interest in women's work, the series is also a loving undertaking. The artist offers us her mother with great pride, both in particular, and on behalf of other mothers overlooked and working out of sight.' The interview offers further insight into Walker's thoughts and working processes in relation to the *Janet* series.

The publication features around eighty illustrations of the preparatory studies and paintings that comprise this new body of work. It was published in an edition of 1,500 copies.

Caroline Walker was born in Dunfermline, Scotland, in 1982. She studied at Glasgow School of Art from 2000-04, before completing her MA at the Royal College of Art in 2009. Recent and forthcoming exhibitions include Kettle's Yard, Cambridge; the Midlands Arts Centre (MAC), Birmingham and the British Art Show 9. She is represented in a number of public collections including the National Museum of Wales, Cardiff; the UK Government Art Collection, London; Kistefos Museum, Jevnaker, Norway and Museum Voorlinden & Kunstmuseum den Haag, in the Netherlands.

Caroline Walker
Hoovering, First Thing, December, 2020
Oil on linen
210 × 160 cm

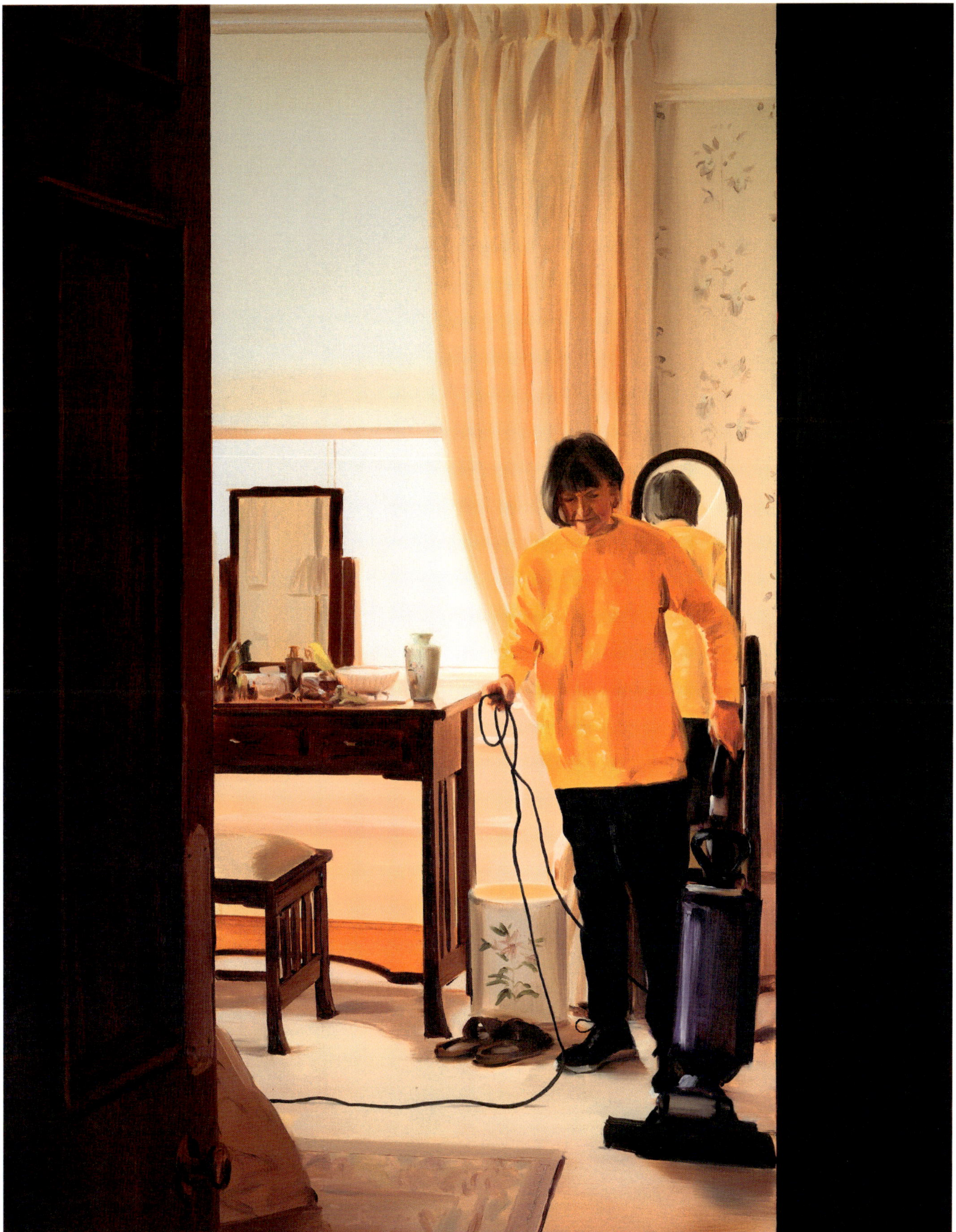

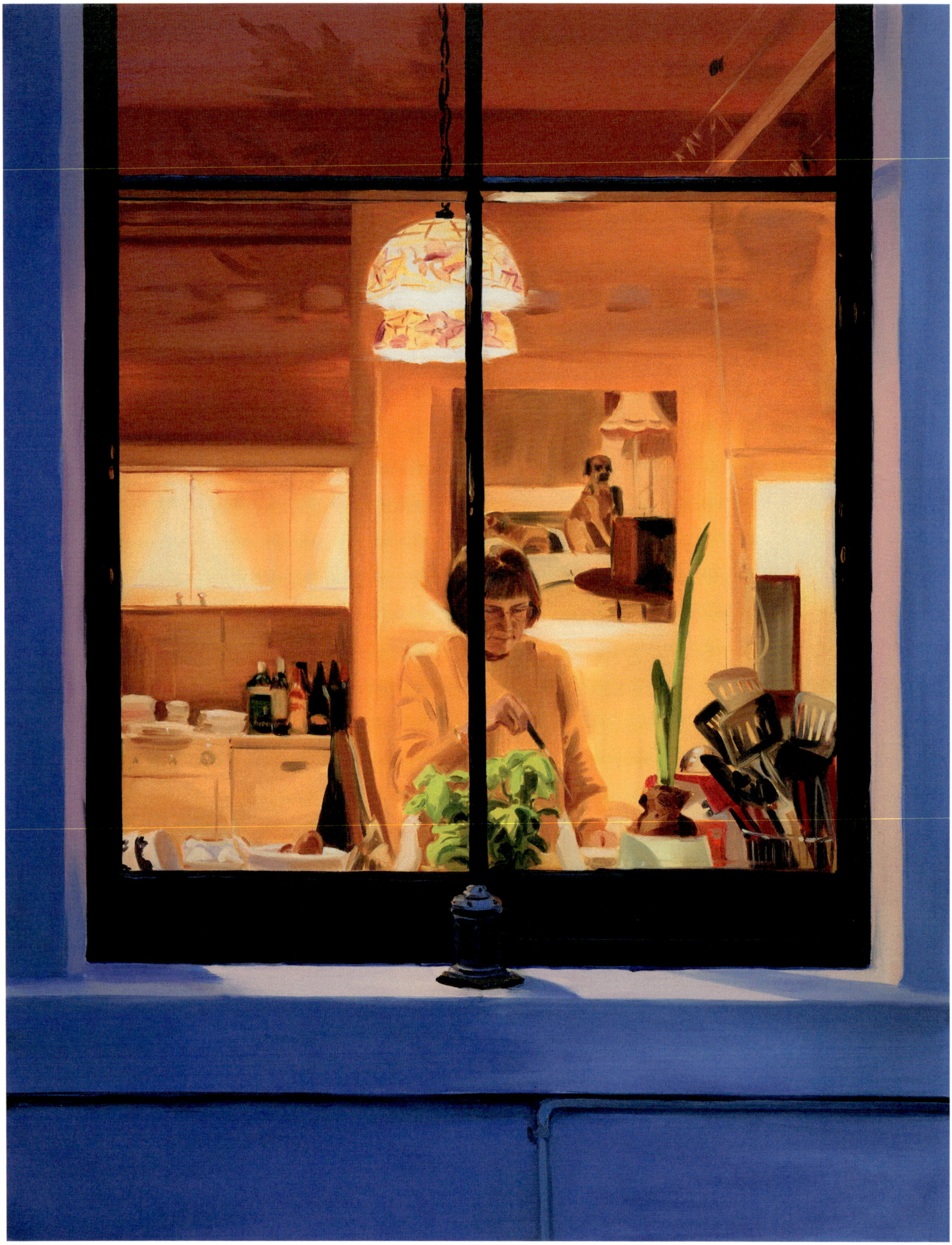

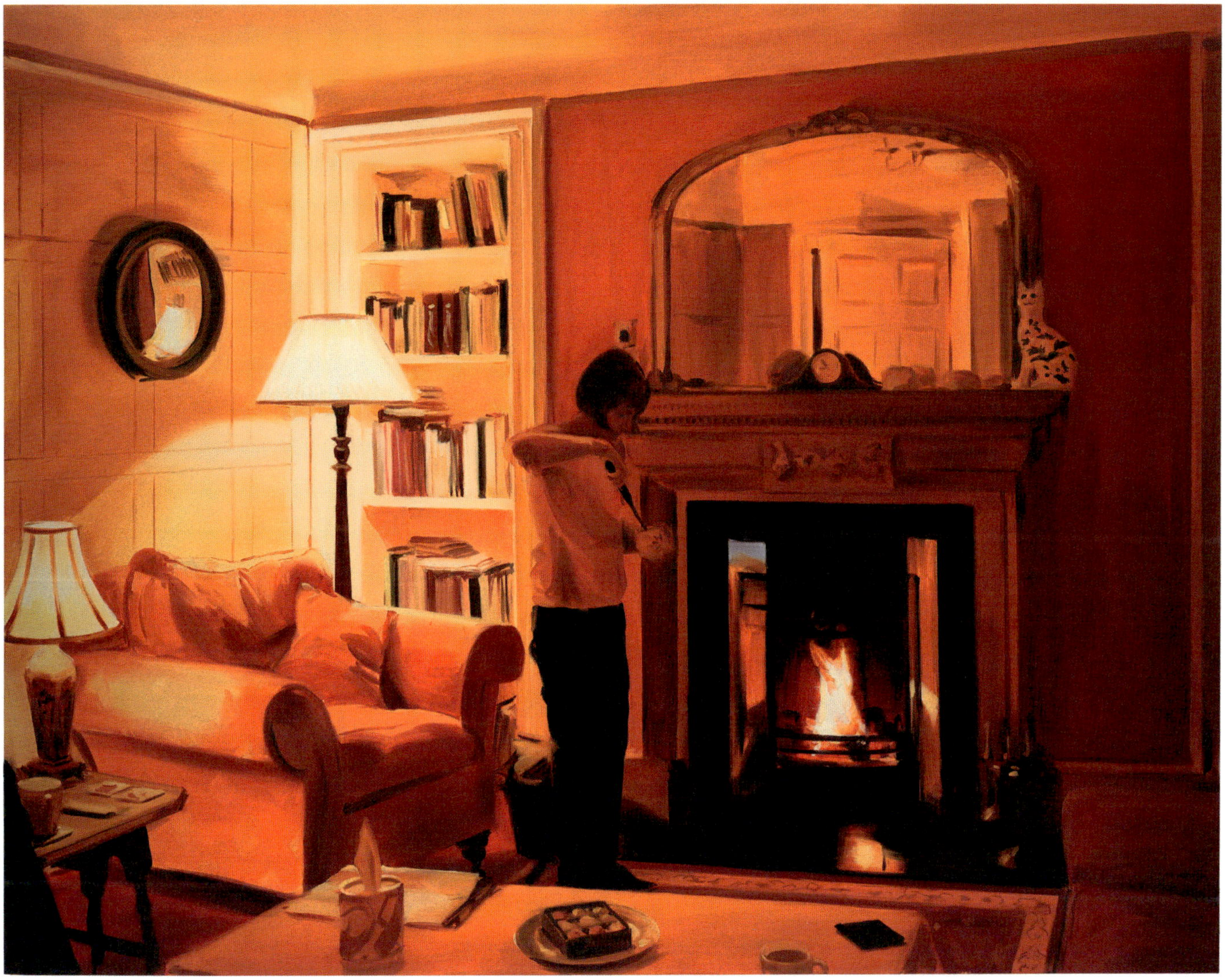

Caroline Walker
Making Fishcakes, Late Afternoon, December, 2019
Oil on linen
210 × 160 cm

Caroline Walker
Lighting Candles, Evening, March, 2019
Oil on linen
180 × 240 cm

All courtesy of the artist and Grimm, Amsterdam | New York
Photos: Peter Mallet

Q&A with... Caroline Walker

Is there a particular book that was significant in terms of your decision to become an artist?

I can't think of a book that was significant as such, but I definitely remember a couple which were really my main frame of reference for understanding anything about contemporary art as a teenager. One was *Art Today* by Edward Lucie-Smith and the other was *Scottish Art in the Twentieth Century* by Duncan MacMillan, which included many of the paintings I was seeing in the public galleries I visited growing up in Scotland.

When you were at art school, were there any books which influenced how you thought or worked?

When I was at Glasgow School of Art, I remember being introduced to Eric Fischl's paintings via *The Krefeld Project*, the book published in conjunction with the series of paintings he made following a three-day photoshoot with actors at the Haus Esters in the Krefelder Kunstmuseen in Germany. I was blown away by these paintings, which had a huge influence on my work over the next decade. I still have the well-thumbed book in my studio, and I was thrilled to see some of the paintings from it in the flesh at Skarstedt Gallery, London, in 2021.

Shortly after graduating from my MA at the Royal College of Art I read *Manet and the Object of Painting* by Michel Foucault. I love Manet's paintings, and I found this little book, which started as a lecture delivered by Foucault in 1971, a fascinating read, making connections between the formal qualities of Manet's paintings and the mechanisms of the culture in which they were made. I've read it many times, and I found it helped me to understand this great artist's work better, and to develop my own painting practice.

What kinds of books do you enjoy reading now?

I rarely read books these days as I have young children and almost no free time! But I do like to listen to audio books while I paint, and I generally tend to listen to things that relate to my work in some way. If that's non-fiction, it might be something which relates to the socio-political and cultural experience of women. Some recent titles which stand out in my mind are *Invisible Women* by Caroline Criado-Perez and *The Double × Economy* by Linda Scott.

What proportion of the books you read are fiction?

I'd say about half the books I read/listen to are fiction. Again, I find myself drawn to novels with subjects that relate to my artistic interests. In the last couple of years my work has been focused on the experience of birth and early motherhood, and a novel I really enjoyed, which circled around this subject beautifully, was *Violets* by Alex Hyde. Sometimes I like something which has no relation to what's going on in the studio, though, and I just finished listening to the *Wolf Hall* trilogy by Hilary Mantel, which I thoroughly enjoyed.

Can you recall a book that made you laugh out loud?

I'm currently reading *My Work* by Olga Ravn in preparation for an in-conversation event with her. The novel is a very honest account of early motherhood, and I was reading a passage last night which made me laugh out loud as its observation of the neurosis and anxieties of being pregnant were so well observed. I'm not sure it was meant to be funny, though!

What are some of your favourite art books?

One of my favourite art books is the exhibition catalogue for a show I didn't even see. It was *Glitter and Doom: German Portraits from the 1920s* at the Metropolitan Museum of Art in 2006. I find that period of German art very interesting as it was such a reflection of the turbulent culture in which it was being made. It's a great book with some really arresting images.

Is there a book you are looking forward to reading that you have not yet had chance to?

I haven't read Lauren Elkin's new book *Art Monsters* yet, but I'm going to hear her speak at the Edinburgh Book Festival so am looking forward to finding out more about it and getting a copy.

I'm also looking forward to seeing Jonathan Wateridge's forthcoming monograph (published by Anomie, of course!). Jonathan and I did an in-conversation for the book last year, so I got a sneak peek then at the images that would be included, but I'll be interested to see how it's come together in the book. I'm also looking forward to reading Marco Livingstone's essay on his work.

Portrait by and courtesy of Peter Mallet.

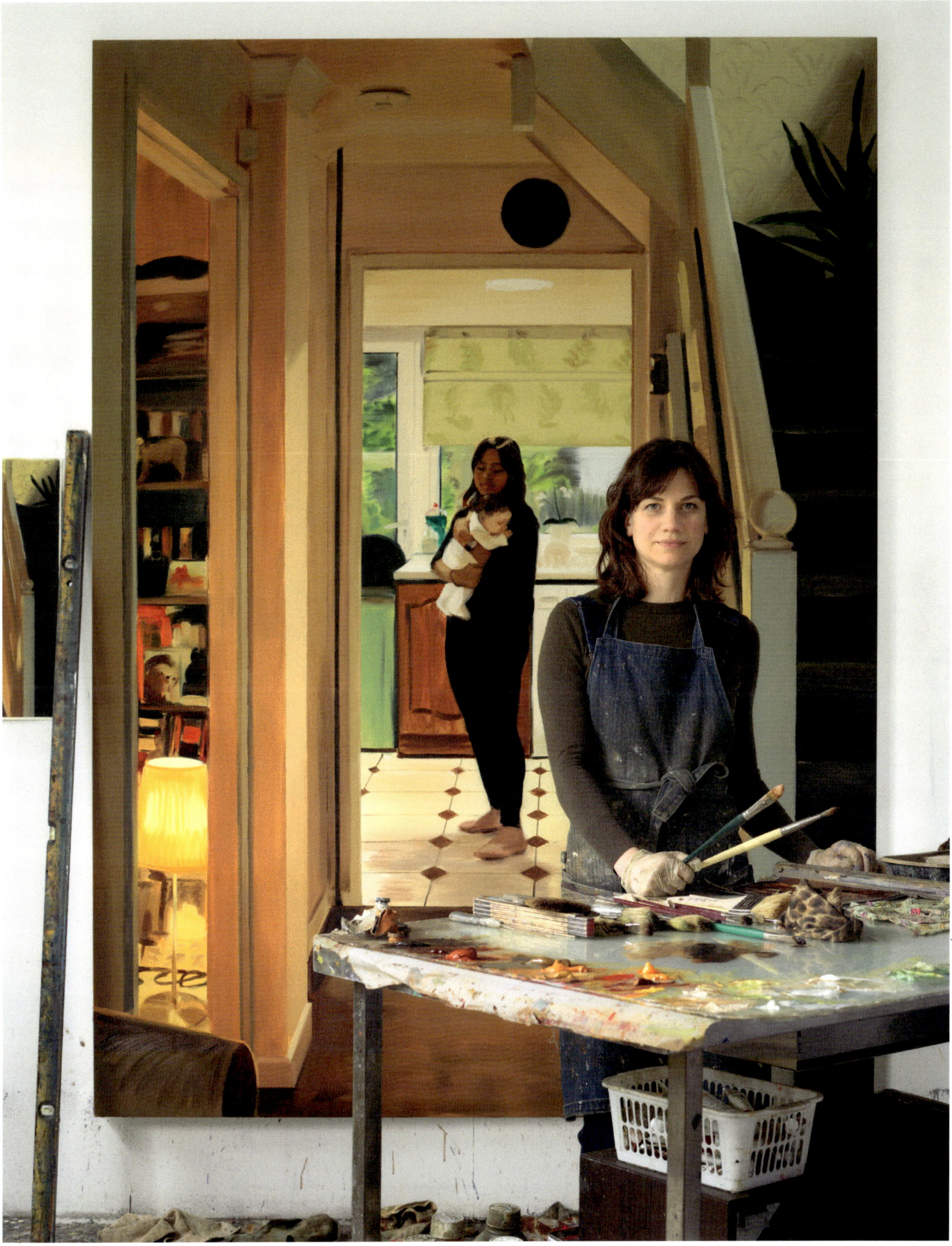

The Eleven Associates of Alma-Marceau

256pp
Hardback, 220 × 165 mm
ISBN: 978-1-910221-19-8
RRP: £20
UK Release: 06 February 2020
Designed by Modern Activity, London
Written and edited by The Old School Writers Circle
Printed by EBS, Verona
Published by Anomie Special Projects, London

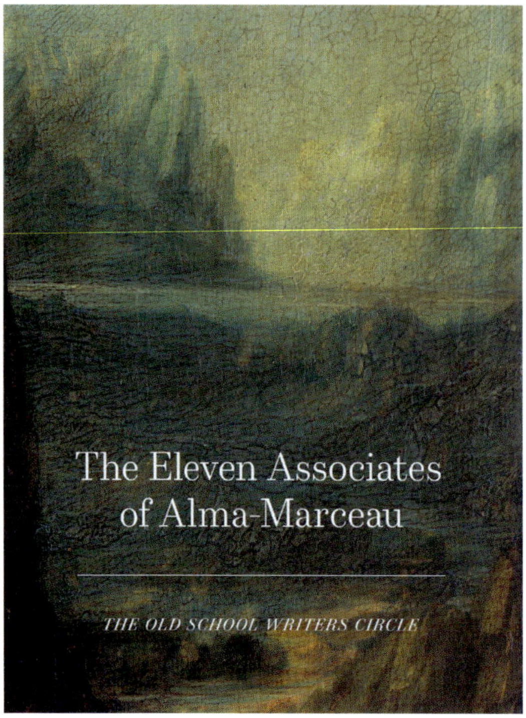

The Eleven Associates of Alma-Marceau is an oddly intoxicating, gently mind-blowing novel that follows a summer in the life of Adam King, a promising young British art student undertaking an internship at a contemporary art museum in Paris. A strange revelation in front of Leonardo's *Mona Lisa* during an evening out with an unusual group of young people who are looking to change the world proves not only to be the cause of intense debate, but also a turning point in a series of interconnected events in which Adam finds himself caught up in much more than his own coming-of-age.

Against a backdrop of late capitalism, media and surveillance, *The Eleven Associates of Alma-Marceau* not only asks questions about how people's images, words and lives are given a platform, used and manipulated in the digital era, but also invites readers to question the very nature of what they perceive. Within this modern-day story about painting, visual communication and how creative ideas are responded to by society, Leonardo, of course, is still ahead of the game, more than five hundred years after his death...

The Old School Writers Circle is a group of friends who periodically meet up to discuss art, writing and books. The current members studied at the same school in Birmingham, UK, in the late 1980s and early 90s, and now live in various locations around England. Famous literary alumni of the school include, somewhat eclectically, J.R.R. Tolkien, Lee Child and Jonathan Coe, all of whom are on the circle's evergrowing list of influences. Projects can be serious as well as playful, confronting surprising and challenging themes through stories that do not necessarily fit squarely within conventional genres.

For their debut publication, *The Eleven Associates of Alma-Marceau*, the starting point was a shared love of Paris and The Louvre – inspired in part by numerous trips across the Channel by members of the circle over the past twenty-five years. The other driving force was the interest of circle member Matt Price in esoterica and unusual optical phenomena in the history of painting – ideas explored by the circle in the form of this curious, engaging and thought-provoking novel.

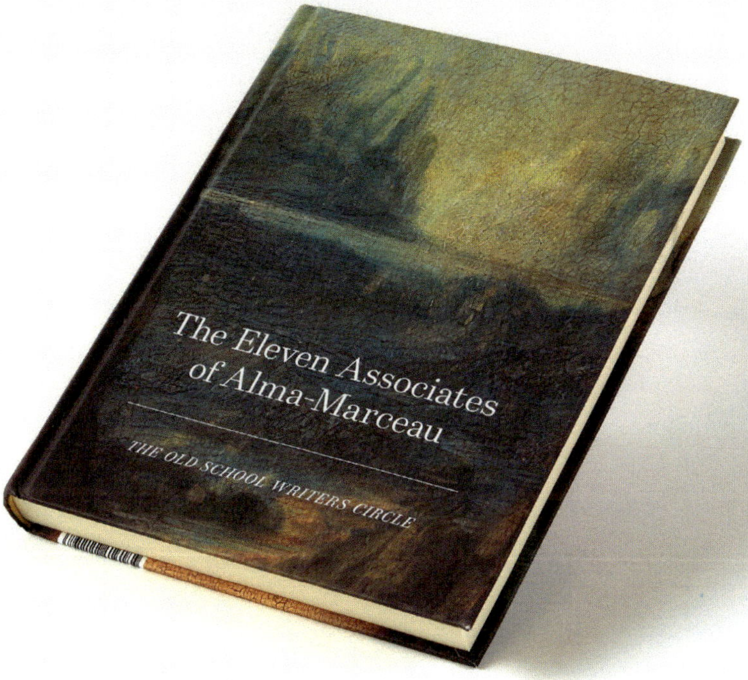

The Eleven Associates of Alma-Marceau
THE OLD SCHOOL WRITERS CIRCLE

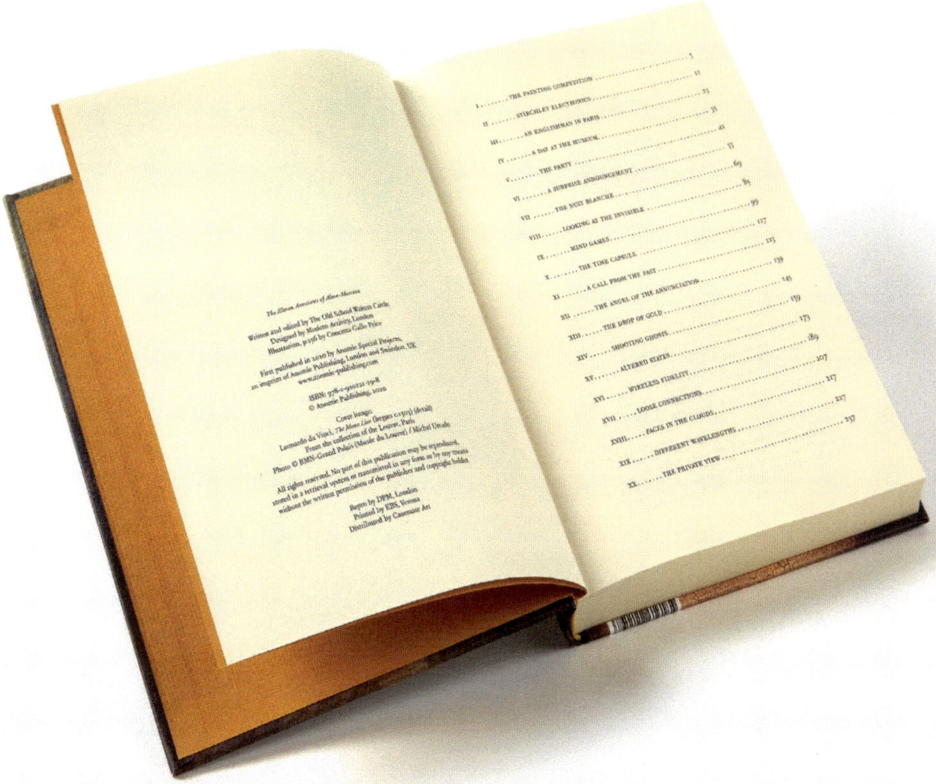

The Eleven Associates of Alma-Marceau
Written and edited by The Old School Writers Circle
Designed by Modern Activity, London
First published in 2020 by Anomie Special Projects,
an imprint of Anomie Publishing, London and Swindon, UK
www.anomie-publishing.com
ISBN: 978-1-910221-19-8
© Anomie Publishing, 2020
Cover image:
Leonardo da Vinci, The Mona Lisa
From the collection of the Louvre, Paris
All rights reserved. No part of this publication may be reproduced, stored in a retrieval system or transmitted in any form or by any means without the written permission of the publisher and copyright holder
Repro by DPM, London
Printed by EBS, Verona
Distributed by Casemate Art
I ...... THE PAINTING COMPETITION
II ...... STIRCHLEY ELECTRONICS
III ...... AN ENGLISHMAN IN PARIS
IV ...... A DAY AT THE MUSEUM
V ...... THE PARTY
VI ...... A SURPRISE ANNOUNCEMENT
VII ...... THE NUIT BLANCHE
VIII ...... LOOKING AT THE INVISIBLE
IX ...... MIND GAMES
X ...... THE TIME CAPSULE
XI ...... A CALL FROM THE PAST
XII ...... THE ANGEL OF THE ANNUNCIATION
XIII ...... THE DROP OF GOLD
XIV ...... SHOOTING GHOSTS
XV ...... ALTERED STATES
XVI ...... WIRELESS FIDELITY
XVII ...... LOOSE CONNECTIONS
XVIII ...... FACES IN THE CLOUDS
XIX ...... DIFFERENT WAVELENGTHS
XX ...... THE PRIVATE VIEW

Gareth Nyandoro

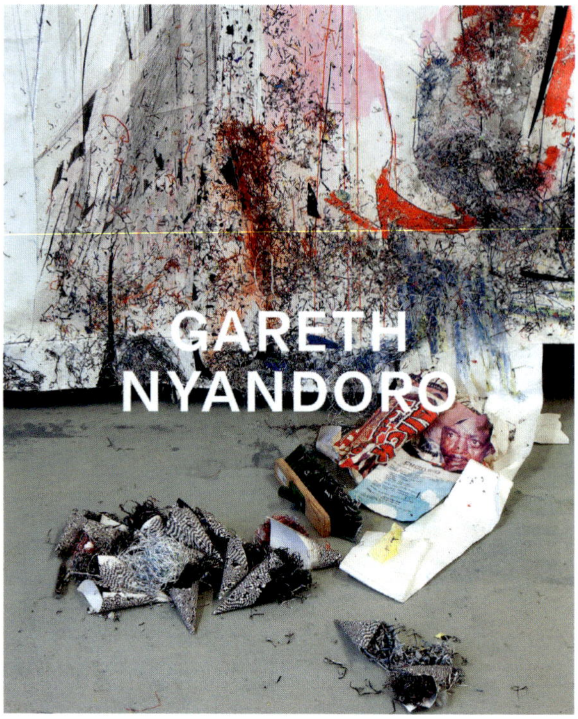

Gareth Nyandoro
Mhofu Motor Spares, 2018
Mixed media on paper, mounted on canvas
208.3 × 165.1 cm

Contributors:
Adélaïde Blanc
Sean O'Toole

96pp
Softback
230 × 190 mm
c. 60 images
ISBN: 978-1-910221-22-8
RRP: £24
UK Release: 23 January 2020
Designed by Joe Gilmore
Edited by Maria Varnava and Eva Langret
Printed in the UK by Pression
Co-published by Tiwani Contemporary and
Anomie Publishing, London

Gareth Nyandoro is noted for his large works on paper, which often spill out of their two-dimensional format and into installations that include paper scraps and objects found in the street markets of Harare, Zimbabwe, where he lives and works. The artist's primary source of inspiration is the rapidly changing urban and cultural panorama of the country. Inspired by his training as a printmaker, and derived from etching, the artist's distinctive technique, 'Kucheka-cheka', is named after the infinitive and present tense declinations of the Shona verb 'cheka', which means 'to cut'. This, the artist's first monograph, documents selected bodies of work created since 2015 and presented in exhibitions at venues including the Palais de Tokyo, Paris; Quetzal Art Centre, Portugal; Tiwani Contemporary, London; Modern Art Oxford and the Rijksakademie, Amsterdam.

The publication features an introduction by curator Adélaïde Blanc, who curated Nyandoro's 2017 solo exhibition *Stall(s) of Fame* at the Palais de Tokyo. The publication also includes a newly commissioned essay from Cape Town-based writer, critic, and editor Sean O'Toole, which discusses notions of 'cutting' and 'spilling' in Nyandoro's practice against a backdrop of both Zimbabwe's colonial past and 'southern urbanism' – city life in the global South.

Gareth Nyandoro was born in 1982 in Bikita, Zimbabwe. He lives and works in Harare, Zimbabwe. Recent solo exhibitions include *...Read All About*, Van Doren Waxter, New York (2018); *Stall(s) of Fame*, Palais de Tokyo (2017); *Stall(s) of Fame*, Tiwani Contemporary (2017). Selected group exhibitions include *Par Amour du Jeu*, Magasins Généraux, Paris (2018); *Drawing Africa on the Map*, Quetzal Art Centre (2018); *Five Bhobh – Painting at the End of an Era*, Zeitz MOCAA, Cape Town (2018); *Kaleidoscope*, Modern Art Oxford (2016) and *Paper Cut*, Tiwani Contemporary (2016). Nyandoro won the FT/ Oppenheimer Funds Emerging Voices award in 2016 and was a resident at the Rijksakademie van Beeldende Kunsten, Amsterdam in 2014-15.

The publication, launched alongside a solo presentation of work by the artist at Art Basel Miami Beach in December 2019, is produced by Tiwani Contemporary with generous support from the A. G. Leventis Foundation, allowing for the production of artists' books and their dissemination to libraries and institutions across the globe.

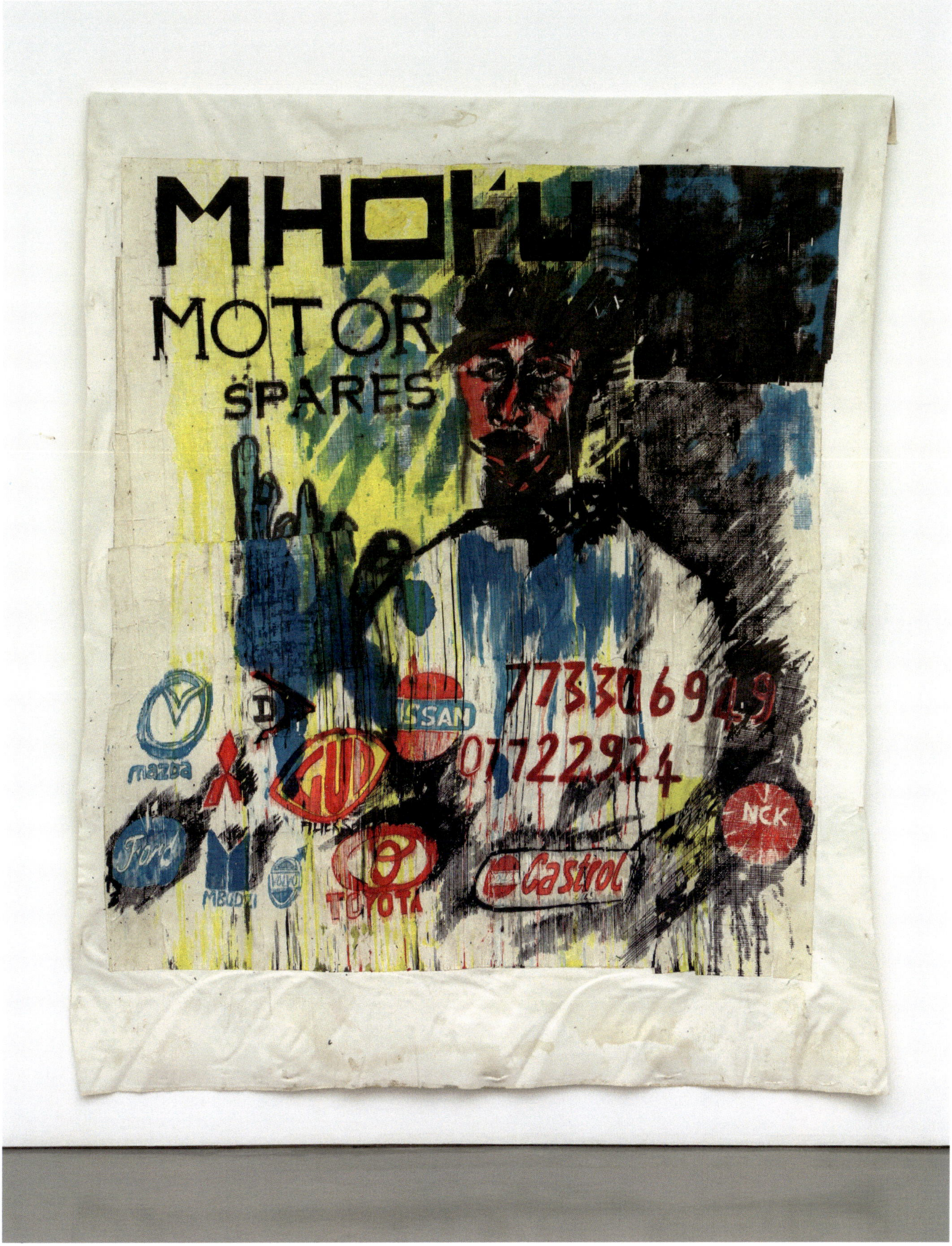
MOTOR
SPARES
mazda
Ford
MBUDZI
TOYOTA
Castrol
NCK

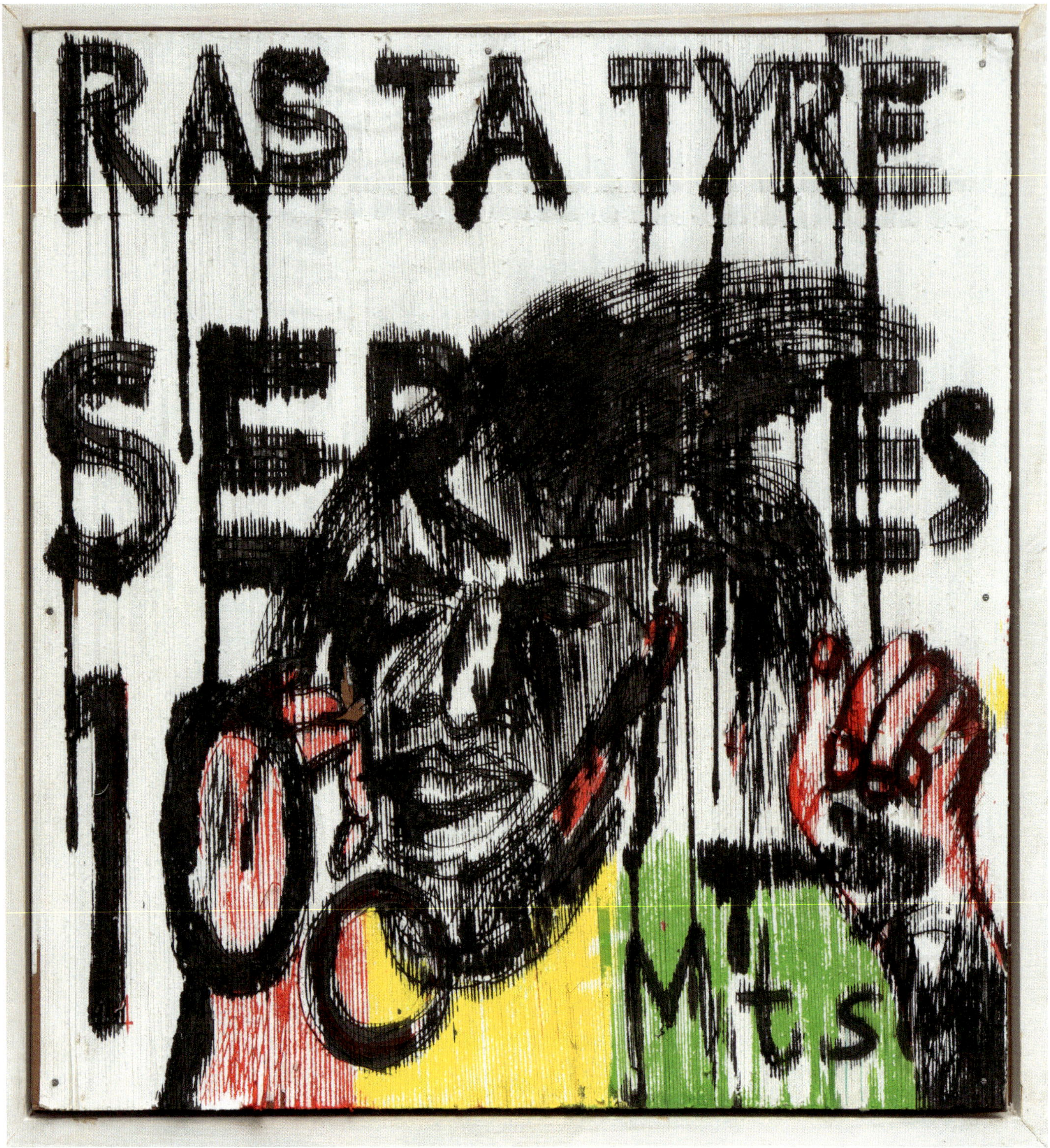

Gareth Nyandoro
Rasta Tyre Services 100mts, 2018
Mixed media on paper, mounted on panel
50.8 × 50.8 cm

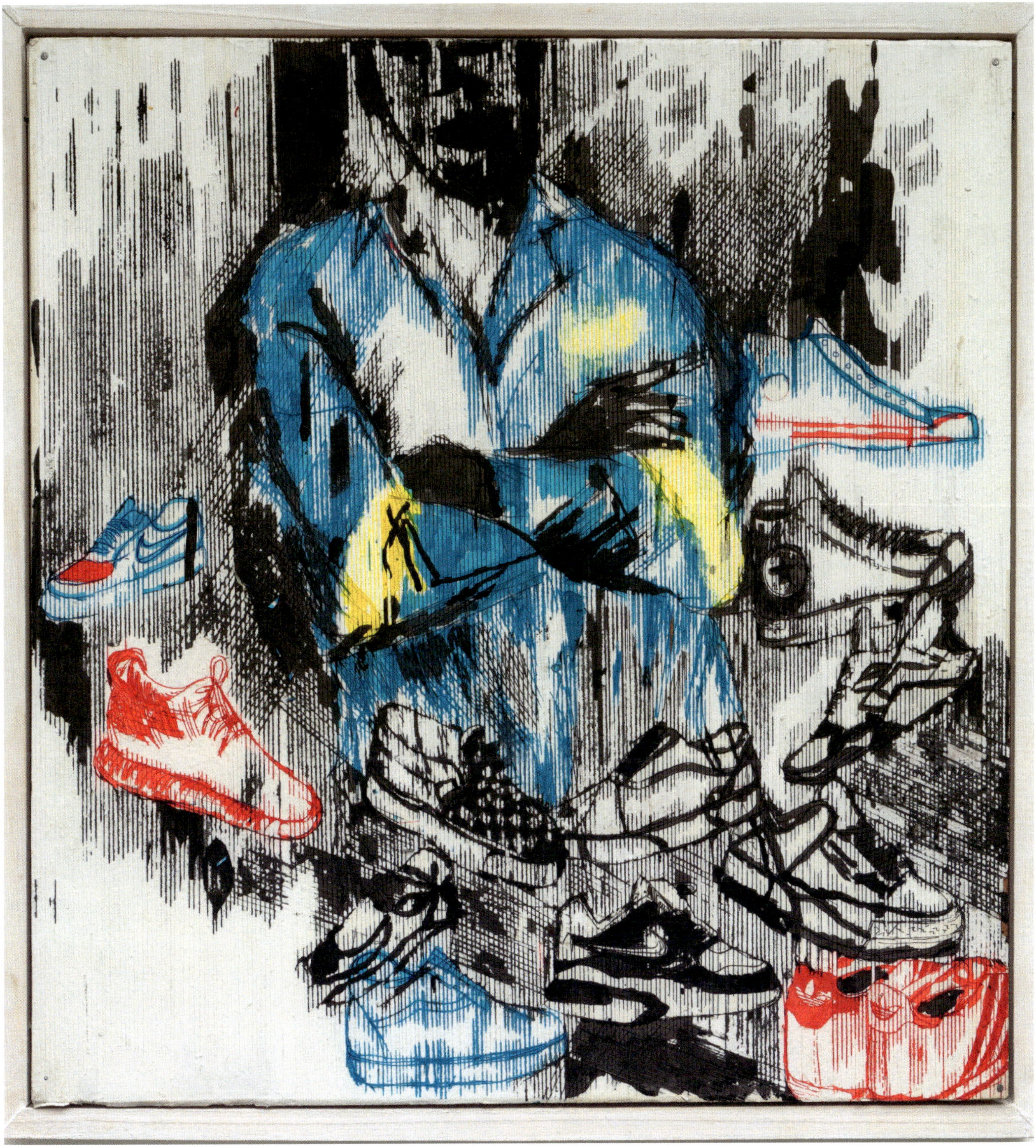

Gareth Nyandoro
USD$Second Hand Sneakers, 2018
Mixed media on paper, mounted on panel
50.8 × 50.8 cm

All courtesy of Van Doren Waxter, New York
Photos: Charles Benton

Jonathan Wateridge
Enclave / Expatria

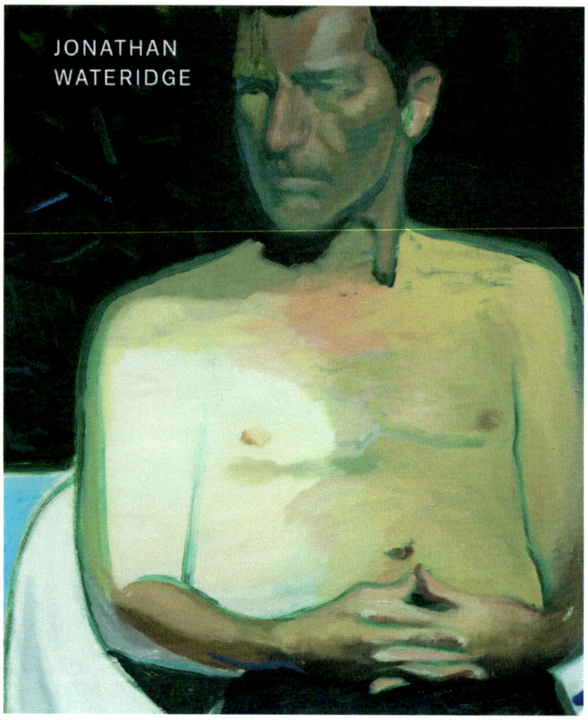

Contributors:
Mark Sanders
Gilda Williams

200pp
Hardback
290 × 245 mm
Clothbound with dust jacket
c. 130 colour and b/w images
ISBN: 978-1-910221-21-1
RRP: £40
UK Release: 25 June 2019
Designed by Peter B. Willberg
Edited by Mark Sanders
Printed in Italy by SiZ
Published by Anomie Publishing, London

Jonathan Wateridge was born in Lusaka, Zambia, in 1972. Today he lives and works in Norfolk, UK. This, the artist's first trade monograph, presents two significant bodies of work, *Enclave* and *Expatria*. In these series, Wateridge returns to his childhood memories of growing up within the privileged white ex-pat communities of Zambia in the 1970s and 80s, during the early years of the country's independence from British rule. 'Having grown up in an apparent world of sunshine and suburban pools, I sought to overlap those aspects of my formative experiences with the wider issues of the West's post-colonial role,' Wateridge has stated. His recent paintings, produced with the artist's characteristic virtuosity and based on elaborate studio stage sets replete with a varied cast of actors, also seek to explore more lyrical figurative languages offered by the medium, adding to the uneasy dynamics that haunt these memorable and accomplished works.

This hardback, clothbound monograph with dust jacket, designed by Peter B. Willberg, has been edited and authored by London-based independent curator, writer and art consultant Mark Sanders. The publication features an essay by Dr Gilda Williams, an author and London correspondent for *Artforum* who also teaches art writing on the MFA Curating programme at Goldsmiths College, University of London. Presenting over 130 paintings and details, this 200-page monograph is essential reading for anybody passionate about contemporary painting, and makes a valuable contribution to discussion of the post-colonial condition in the visual arts.

Recent solo exhibitions include: *Swimmer*, Galerie Haas, Zurich (2017); *Enclave*, Pace London / HENI, London (2016); *Colony*, Galerie Michael Haas, Berlin (2016); *Monument*, Wilkinson, London (2014). Recent group exhibitions include: *Painting Still Alive*, Centre of Contemporary Art, Torun, Poland (2018); *Disrupted Imagination*, Central Museum, Szentendre, Hungary (2017); *Proof of Life*, Weserburg Museum of Art, Bremen, Germany (2017); *Disrupted Imagination*, House of Arts, Ostrava, Czech Republic (2017); *The Good, the Bad and the Ugly*, Charlie Smith, London (2016) and *Blow Up*, Parafin, London (2015).

Jonathan Wateridge
Two Women, 2018
Oil on linen
175 × 110 cm

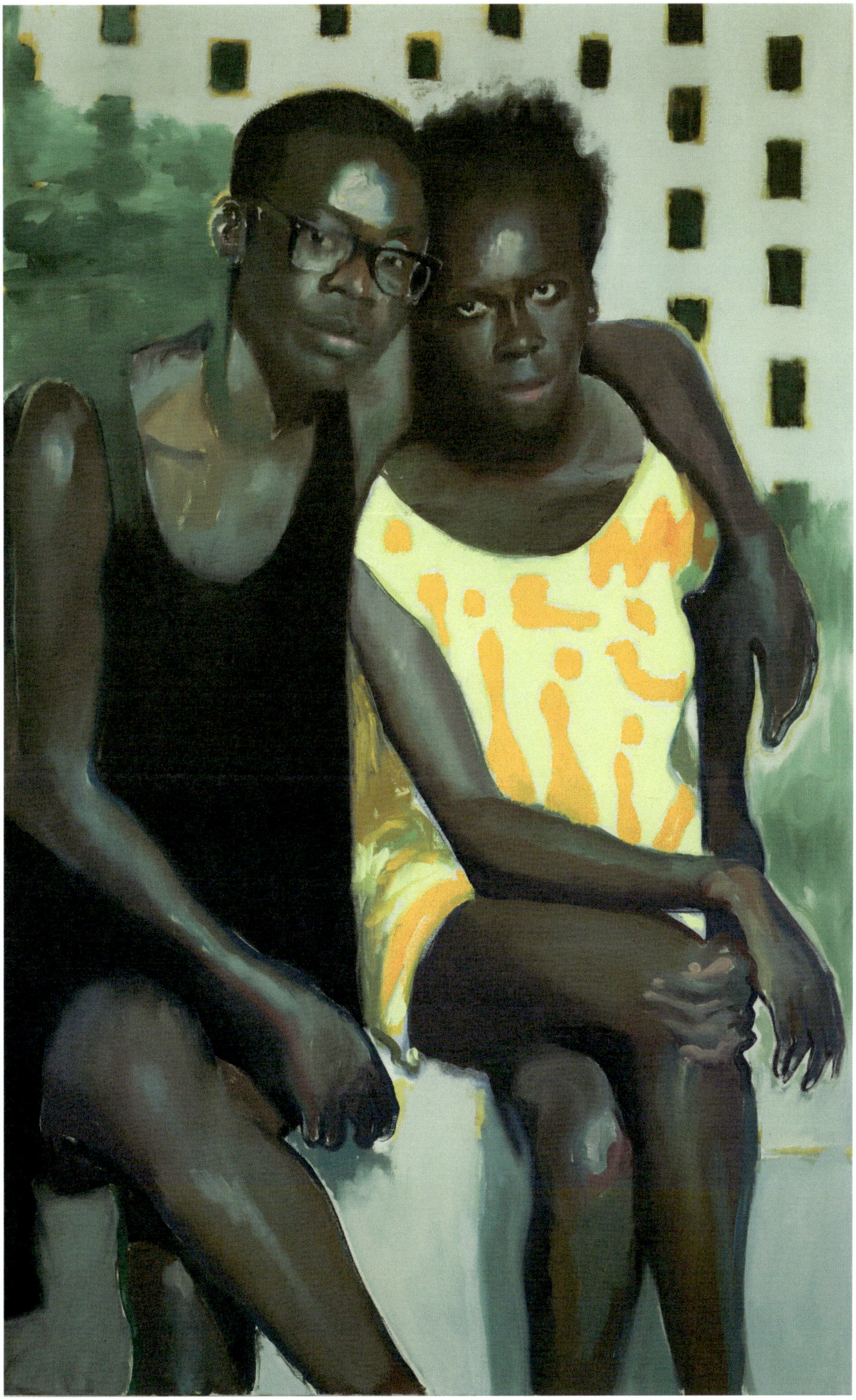

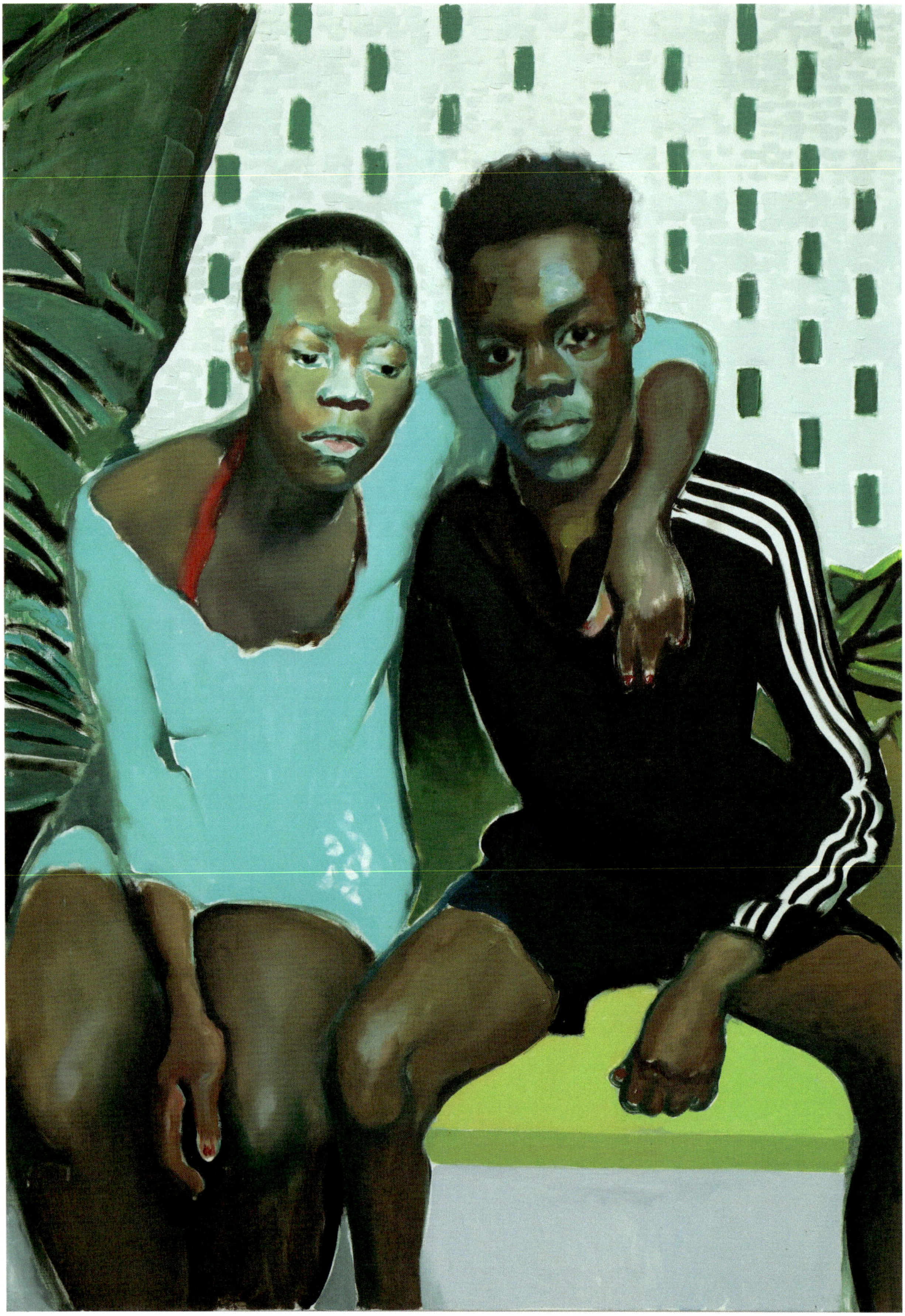

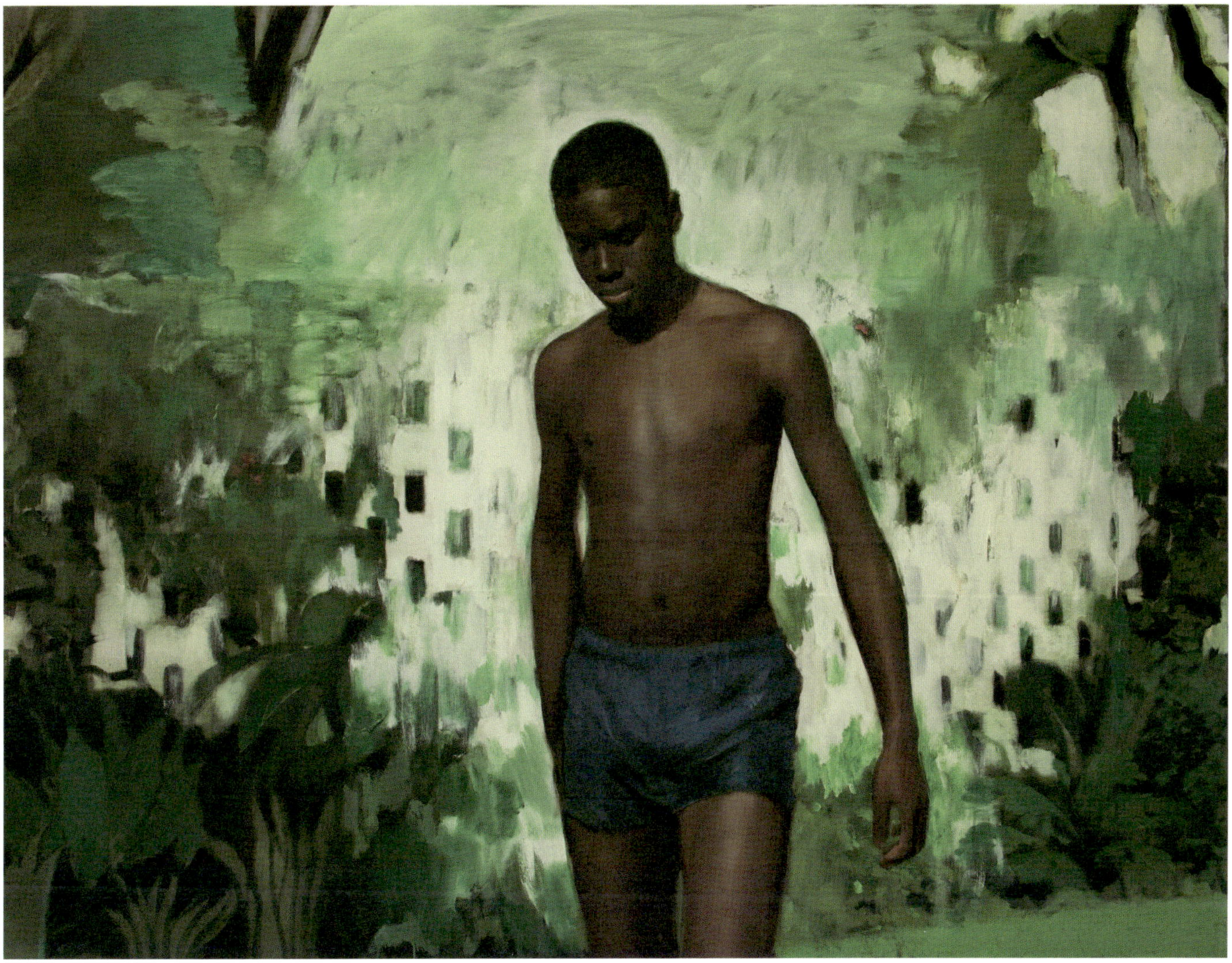

Jonathan Wateridge
Couple by Wall, 2018
Oil on linen
170 × 120 cm

Jonathan Wateridge
Swimmer, 2017
Oil on linen
135 × 180 cm

All © Jonathan Wateridge
Courtesy of Mark Sanders Art Consultancy Ltd.

Greg Rook
Honyocker

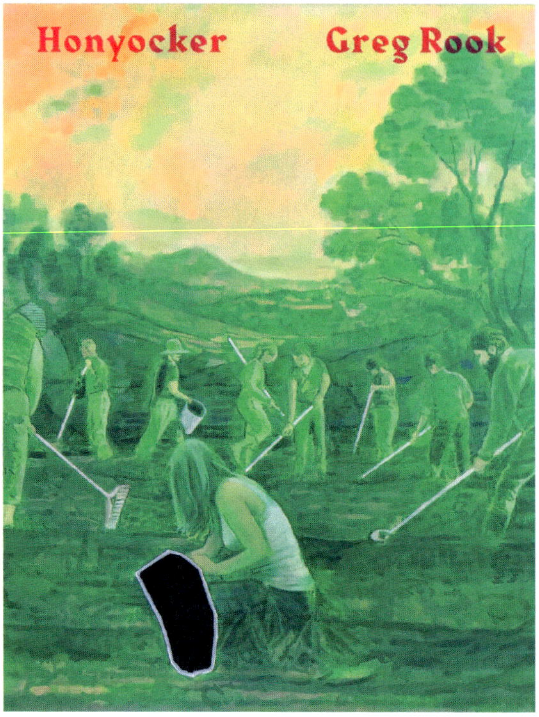

Contributors:
Andrea Vento
Michele Robecchi
Matt Price

64pp
Hardback
255 × 195 mm
English and Italian language
c. 50 colour and b/w images
ISBN: 978-1-910221-20-4
RRP: £25
UK Release: 23 May 2019
Designed by Joe Gilmore
Edited by Vento & Associati and Anomie
Printed by Tempo Libro Srl, Milan
Co-published by Vento & Associati, Milan, and
Anomie Publishing, London

The practice of Chelsea School of Art and Goldsmiths College graduate Greg Rook (b. 1971, London) explores the rich visual history, curious cultural politics and often complex ideologies of those who seek to start a new life or wish to lead alternative lifestyles. From pioneers travelling to new continents to those wanting to stay put and live self-sufficiently, Rook invites us to join him on his own aesthetic and critical journey through a world of colonies, communities, communes and cults.

By means of figurative painting that pushes the boundaries between realism and lyricism, Rook captures something profoundly revealing in terms of the hopes, dreams and successes as well as the disappointments, disillusionment and disasters that radical departures from home life and mainstream society can entail. For some, utopias can turn to dystopias, the Romantic imaginary can turn to tragedy, the sublime can turn to misery. For those fleeing oppression, however, it can, on occasion, be completely the opposite – newfound freedom, affluence and happiness. Rook's oeuvre, which incorporates cowboys and communists, agrarians and anarchists, believers and book-burners, depicts how the relationship between people and land is regularly fraught with issues, especially when migration and a clash of mindsets or ways of life is involved. What are brave new worlds for some are threatened old worlds for others...

This hardback publication, the first to be devoted to the work of Greg Rook, was co-published by Vento & Associati and Anomie to coincide with a substantial mid-career survey exhibition of the artist's work being staged by Vento & Associati at the Fabbrica del Vapore in Milan in spring 2019. Featuring approximately 50 illustrations of works made by Rook since 2006, along with an introduction by London and Milan-based critic and curator Michele Robecchi and a significant newly commissioned essay by Matt Price, the publication offers an engaging commentary on Rook's long-standing painterly investigation into how people choose to live their lives.

Greg Rook is an artist working in London and Surrey. He graduated with a BA from Chelsea School of Art in 2000, before completing an MA in Fine Art at Goldsmiths College, University of London, in 2002. Since then he has held over a dozen solo exhibitions and featured in more than forty group exhibitions in Britain and internationally.

Greg Rook
And this, too, shall pass away 5, 2009
Oil on linen
198 × 152 cm
Courtesy of the artist and David Roberts Collection, London
Photo: Andy Keate

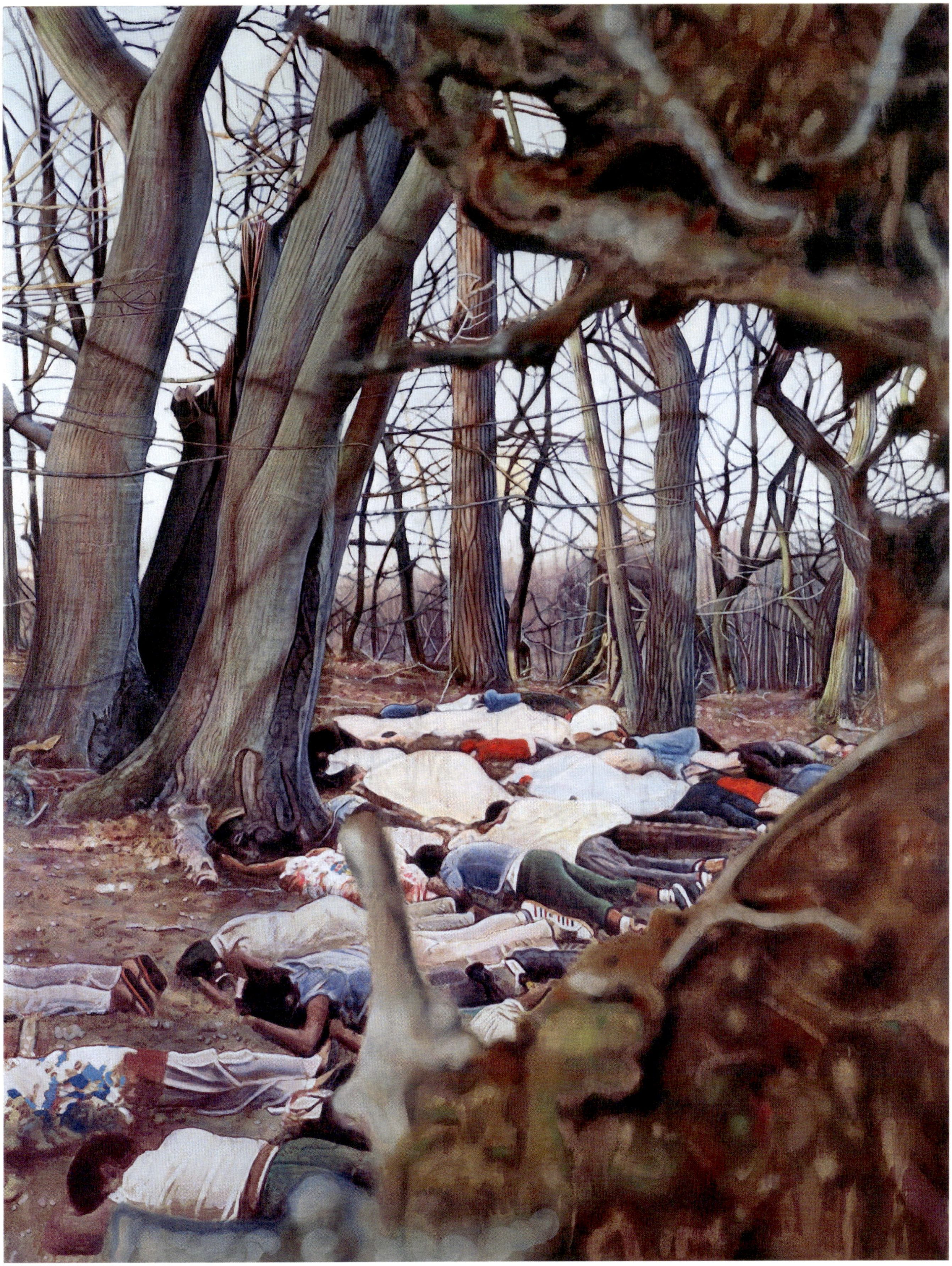

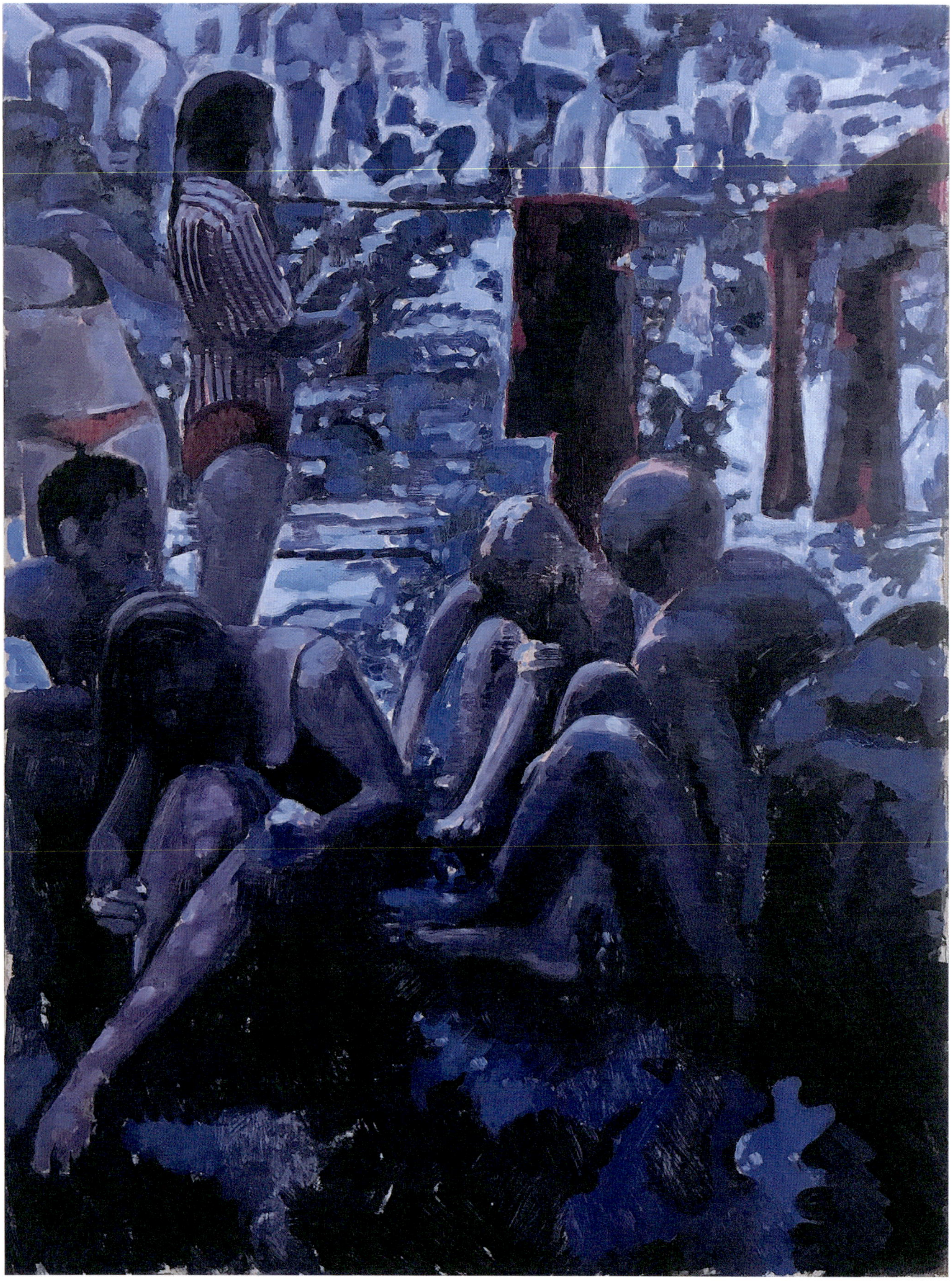

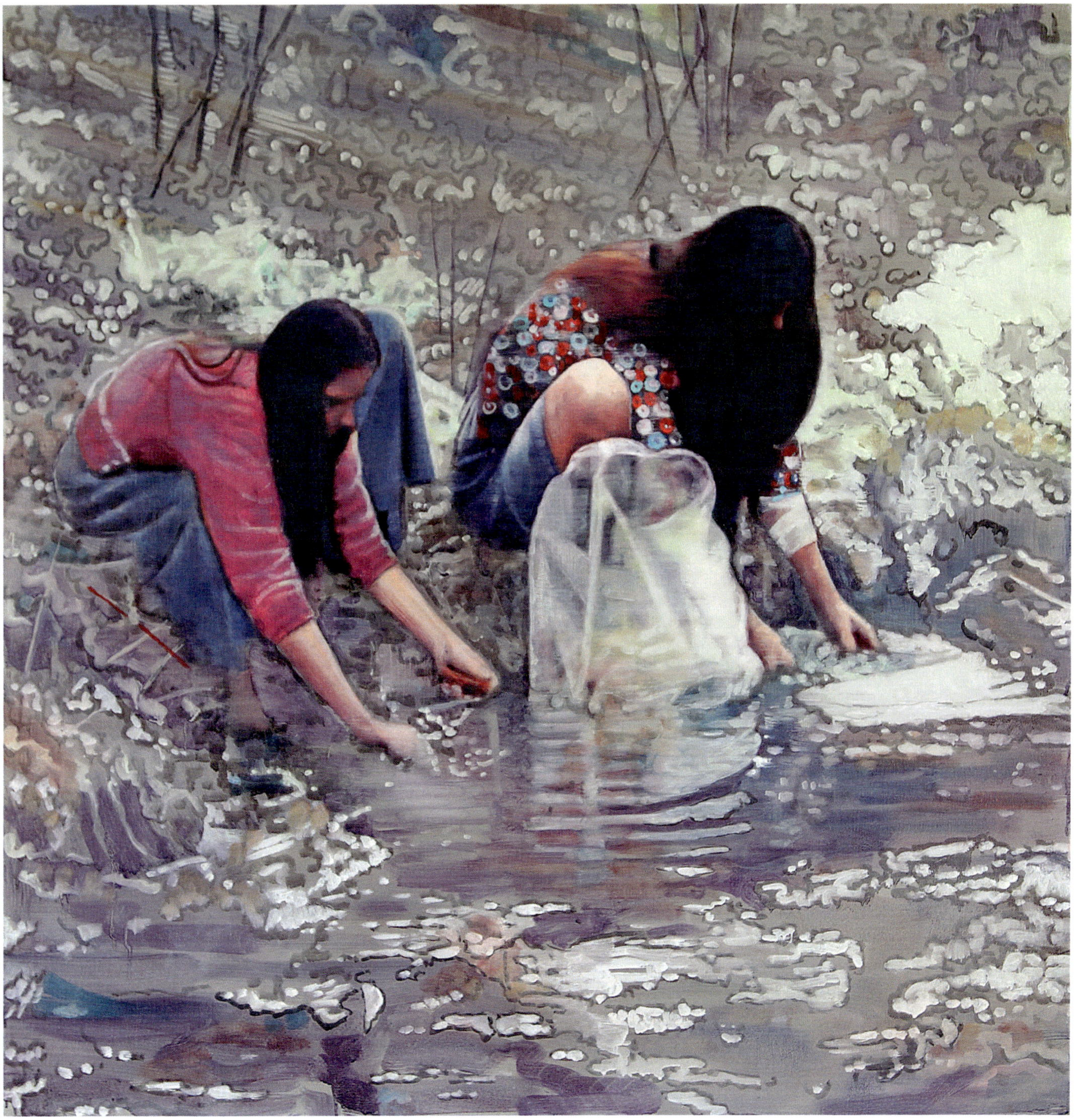

Greg Rook
Communal wash, 2018
Oil on linen
61.5 × 46 cm
Courtesy of the artist
Photo: Studio Greg Rook

Greg Rook
Weird science, 2013
Oil on linen
106.5 × 106.5 cm
Private collection
Photo: Studio Greg Rook

Emily Andersen
Portraits: Black & White

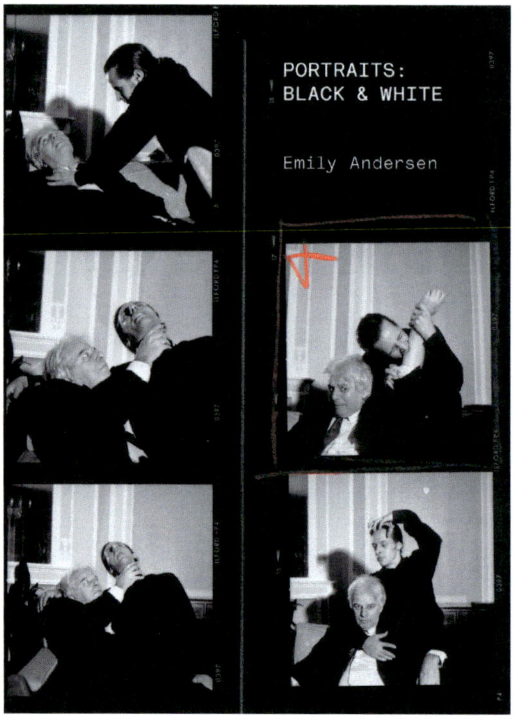

Contributors:
Emily Andersen
Jonathan P. Watts

120pp
Hardback
230 × 180 mm
c. 70 black and white images
ISBN: 978-1-910221-17-4
RRP: £30
UK Release: 18 October 2018
Designed by Melanie Mues / Mues Design
Printed by EBS, Verona
Published by Anomie Publishing, London

Emily Andersen has been making photographic portraits of the international avant-garde since graduating from the Royal College of Art in the early 1980s. Having started out by finding her way into some pretty cool-sounding private parties in London and New York, she began convincing artists and musicians to pose for her – from Nan Goldin to Nico. Over the past thirty-five years, she has built up a remarkable and beautiful portfolio that includes many high-profile writers, poets, film directors, actors and architects, with Peter Blake, Michael Caine, Derek Jarman, Zaha Hadid, Arthur Miller, Helen Mirren, Michael Nyman and Eduardo Paolozzi among those featured in this new publication devoted to her black-and-white portraits.

In addition to celebrities, Andersen has documented many interesting and inspiring figures who are celebrated and respected within their fields. An illuminating essay by critic Jonathan P. Watts not only explores the lives of some of Andersen's many sitters and the photographs she has taken of them, but also get to grips with ideas such as the nature of portraiture, photojournalism and the limitations of the documentary photograph, framing them within debates from the late 1980s onwards.

Beyond capturing the essence of these figures and the times in which they are living, Andersen has a particular talent for entering into their private lives, often being invited into her sitters' homes. By photographing family members and friends, she gets an angle on them that is often deeply personal, sensitive and honest. Creating works that are carefully composed and choreographed and yet regularly informal and relaxed, there is always a sense that Andersen is more interested in encouraging her subjects to speak through her images than in imposing her own impressions upon them.

Andersen has been commissioned for many magazines and newspapers including the *New Musical Express (NME)*, *The Face*, *Elle Deco*, *Domus*, *The Times*, *The Guardian*, *The Sunday Telegraph* and *The Economist*. Her works have been exhibited internationally in venues including The Photographers' Gallery, London; The Institute of Contemporary Art, London and The Scottish National Portrait Gallery, Edinburgh. A winner of the John Kobal prize for portraiture, she has a number of works in The National Portrait Gallery, London and in other public collections including The British Library, London and The Contemporary Art Society, London. Andersen is a senior lecturer in photography at Nottingham Trent University.

This monograph has been released in both a trade edition and as an artist's limited edition of fifty signed and numbered copies, accompanied by an original print. The cover image is of Chilean-French filmmaker Alejandro Jodorowsky and his son, Axel, London, 1989.

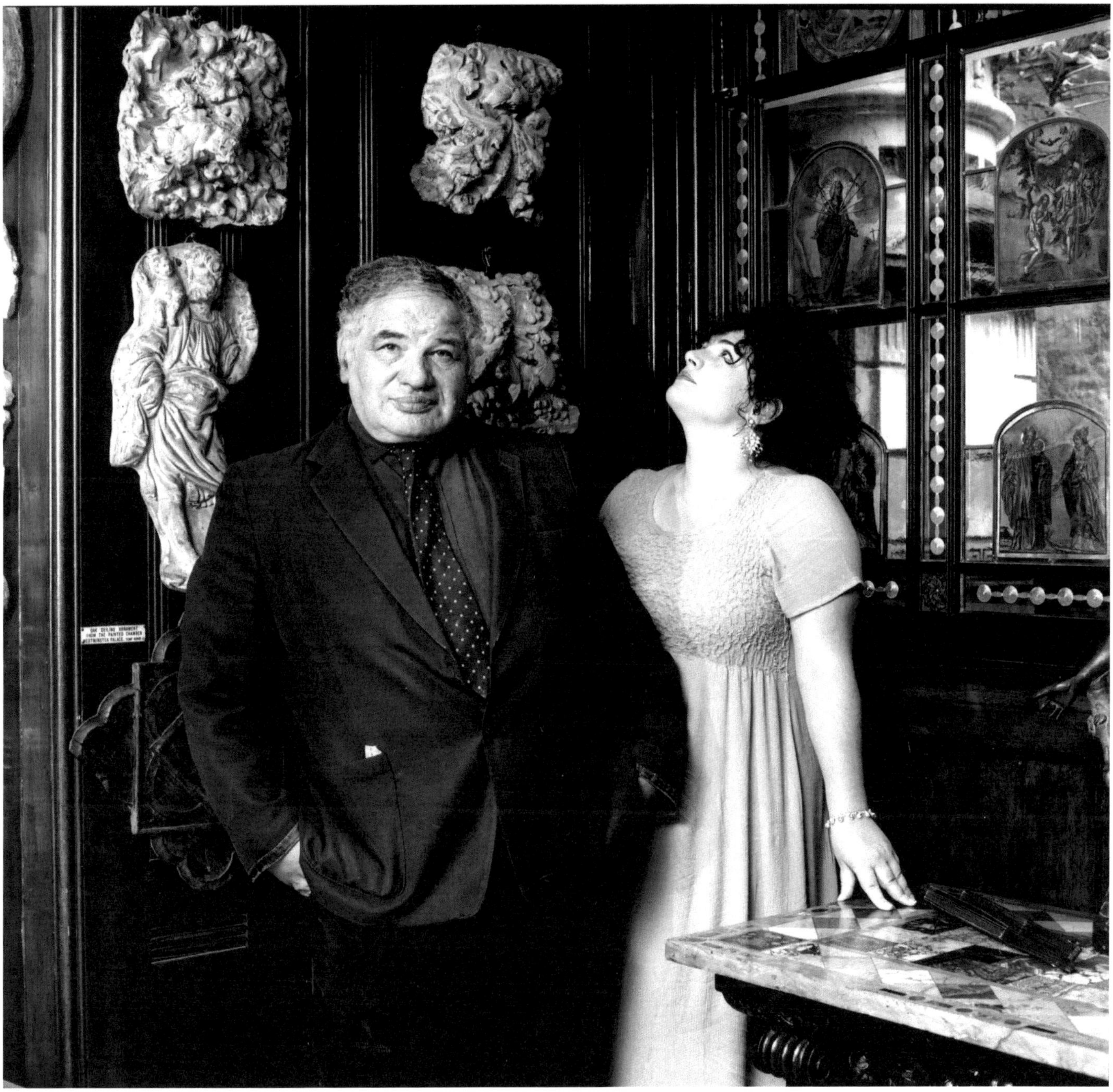

Emily Andersen
Anna and Eduardo Paolozzi,
London, 1995

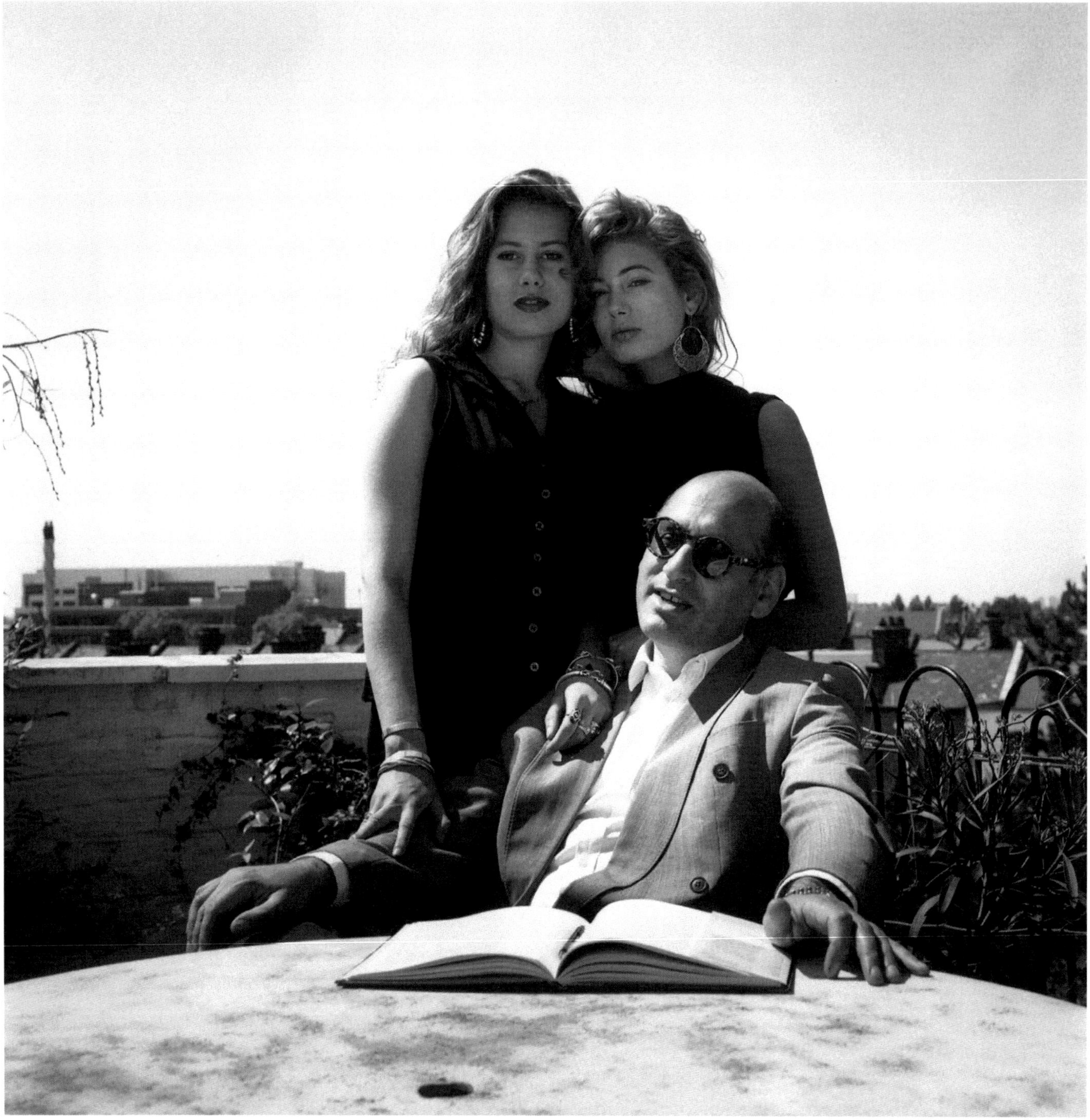

Emily Andersen
Molly, Martha and Michael Nyman, London, 1990

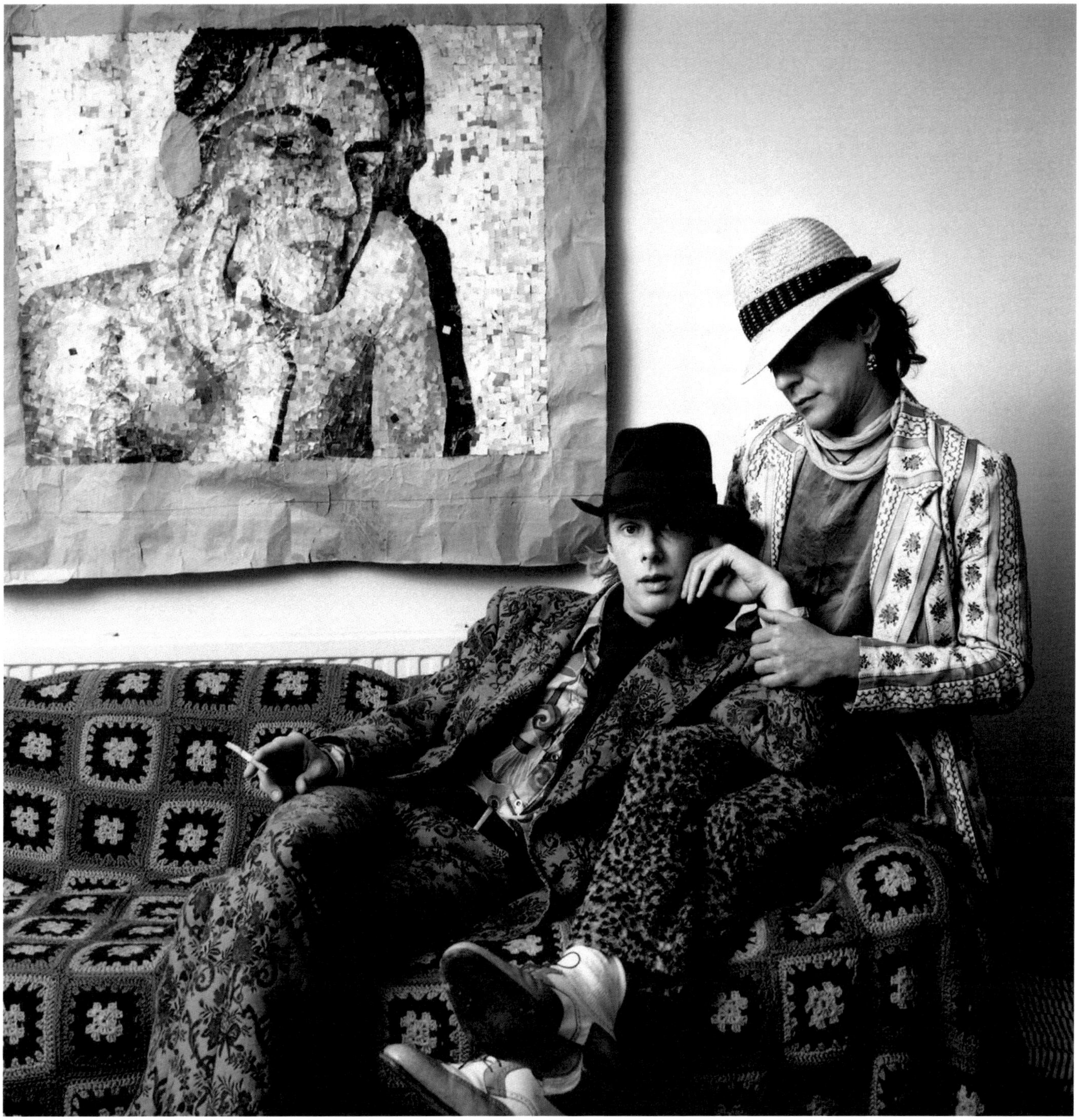

Emily Andersen
Bill and Sanso, London, 1994

All © Emily Andersen
Courtesy of the artist and Anomie Publishing

Caroline Walker
Picture Window

Contributors:
Marco Livingstone
Andrew Nairne
Rina Arya
Lauren Elkin

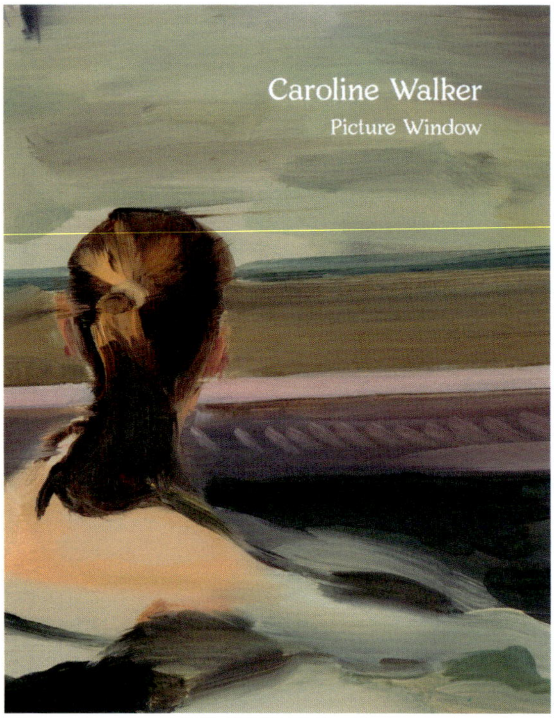

312pp
Softback
290 × 232 mm
c. 170 images
ISBN: 978-1-910221-18-1
RRP: £35
UK Release: 04 October 2018
Designed by GRIMM (Sebastiaan Brandsen & Tamara van Latum)
Printed by Aeroprint, Ouderkerk aan de Amstel, Amsterdam
Co-published by GRIMM, Amsterdam / New York, and Anomie Publishing, London

Caroline Walker's practice explores myriad social, cultural, economic, racial and political factors that affect women's lives today. From the luxurious hotels of Los Angeles and Palm Springs to the temporary social housing of female asylum seekers arriving in Europe from Africa and Asia, from the nail bars of London to the private pools and nighttime parties of the European elite, Walker deftly broaches both everyday and more provocative subjects ranging from the pay gap to migrant workforces, the beauty industry to domestic roles, gender stereotypes to ageism. By addressing such themes and through her painterly virtuosity, Walker is rapidly becoming established as one of the leading British painters of her generation.

The publication features both a significant newly commissioned essay and an in-depth interview with the artist by art historian Marco Livingstone, exploring topics such as nineteenth-century French painting, twentieth-century modernist architecture, Walker's carefully choreographed staging of photoshoots with models in various locations around the world, and the role of photography and studies in the development of her major works. Another new text, by Andrew Nairne, Director of Kettle's Yard, University of Cambridge, addresses the body of work *Home* that was commissioned and first presented at Kettle's Yard in spring 2018. For this series, Walker worked with the charity Women for Refugee Women, depicting the lives of asylum-seeking women in temporary accommodation in London. Dr. Rina Arya, a Professor of Visual Culture at the University of Huddersfield, focusses in her text on Walker's paintings of nail bars. Continuing the publication's consideration of how Walker represents the realities of women's lives in different urban and suburban contexts today, a text by Paris-based writer Dr. Lauren Elkin offers an introduction to Walker's glimpsed scenes of women at work, whether in hair salons, restaurants or office buildings – the result of the artist's own record of walking the city.

Picture Window is the most comprehensive publication to date on the work of London-based, Scottish artist Caroline Walker (b. 1982, Dunfermline). A graduate of the Glasgow School of Art and the Royal College of Art, London, selected solo exhibitions include Kettle's Yard, Cambridge; GRIMM, Amsterdam and New York; Anat Ebgi, Los Angeles; ProjectB, Milan; and Space K, Gwacheon.

Picture Window is illustrated by around 170 images including paintings, studies, drawings and photographs, many published here for the first time. The publication was launched to coincide with a presentation of Walker's works at Frieze London in autumn 2018.

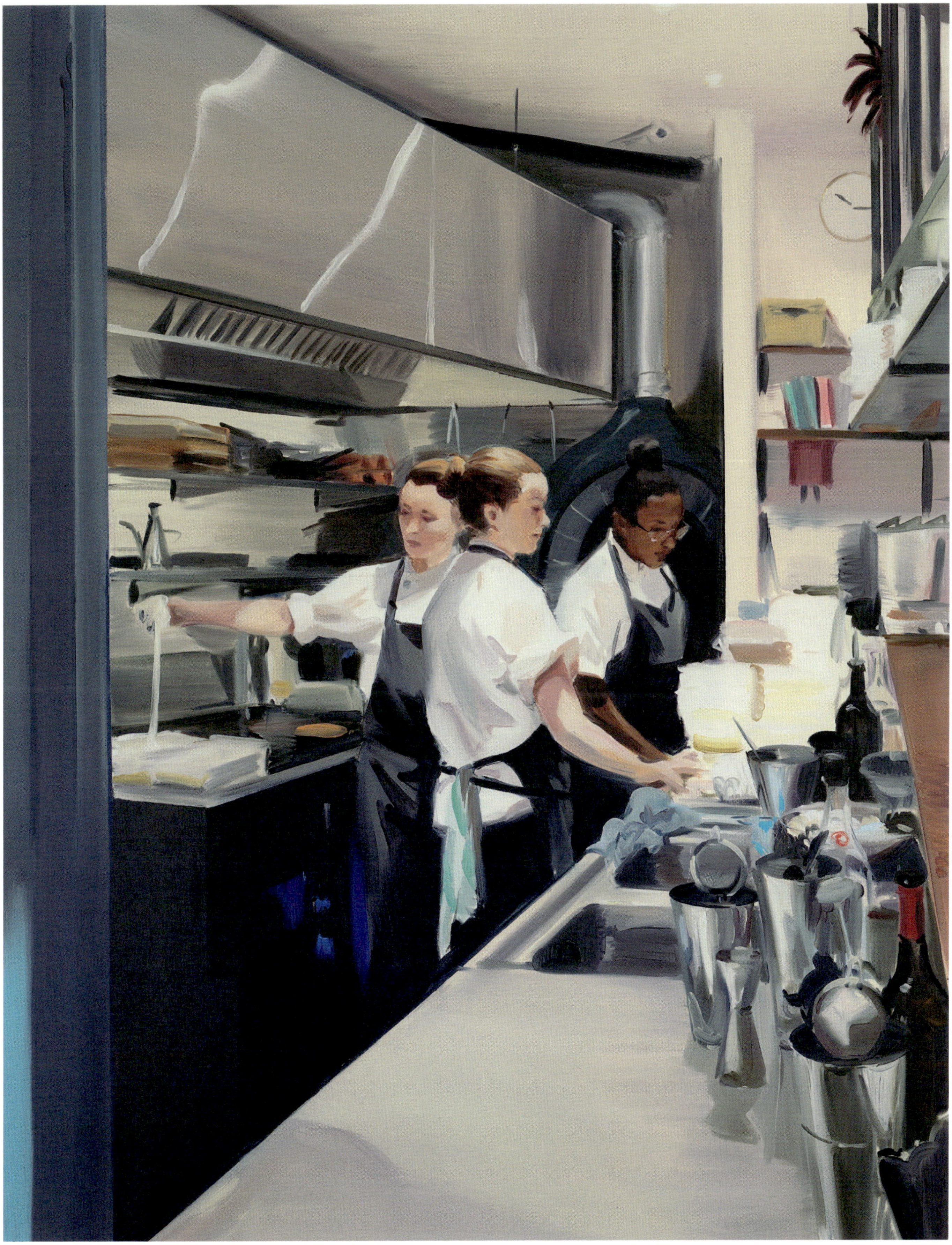

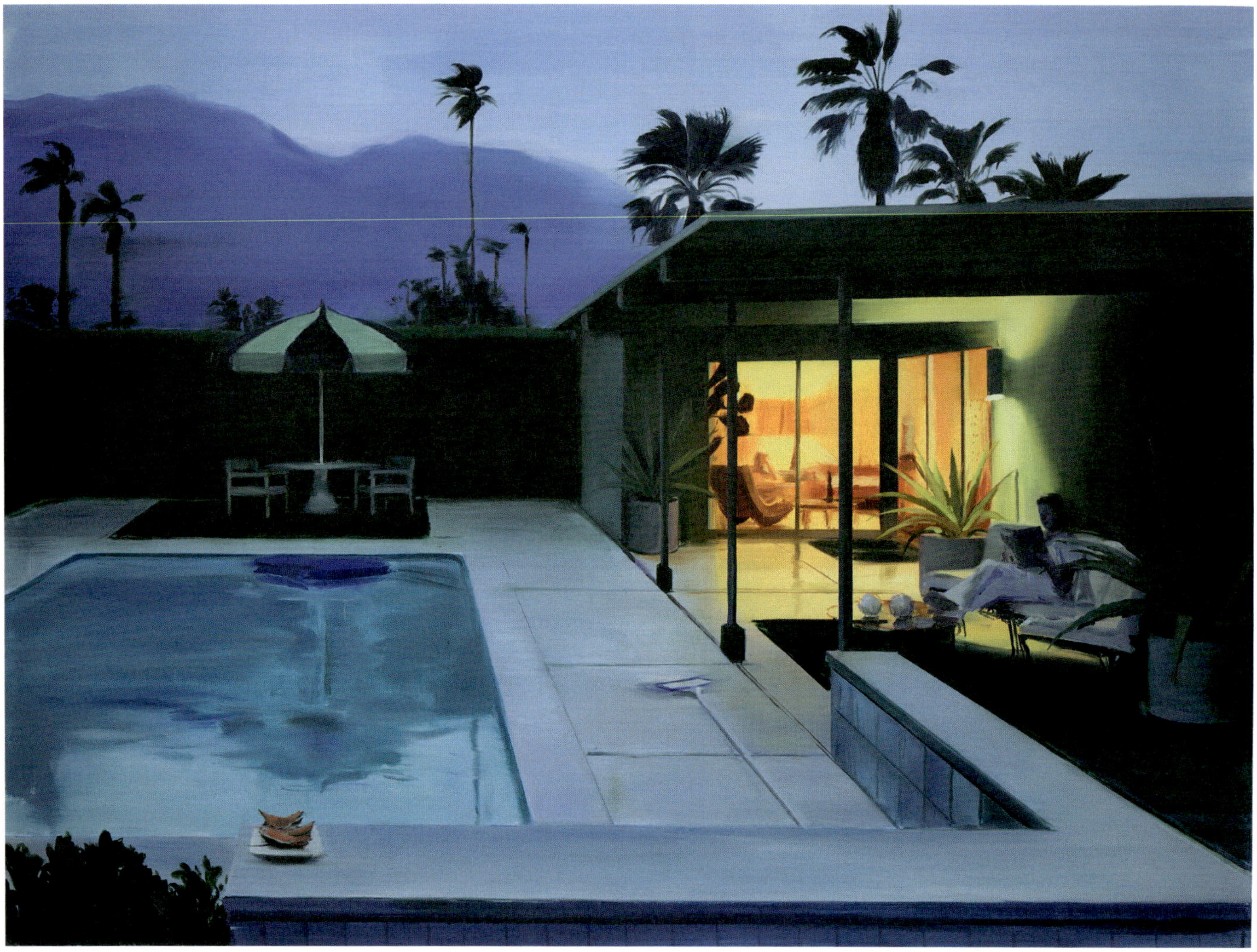

p. 139
Caroline Walker
Service, 2018
Oil on linen
180 × 140 cm

Caroline Walker
Desert Modern, 2016
Oil on linen
230 × 325 cm

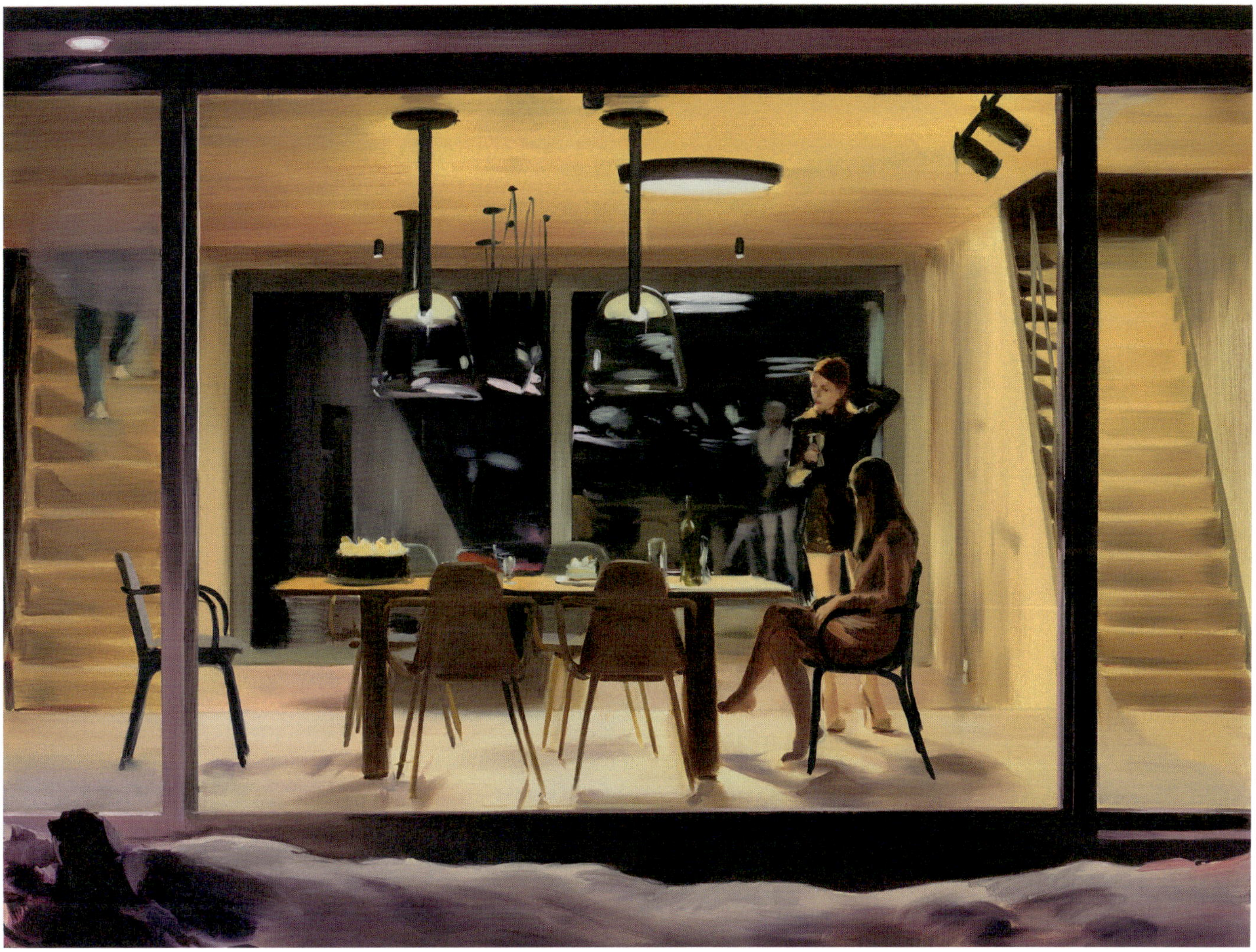

Caroline Walker
Birthday Party, 2017
Oil on linen
200 × 270 cm

All © Caroline Walker
Courtesy of the artist and GRIMM, Amsterdam
and New York
Photos: Peter Mallet

The Anomie Review of Contemporary British Painting

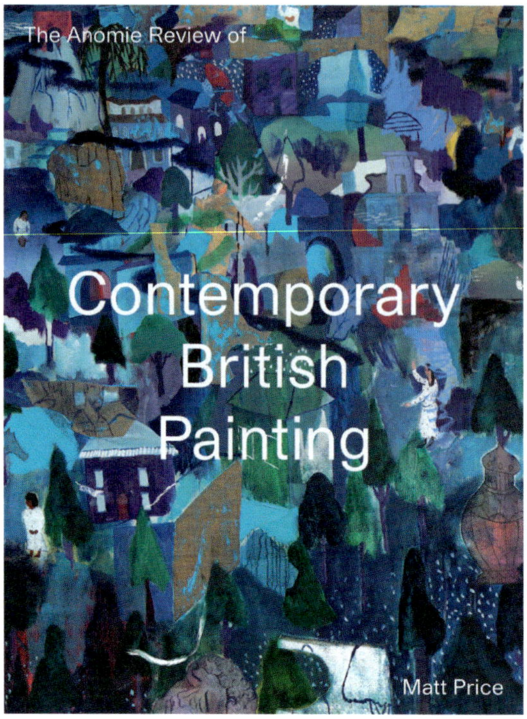

Contributors:
Matt Price

160pp
Softback
280 × 210 mm
c. 160 images
ISBN: 978-1-910221-16-7
RRP: £30
UK Release: 20 September 2018
Designed by Joe Gilmore
Copy-editing by William Lambie
Printed by S&G, Merthyr
Published by Anomie Publishing, London

There has been a huge injection of energy within contemporary painting in Britain in the past few years – part of a wider international dynamic that has seen the medium of paint explored with a renewed sense of interest, excitement and enjoyment. It is an energy that can be sensed all the way through the industry, from the art schools and the grass-roots painting community to the leading galleries, major museums and prominent festivals, biennials and art fairs. *The Anomie Review of Contemporary British Painting* considers and celebrates the work of forty artists whose practices have been shaping and defining Britain's contribution to current painting on the national and international stage.

The anthology documents the work of the invited artists by means of forty solo exhibitions in public museums and galleries, as well as in independent, university, commercial and artist-led spaces, both in Britain and abroad, during 2017. The publication presents around 160 images, including installation views from many of these exhibitions, giving both context and a sense of scale to the works.

The anthology features the work of forty artists, born or living in Britain, at various stages in their careers, from high-profile, internationally renowned artists to up-and-coming names. Featured artists and exhibitions include: Tom Anholt at Mikael Andersen, Copenhagen; Gillian Carnegie at Cabinet, London; Peter Doig at Michael Werner, London; Kaye Donachie at Le Plateau, Frac Ile de-France, Paris; Jadé Fadojutimi at Pippy Houldsworth, London; Nick Goss at Josh Lilley, London; Lubaina Himid at Badischer Kunstverein, Karlsruhe; Ryan Mosley at Eigen + Art, Leipzig; Chris Ofili at Victoria Miro, Venice; George Shaw at Maruani Mercier, Brussels; Raqib Shaw at The Whitworth, Manchester; Clare Woods at DCA, Dundee; Rose Wylie at Serpentine Galleries, London and Lynette Yiadom-Boakye at the New Museum, New York.

The anthology has been compiled and written by Matt Price, who in addition to editing around fifty monographs, catalogues and books including Phaidon's international anthologies of painting and drawing *Vitamin P2* and *Vitamin D2*, has written for magazines including *Art Monthly*, *Art Quarterly*, *ArtReview*, *Flash Art*, *Frieze* and *Modern Painters*.

Gillian Carnegie
Aminadab, 2016
Oil on board
74 × 58 cm
© Gillian Carnegie
Courtesy of the artist and Cabinet, London

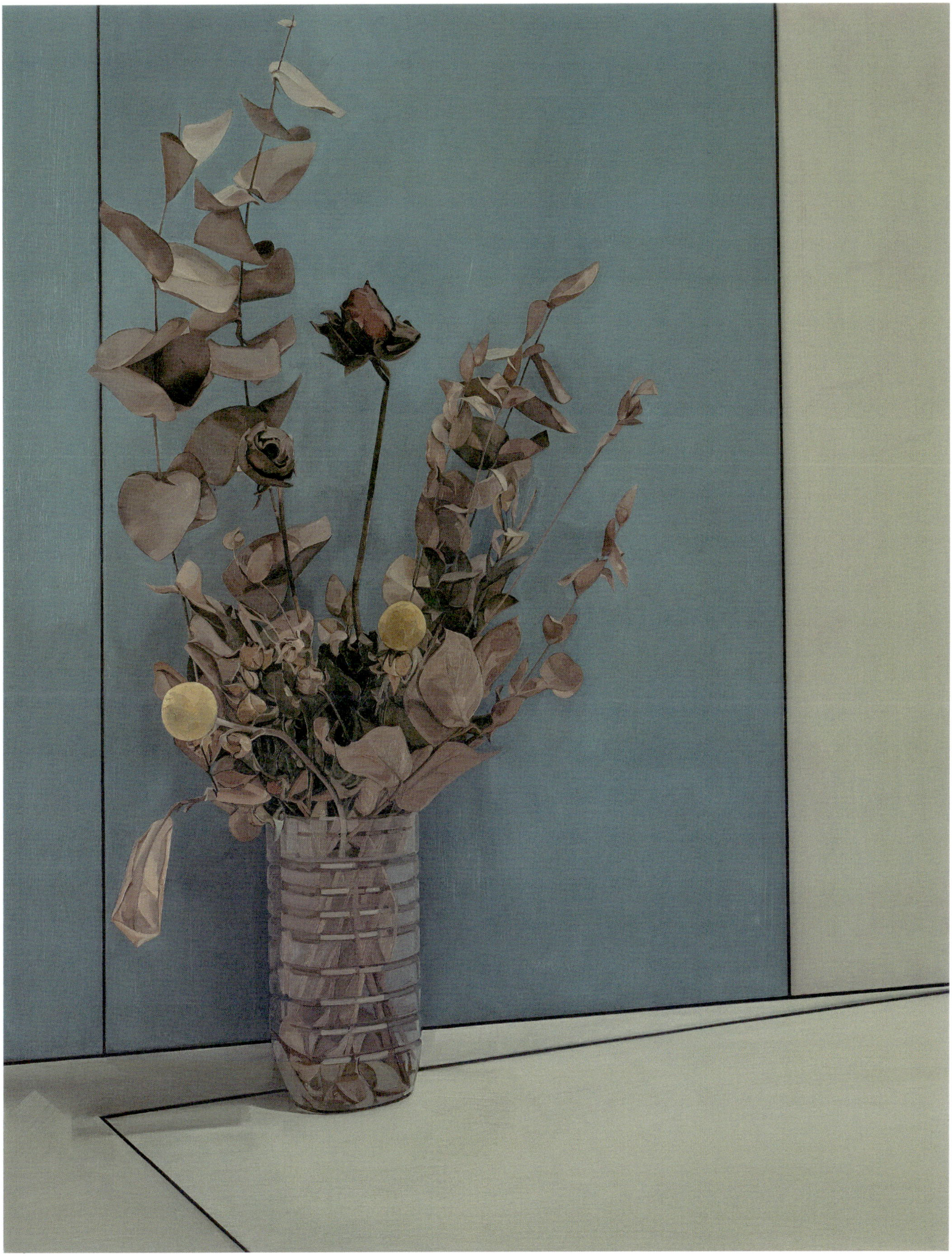

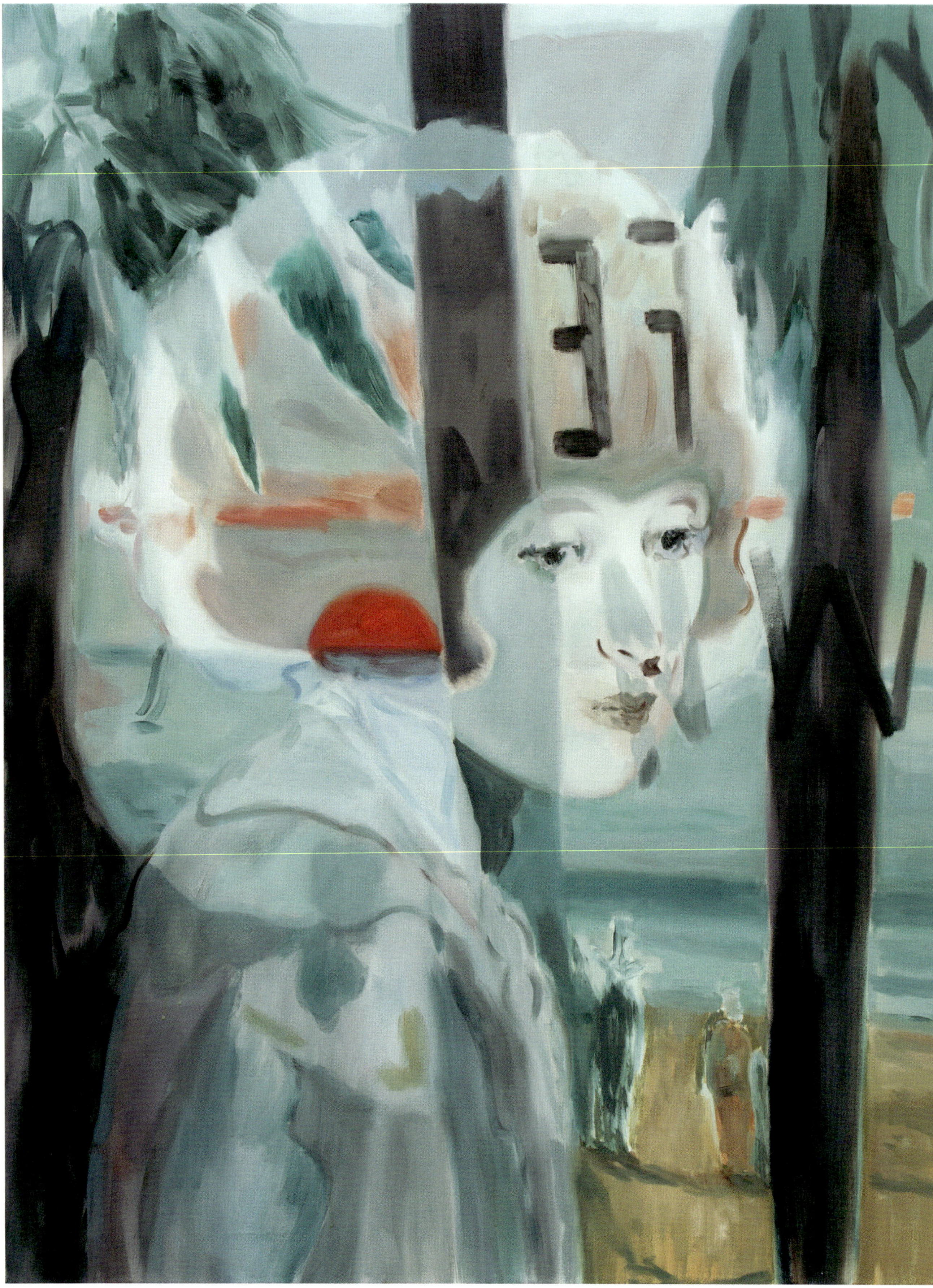

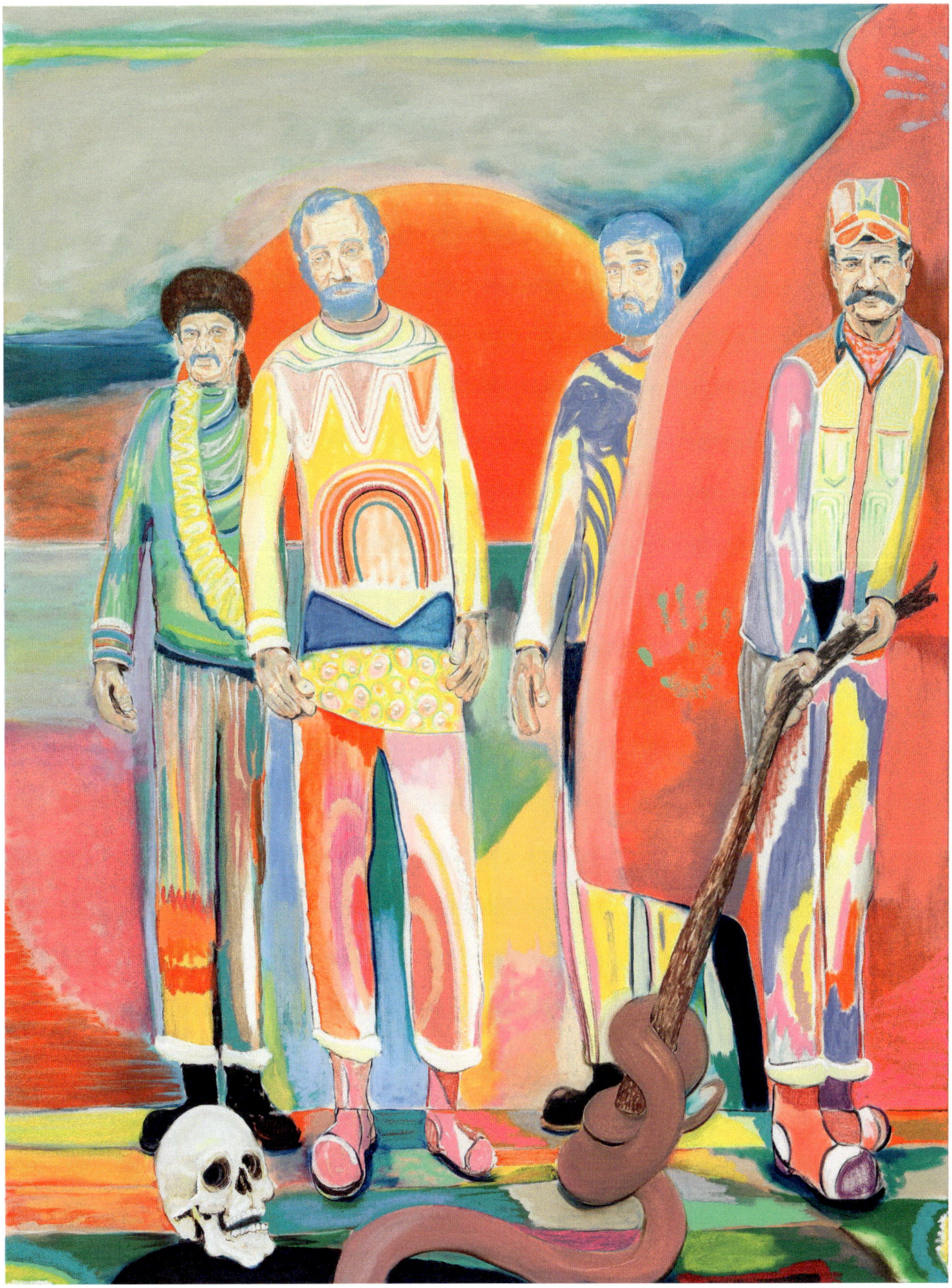

Kaye Donachie
A world in your image, 2017
Oil on canvas
150 × 115 cm
© Kaye Donachie
Courtesy of Maureen Paley, London

Ryan Mosley
From the Verges, 2017
Oil on canvas
215 × 165 cm
© Ryan Mosley
Courtesy of Galerie EIGEN + ART Leipzig/Berlin
Photo: Dave Morgan

Anna Freeman Bentley
Exclusive – Paintings of Private Members Clubs

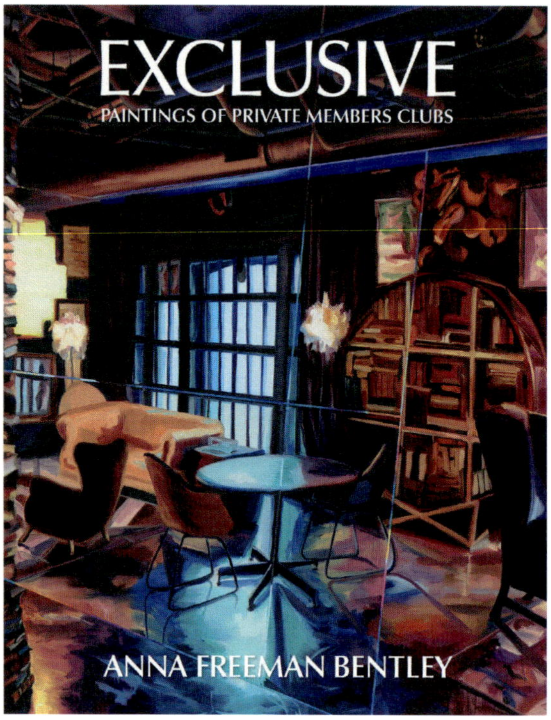

Contributors:
Roberta Ahmanson
John Silvis
Jane Neal

64pp
Hardback
315 × 250 mm
c. 40 images
ISBN: 978-1-910221-15-0
RRP: £30
UK Release: 14 June 2018
Designed by Reynolds Wulf Inc., Oregon
Edited by Ann Hirou
Printed and bound in the USA
Co-published by Pinatubo Press, Inc., and
Anomie Publishing, London

In this publication, Anna Freeman Bentley presents a series of new paintings and works on paper documenting her journey into the exclusive realm of private members clubs. Having started out in London, her research took her to California, and in particular to some of the most desirable clubs of Los Angeles, where through friends, professional networks and a number of courteous emails, doors were temporarily opened to her. In places where photography is often strictly forbidden, Freeman Bentley was authorised to document some of the many luxurious lounges, well-stocked bars and high-end restaurants that are second homes to the members who pay considerable fees to use them. Freeman Bentley uses the photographs she takes of these spaces out of hours as the starting point for unpeopled drawings, collages and painted sketches, transforming her studies into complex paintings that hover between reality and invention.

Freeman Bentley is known for her paintings of architecture and interiors, not only exploring the physical attributes of the built environment, but also raising questions about how and why they are used, and how this is reflected in the ambiance and dynamics of a given space. At a time of heightened awareness of wealth inequality, through her painterly works Freeman Bentley gives us a glimpse inside the spaces of the social milieu of the financially successful, the movers and shakers, the leaders and trend setters, inviting us to respond as viewers as we choose. For some, it may be a matter of curiosity or of desire and aspiration; for others the very idea of members clubs might be elitist. Yet for others it might be an occasional treat, or simply the norm. With her characteristic combination of matter-of-fact observation, critical reflection and atmospheric perception, Freeman Bentley presents us with a body of work that is as enigmatic as it is intriguing, asking us not only about issues of individuality and communality, private and public life, exclusivity and inclusivity, but also about how we each fit into such dialectics, and what this says about our inner and outer lives. *Exclusive* has been co-published by Pinatubo Press, Inc., and Anomie Publishing, and was released to coincide with an exhibition of the same name at the Ahmanson Gallery, Irvine, California, in spring 2018. This hardback publication showcases images of approximately twenty paintings and as many works on paper, alongside a foreword from collector and patron Roberta Ahmanson, an introduction by the exhibition curator John Silvis and a specially commissioned essay from critic Jane Neal.

Anna Freeman Bentley (b. 1982) is an artist based in London. She studied painting at Chelsea College of Art and Design before graduating with an MA from the Royal College of Art in 2010. She has had solo exhibitions at venues including Wolfson College, Oxford (2017); Husk Project Space, London (2015); Workshop Gallery, Venice (2012) and Galerie Kollaborativ, Berlin (2007).

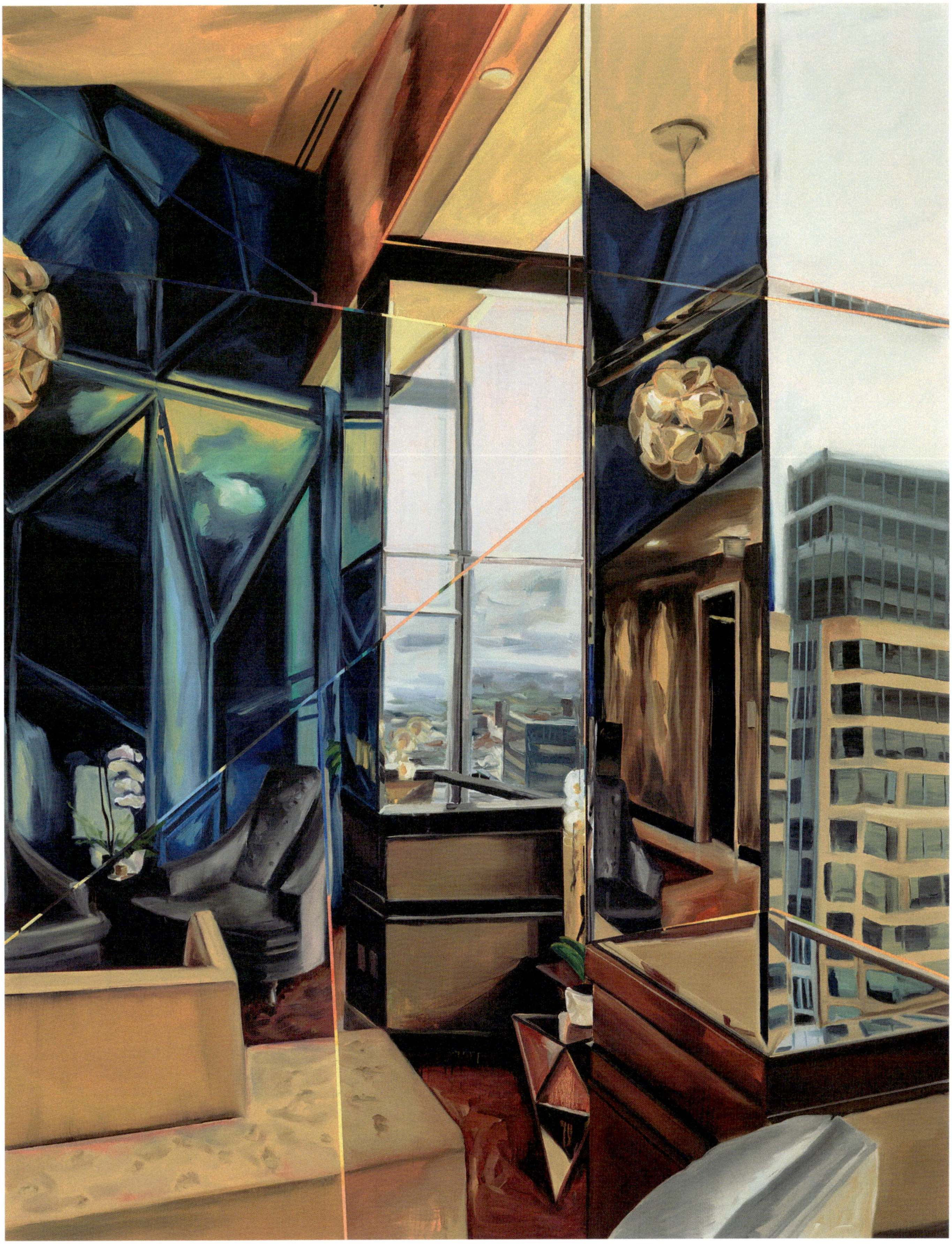

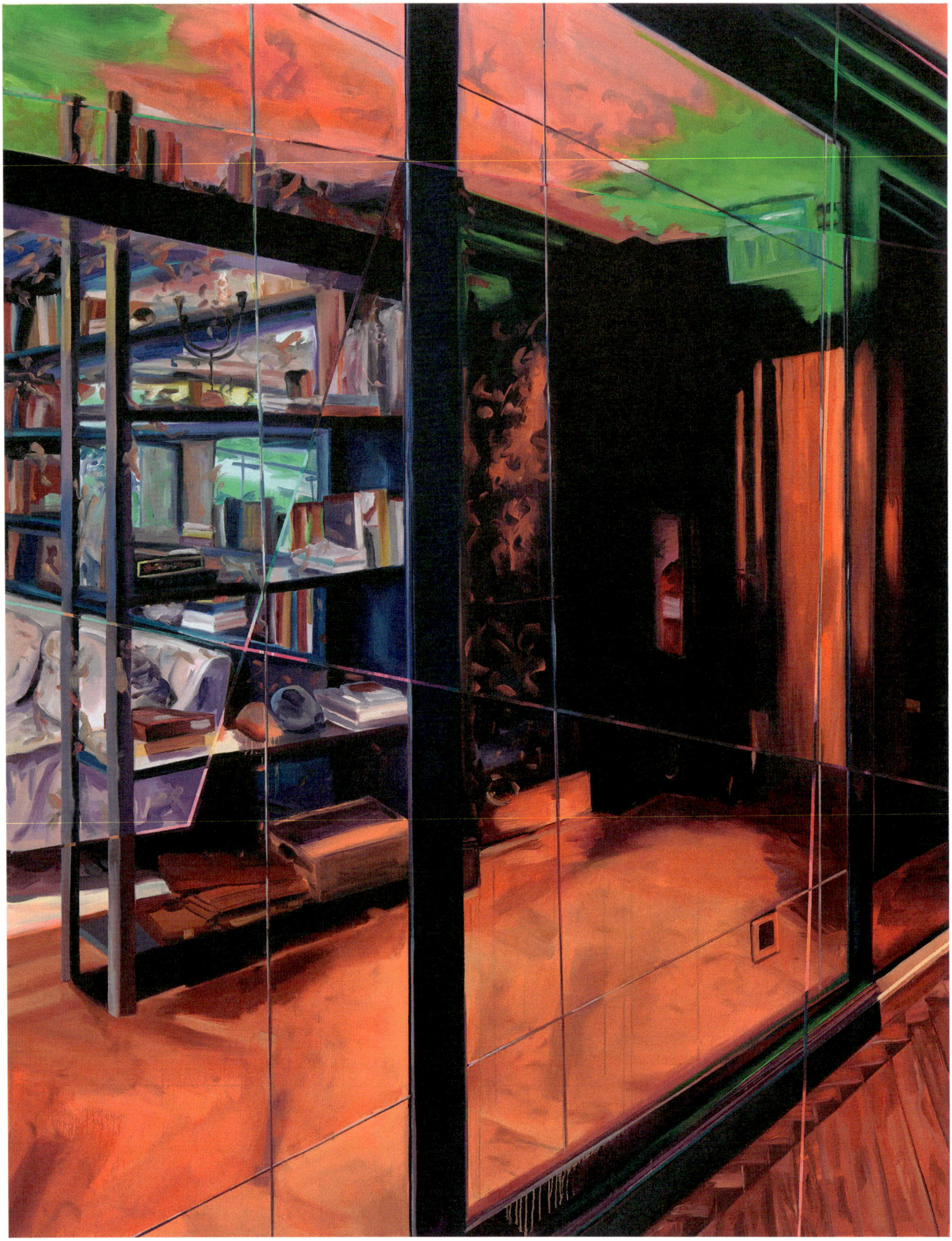

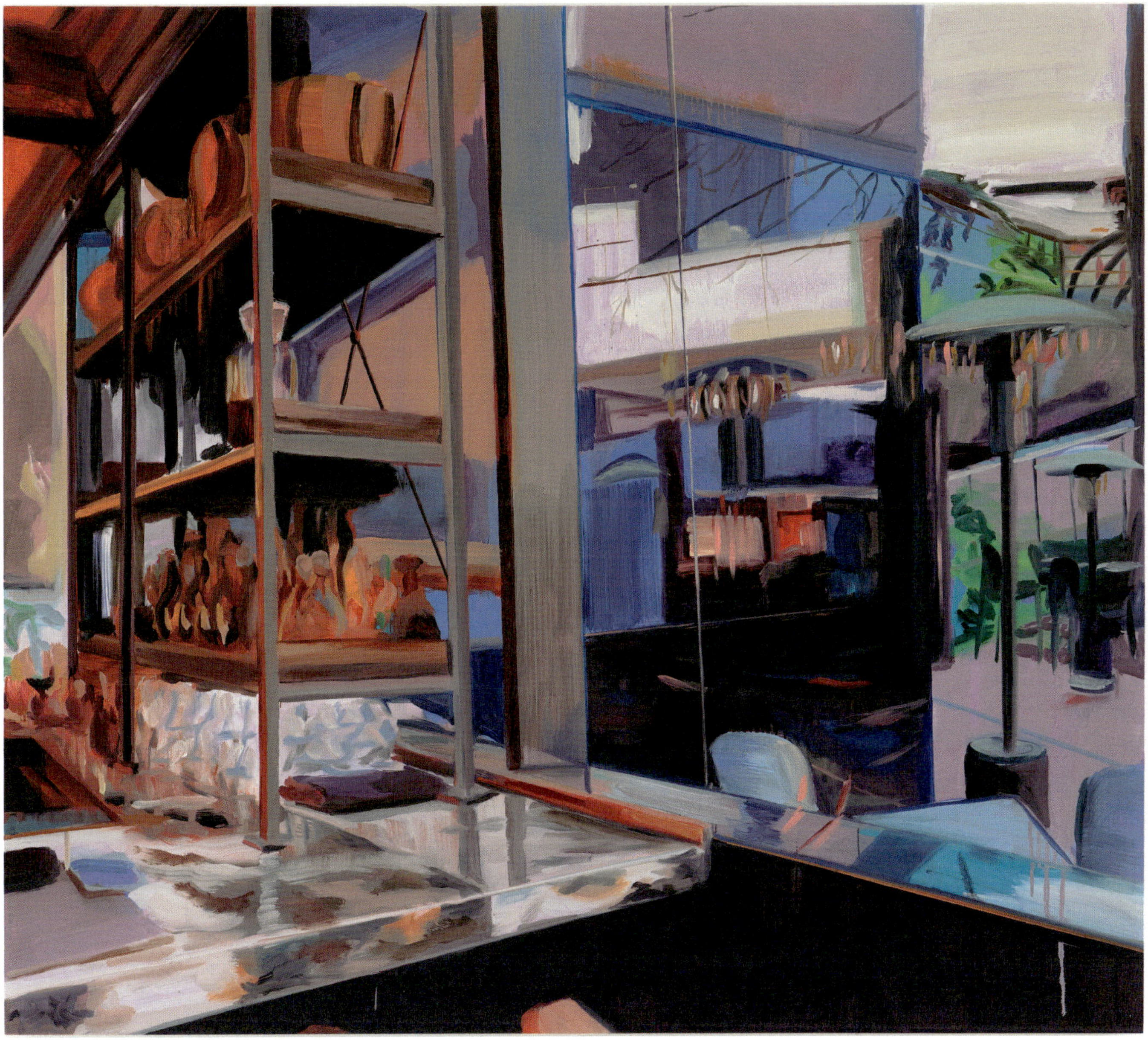

p. 147
Anna Freeman Bentley
Exclusive (II), 2017
Oil and acrylic on canvas
230 × 180 cm

Anna Freeman Bentley
Exclusive (I), 2017
Oil and acrylic on canvas
230 × 180 cm

Anna Freeman Bentley
Outlook, 2017
Oil and acrylic on board
113 × 131cm

All © Anna Freeman Bentley
Photos: Anna Arca

Justin Mortimer
Hoax

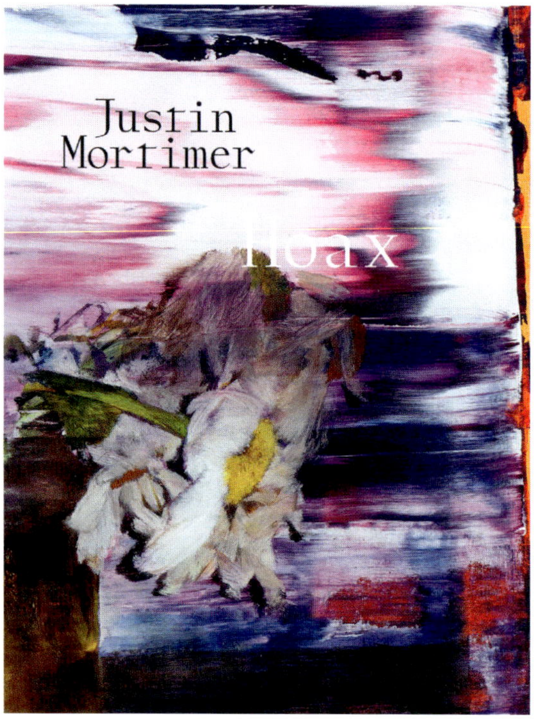

Contributors:
Freya Cooper Kiddie

88pp
Hardback
255 × 195 mm
c. 45 images
ISBN: 978-1-910221-14-3
RRP: £30
UK Release: 19 April 2018
Designed by Modern Activity, London
Edited by Matt Price
Printed by EBS, Verona
Published by Anomie Publishing, London,
in a first edition of 500 copies

Published to coincide with a solo presentation of the new *Hoax Suite* by British painter Justin Mortimer at The Armory Show in New York in spring 2018 with London-based gallery Parafin, the publication presents the thirty works that comprise this exceptional series of paintings depicting dead and dying flowers, offering an intense and accomplished exposition of still life, or perhaps more aptly, nature morte. From one direction, pure abstraction threatens to rupture into physical space and matter; from the other, figuration almost collapses into the abstraction that engulfs it. With Mortimer's characteristic combination of darkness and beauty, melancholy and metaphysics, observation and interpretation, the series is not only a significant body of work within the artist's oeuvre, but one of the most significant series of paintings of flowers in our time.

Alongside new photography of all the paintings, the book features a commissioned essay by writer Freya Cooper Kiddie, in which she discusses the genesis and evolution of the suite of paintings, its connections to Mortimer's wider practice and to art history, and opens up critical lines of enquiry ranging from twentieth-century experimental film to existential notions of mortality, from altered states of mind to the concept of still life as portraiture. Cooper Kiddie investigates the techniques and aesthetics of a series that fuses decaying organic matter with corrupted digital technology. While the *Hoax Suite* of paintings can be read as an exploration of the medium of paint and of the dialogue between figuration and abstraction through a single subject, its themes are manifold, from the contemplation of mortality to faded beauty and lost love – fragrant flowers in full bloom, as if to deceive us, soon decay. Here, in these dank, acrid, darkly psychedelic works, Mortimer shines a flashlight on the spectral beauty of death, and in doing so, reminds us that life is the agonising yet ecstatic explosion of colour that fleetingly fills the void.

Justin Mortimer graduated from the Slade School of Art in 1992 and lives and works in London. Recent solo exhibitions include Parafin, London (2017 and 2015); Djanogly Gallery, Lakeside Arts, University of Nottingham (2015); Future Perfect, Singapore (2015); Haunch of Venison, London (2012) and Mihai Nicodim Gallery, Los Angeles (2011). Recent group exhibitions include *The New Frontiers of Painting*, Fondazione Stelline, Milan (2017-18); *Disruptive Imagination*, Gallery of Fine Arts, Ostrava, Czech Republic (2017); *This Side of Paradise*, Sotheby's S/2, London (2014); *Are you alright?* MOCCA, Toronto (2013); *Nightfall*, MODEM Centre for Modern and Contemporary Arts, Debrecen, Hungary (2012) and the 5th Prague Biennial (2010). His work is in collections including the National Portrait Gallery, London; the Royal Society for the Arts; Bank of America; NatWest Bank and Flash Art Museum of Contemporary Art in Trevi, Italy.

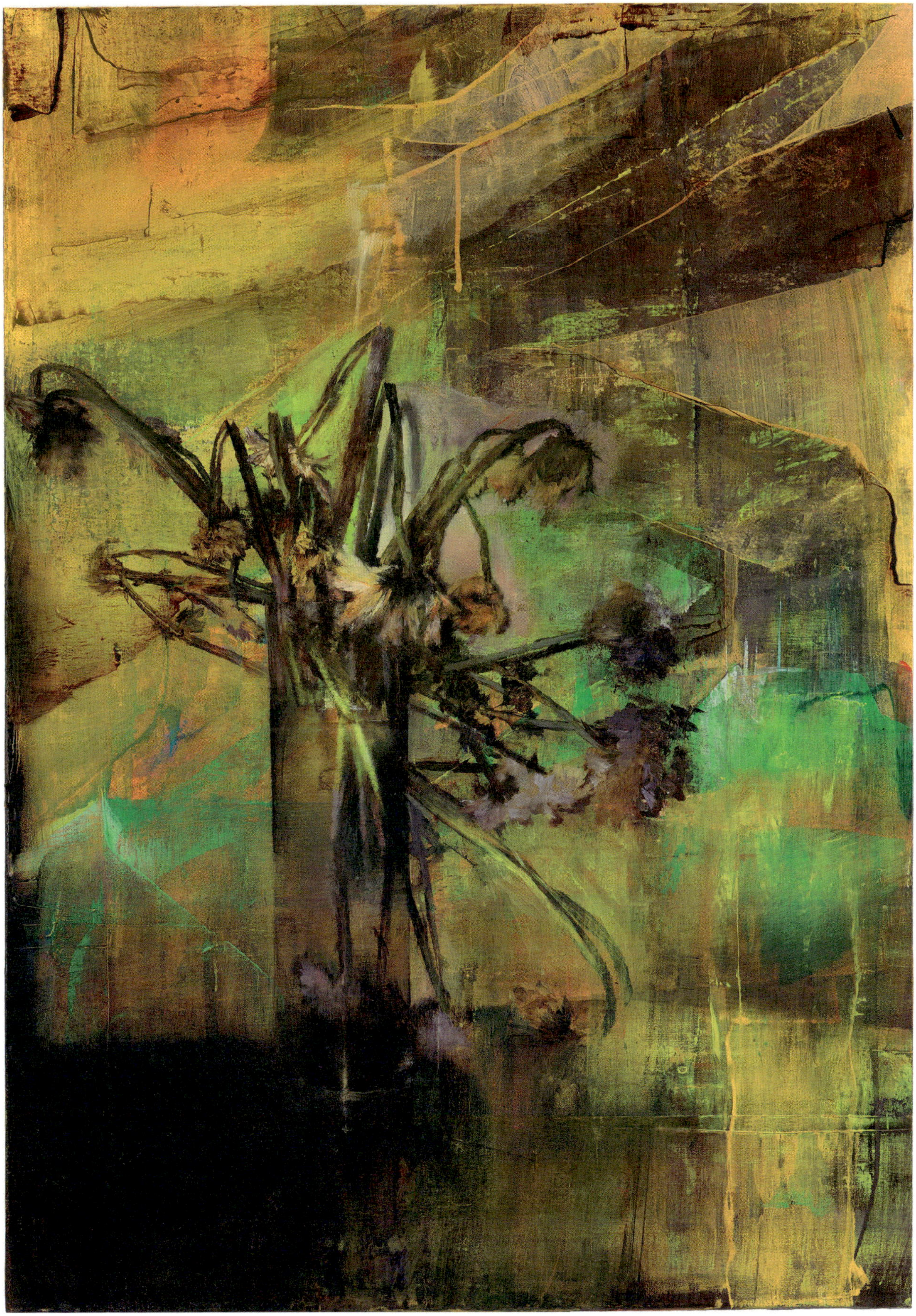

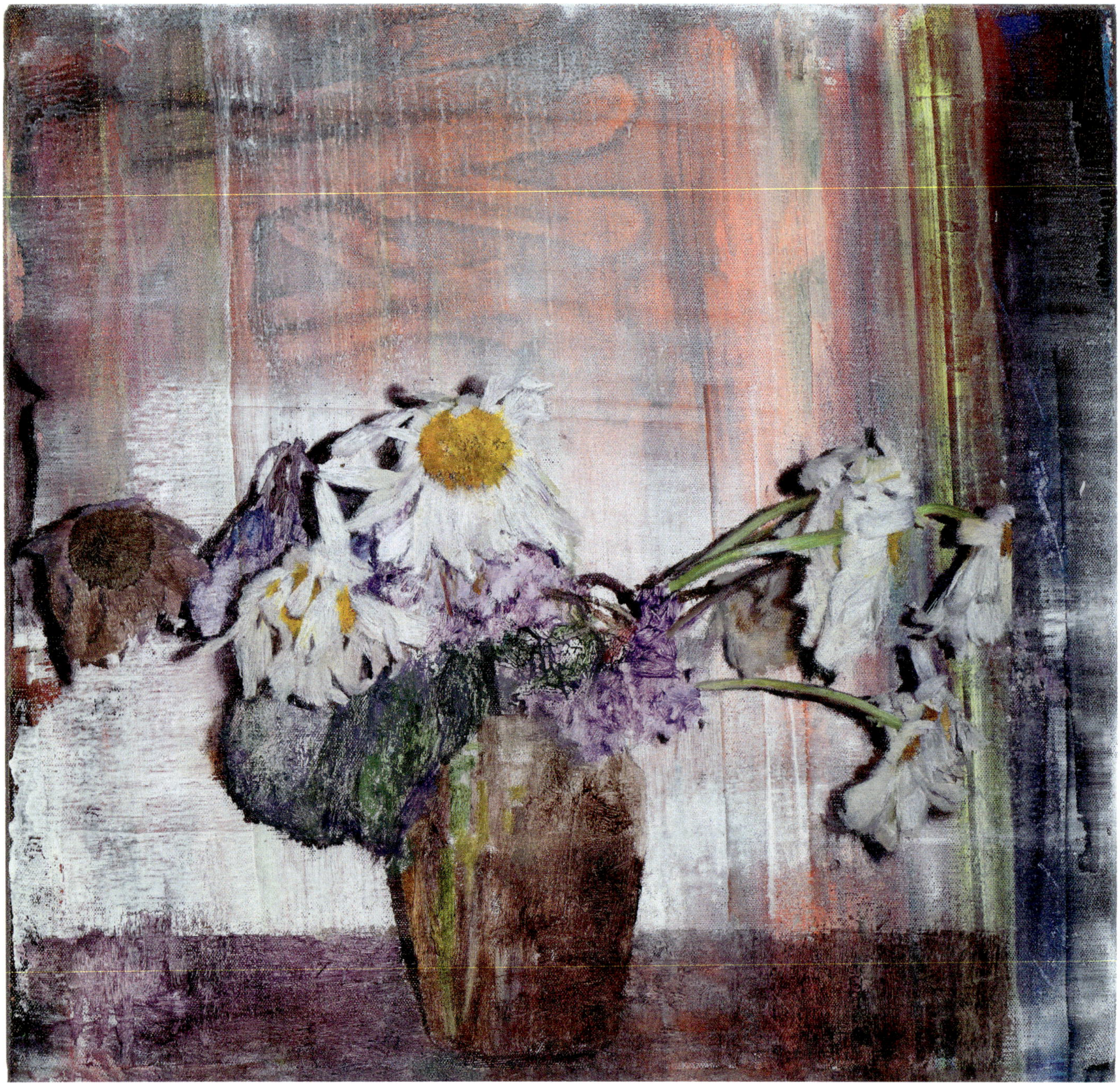

p. 151
Justin Mortimer
Hoax 22, 2017
Oil and acrylic on canvas
laid on panel
100 × 70 cm

Justin Mortimer
Hoax 5, 2017
Oil and acrylic on canvas
51 × 51 cm

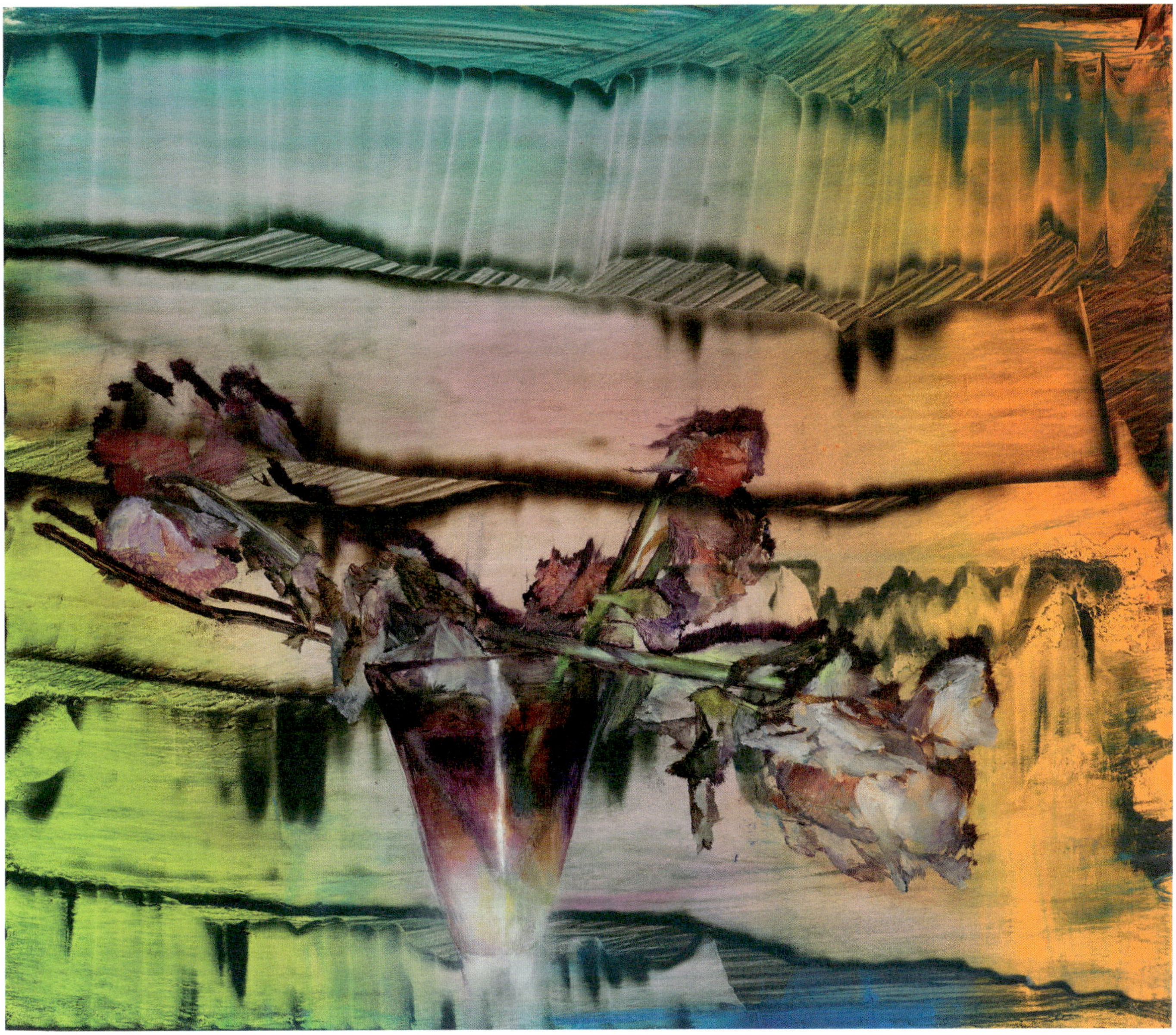

Justin Mortimer
Hoax 26, 2017
Oil and acrylic on panel
50 × 60 cm

All © Justin Mortimer
Courtesy of the artist and Parafin, London
Photos: Peter Mallet

Louise Giovanelli
In Conversation

Contributors:
Paulette Terry Brien
Charlotte Keenan McDonald

78pp
Softback
245 × 171.5 mm
c. 35 images
ISBN: 978-1-910221-13-6
RRP: £18
UK Release: 23 March 2017
Designed by Textbook Studio
Edited by Linda Pittwood and Guy Tindale
Printed by Pression, Leeds
Published by Anomie Publishing, London, in a first edition of 500 copies

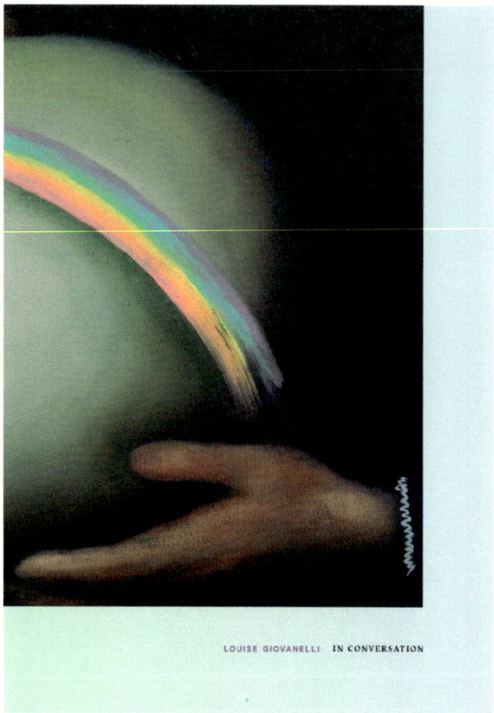

Louise Giovanelli is one of Britain's most promising young painters. This, the artist's first monograph, documents her first three solo exhibitions, staged in 2016-17 at The International 3, Salford, the Grundy Art Gallery, Blackpool and Touchstones Rochdale. Featuring a foreword by Paulette Terry Brien, co-founder and co-director of The International 3, and an essay and an interview by Charlotte Keenan McDonald, Curator of British Art at the Walker Art Gallery, Liverpool, this publication has been beautifully designed by Textbook Studio and published by Anomie in a first edition of 500 copies.

Paintings, both contemporary and spanning the history of art, are Giovanelli's primary subjects within her own paintings. Picking out sections or details from existing works – some well-known but mostly lesser-known – she reworks and represents them, focussing on aspects that attract her eye and critical attention. These might be unusual or odd formal elements – a neckline or a detail such as a pocket on an item of clothing – or can equally be things that are extraneous to the original, such as how candlelight might fall on a painting, or how sections might appear during restoration work by a conservator. Considering the position of the viewer as much as the painter, Giovanelli explores the history of painting as object, the context of its display and reception, and the very mechanics of painting itself to investigate languages of painting both past and present, resulting in works that are cryptic, other-worldly and strangely enchanting. Indeed, it could be said that the history of painting is curiously deconstructed and reframed in her unique and engaging contemporary practice.

Louise Giovanelli (b. 1993, London) graduated in BA (Hons) Fine Art (Painting) from Manchester School of Art in 2015. Her previous group exhibitions include: BEEP, Wales' international painting prize; *Institution / Outstitution* at The International 3; *Pleasure Islands* at Art Work Atelier, Salford; *The Painted World*, Saatchi Art Showdown Final, Los Angeles; and *Ones to Watch*, Galerie Sarow, Pforzheim, Germany. In 2016 Giovanelli had her first solo exhibition *Prima Donna* at The International 3, followed by *From Here to Here* at Grundy Art Gallery, Blackpool, *Slow to Respond* at Touchstones Rochdale and in 2017 a solo exhibition at Warrington Museum and Art Gallery. Giovanelli has been the recipient of a number of prizes including The Leonard James Fine Art Prize, The Manchester Academy of Fine Art Award, and The Ken Billany Painting Prize. In 2015 she was awarded second place in the Saatchi Art Showdown and in 2017 she undertook a residency at Griffin Gallery, London. Her work is held in private collections in the UK, USA, Canada, China, Germany, Slovakia and Italy.

Louise Giovanelli
Neckline (from the Tiergarten), 2016
Oil on canvas
50 × 40 cm
Courtesy of the artist

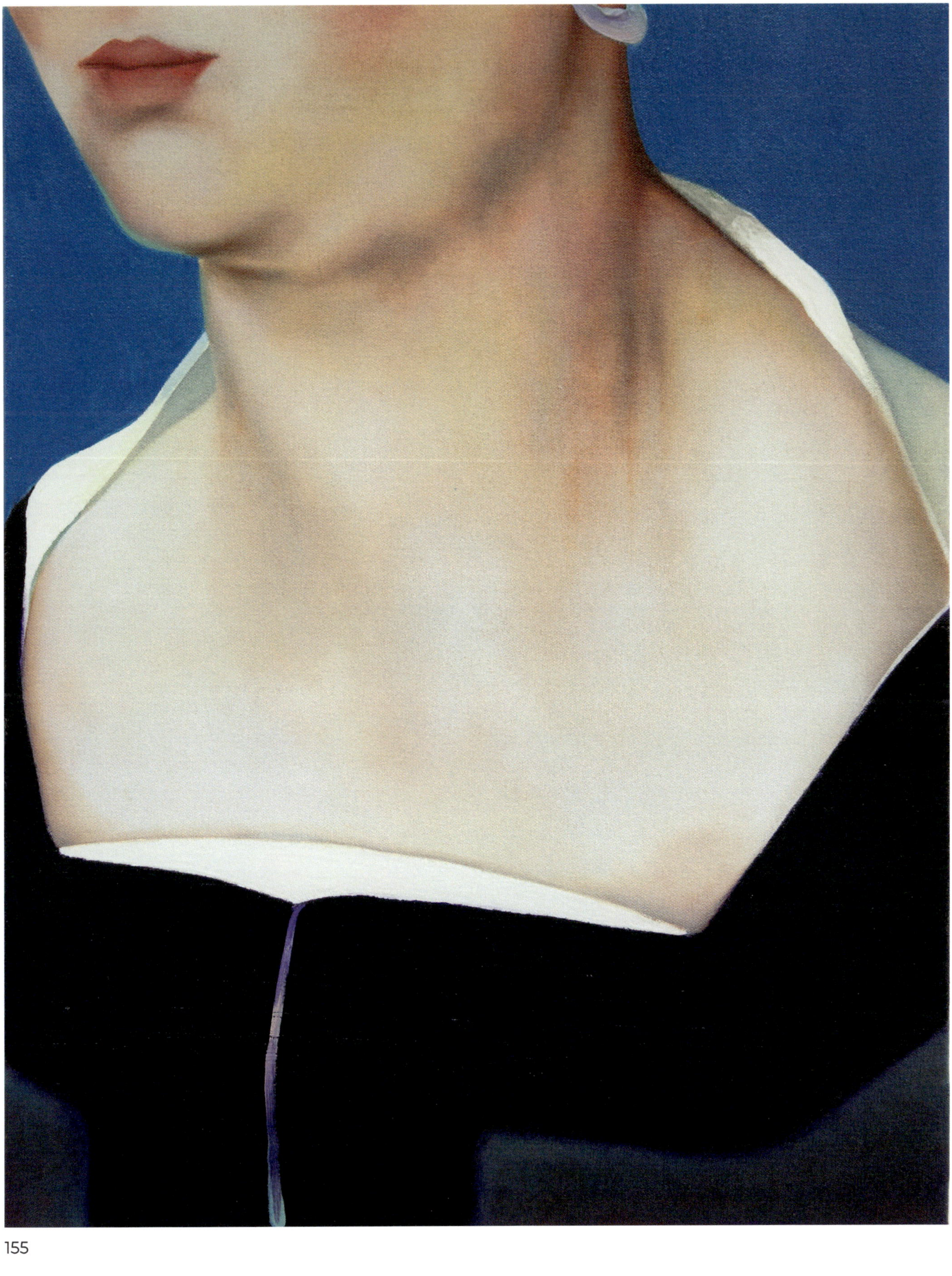

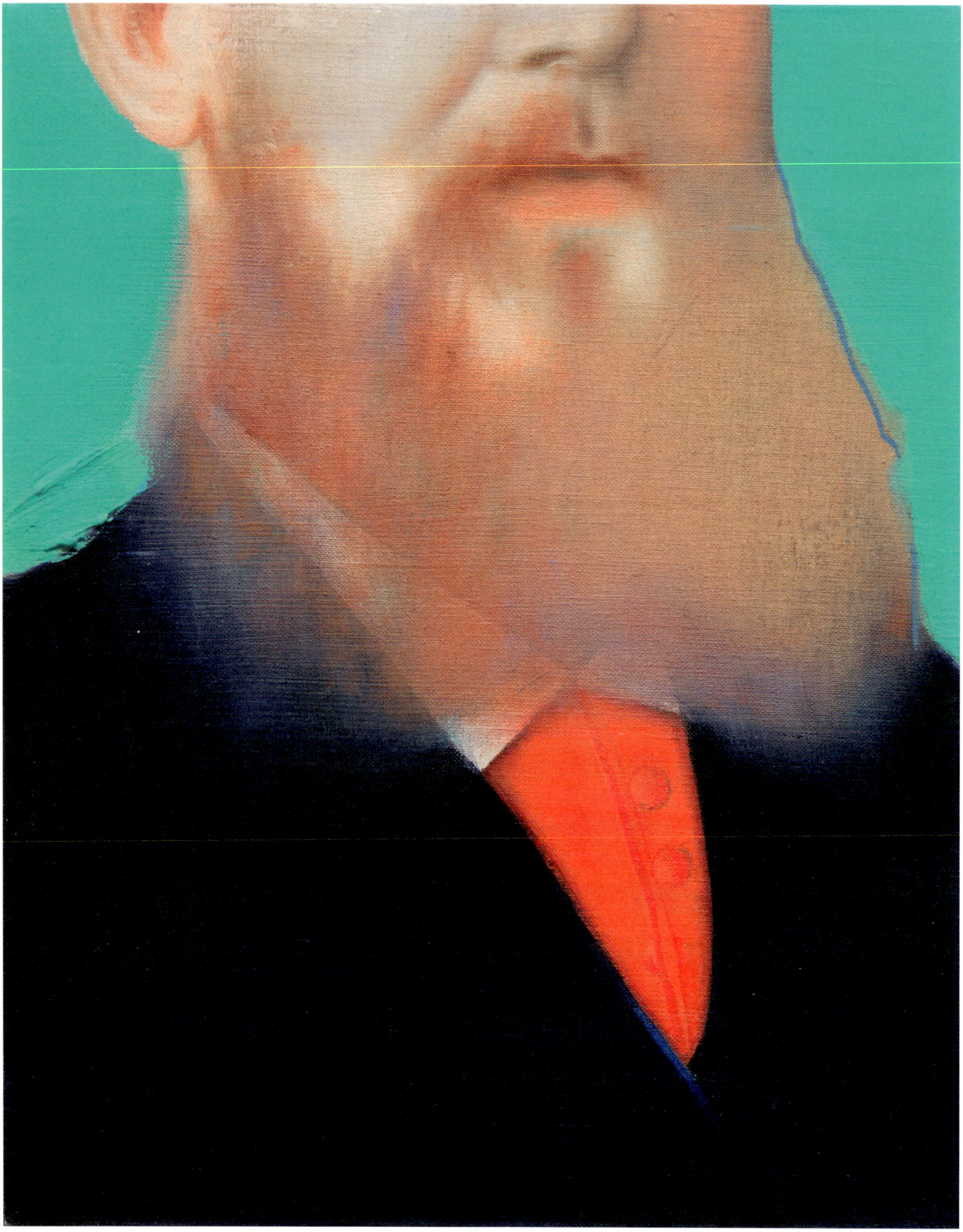

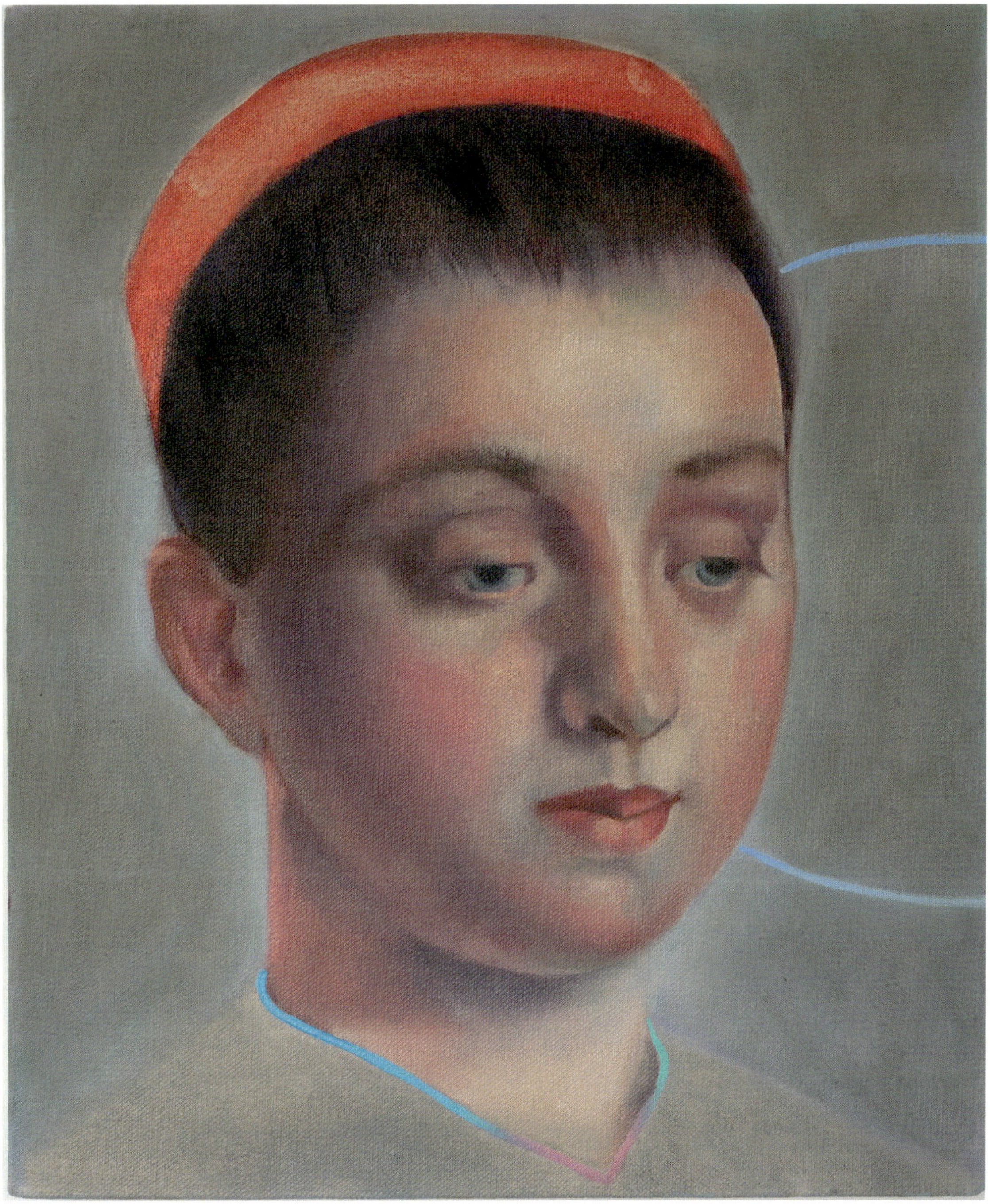

Louise Giovanelli
Watcher, 2016
Oil on canvas
35 × 29.5cm
Courtesy of the artist

Louise Giovanelli
The Beard III, 2016
Oil on linen
30 × 24.5cm
Courtesy of the artist

All photos: Pantling Studio

Richard Patterson
Matters of Life and Death

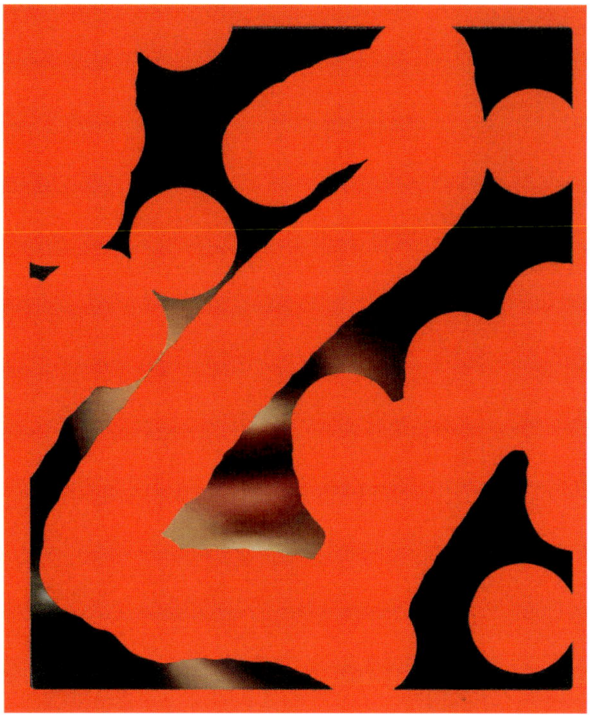

Contributors:
Paul Moorhouse
Jane Neal
James Cahill

104pp
Hardback in a hardback slipcase
292 × 245 mm
c. 49 colour and b/w images
ISBN: 978-1-910221-12-9
RRP: £75
UK Release: 23 February 2017
Designed by Modern Activity
Edited by Matt Price and Kat Sapera
Printed by EBS, Verona
Published by Anomie Publishing, London, in an edition of 500 copies

Matters of Life and Death is a limited-edition publication documenting the remarkable new and recent paintings of celebrated Dallas-based British artist Richard Patterson.

An introduction by Paul Moorhouse, Senior Curator at the National Portrait Gallery, London, discusses the dynamic and complex relationship between figuration and abstraction in Patterson's oeuvre. Moorhouse observes: 'Visual ambiguity defines Patterson's art, and its most conspicuous feature is the interaction between figurative painting, abstraction and photography ... From the outset he moved between these disparate visual languages, combining them in ways that seemed deliberately oppositional and subversive.' Patterson's latest works are as provocative as ever, and as he enters mid-career, have become increasingly accomplished, cryptic and, at times, haunting.

An illuminating essay by art historian James Cahill explores the subject of portraiture within the artist's works, asserting that 'his strategy of distancing his figures – whether through a broken veil (or enclosing frame) of abstract paint, or the gauze-like intercession of a photographic source – throws into relief the idea that selfhood is ultimately a succession of masks.'

Curator and critic Jane Neal deftly navigates ideas of gender and sexuality in Patterson's practice, taking us into the realms of fetish and the male gaze, proposing that his painting overtly 'points towards the patriarchal and often misogynistic attitude to women's bodies still prevalent in magazines, films and social media, even in the twenty-first century. Patterson sets us up to confront the darkness that often underlies the male gaze, even affording it physical form.'

Featuring a selection of works executed between 2013 and 2016, many of which are published here for the first time, the cloth-covered book is presented in a specially printed hard slipcase and has been published in an edition of just 500 copies.

Born in 1963, Patterson graduated from Goldsmiths College in 1986. He featured in Damien Hirst's renowned *Freeze*, Surrey Docks, London (1988); as well as *Sensation: Young British Artists from the Saatchi Collection*, Royal Academy of Arts, London and touring (1997-2000). Other exhibitions include *Painting Pictures*, Kunstmuseum Wolfsburg, Germany (2003); *Nexus Texas*, Contemporary Arts Museum Houston, Texas (2007) and *Attention to Detail*, the FLAG Art Foundation, New York. He has had solo exhibitions at Anthony d'Offay Gallery, London (1997); James Cohan Gallery, New York (1999 and 2002); Dallas Museum of Art, Texas (2000; Timothy Taylor Gallery, London (2005, 2008 and 2013); the Goss-Michael Foundation, Dallas (2009); and the FLAG Art Foundation (2014).

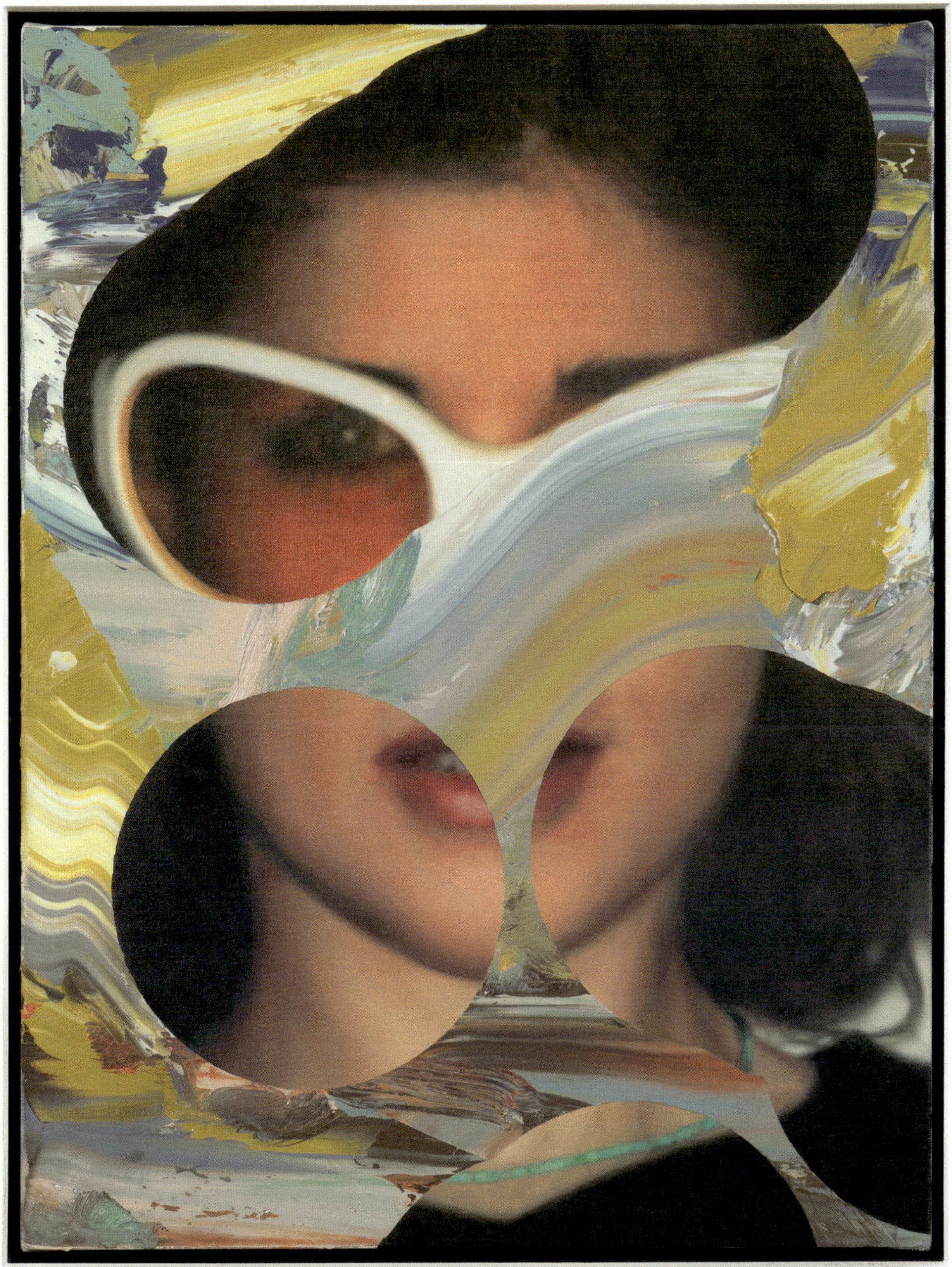

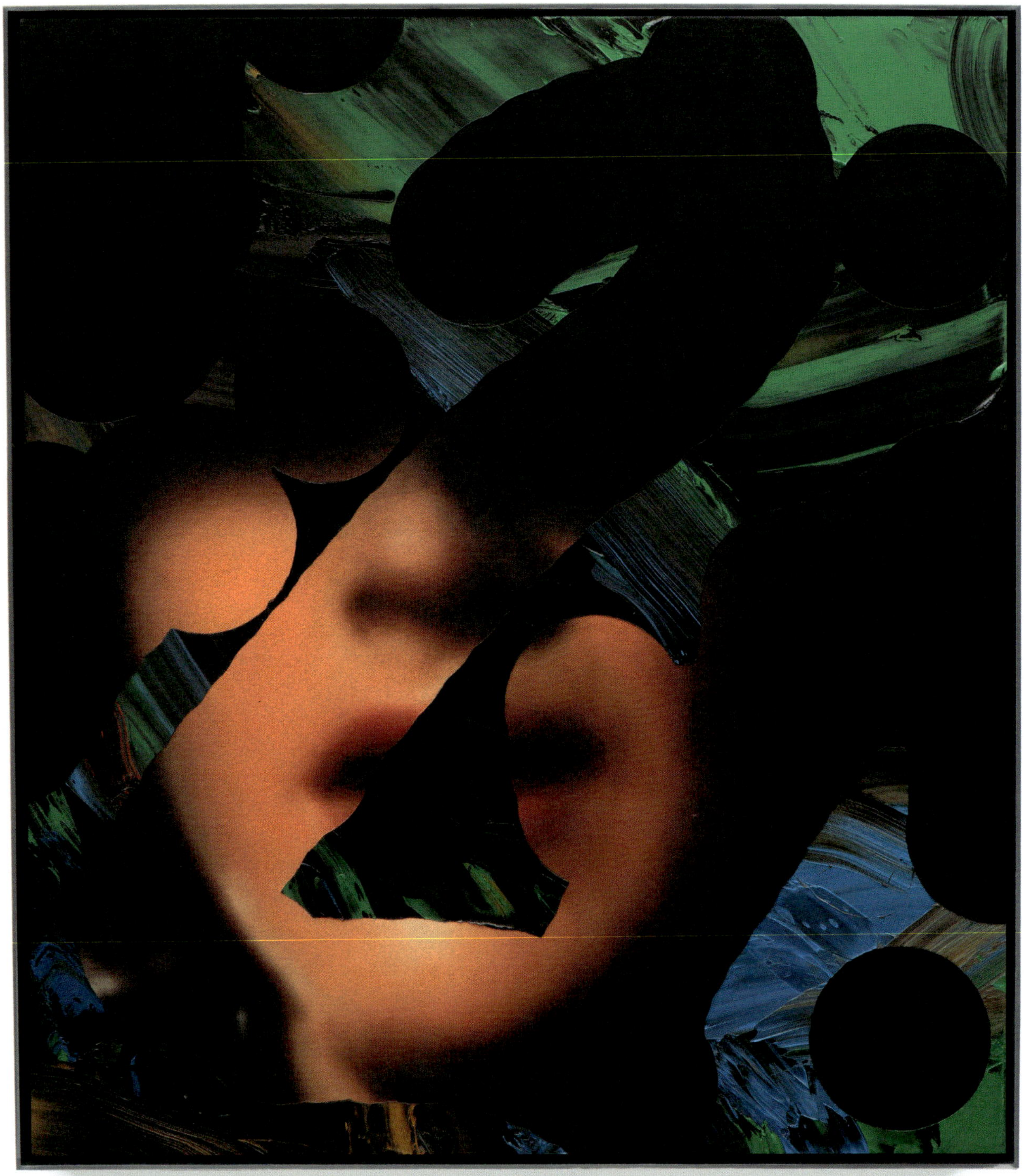

p. 159
Richard Patterson
Christina with Yellow Glasses, 2014
Oil on canvas
66.4 × 51.1 cm
Courtesy of private collection
Photo: Todd-White Art Photography, London

Richard Patterson
That sunny dome! those caves of ice!, 2015
Oil on canvas
66 × 58.4 cm
Courtesy of Timothy Taylor, London
Photo: Prudence Cuming Associates, London

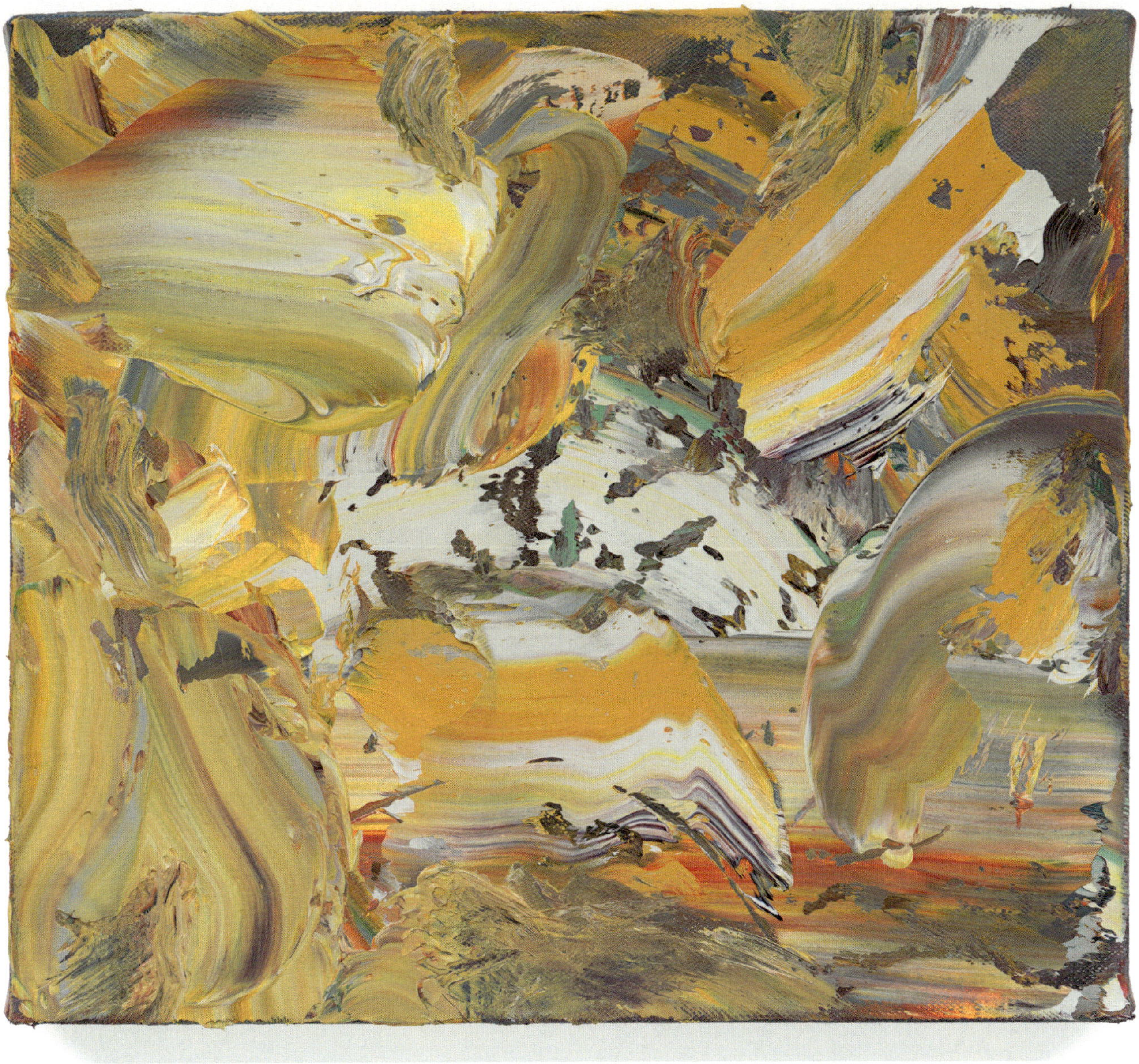

Richard Patterson
Country Life, 2014
Oil on canvas
25.5 × 31 cm
Courtesy of Timothy Taylor, London
Photo: Genevieve Hanson Photography

All © Richard Patterson

Daphne Oram
An Individual Note of Music, Sound and Electronics

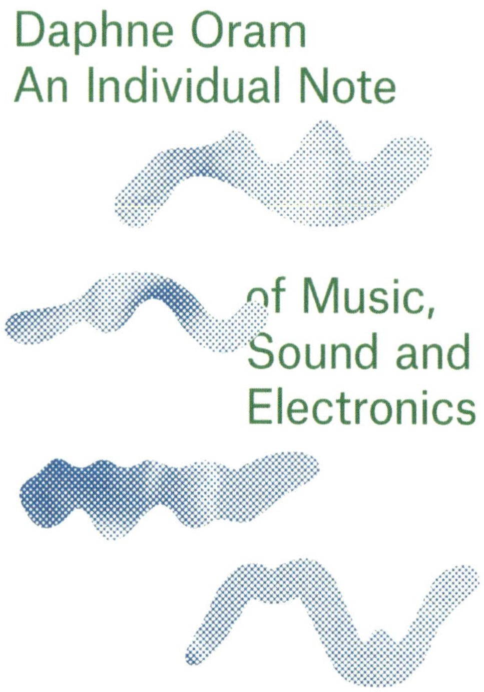

Contributors:
Sarah Angliss

176pp
Hardback
220 × 165 mm
c. 20 b/w images
ISBN: 978-1-910221-11-2
RRP: £20
UK Release: 23 November 2016
Designed by Joe Gilmore
Edited by Matt Price
Printed by EBS, Verona
Co-published by Daphne Oram Trust / Anomie Academic, UK

Daphne Oram (1925–2003) was one of the central figures in the development of British experimental electronic music. Having declined a place at the Royal College of Music to become a music balancer at the BBC, she went on to become the co-founder and first director of the BBC Radiophonic Workshop. Oram left the BBC in 1959 to pursue commercial work in television, advertising, film and theatre, to make her own music for recording and performance, and to continue her personal research into sound technology – a passion she had had since her childhood in rural Wiltshire. Her home, a former oasthouse in Kent, became an unorthodox studio and workshop in which, mostly on a shoestring budget, she developed her pioneering equipment, sounds and ideas. A significant part of her personal research was the invention of a machine that offered a new form of sound synthesis – the Oramics machine.

Oram's contribution to electronic music is receiving considerable attention from new generations of composers, sound engineers, musicians, musicologists and music lovers around the world. Following her death, the Daphne Oram Trust was established to preserve and promote her work, life and legacy, and an archive created in the Special Collections Library at Goldsmiths, University of London. One of the Trust's ambitions has been to publish a new edition of Oram's one and only book, *An Individual Note of Music, Sound and Electronics*, which was originally published in 1972. With support from the Daphne Oram Archive, the Trust has now been able to realise this ambition.

When commissioned to write a book, she was keen to avoid it becoming a manual or how-to guide, preferring instead to use the opportunity to muse on the subjects of music, sound and electronics, and the relationships between them. At a time when the world was just starting to engage with electronic music and the technology was still primarily in the hands of music studios, universities and corporations, her approach was both innovative and inspiring, encouraging anyone with an interest in music to think about the nature, capabilities and possibilities that the new sounds could bring. And her thinking was not limited to just the future of the orchestra, synthesizer, computer and home studio, but ventured, with great spirit and wit, into other realms of science, technology, culture and thought. *An Individual Note* is a playful yet compelling manifesto for the dawn of electronic music and for our individual capacity to use, experience and enjoy it.

This new edition of *An Individual Note* features a specially commissioned introduction from the British composer, performer, roboticist and sound historian Sarah Angliss. It has been co-published by The Daphne Oram Trust and Anomie Academic, an imprint of Anomie Publishing, London.

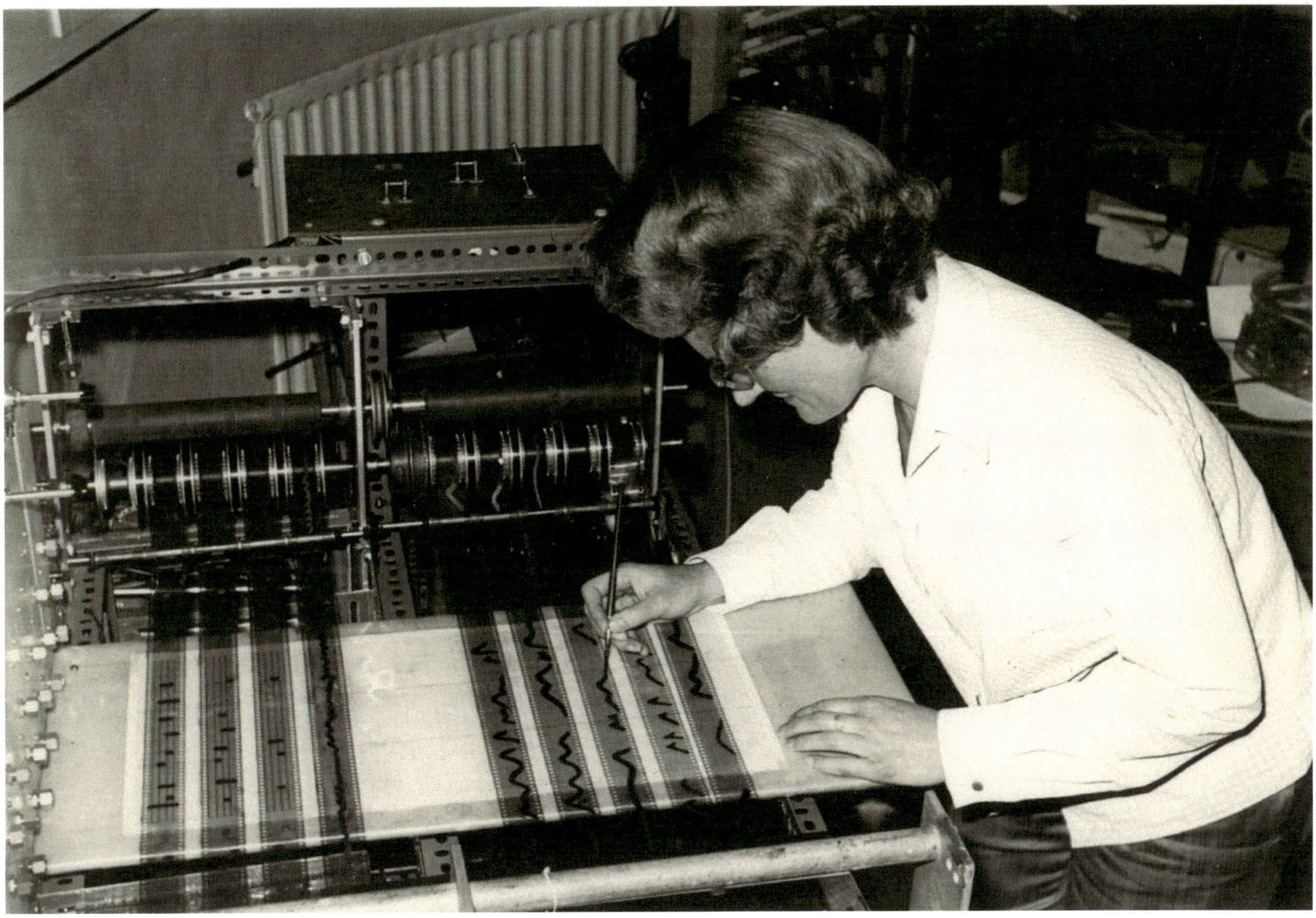

Daphne Oram drawing timbres on the
Oramics machine
© Daphne Oram Trust and Fred Wood
Courtesy of Goldsmiths Special Collections
& Archives

Oliver Clegg

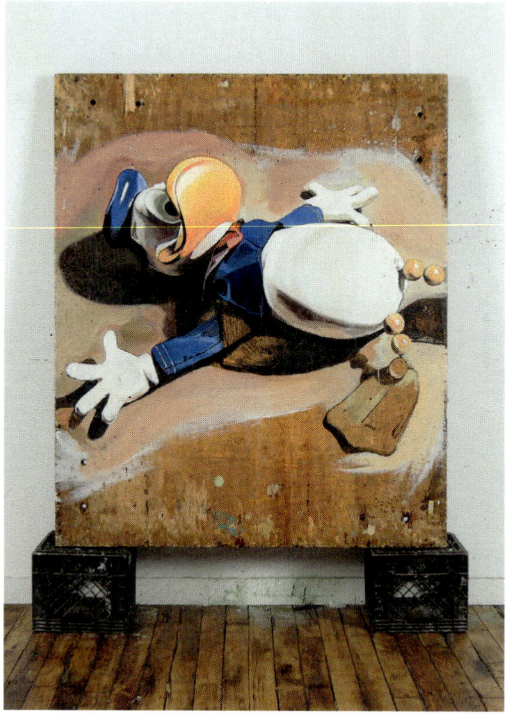

Contributors:
Martin Herbert
Sina Najafi
Matt Price

288pp
Hardback
305 × 220 mm
c. 135 colour and b/w images
ISBN: 978-1-910221-07-5
RRP: £30
UK Release: 07 July 2016
Designed by Dominique Clausen
Edited by Matt Price
Printed by Asia Pacific Offset, China
Published by Anomie Publishing, London

Featuring an interview with Sina Najafi, an essay by Martin Herbert, and designed by Dominique Clausen, this is the first major monograph on the British-born, New York-based artist Oliver Clegg. An eclectic, polyphonic and multidisciplinary artist, Clegg's oeuvre stretches from painting, drawing and printmaking to sculpture, installation, site-specific art, participatory projects and beyond. Indeed, his practice is in many ways a shining example of 'post-medium' creativity today, pursuing the essence of art itself beyond any specific medium or art form. The irony is, he's pretty damn good with each art form too.

With his erudite, surprising and striking repertoire, and his diverse materials and methods (from glass, wood and steel to neon, resin and concrete, weaving and casting to engraving and industrial manufacture), Clegg offers the viewer a complex, sometimes playful, other times moving journey into existential and ontological notions of objecthood and matter, images and signs, language and communication, creation and being. From the studio and gallery walls to the streets of London and New York, from Freud's house to the Joshua Tree National Park, from foosball tables to state asylums, Clegg turns up to do remarkable things with the fabric of spacetime.

And yes, it's an emotional rollercoaster of a ride – in fact, Clegg's oeuvre spans a significant proportion of the spectrum of human emotion, his unique trans-Atlantic blend of humour, sarcasm and wit coming face to face with the much more serious matters of memory, psychology, truth, belief, meaning, love, life and death. Nostalgia, childhood, games, play and sentimentality career headlong into the realms of kitsch, Pop and the history of the avantgarde, resulting in a delightful yet challenging range of responses from the viewer, whether amusement, camaraderie, joy, bemusement, outrage, disillusionment or a call to arms. Clegg is an artist with great energy, incredible spirit, and one of the most engaging, curious, cryptic and entertaining oeuvres currently making waves in the world of art.

In many ways an exploration of the id, ego and superego, Clegg's practice plays out the struggle between our basic desires, our rational minds, and the underlying mores that keep us in check. Not unlike Freudian notions of the psyche, Clegg's practice articulates the battle that takes place inside us all on a daily basis, spilling into the outside world in myriad ways. It is a fight, yes, but it is play too.

Oliver Clegg
Egg Head, 2015
Oil, emulsion and acrylic on board
127 × 111.7 cm
Photo: Richard Evans

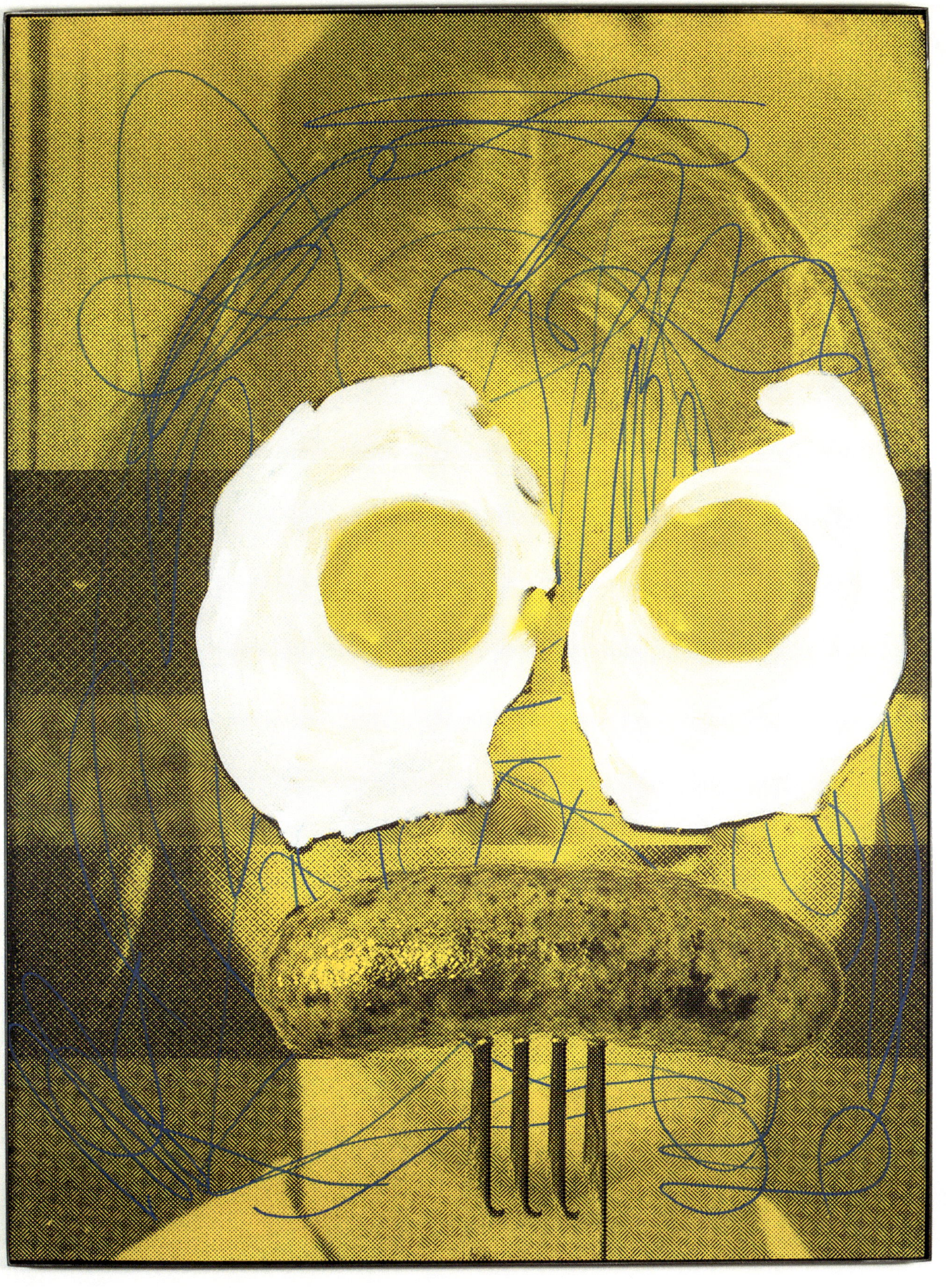

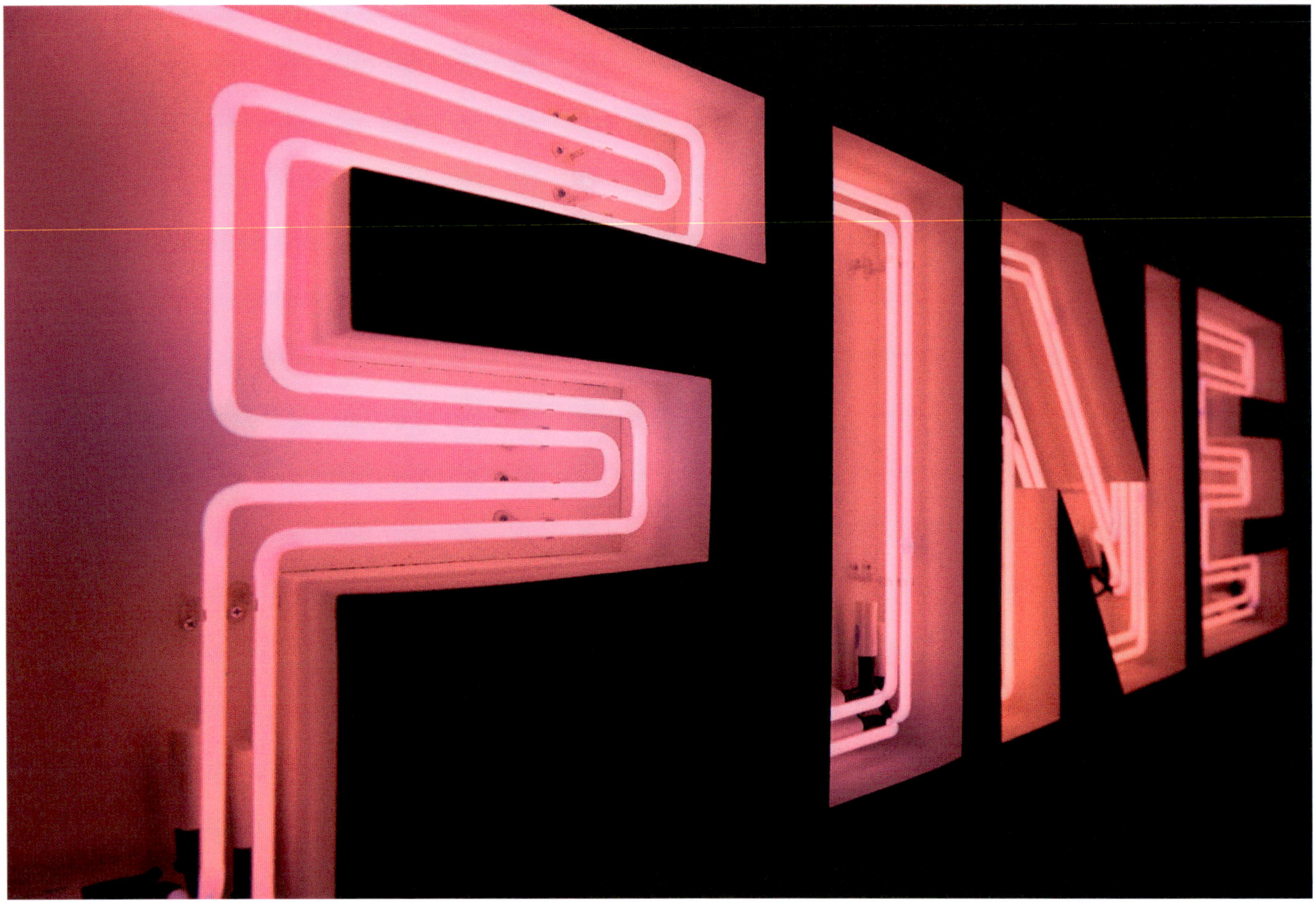

Oliver Clegg
Fine, 2014
Neon, aluminium, steel
69.2 × 226.6 cm
Photo: Christian Harder

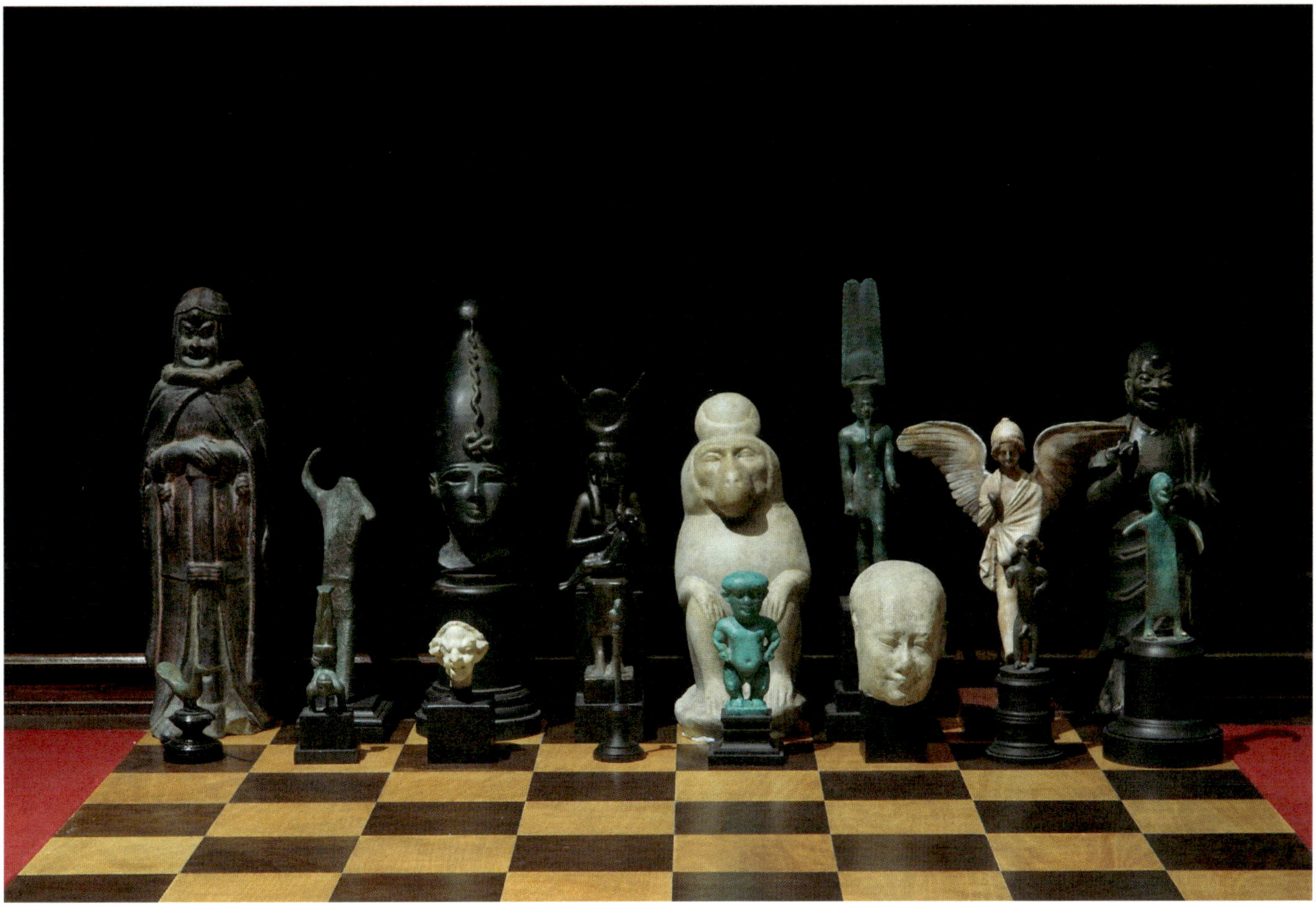

Oliver Clegg
Everytime I think I have discovered something I realise a poet has been there before me, 2008
Mixed media, various dimensions
Photo: Andy Keate

All © Oliver Clegg
Courtesy of the artist and Anomie Publishing

Sensory Systems

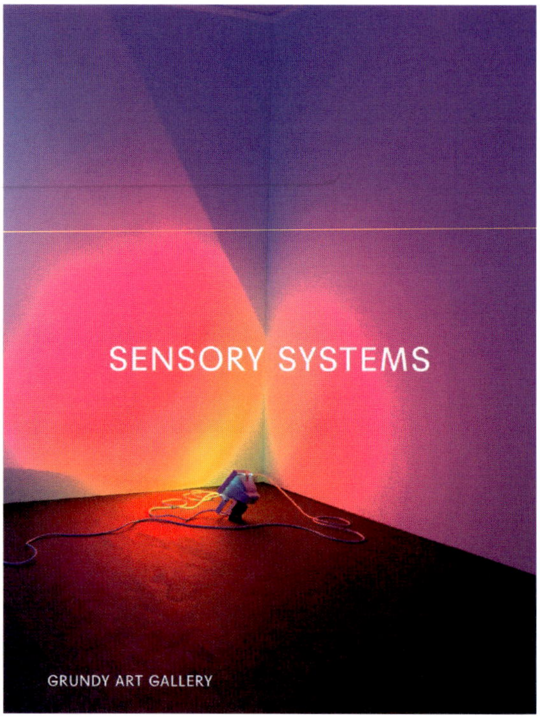

Contributors:
Richard Parry
Luke Skrebowski

64pp
Softback
305 × 235 mm
c. 30 colour and b/w images
ISBN: 978-1-910221-10-5
RRP: £18
UK Release: 31 March 2016
Designed by Joe Gilmore
Edited by Richard Parry
Printed by Team Impression, Leeds
Co-published by Grundy Art Gallery, Blackpool,
and Anomie Publishing, London

Sensory Systems documents an engaging group exhibition presented at the Grundy Art Gallery, Blackpool, in autumn 2015. The exhibition was the first in an annual programme by the gallery to revolve around the theme of light, and timed to coincide with the famous Blackpool Illuminations – a six-mile-long outdoor display of lights that has drawn many visitors to the town each year since it was first switched on in 1912.

The exhibition and publication feature works by internationally acclaimed artists interested in the technology and science of light, and how this can be used to affect our perceptual experiences of space. Whether through sculpture, projection or immersive architecture, each artwork presented in the exhibition invited a dialogue with the viewer, utilising colour, pattern, movement and other factors to evoke a variety of spatial and sensory experiences.

The selection of prominent figures working internationally today who feature in the exhibition and publication are: Angela Bulloch, Rafael Lozano-Hemmer, Ann Veronica Janssens, Anthony McCall and Conrad Shawcross. Among these, Anthony McCall was one of the early pioneers in the field, alongside figures such as James Turrell, Mary Corse, Robert Irwin, Carlos Cruz-Diez and Dan Flavin. McCall, who moved to New York from England in the early 1970s, was highly influential with his 'solid light' installations. In this exhibition and publication, McCall presents *You and I, Horizontal* (2005), a slowly evolving, curving sculpture made of light.

The publication includes a foreword by Richard Parry, Curator at the Grundy Art Gallery and an essay by Dr Luke Skrebowski, Director of Studies in History of Art at Churchill College at the University of Cambridge. The project has been supported by Blackpool Council, Coastal Communities Fund, Arts Council England, and is co-published by the Grundy Art Gallery and Anomie Publishing.

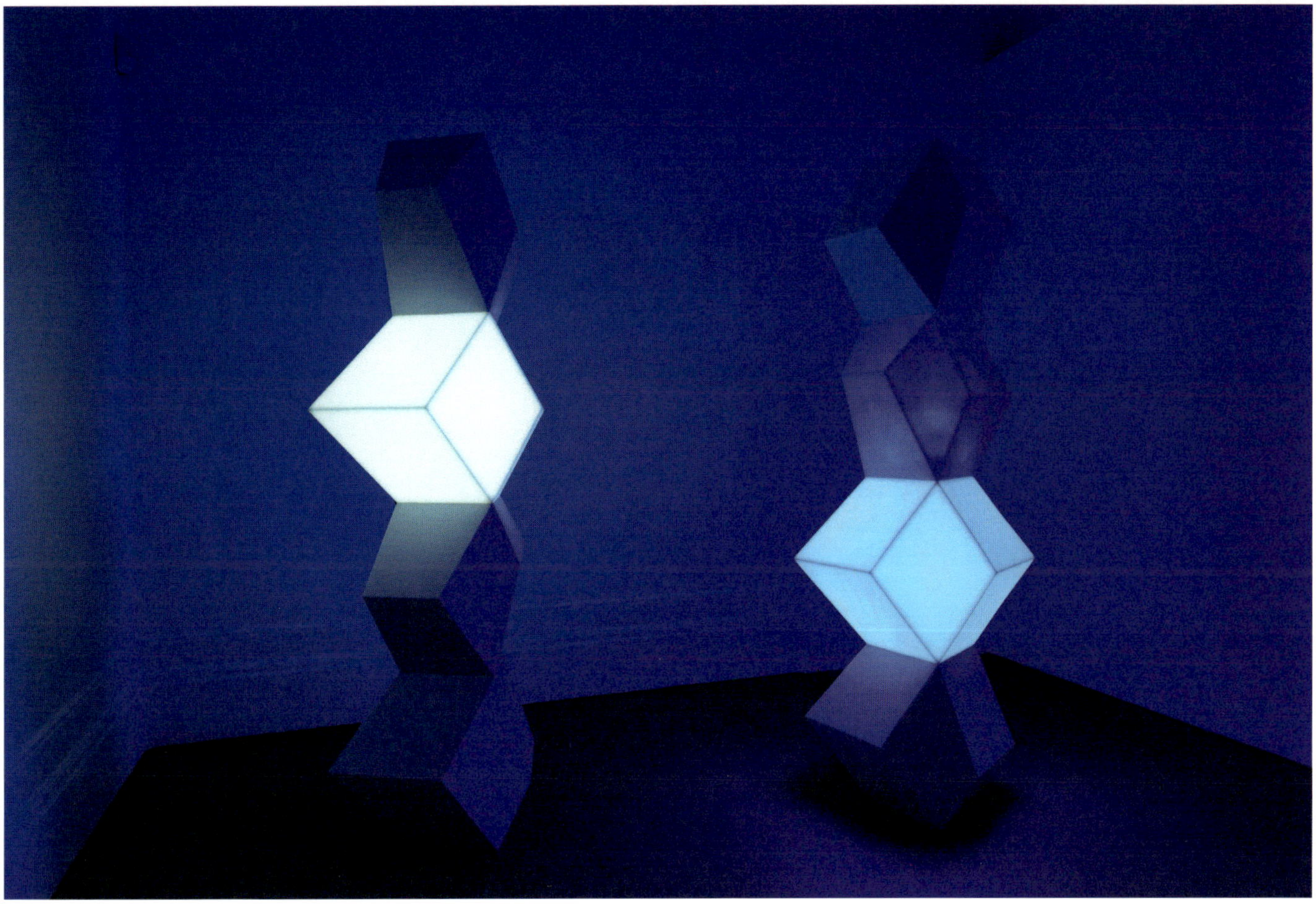

Angela Bullock
Anima Eve and *Animus Ernest*, both 2015
Courtesy of the artist and Simon Lee Gallery,
London and Hong Kong

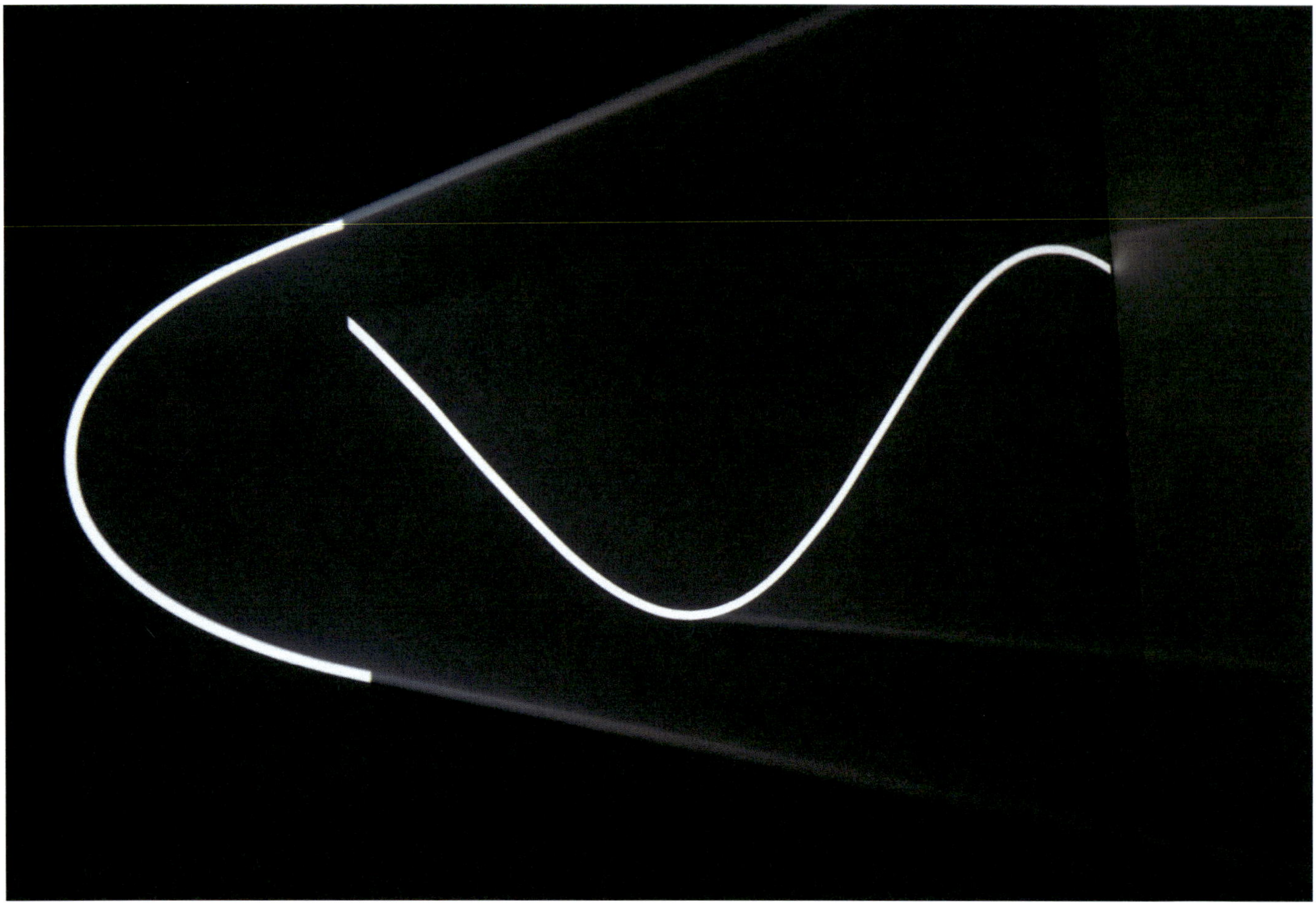

Anthony McCall
You and I, Horizontal, 2005
Courtesy of the artist

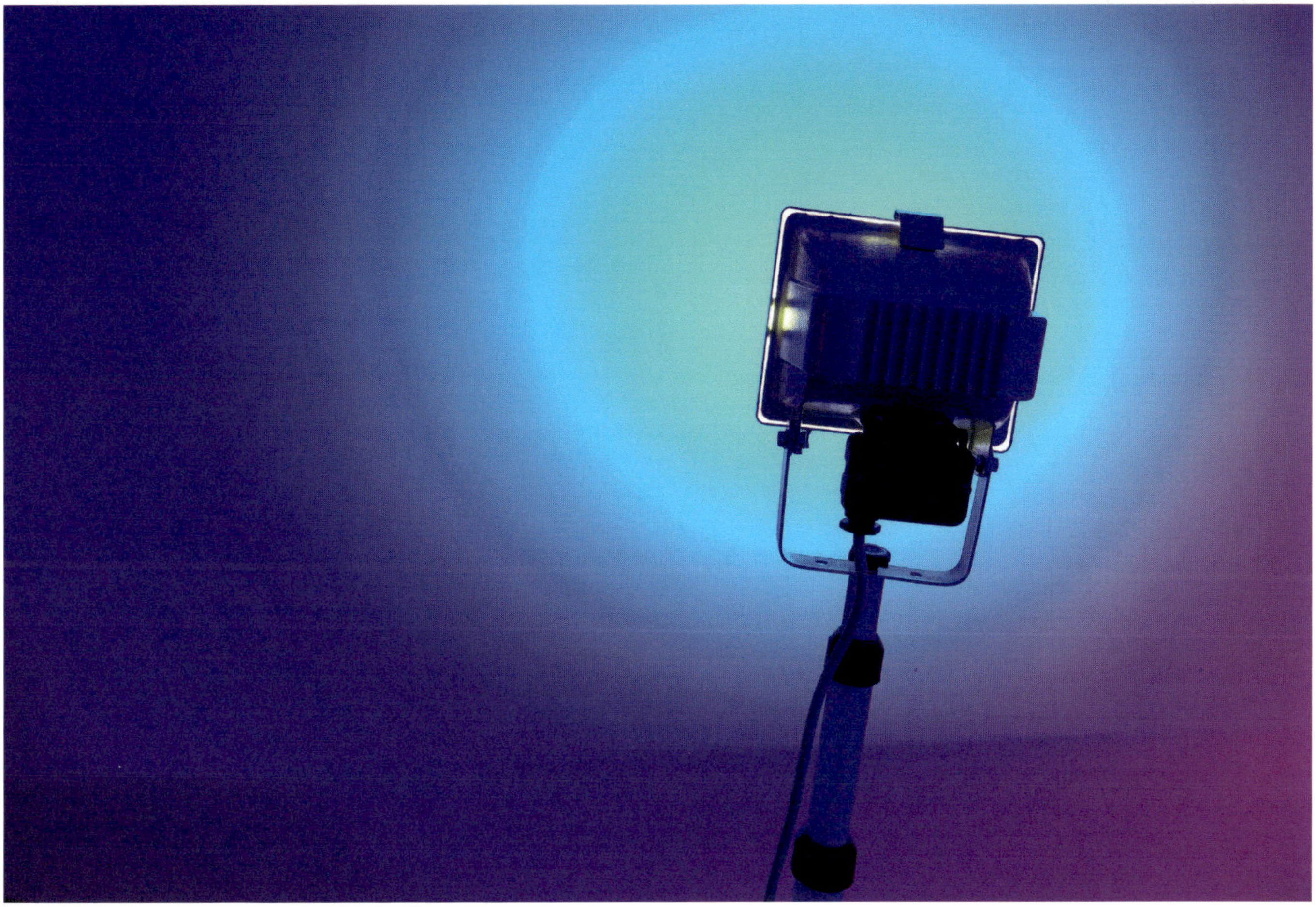

Ann Veronica Janssens
Red & Turquoise, 2005
Courtesy of the artist and Esther Schipper, Berlin

All photos © Grundy Art Gallery

Wolfe von Lenkiewicz

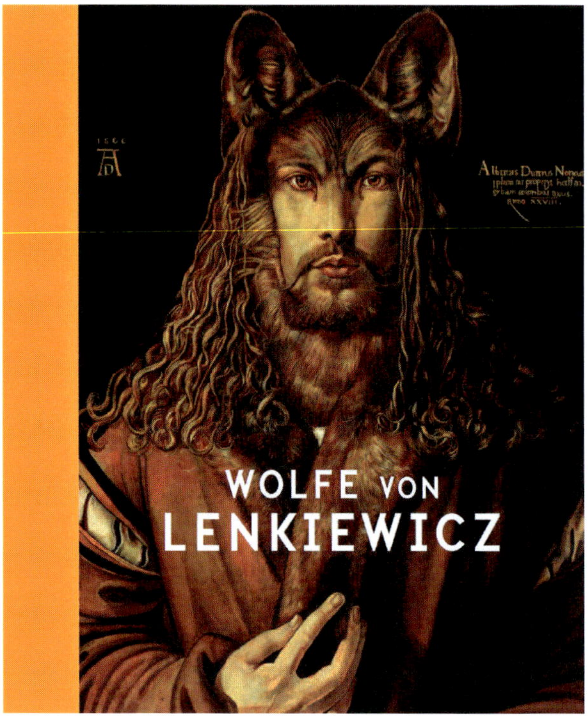

Contributors:
Richard Dyer
Edward Lucie-Smith

236pp
Hardback
320 × 268 mm
c. 150 colour and b/w images
ISBN: 978-1-910221-09-9
RRP: £45
UK Release: 21 January 2016
Designed by Peter B. Willberg with James Sutton
Edited by Mark Sanders
Printed by Castelli Bolis, Italy
Published by Anomie Publishing, London

This is the first major monograph on the work of one of Britain's most dynamic artists, Wolfe von Lenkiewicz. His striking paintings and drawings mine the hallowed halls of art history and popular culture in search of visual languages, imagery, themes and motifs that he can appropriate, adapt, use and abuse, bringing together different movements, genres, periods and styles in dialogues that are surprising, innovative, challenging and sometimes provocative.

Lenkiewicz's imagination and energy seem to be inexhaustible, concocting endless amazing hybrids such as iconic Renaissance paintings invaded by characters from nineteenth-century Japanese woodblocks, French Revolutionary masterpieces spliced with German Romanticism and the sublime, or Cubism infiltrated by Victorian children's illustration. The result is a peculiar and fantastical cast of characters and scenarios, whether Nazi soldiers trampling through the snow towards a crashed UFO in the middle of a village scene by Pieter Bruegel the Elder, Snow White making an uncomfortable guest appearance in an already troubling Balthus interior, or a guillotined head assuming a cameo role in an otherwise serene still life.

These painterly chimera are cultural mash-ups. Sometimes irreverent, sometimes witty, other times simply beautiful, odd and arresting amalgams, they are always poignant, pertinent and decidedly thought-provoking, inviting the viewer to think across time, cultures, countries and ideologies about the many languages of art.

In the process, Lenkiewicz has established his own distinctive oeuvre, one that perhaps perfectly illustrates the notion of post-modernity within painting – an oeuvre of juxtapositions and non-sequiturs, semantics and semiotics, binary oppositions and the uncanny, pastiche and deconstruction, ruptures and elisions, the real and the irrational. As well as encouraging us to look at works from the history of art with fresh eyes, Lenkiewicz's practice demands that we think about visual culture today, raising questions about how our understanding of the past and the present rests on shifting sands.

With an introduction by distinguished art critic Edward Lucie-Smith and a major new essay by writer and editor Richard Dyer, this beautiful clothbound hardback book presents an impressive selection of works produced by the artist between 2009 and 2015.

Born in 1966 and based in London, Lenkiewicz is of German and Polish descent; he studied philosophy at York University, graduating in 1990, and is the son of the painter Robert Lenkiewicz and great grandson of Baron von Schlossberg, court painter to King Ludwig II of Bavaria, the Swan King.

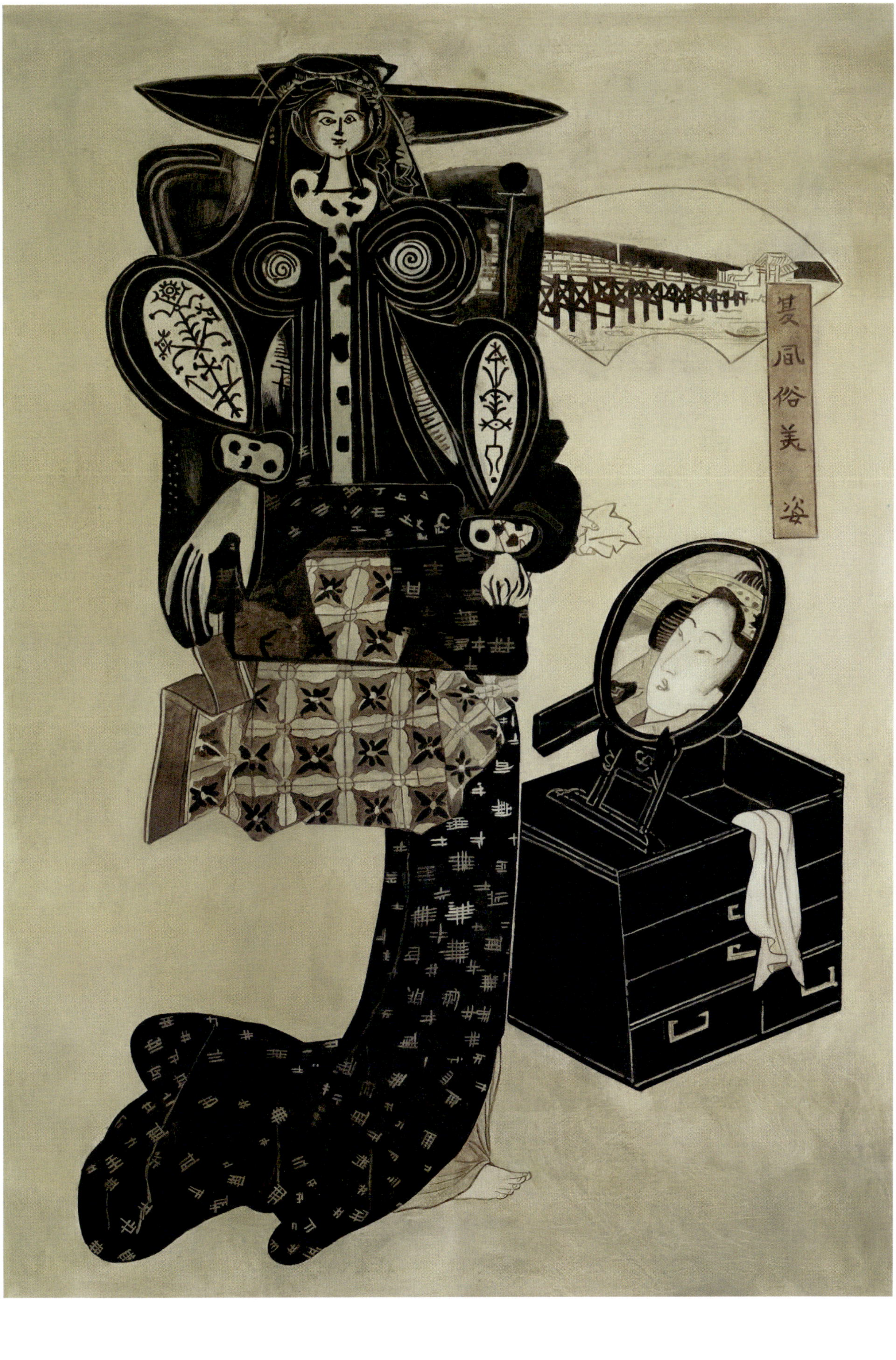
風俗美姿

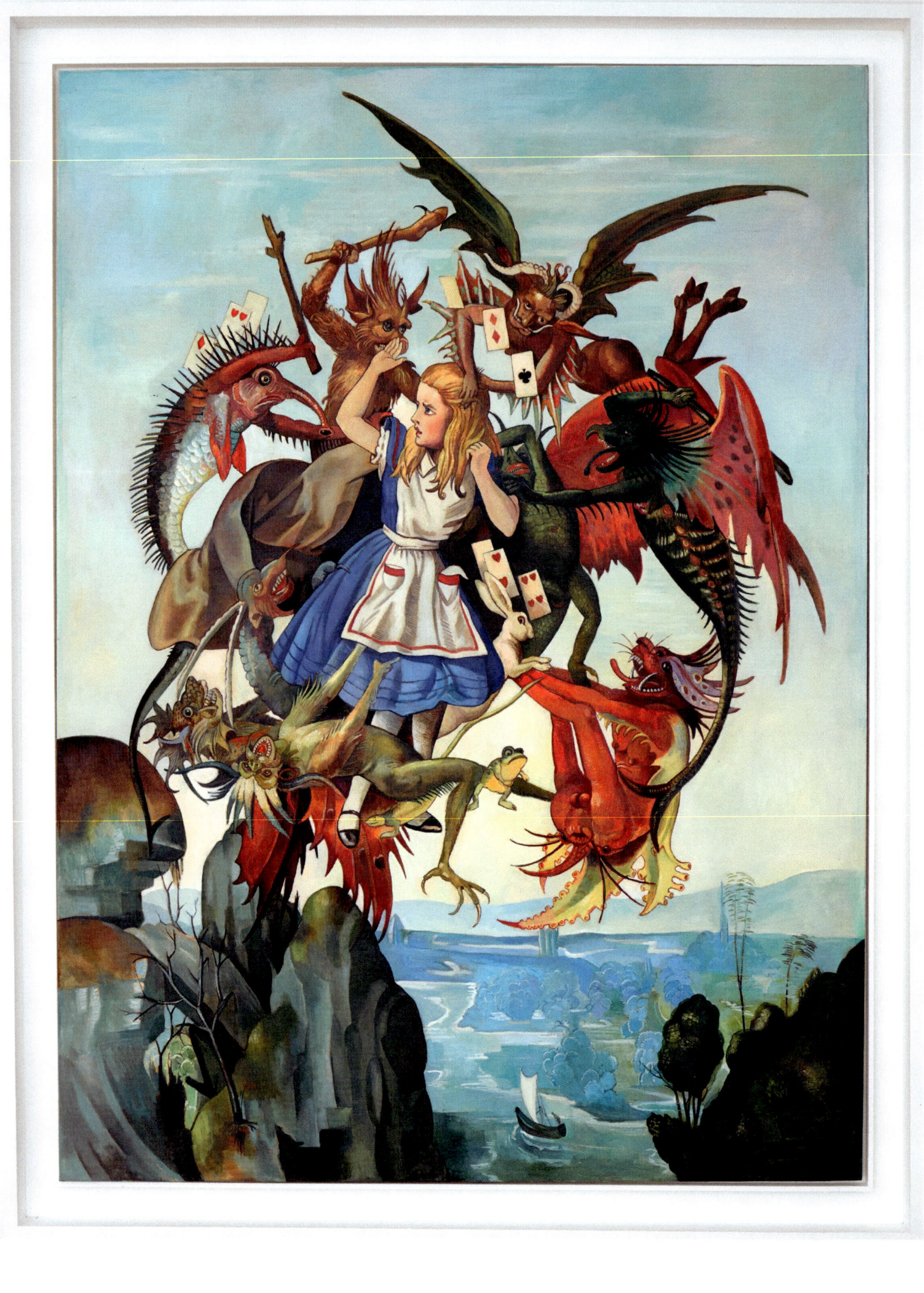

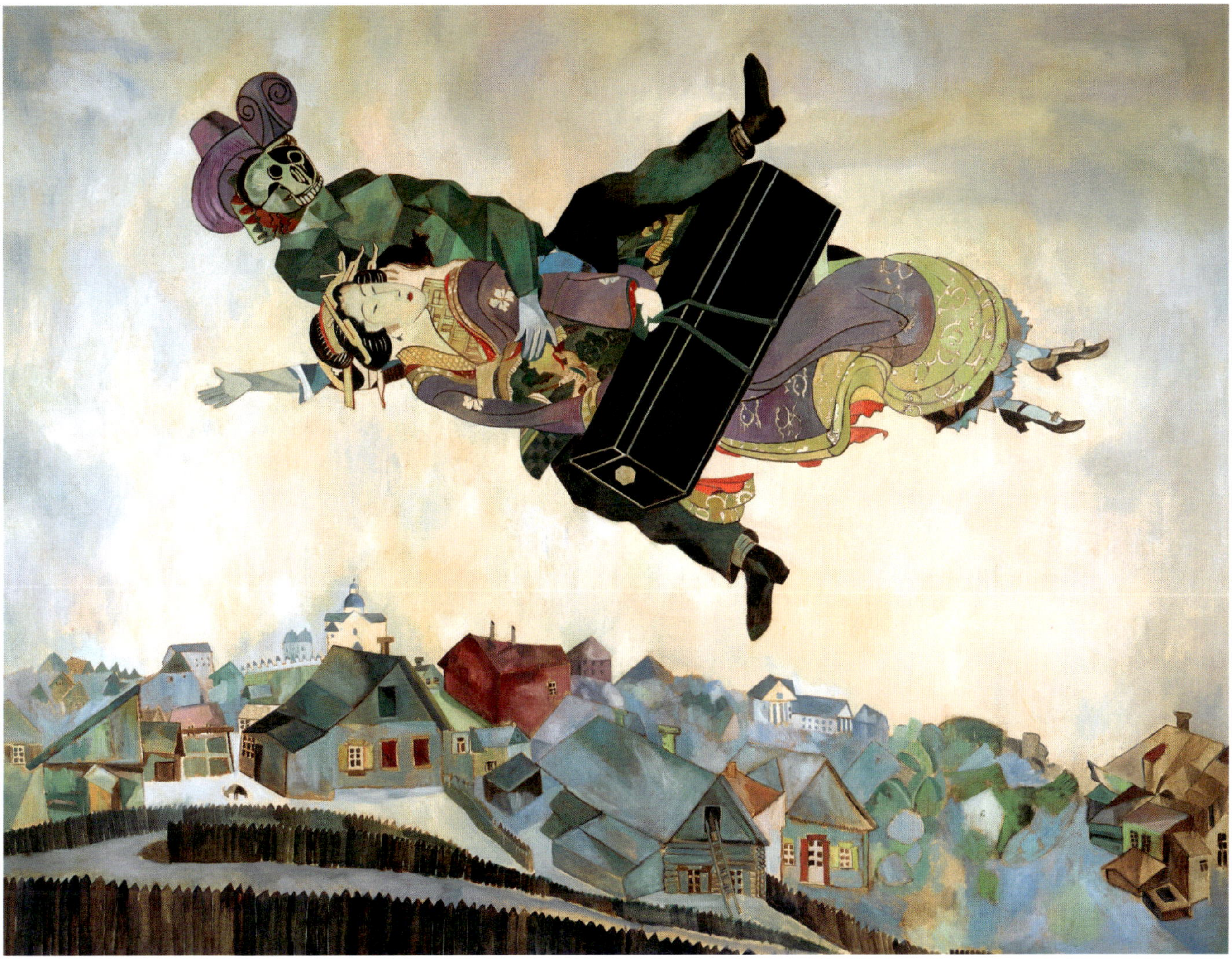

Wolfe von Lenkiewicz
You're Nothing but a Pack of Cards, 2011
Oil on canvas
190 × 140 cm
Photo: Tessa Angus

Wolfe von Lenkiewicz
Over the Town, 2009
Oil on canvas
280 × 370 cm
Photo: Tessa Angus

p. 173
Wolfe von Lenkiewicz
Girl before the Mirror, 2015
Oil on canvas
300 × 200 cm
Photo: Andy Romer

All courtesy of Wolfe von Lenkiewicz

LightScape: James Turrell at Houghton Hall

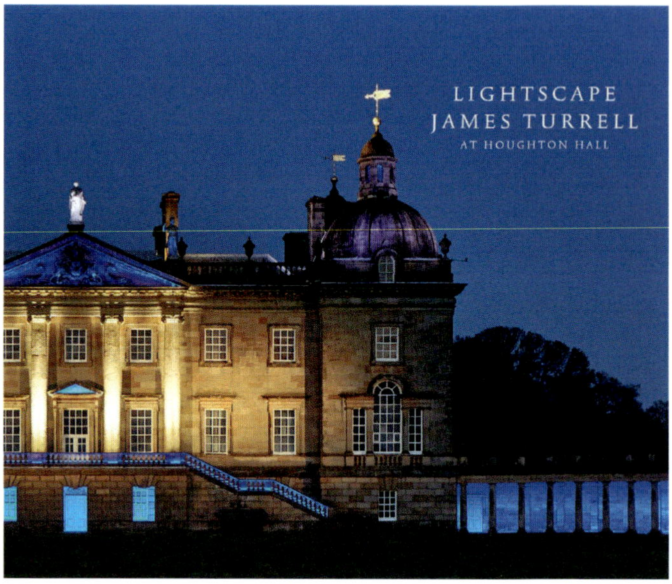

Contributors:
Peter Murray
Hiram C. Butler
David Cholmondeley

102pp
Hardback, clothbound with dustjacket
260 × 300 mm
c. 60 colour and b/w images
ISBN: 978-0-9932882-0-3
RRP: £35
UK Release: 10 December 2015
Designed by Peter B. Willberg
Edited by David Cholmondeley
Published by Houghton Hall in association with
Anomie Publishing, London

James Turrell is widely acknowledged as one of the most important artists working today. From the mid 1960s onwards his principal concern has been the way we apprehend light and space. His study of mathematics and perceptual psychology, as well as his Quaker upbringing and background as a pilot, inform his practice. His first exhibition in 1967 of 'projection pieces' used high-intensity light projectors to give the illusion of a solid geometrical object, often seemingly floating in space. From these investigations of light, Turrell went on to begin his series of *Skyspaces*. These are enclosed viewing chambers that affect our perception of the sky.

Since then he has continued to create works using light as his medium. Perhaps his most celebrated works are his *Ganzfeld chambers*, whole spaces immersed in light, as well as his more recent *Tall Glass* series, which resemble windows of slowly changing colour. Meanwhile, Turrell continues work on a monumental project at Roden Crater, an extinct volcano in Arizona. Here he has created a series of viewing chambers, tunnels and apertures to heighten our sense of the heavens and earth in one of the most ambitious artistic endeavours of modern times.

In summer/autumn 2015, Houghton Hall, Norfolk, hosted an ambitious and significant exhibition of James Turrell's light pieces, many collected by the Marquess of Cholmondeley, owner of Houghton, who has long been an admirer of his work. This publication was produced to document and accompany the exhibition. A project devoted to James Turrell's work had been a long-held ambition of Lord Cholmondeley, who discovered it twenty years ago, and who in 2000 invited him to Houghton Hall to install a *Skyspace* among the trees on the west side of the house. Soon afterwards, a rusty water tank was removed from an eighteenth-century folly in the park to make way for his atmospheric interior space, *St Elmo's Breath*.

The exhibition was centred around works from the Houghton collection, which also includes projections, a *Tall Glass*, holograms and prints. The exhibition was complemented by further loans to help illustrate the broad spectrum of Turrell's work, and a unique, site-specific installation was created especially for Houghton – *The Illumination* – lighting the whole west façade of the house that could be viewed from dusk.

LightScape follows three highly acclaimed exhibitions by Turrell in 2013/14 at the Guggenheim, New York, the Los Angeles County Museum of Art and the Museum of Fine Arts, Houston. The publication, which was supported by Christie's and PACE, is essential reading for all admirers of Turrell's oeuvre.

James Turrell
Shirim, 2015

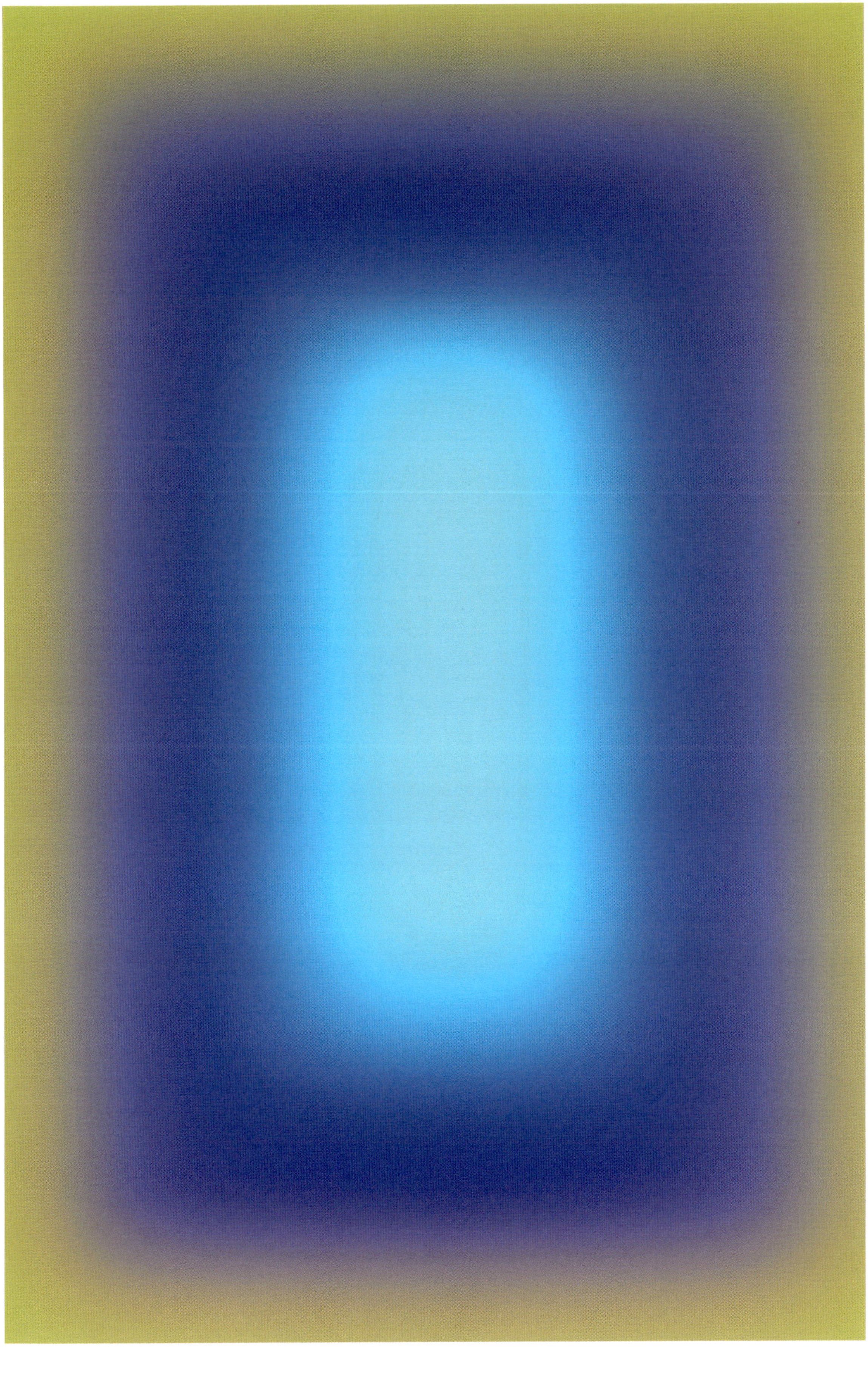

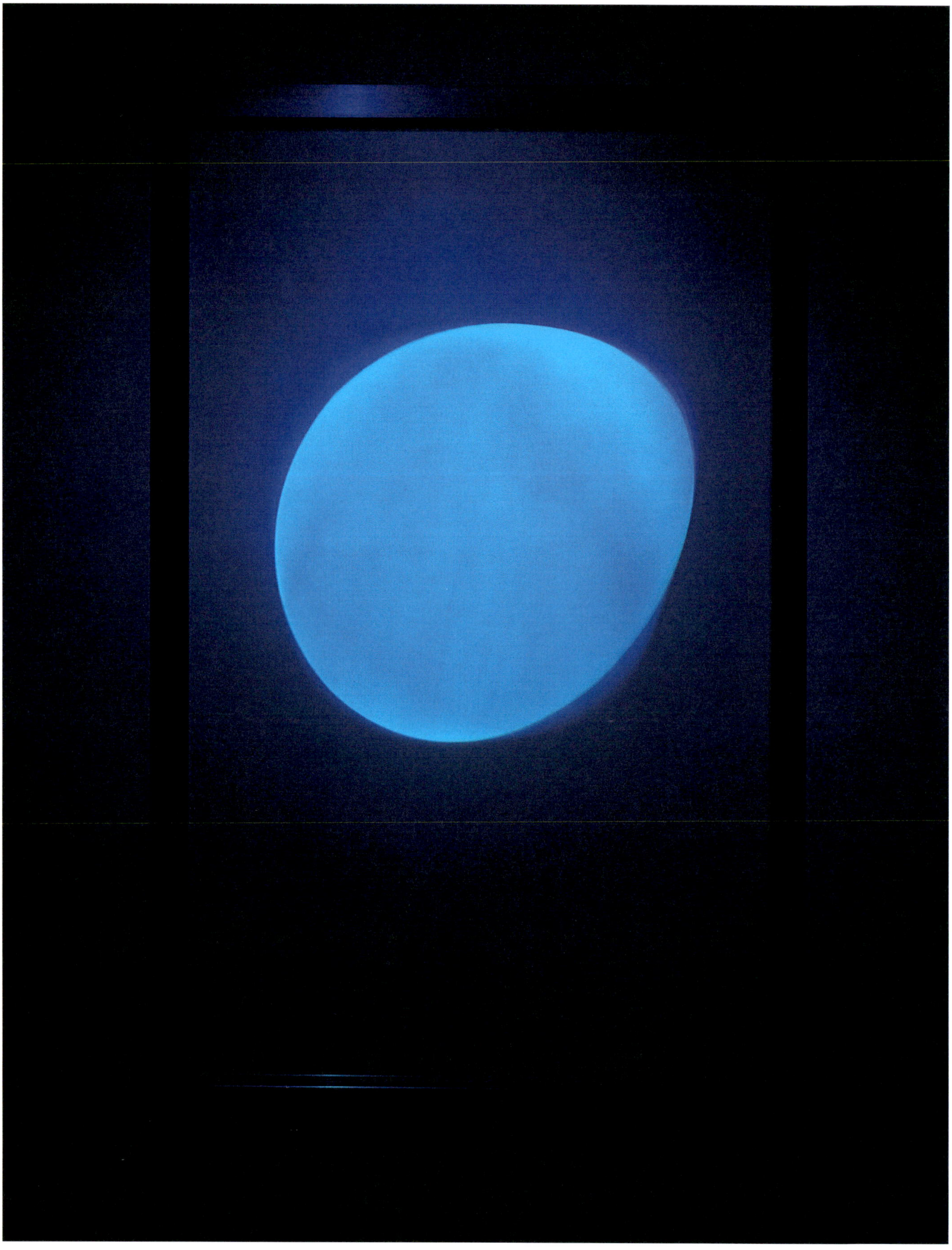

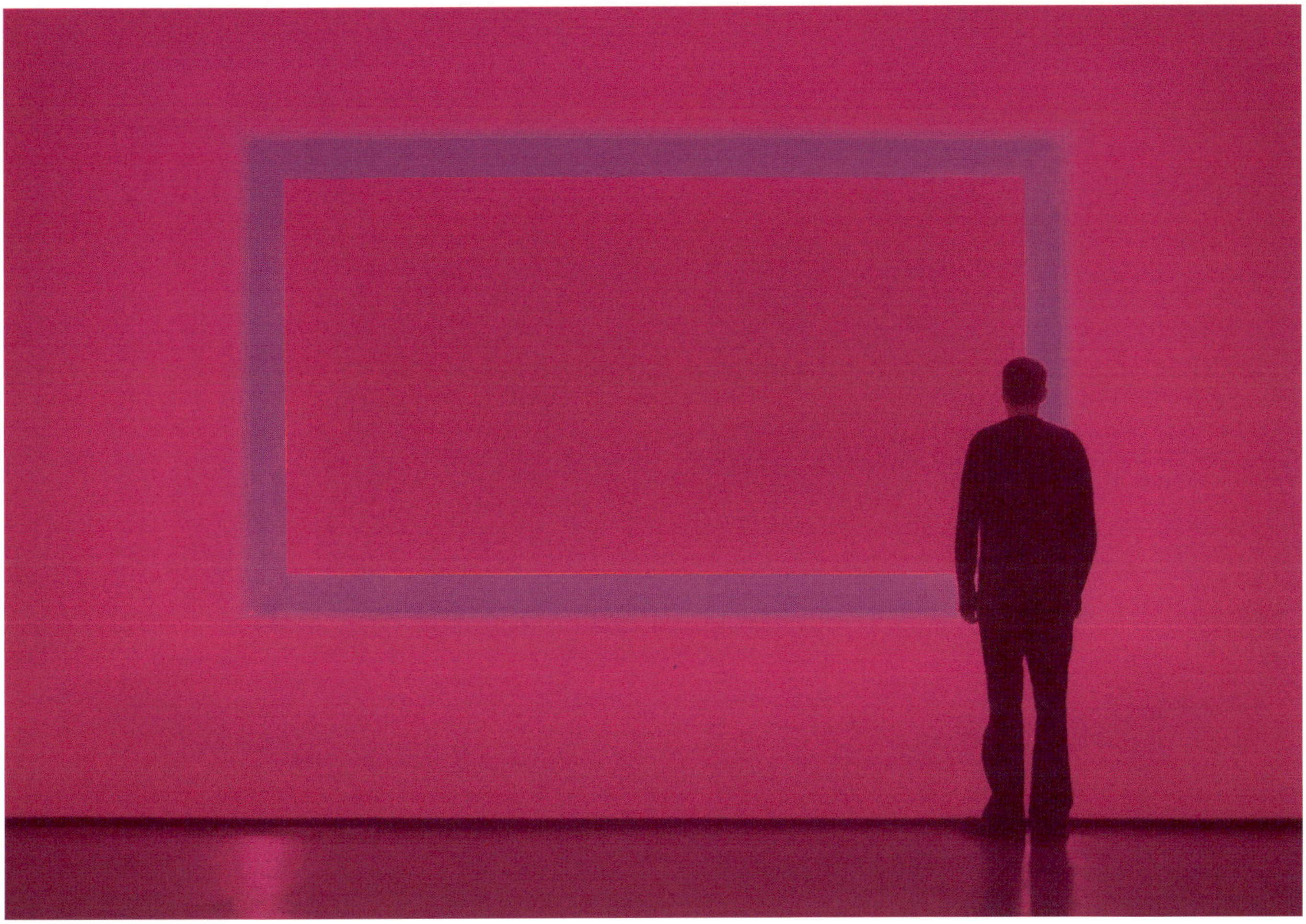

James Turrell
Untitled, 2010

James Turrell
Raemar Magenta, 1970

All © James Turrell
Photos: Pete Huggins

Nathan Coley
to the Bramley Family of Frestonia

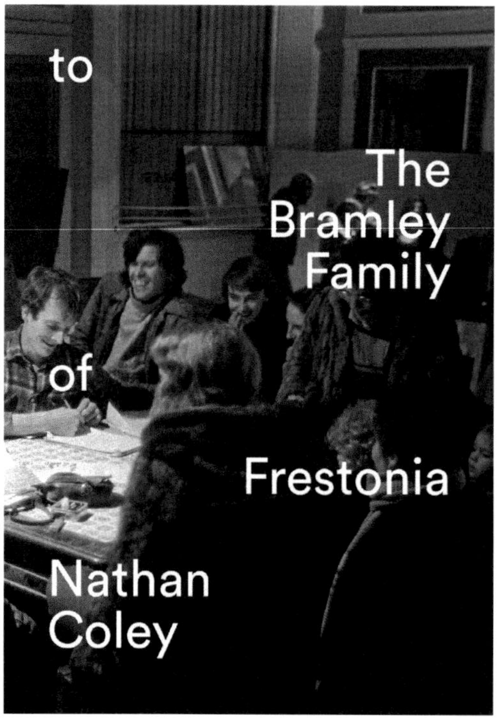

Contributors:
Nathan Coley

190pp
Softback
210 × 148 mm
c. 60 colour and b/w images
ISBN: 978-1-910221-05-1
RRP: £24
UK Release: 11 September 2015
Designed by Hector Pottie
Edited by Moira Jeffrey
Printed by Identity Print, UK
Published by Anomie Publishing, London

to the Bramley Family of Frestonia is a publication documenting a public art project in London by Glasgow-based artist Nathan Coley.

In the mid-late 1960s, the Greater London Council moved local authority tenants out of their run-down terraced houses in the Freston Road area of the Royal Borough of Kensington and Chelsea and into newly built blocks of flats nearby. The Greater London Council was planning to knock down the terraced houses and to regenerate the area, but the plans were beset by delays so the houses lay derelict for almost a decade. During the 1970s a group of squatters began moving in – there were around 150 people living in 35 houses at one point. The group, which was an eclectic mixture of free-thinkers, hippies, creatives, drop-outs and activists, became a somewhat radicalised community calling themselves the 'Free Independent State of Frestonia', taking the name from Freston Road. The squatters printed their own stamps, had their own passports and even applied to the UN for independence from the rest of the United Kingdom. In a legal manoeuvre to prevent the authorities from evicting them without rehousing them, the members of the community made themselves into one large family and changed their surname to Bramley, the name of another road on the estate. The residents of Frestonia developed a strong social fabric and complex cultural life before it fell into decline due to crime, drugs and social problems.

In late summer 2015, on the site where Frestonia once stood, the first phase of apartments designed by Haworth Tompkins Architects and built by the charitable organisation The Peabody Trust was completed and its new residents moved in. With a third of the properties for sale, a third for rent, and a third under the management of the Housing Association, the complex, called The Silchester (More West) development, consists of 112 apartments.

Nathan Coley (b. 1967) was commissioned to make new artwork for the site. With its shapes and forms based on those of an apple tree – inspired by the history of the Bramley apple that gave its name to the Frestonia residents – Coley not only made a striking steel and gold leaf rooftop sculpture, but also 112 small versions of the same sculpture that were given to each of the residents as a house-warming present. In so doing, Coley not only connected the new housing complex and its residents with its history, but to wider discourses of modernism and sculpture, art and society, capitalism and alternative modes of living, hegemony and dissent.

The publication, which forms part of the artist's commissioned project, presents a variety of texts, images and documentation relating to the new housing development, to the history of the Bramley apple and to Frestonia – including a selection of archive photographs of Frestonia taken by former resident Tony Sleep.

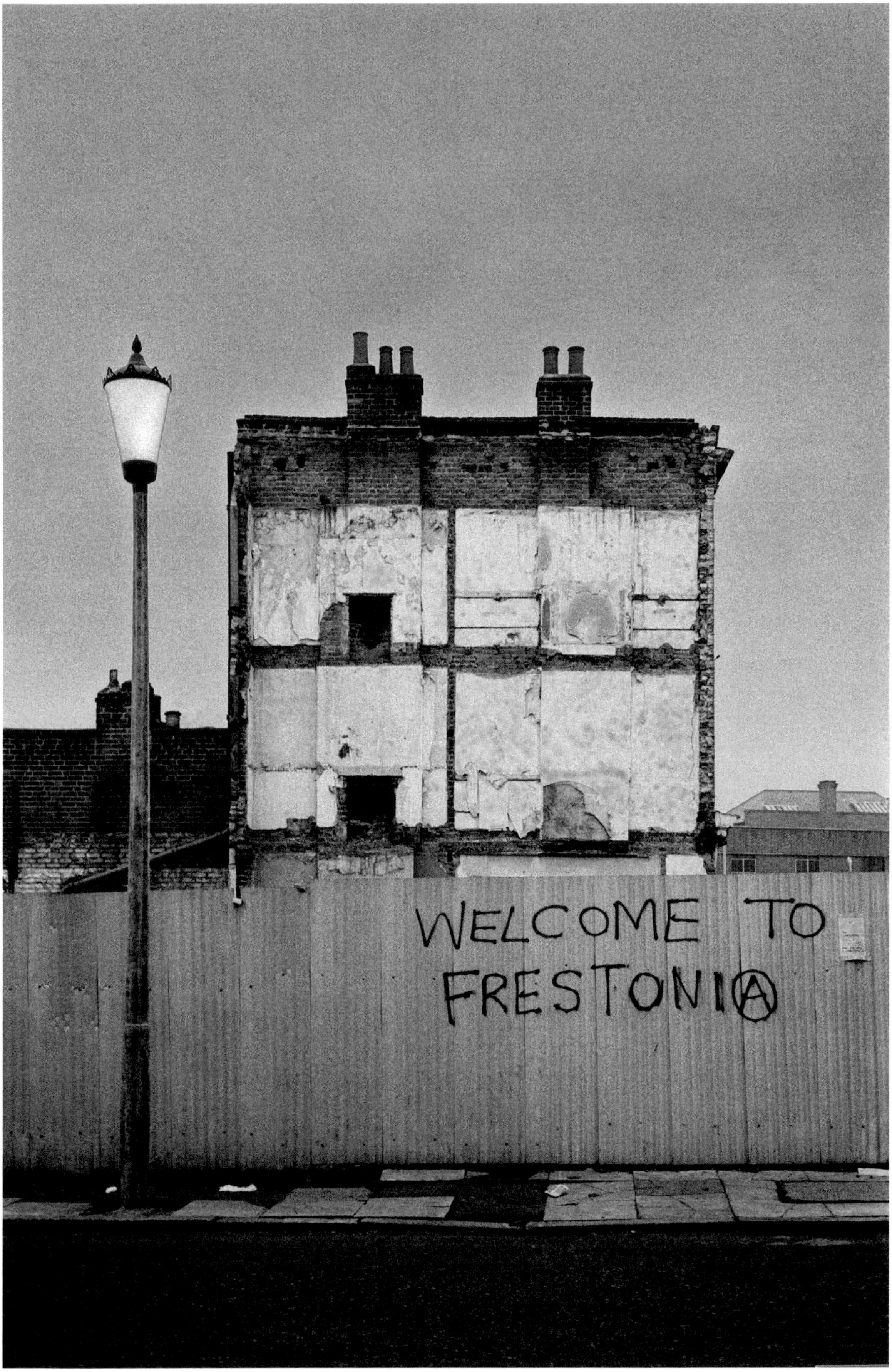
WELCOME TO
FRESTONIA

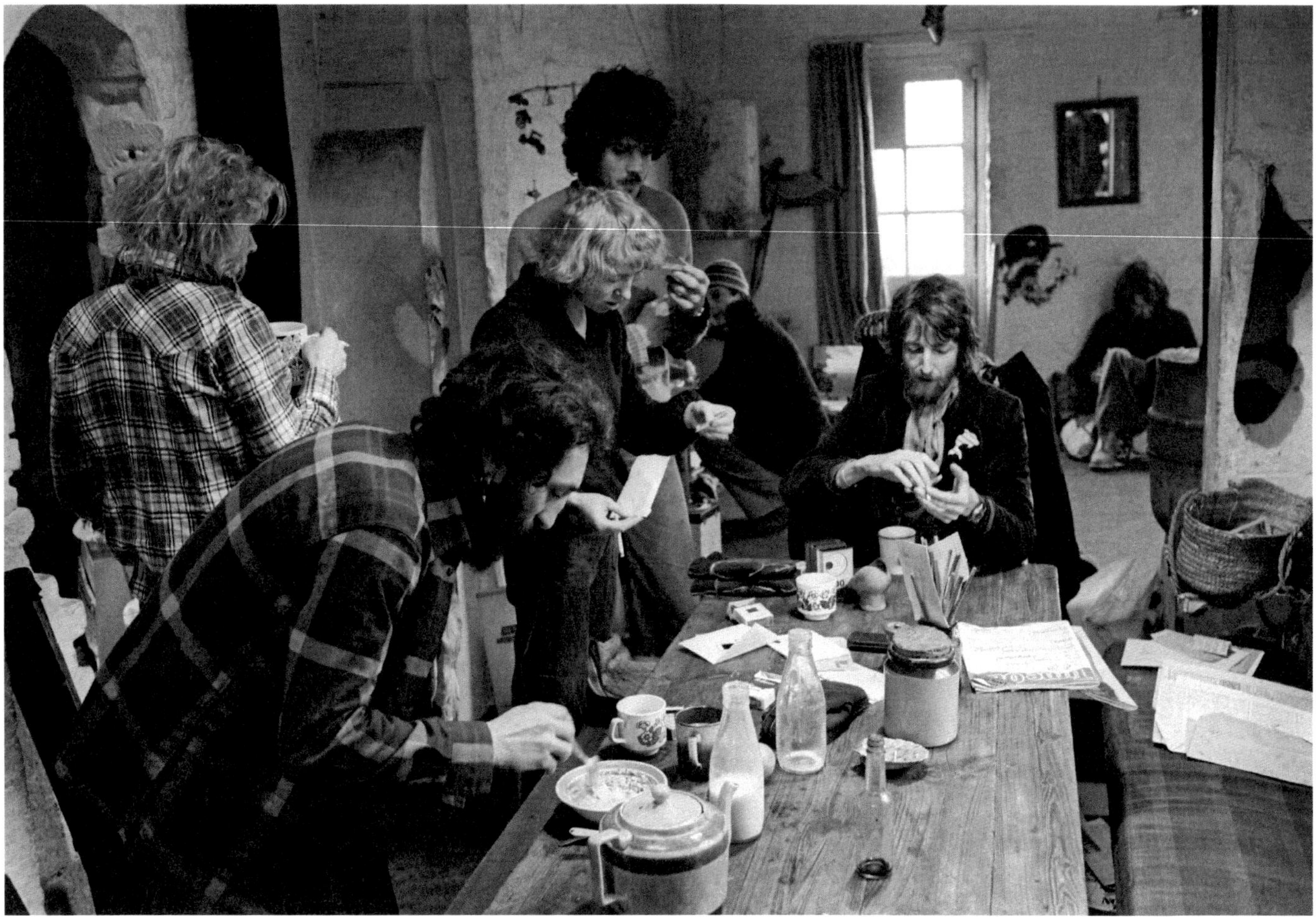

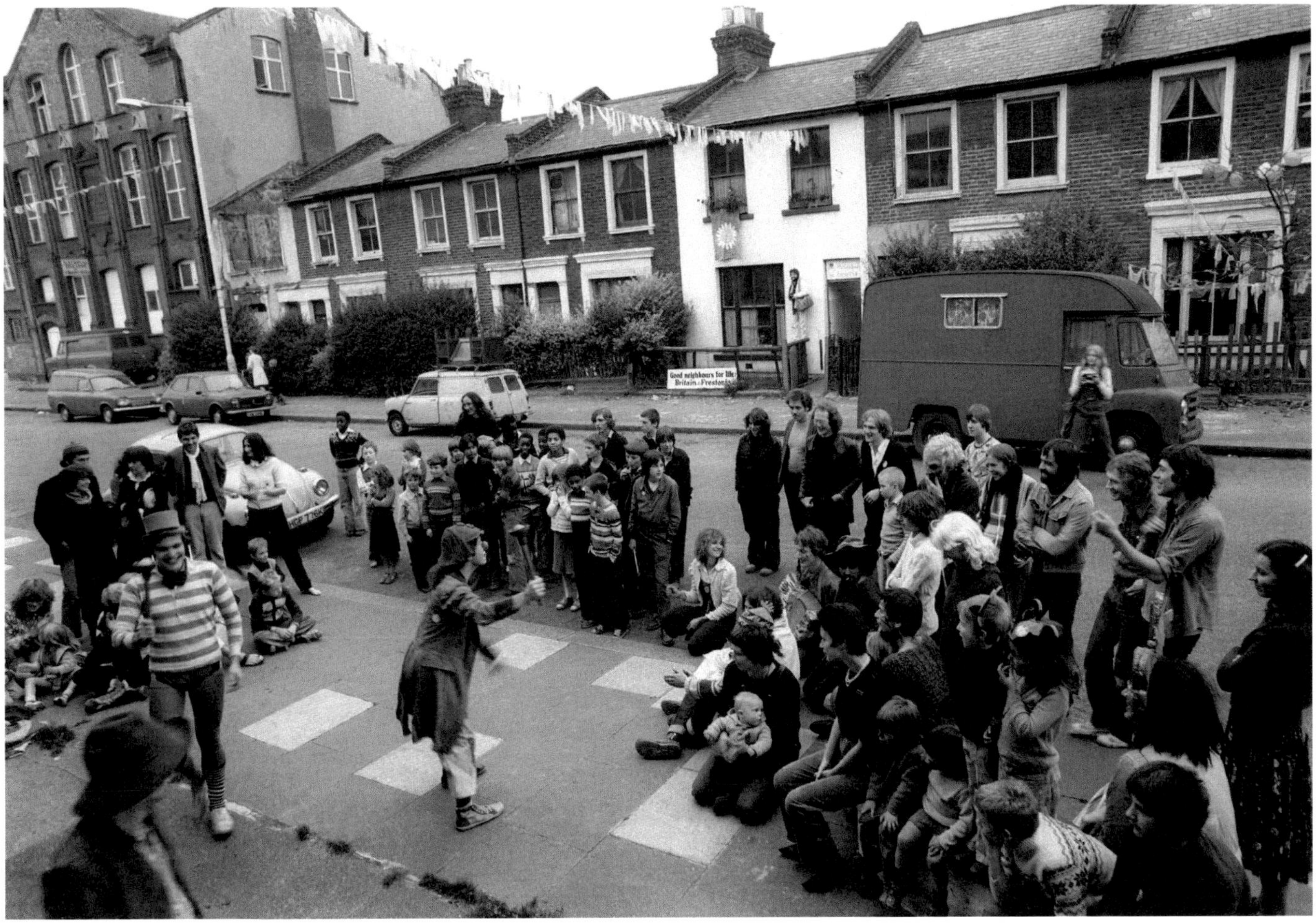

Photographic documentation of Frestonia,
mid-late 1970s by former Frestonia resident
Tony Sleep
© Tony Sleep

Benjamin Senior
Breathless

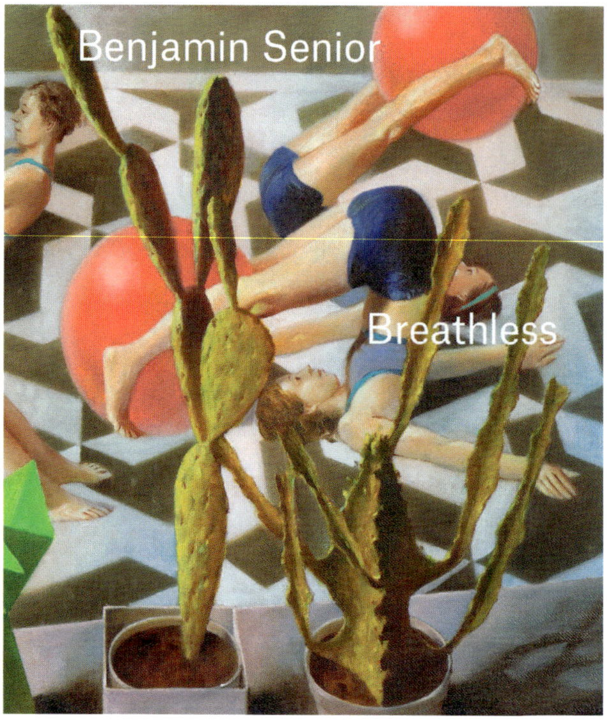

Contributors:
Sacha Craddock
Ben Street
Gabor Gyory

100pp
Hardback
225 × 195 mm
c. 60 images
ISBN: 978-1-910221-06-8
RRP: £25
UK Release: 9 July 2015
Designed by Joe Gilmore
Printed by Pression, UK
Published by Anomie Publishing, London

Breathless is the first monograph on the emerging British painter Benjamin Senior. His paintings conjure up a world that is delightful, curious, quirky and distinctly his own. It is a world in which bathers lounge around pools and swimmers limber up before finally diving in; where we find people doing yoga and various exercise routines both indoors and out; where walkers and joggers take us out into the countryside, or into the city with their dogs. These physical activities – both leisure and sporting – would undoubtedly leave some of their protagonists out of breath, as the title of the monograph suggests, and may well inspire some viewers to shake off any lethargy and get physical, too.

But despite their clear iconography and endorphin-rousing semiotics, Senior's paintings are no mere campaign to get, or to keep, art lovers fit and healthy. For they are also carefully conceived and meticulously executed studies of the human body, of shape, line and form, of colour, tone, light and shadow. They are engaging explorations of composition and colour, pattern and geometry, textures and materials, the natural and the manmade. This interplay between the natural and synthetic is played out in surprising juxtapositions, such as blue rubber exercise balls in dialogue with various-sized cacti, or between the materials and designs of sports clothing in contrast to the rolling hills of a spring landscape, or to autumnal trees at sunset.

There are many other intriguing devices and recurring motifs within Senior's repertoire, from cast iron grilles to unorthodox hats and hairstyles, perhaps leading his stylised vocabulary into the realms of nineteenth-century symbolist painting as much as into the health clubs, spas, leisure centres and parks of today. There is a strange sense of timelessness to Senior's practice that is matched by a captivating sense of silence, loneliness and isolation, despite the figures often being present in couples, clusters or small groups. Behind their toned physiques, stripy towels and goggles, underneath their cagoules and peaked caps, there are, perhaps, some small glimmers of inner lives – of sentient, intellectual, cultured, emotional, sexual beings trapped within. Senior's oeuvre is preoccupied with repression and expression, freedom and conformity, motion and stasis, balance and inertia, engagement and disengagement. One might even describe it as a bittersweet analogy of the human body for states of mind, for energy versus futility, effort versus relaxation, health versus decline.

Senior completed a BA in Painting at Wimbledon School of Art before graduating with an MA in Painting from the Royal College of Art in 2010. Recent solo exhibitions include at Grey Noise, Dubai; Studio Voltaire, London; Galleria Monica de Cardenas, Milan; James Fuentes, New York and BolteLang, Zurich.

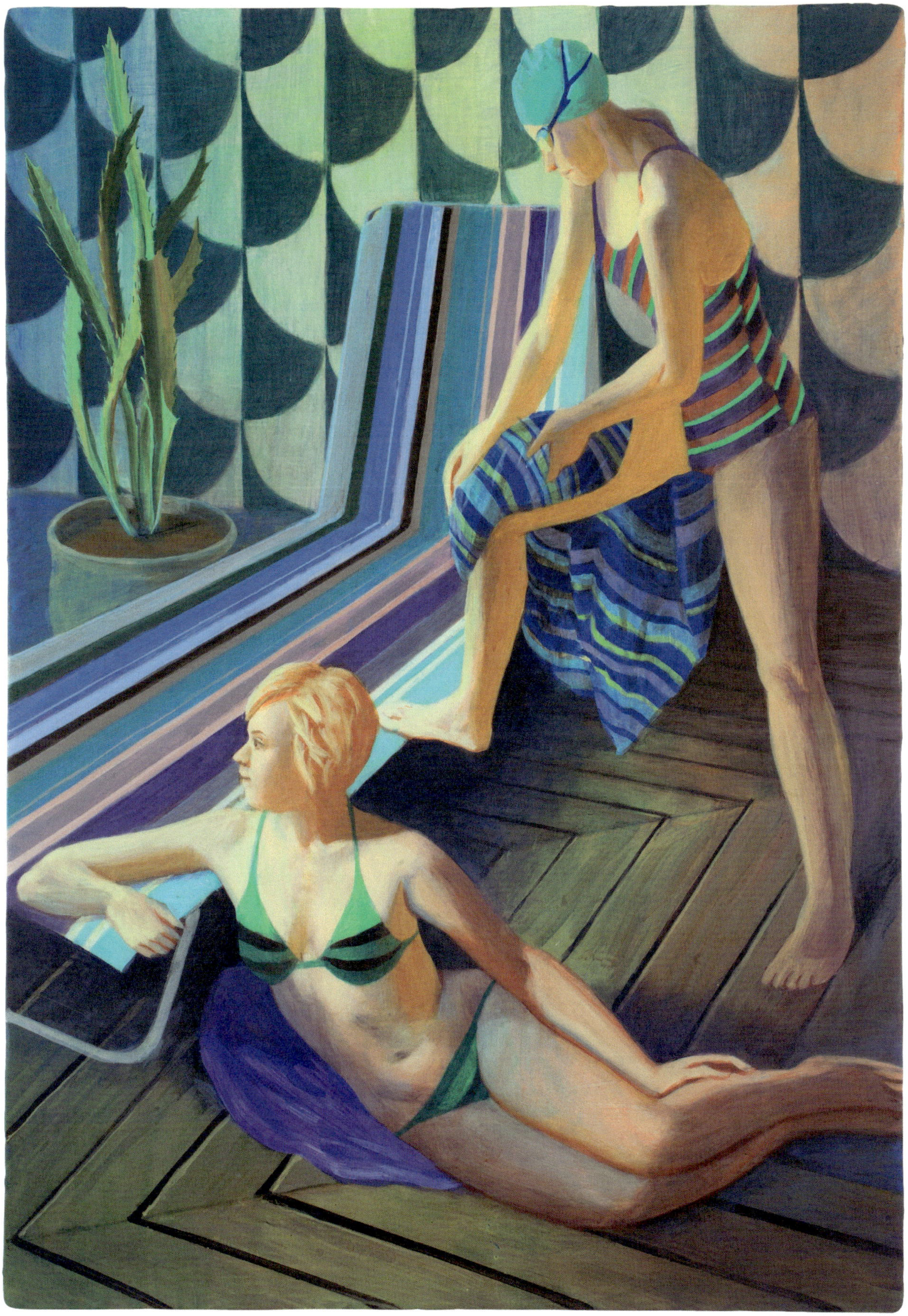

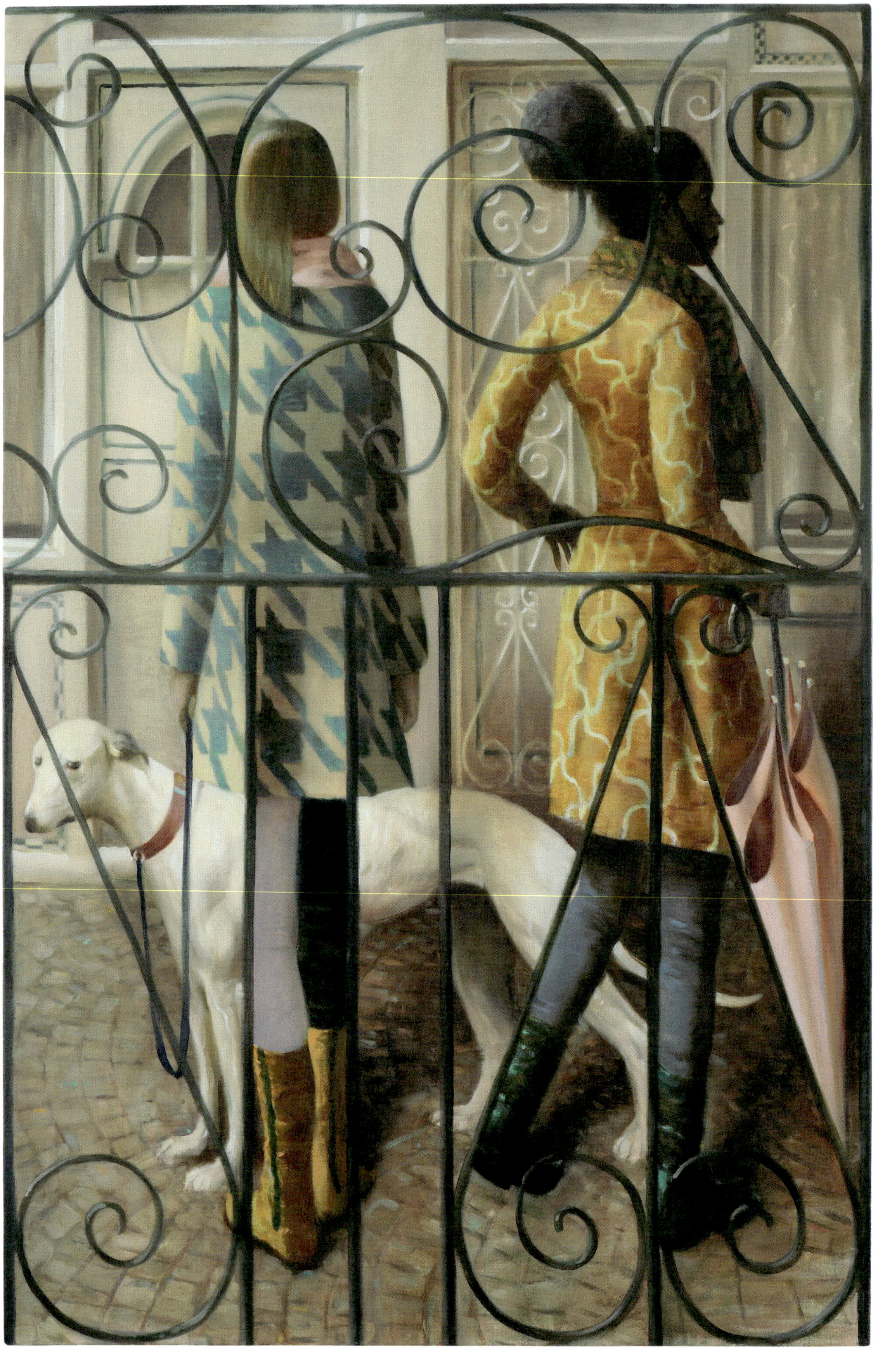

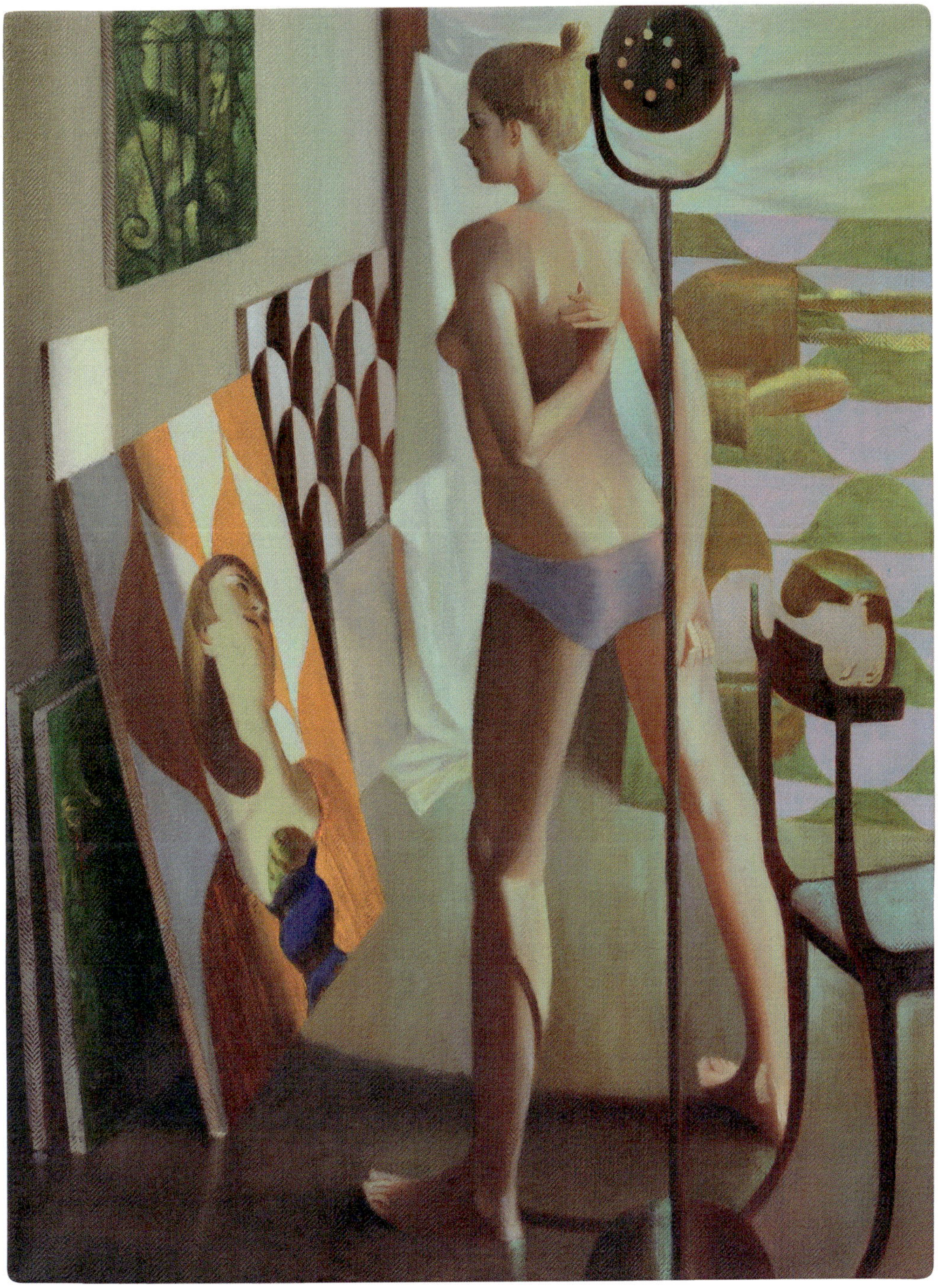

p. 187
Benjamin Senior
Sunbomb, 2012
Egg tempera on cotton on aluminium
60 × 40 cm
Photo: Jason Mandella

Benjamin Senior
Dogtooth Dog Walker, 2015
Oil on linen
150 × 100 cm
Photo: Andy Keate

Benjamin Senior
The Olive Studio, 2014
Oil on linen
82 × 52 cm
Photo: Dave Morgan

All courtesy of the artist and Anomie Publishing

Tamara Tracz
Three Books

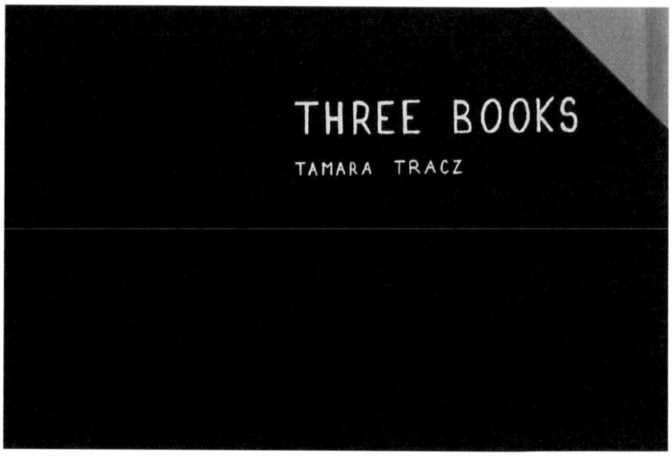

Contributors:
Tamara Tracz

3 volumes, each 72pp
Hardback in slipcase
135 × 210 mm
c. 15 colour and b/w images
ISBN: 978-1-910221-04-4
RRP: £35
UK Release: 1 July 2015
Designed by Tamara Tracz with Herman Lelie
Printed by EBS, Italy
Co-published by Anomie Publishing, London and Parkholme Press

Three Books by Tamara Tracz is a very special three-volume slipcased book. It is a story that follows several generations of a family as their lives unfold in various cities, countries and continents during the course of the twentieth century. It is a story with a cast of characters, some exceptional, some familiar, some curious. It is a story of births and deaths, of lives led and of the forces that shape them.

The family in *Three Books* is Jewish, and the story is one of emigration and persecution that was profoundly affected by the Holocaust. It is a story that is shared with many thousands of other families – of taking flight from the Nazi regime, of German forces arriving in towns and villages and searching out the Jewish inhabitants, of summary executions and mass graves. It is a story of branches of the family destroyed, and of the survival of others. It is as distressing a story as one might fear to read of the plight of the Jews last century.

But *Three Books* is not written in the usual form of family biography, and is not only the story of this family's history. It is also a story about stories, about the passing on of information between generations, and between different branches of a family over time. It is a story about the impossibility of ever being able to tell a complete or truly objective family history. It is a story of fragments and recollections, of oral histories and letters sent, of trying to piece things together to fill in gaps.

Three Books is also partly autobiography, as it is Tracz's own family that is its subject. Indeed, the reader can glean much about the author's life as Tracz consciously lets us in to her immediate family circle, to their happy family life today. With a particular focus on her young children, Riva and Constantin, she shares her fears about being a mother, of the thought of losing her children. These are the thoughts of almost any mother, especially any mother who has heard the stories of mothers, daughters and sisters in her own family's past who experienced such separations and losses through oppression and genocide. It is a story about living and loving, of family, and of the things that remain and the things that slip away.

But while Tracz is in some respects every woman, every mother and every daughter – and a Jewish woman in particular – she is also, quite inimitably, Tamara Tracz. A unique, remarkable and inspiring person, a writer, filmmaker and artist based in London, she does things in ways that only she can. For every word in this book has been handwritten, and reproduced as she planned and drew it. The text does not, therefore, flow as regular lines and pages, but in all manner of configurations, arrangements and patterns, and in such a way as to emphasise the mind's reading of the text just as the voice adds when reading a story aloud. As such, *Three Books* is a form of artist's book, a creative work, a story, a journey and an experience that is not easily forgotten.

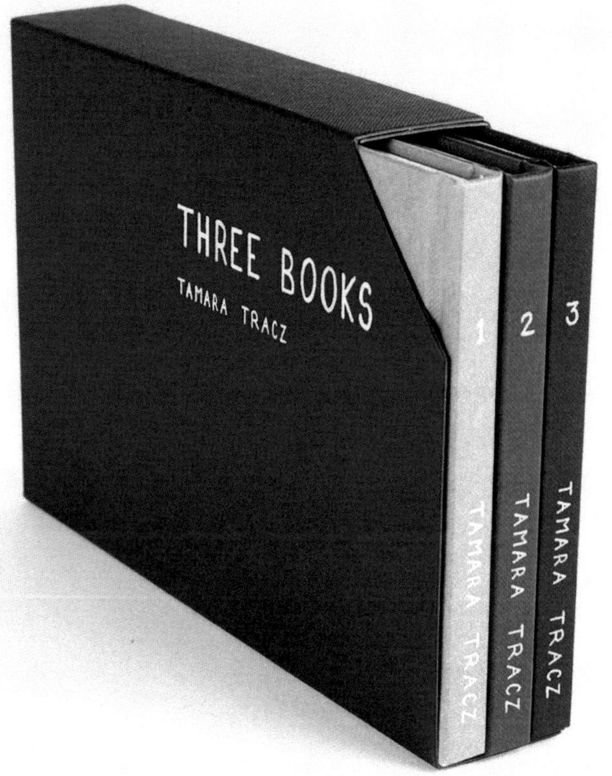
THREE BOOKS
TAMARA TRACZ
1
2
3
TAMARA TRACZ
TAMARA TRACZ
TAMARA TRACZ

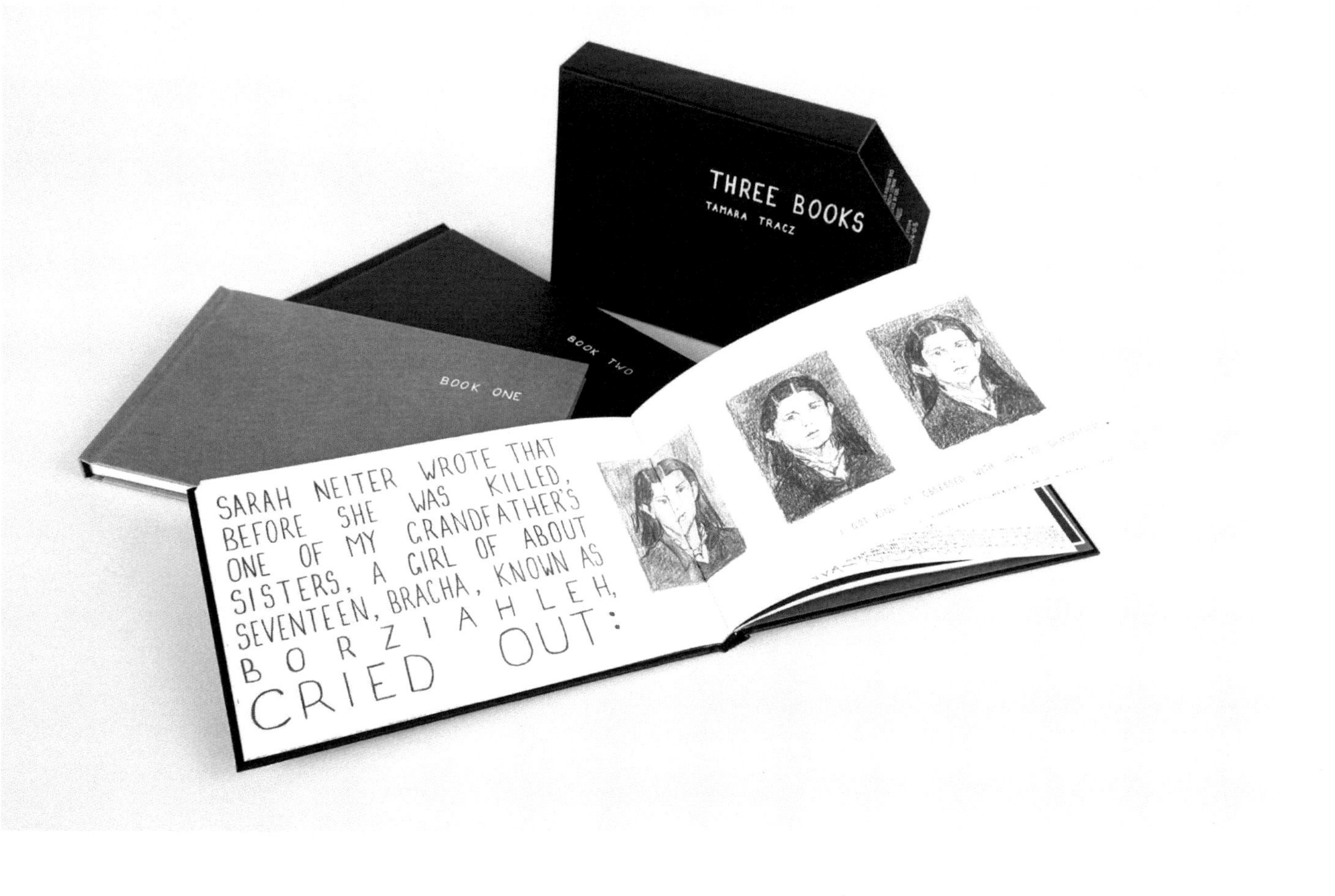
THREE BOOKS
TAMARA TRACZ
BOOK TWO
BOOK ONE
SARAH NEITER WROTE THAT BEFORE SHE WAS KILLED, ONE OF MY GRANDFATHER'S SISTERS, A GIRL OF ABOUT SEVENTEEN, BRACHA, KNOWN AS B O R Z I A H L E H, CRIED OUT:

Sarah Medway
Voyage

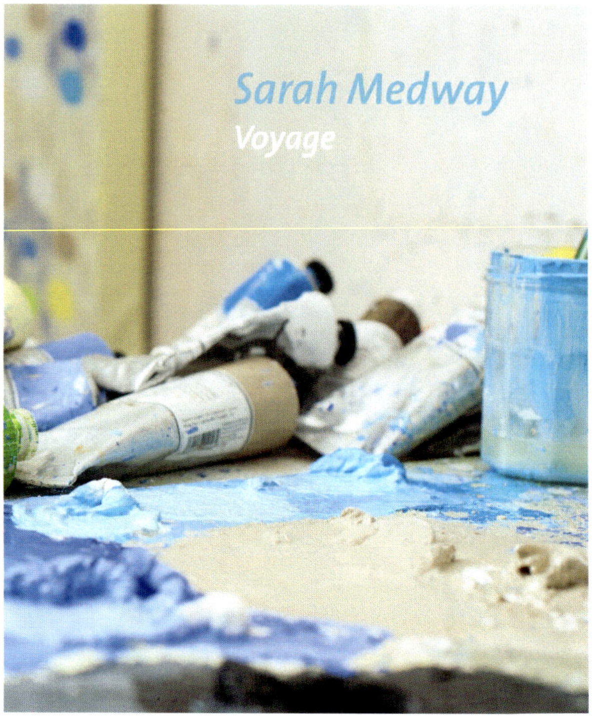

Contributors:
Andrew Lambirth
Sue Hubbard

112pp
Flexibound
260 × 225 mm
c. 75 images
ISBN: 978-1-910221-08-2
RRP: £20
UK Release: 11 June 2015
Designed by Peter B. Willberg with James Sutton
Printed by Castelli Bolis, Italy
Published by Anomie Publishing, London

This publication presents a major body of work by the British artist Sarah Medway commissioned for the new P&O Cruises Britannia. Named by Her Majesty the Queen in spring 2015, the Britannia is the largest and highest-specification cruise ship built by the company to date, making regular voyages into the Med, to the Fjords, to the Canaries, the Caribbean and beyond. This substantial commission – comprising fifty-six paintings – is one of the latest in a long line of commissions by P&O of original works of art by living artists.

Sarah Medway's abstract paintings are a delicate, evocative and sincere investigation into the nature of light as it manifests itself through the myriad environments that surround us. She navigates us through the different seasons, sometimes on foreign shores – from the Mediterranean to Scandinavia and beyond – other times closer to her canal-side studio in central London. She leads us through different times of day and night, from dawn to dusk and long into the night. She takes us up to the skies, into sunlight and shade, clouds and fog, rainbows and sunsets. She takes us into fields, along the coastline, and far out to sea. With her distinctive vocabulary of abstract marks and shimmering palettes, her works build into complex webs of patterns and textures that capture something of the experience of perceiving light, colour and shapes as they filter through the atmosphere into our eyes, minds, memories and subconscious.

Specially commissioned texts by Andrew Lambirth and Sue Hubbard offer an illuminating and insightful introduction to Medway's oeuvre and to this significant new series of paintings. Andrew Lambirth is a writer, critic and curator who has written for a number of publications including *The Sunday Telegraph*, *The Spectator*, *The Sunday Times*, *Modern Painters* and *RA*, the Royal Academy's magazine. He was art critic of *The Spectator* 2002–14. Sue Hubbard is a freelance art critic, novelist, award-winning poet, lecturer and broadcaster. She has written for publications including *Time Out*, *The Independent*, *The New Statesman*, *The Times*, *The Guardian*, *Apollo*, *Tate* and *RA*, the Royal Academy's magazine.

In addition to having participated in group exhibitions at Tate Britain, the Whitechapel, the Royal Academy, the World Trade Center and Austin Museum of Art, Medway has had solo exhibitions at venues including Flowers East, London; Chelsea Hotel, New York; Kienbaum Gallery, Frankfurt; The Mandalai, Thailand and Atelier Gallery, Spain. She has works in many public, private and corporate collections in the UK, US, Germany, Italy, Spain, Belgium, Hong Kong and Thailand.

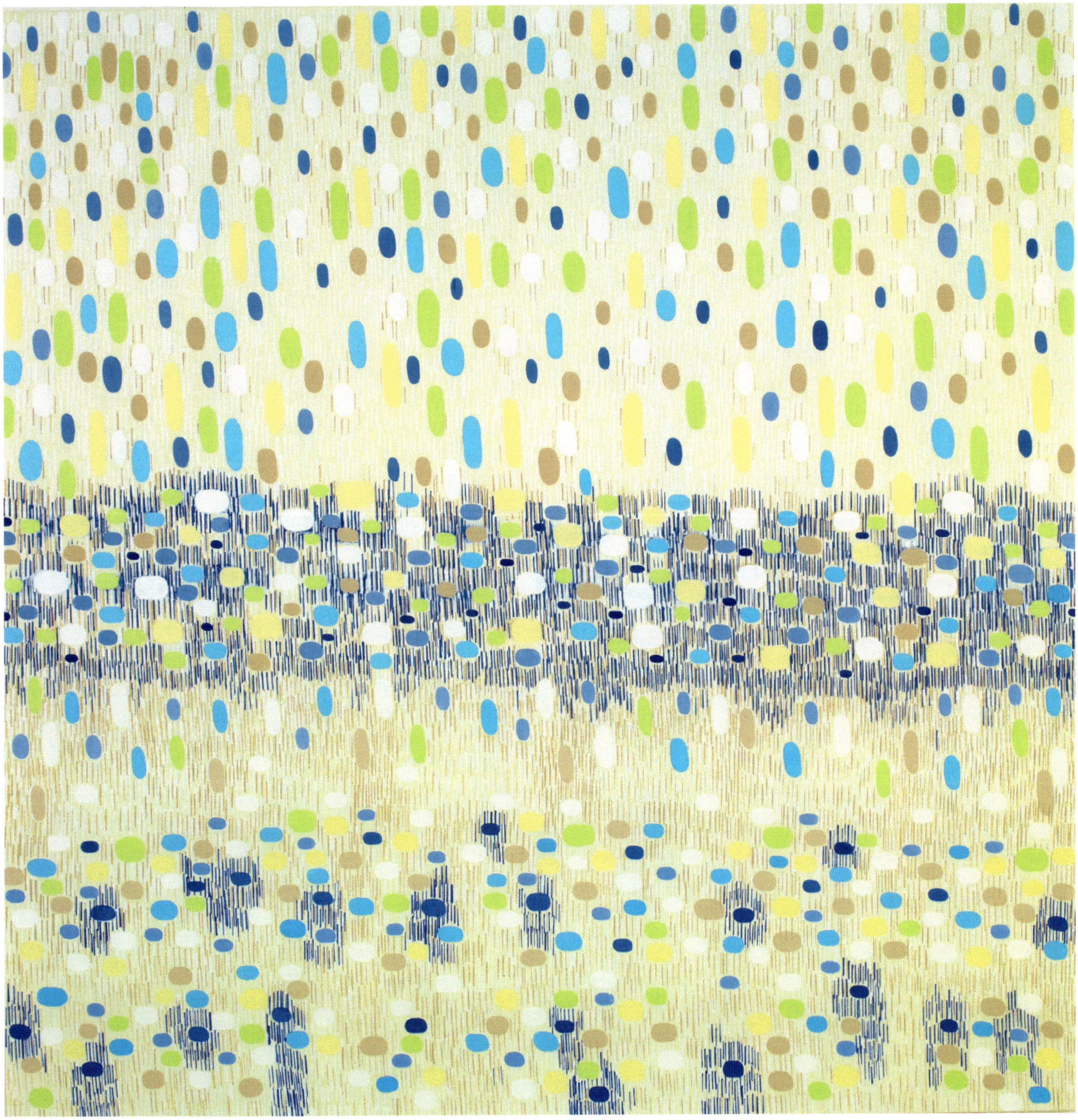

Sarah Medway
Spring Calm II, 2015
Oil on linen
152 × 152 cm

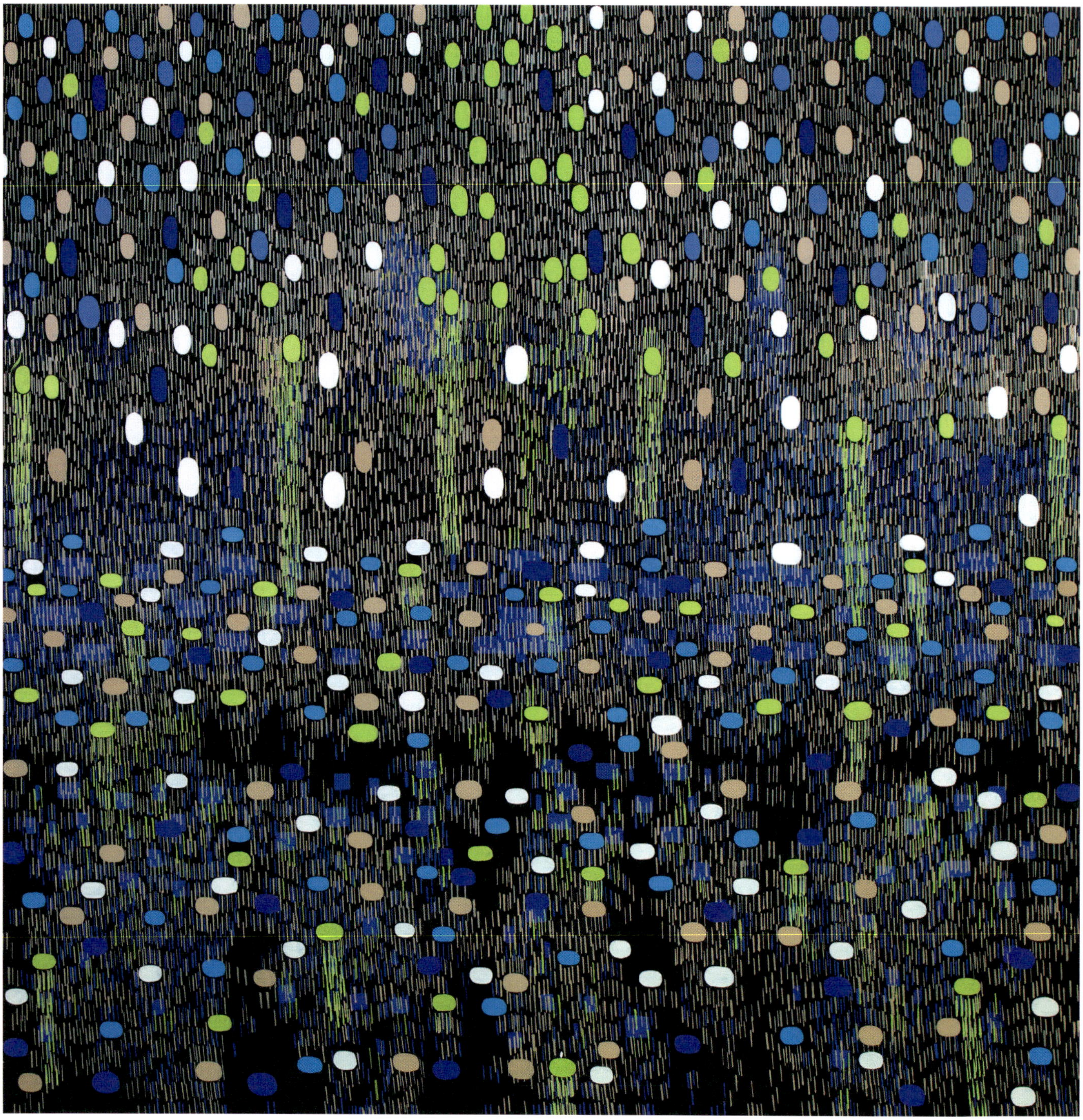

Sarah Medway
Oceanscape Night, 2015
Oil on linen
152 × 152 cm

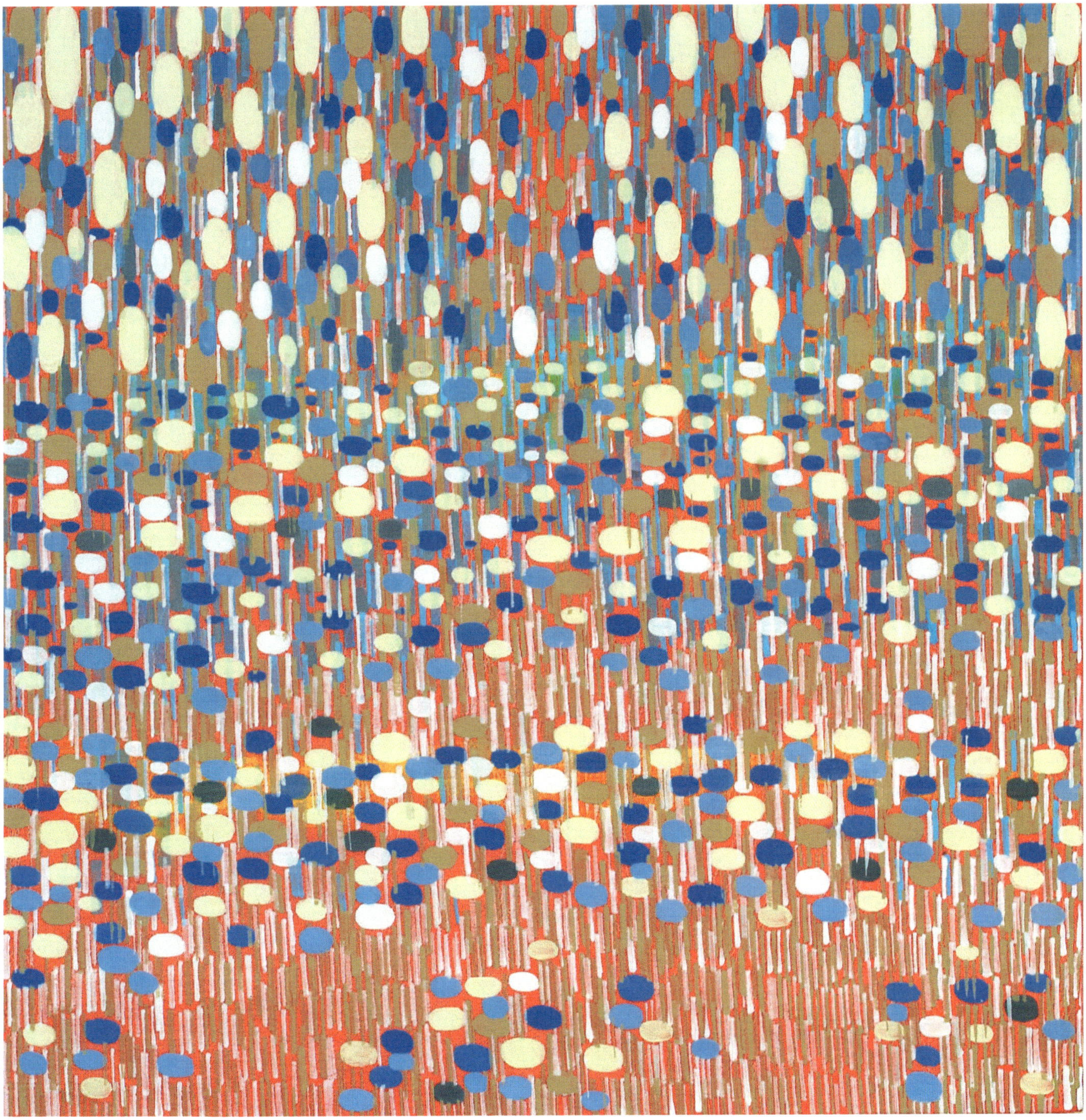

Sarah Medway
Sunset Warm, 2015
Oil on linen
60 × 60 cm

All © Sarah Medway
Courtesy of Anomie Publishing

Anna Freeman Bentley
Mobility and Grandeur

Contributors:
Michele Robecchi
Marina Cashdan
Ben Quash

98pp
Hardback
220 × 190 mm
c. 75 colour
ISBN: 978-1-910221-03-7
RRP: £24
UK Release: 12 February 2015
Edited by Matt Price
Designed by Joe Gilmore
Printed by Pression, Leeds
Published by Anomie Publishing, London

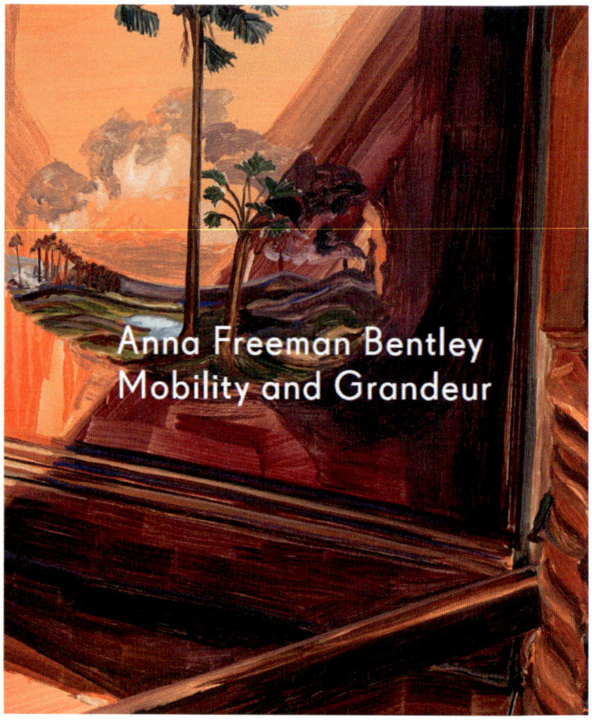

Anna Freeman Bentley is a painter based in London. Her practice explores the built environment, architecture and interiors, inviting emotive, psychological and semiotic readings of space. With an intense, regularly dark palette and energetic yet often intricate brushwork, her paintings depict all manner of places – derelict factories and warehouses, baroque buildings, shops, cafes, and modern industrial and corporate architecture. With a particular focus on the relationships between the design of architecture, its function and use, how these uses change over time, and how streets, areas, communities and cities decline, regenerate and gentrify, Freeman Bentley's practice documents the changing vocabulary of architecture and captures some of the complex dynamics, atmospheres, politics and states of mind that these places engender.

This, the artist's first monograph, features over seventy works spanning her career to date, offering a journey through the built environment that takes the viewer into realms as diverse as psychogeography and heterotopias, romanticism and modernism. From the needs and desires of individuals to those of the different communities that make up urban life in cities and towns today, her paintings open up questions about displacement and replacement, decay and rebirth, change and transformation, public and private space, social and economic mobility, aspiration and desire, buildings and people. Seeking to go beyond the visible and tangible and to explore ideas of faith and the sacred within space, Freeman Bentley's work looks through the fabric of our physical environment to ask about what lies behind, into the dialogue between matter and spirit.

The publication features newly commissioned texts by London-based curator and writer Michele Robecchi, New York-based art writer and editor Marina Cashdan, and Ben Quash, Professor of Christianity and the Arts at King's College London. Edited by Matt Price, this hardback monograph presents the arresting and engaging work of one of the UK's most promising emerging painters.

Anna Freeman Bentley (b. 1982) studied painting at Chelsea College of Art and Design before graduating with an MA from the Royal College of Art in 2010. She has had solo exhibitions in Berlin, Venice and California, residencies in London with the Florence Trust and with Pied à Terre Michelin-starred restaurant, and has participated in group exhibitions including Bloomberg New Contemporaries (2009); the Prague Biennale 5 (2011) and the inaugural East London Painting Prize (2014).

Anna Freeman Bentley
Darkness Passing, 2011
Oil on board
170 × 110 cm (2 panels, 170 × 55 cm each)
Photo: Gustavo Valdes

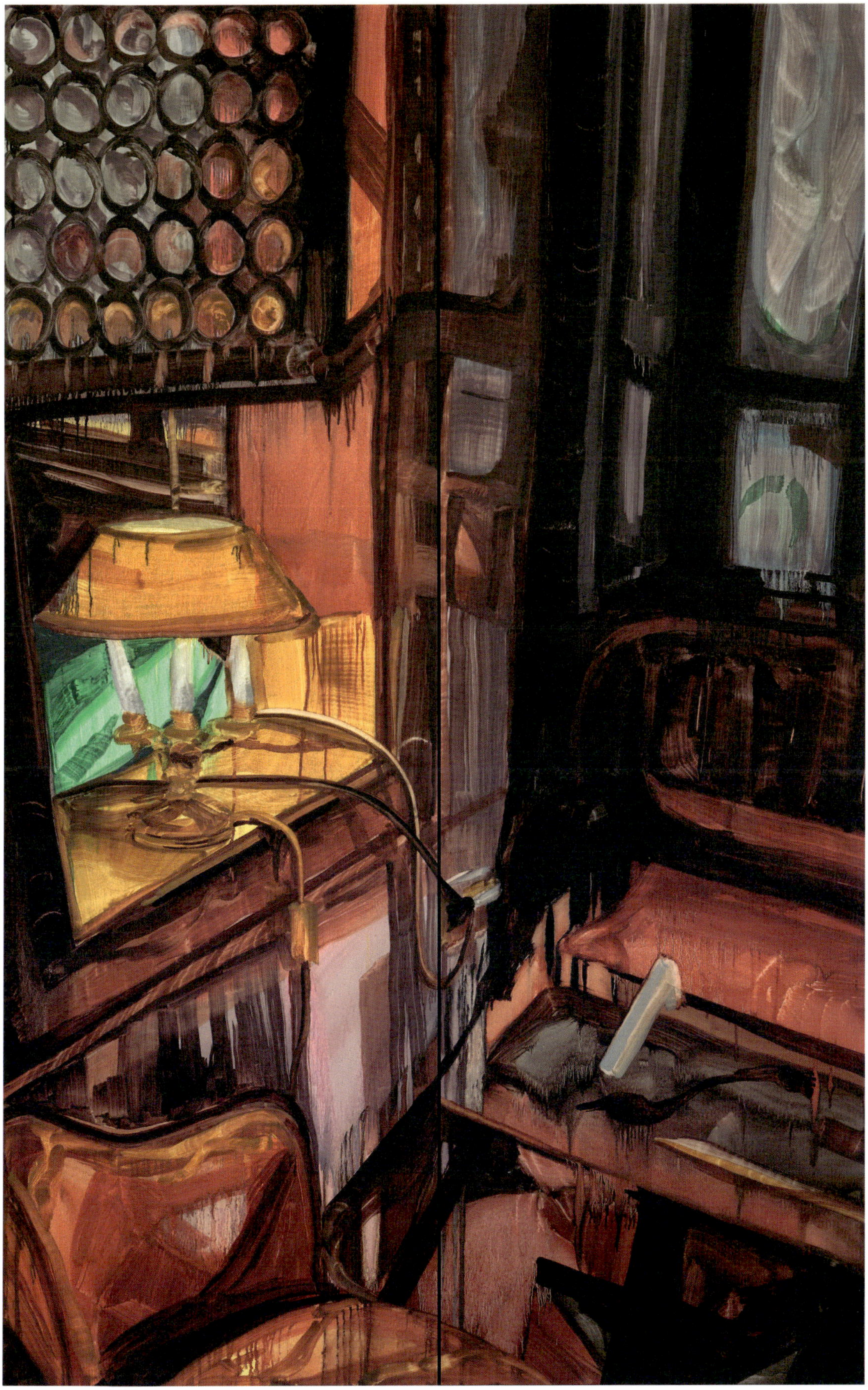

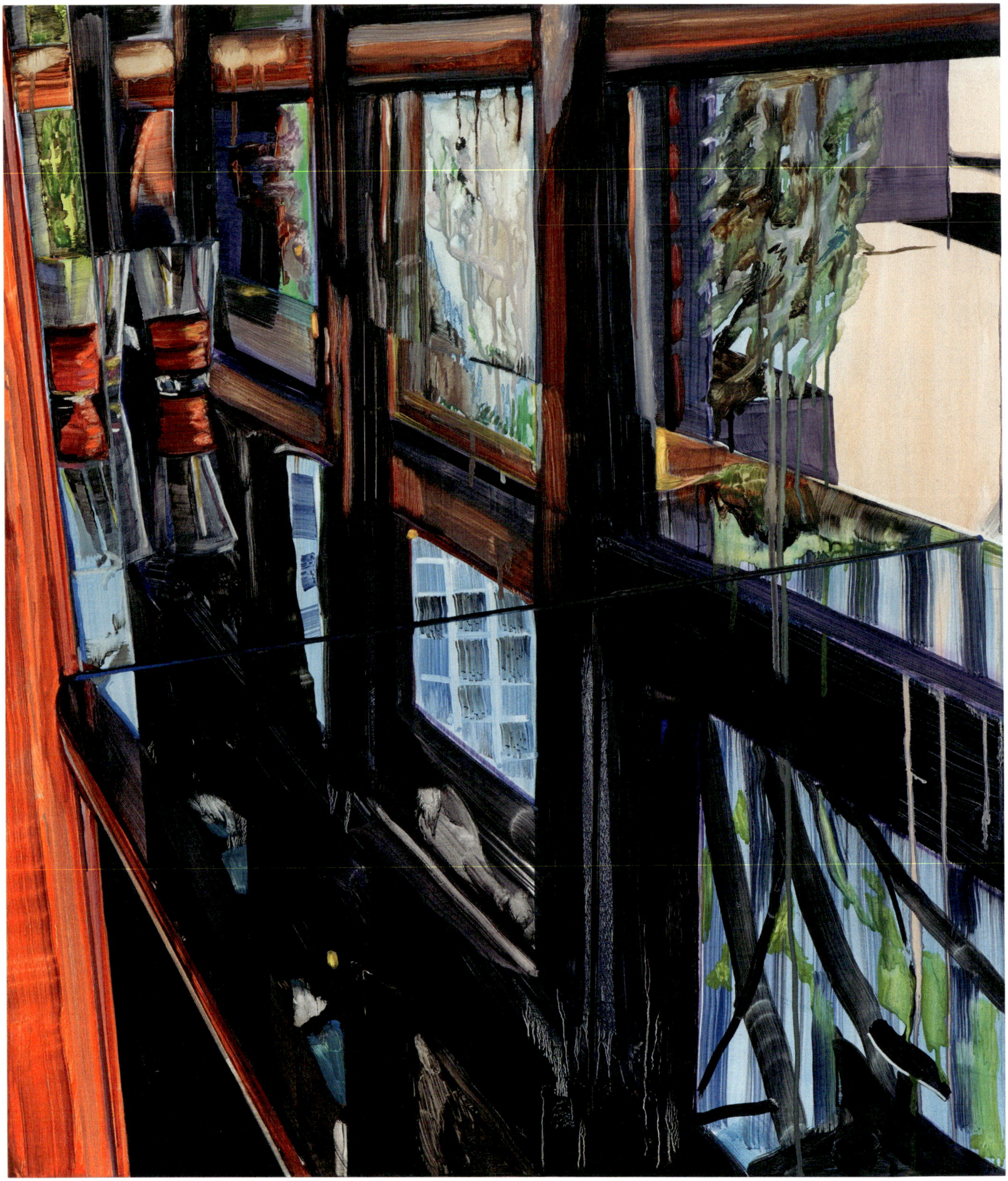

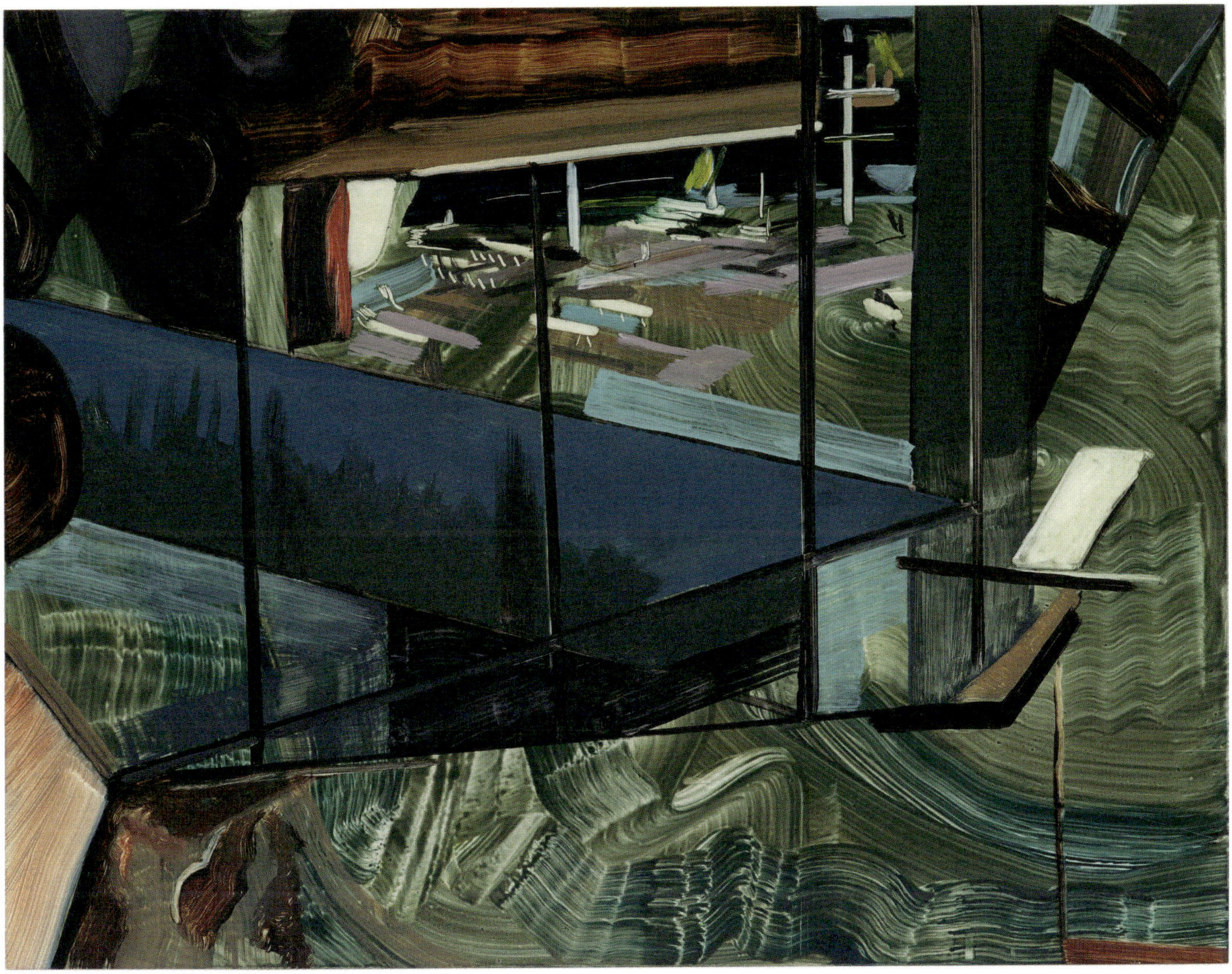

Anna Freeman Bentley
Recharging, 2014
Oil on board
80 × 70 cm
Photo: Anna Arca

Anna Freeman Bentley
Build up, 2013
Oil on board
40 × 52.5cm
Photo: Anna Arca

All © Anna Freeman Bentley
Courtesy of Anomie Publishing

Paul Simonon
Wot No Bike

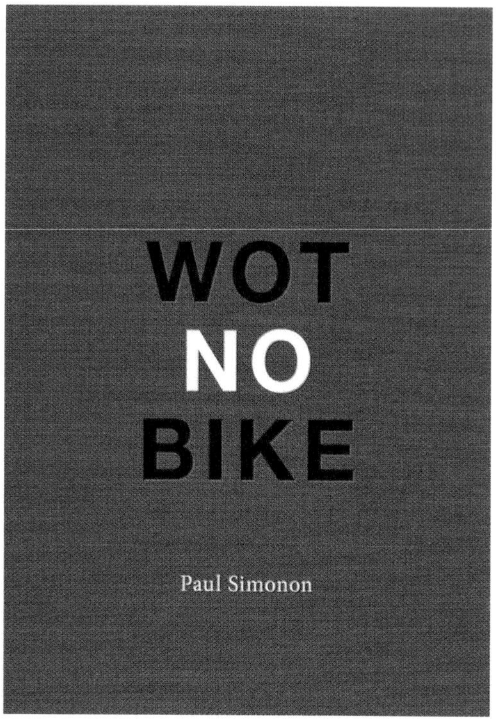

Contributors:
David Lancaster
Tim Marlow

64pp
Hardback
285 × 200 mm
c. 22 colour and b/w images
ISBN: 978-1-910221-02-0
RRP: £30
UK Release: 28 January 2015
Edited by Bruce Cameron and Serena Rees
Designed by Martin Bell / Fruitmachine
Printed by Grafiche Antiga, Italy
Published by Anomie Publishing, London

Wot No Bike is a new limited edition publication of the work of Paul Simonon (b. 1955). Simonon is a London-based artist and musician who came to prominence with the Punk band The Clash in the late 1970s, with whom he played bass guitar. Simonon began studying at art school, but became disillusioned and left. He bumped into Mick Jones who asked if he wanted to form a band. As an aspiring painter who had never previously played bass, he first took a lead role in the band's visual identity, learning to play the instrument as he went along. Simonon has always been passionate about art, and since the band split in the mid 1980s, painting has become as important as his music career.

Simonon's passion for painting began as a boy – his father was an avid amateur painter and Paul spent a lot of time in his studio. Here, surrounded by books and pictures pinned to the walls, he encountered nineteenth- and twentieth-century movements, from Impressionism to Cubism and beyond. In addition to these, Simonon's painting practice has been heavily influenced by twentieth-century realism, particularly the American Ashcan School, which documented New York's working class life at the turn of the century, and the British 'Kitchen Sink' school of painters of the 1950s. The latter formed a part of the wider social realism movement, both in the arts and popular culture, that focused attention on the living conditions of the working classes in post-war Britain.

Growing up in London in the 1960s, Simonon's first experiences of subculture came through Teds, Bikers and Rockers – groups which in their different ways were precursors of Punk culture in the 1970s. Simonon has been a Biker since he was old enough to ride one – his first was a white and gold Triumph 3TA, and it was this, along with subsequent bikes, that established him in the 1970s within the remarkable community of Bikers discussed in David Lancaster's introduction to the publication. The bikes, jackets, boots, helmets, gloves and other biking paraphernalia that feature in Simonon's paintings are his own possessions, things that he uses daily. As such, the paintings are as much in the tradition of self-portraits as still lifes: 'It's like writing a diary, in a way, but in paint,' says Simonon during the conversation with art historian Tim Marlow.

With an independent-minded, outsider spirit, Simonon's paintings in *Wot No Bike* bring British subcultures of the 1950s to 1970s into dialogue with modernist and realist painting traditions, particularly the social realism that came to the fore as these subcultures were emerging. Bound up in the middle of this is Simonon himself – his early life and adolescence, his adult life, social life and his music.

Wot No Bike was published to coincide with an exhibition of Simonon's works at the ICA, London, in January-February 2015.

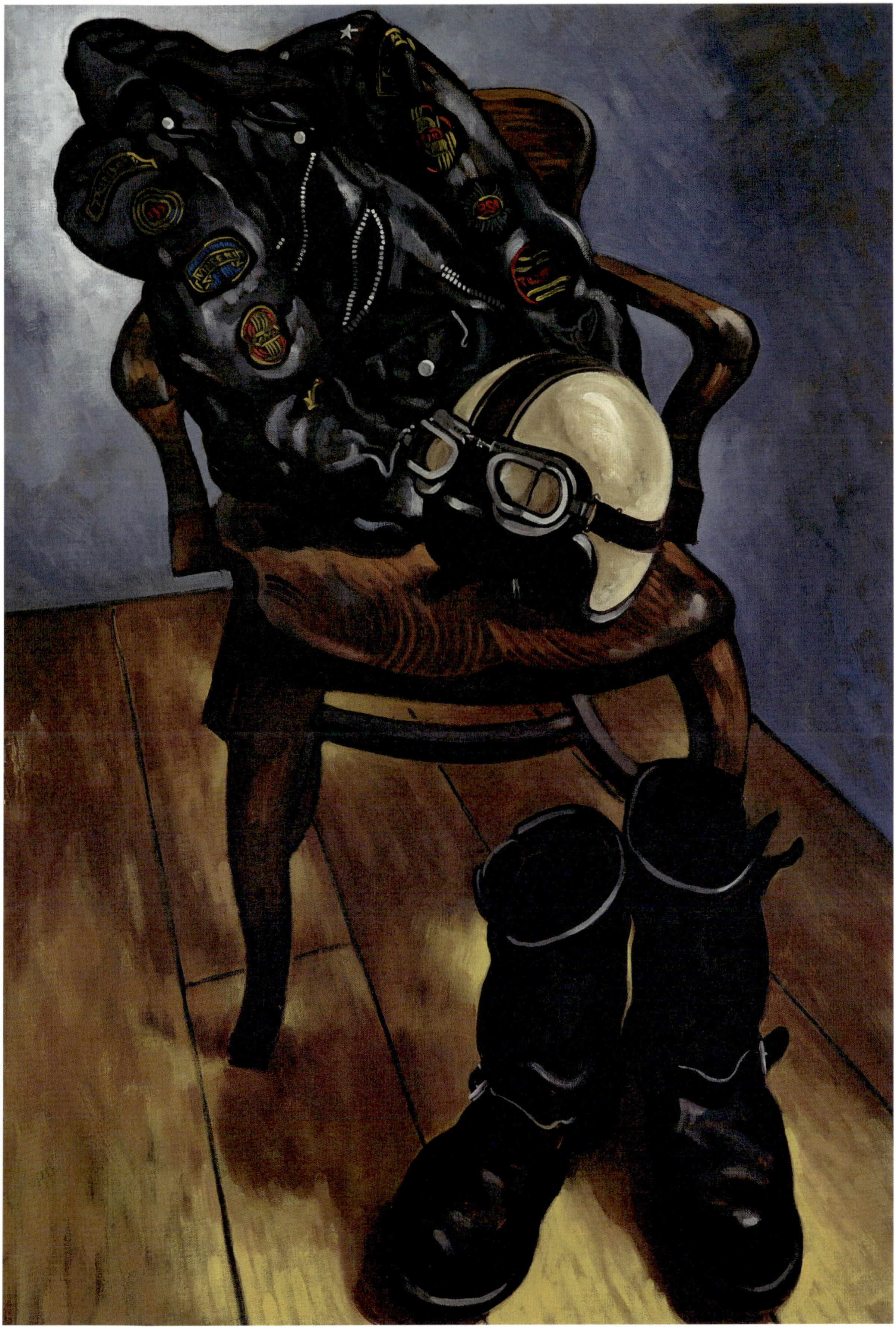

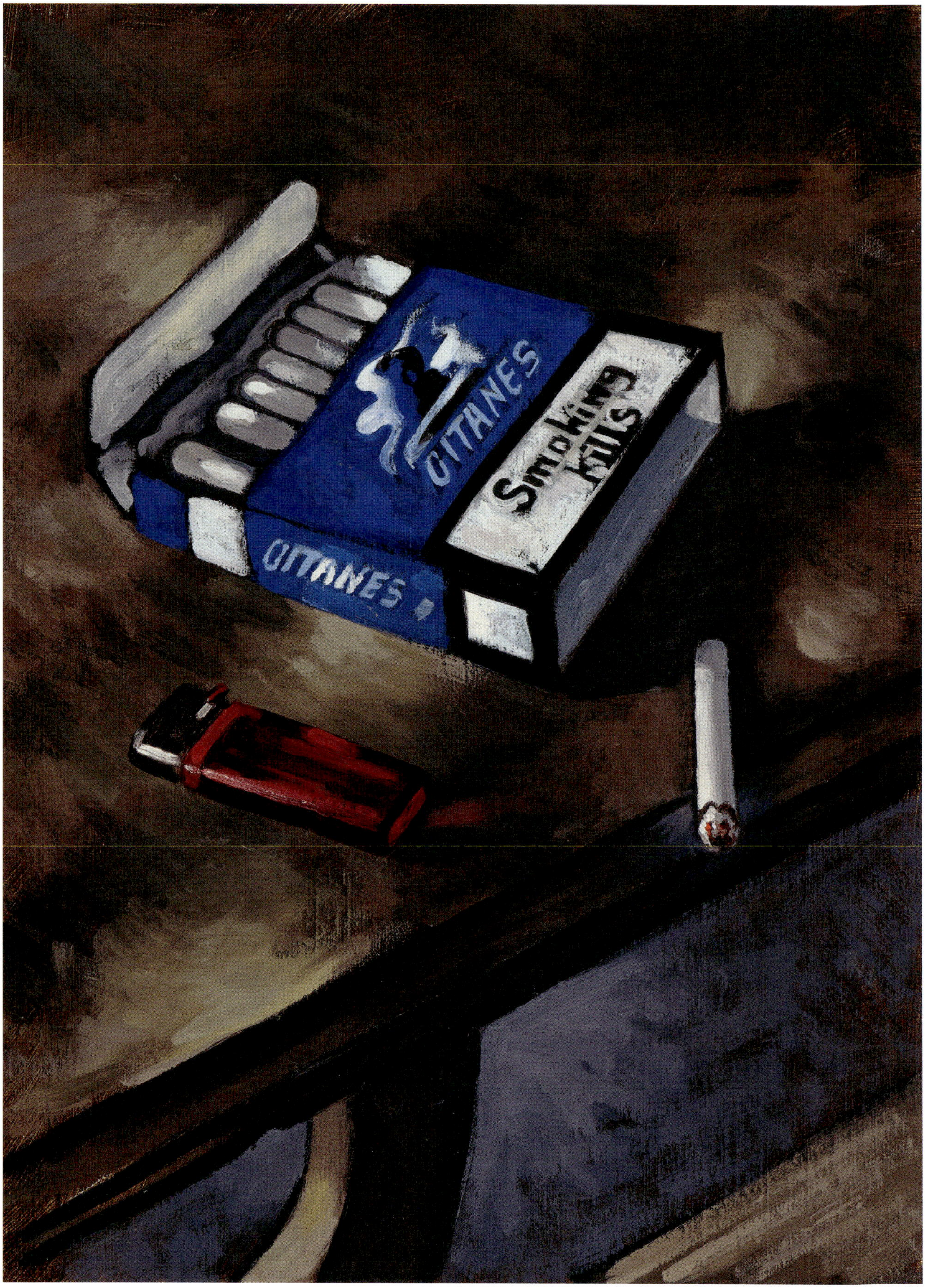
GITANES
Smoking kills
GITANES

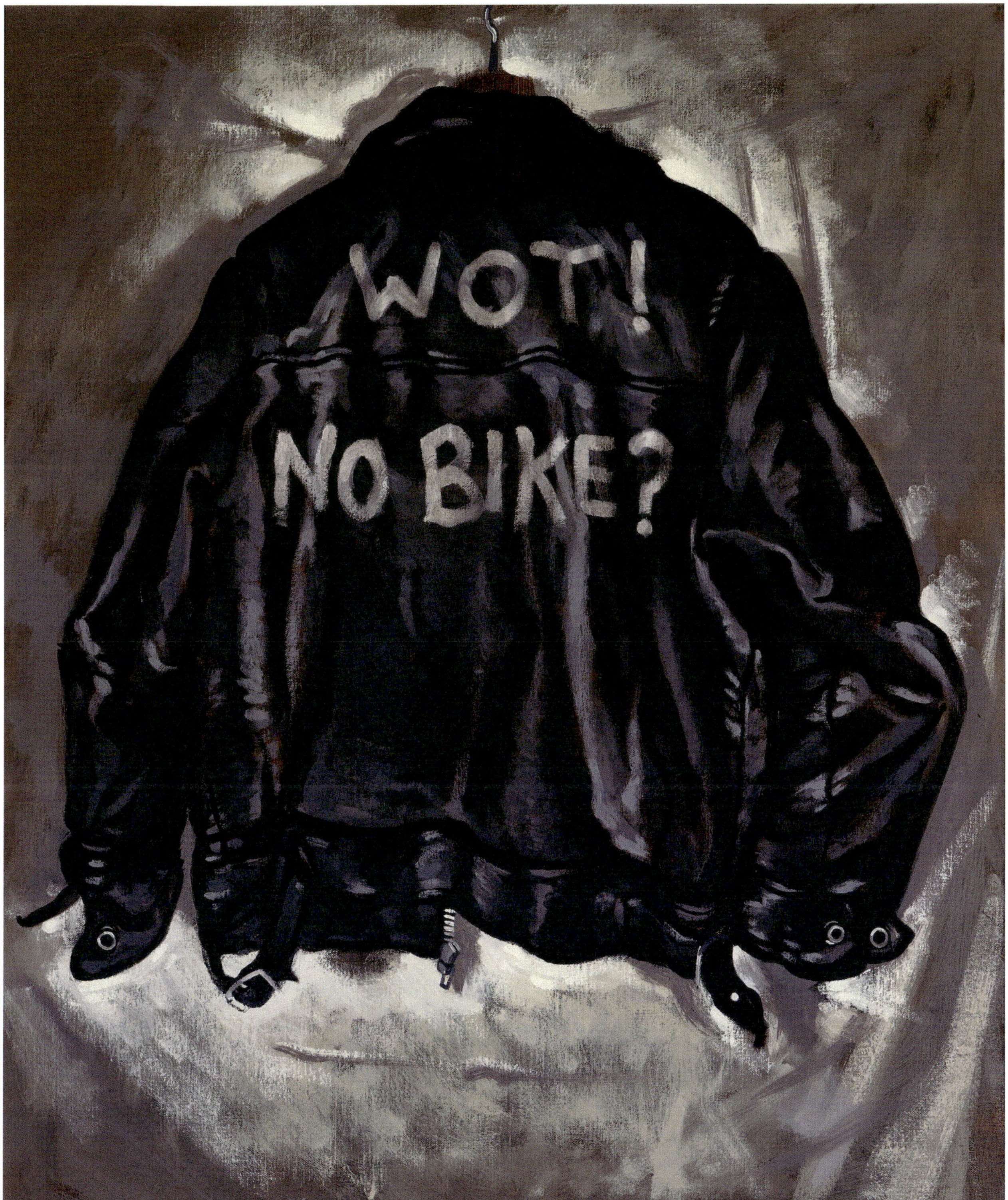

p. 199
Paul Simonon
Boots and Jacket, 2014
Oil on canvas
101.6 × 71.1 cm

Paul Simonon
Gitanes, 2014
Oil on canvas
40.6 × 30.5 cm

Paul Simonon
Wot! No Bike?, 2014
Oil on canvas
71.1 × 61 cm

All © Paul Simonon
Courtesy of Anomie Publishing

Rachel Kneebone
Regarding Rodin

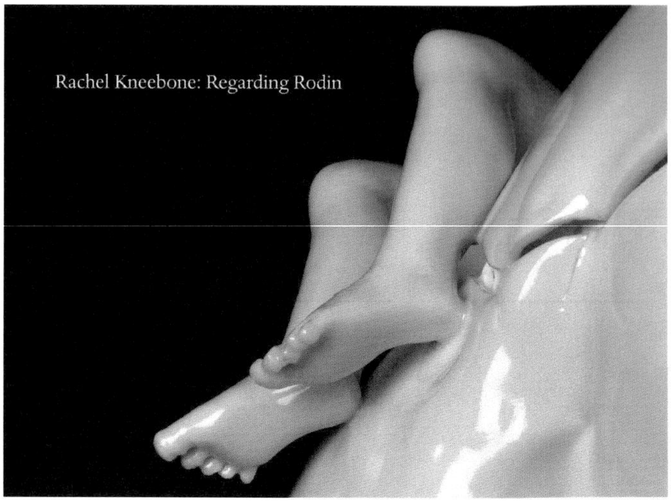

Contributors:
Ali Smith
Catherine Morris

88pp
Hardback
170 × 235 mm
c. 50 images
ISBN: 978-1-910221-01-3
RRP: £24
UK Release: 21 August 2014
Designed by Herman Lelie
Layouts by Stefania Bonelli
Produced by fandg.co.uk
Published by Anomie Publishing, London

Rachel Kneebone (b. 1973, Oxfordshire) is a London-based artist internationally renowned for her porcelain sculptures that intricately fuse human, natural and abstract forms in ways that are both serene and cacophonous, beautiful yet grotesque, otherworldly yet full of humanity. Exploring themes such as sexual desire, mortality, anguish and despair, Kneebone's sculptures are contemporary visions of eternal truths, conveyed with endless imagination and impressive artistry.

Launched in anticipation of *399 Days*, Kneebone's presentation at White Cube, London, in summer 2014, this publication features sculpture from the artist's acclaimed solo exhibition at Brooklyn Museum in 2012, which included the artist's works in dialogue with bronze sculptures by Auguste Rodin. Curated by Catherine Morris, Sackler Family Curator at the Elizabeth A. Sackler Center for Feminist Art at Brooklyn Museum, the exhibition was Kneebone's debut museum show, highlighting the two artists' shared interest in mourning, ecstasy and death in figurative sculpture.

The centrepiece of the exhibition and publication is a work entitled *The Descent* (2008). In part inspired by Dante's *Divine Comedy*, Kneebone's white porcelain sculpture depicts myriad small mutant figures standing on the rim of a strange pit, teeming with wretched limbs on the slopes below. With references ranging from Bataille to Cormac McCarthy, this apocalyptic vision of humanity captures souls condemned to eternal damnation in a sculpture that is as affecting as it is unforgettable.

Other sculptures by Kneebone include *For Beauty's nothing but beginning of Terror we're still just able to bear* (2011), which takes the form of a two-tier configuration of human limbs, evocative of classical myths and a history of aberrations; and *Eyes that look close at wounds themselves are wounded* (2010), which renders a pitiable naked female form transmogrified through her anguish into an almost abstract pile of flesh, bones and organs. Beautiful, disturbing, remarkable – the gleaming white porcelain surfaces of Kneebone's exquisite sculptures belie their dark, despairing iconography, unleashing an orgiastic nightmare of elegant depravity and classical desolation.

'Am I the only person who sees past the dark, the classical desolation that critics like to see in Kneebone's work?' asks Ali Smith in her thought-provoking text, which takes us from Apollo to Lacan on a mind-expanding journey that starts by skinning satyrs alive and ends by proclaiming the lifeforce that can be found even in prehistory's primordial slime.

Having undertaken a BA at UWE, Bristol, Kneebone graduated with an MA from the Royal College of Art, London, in 2004. She is represented by White Cube.

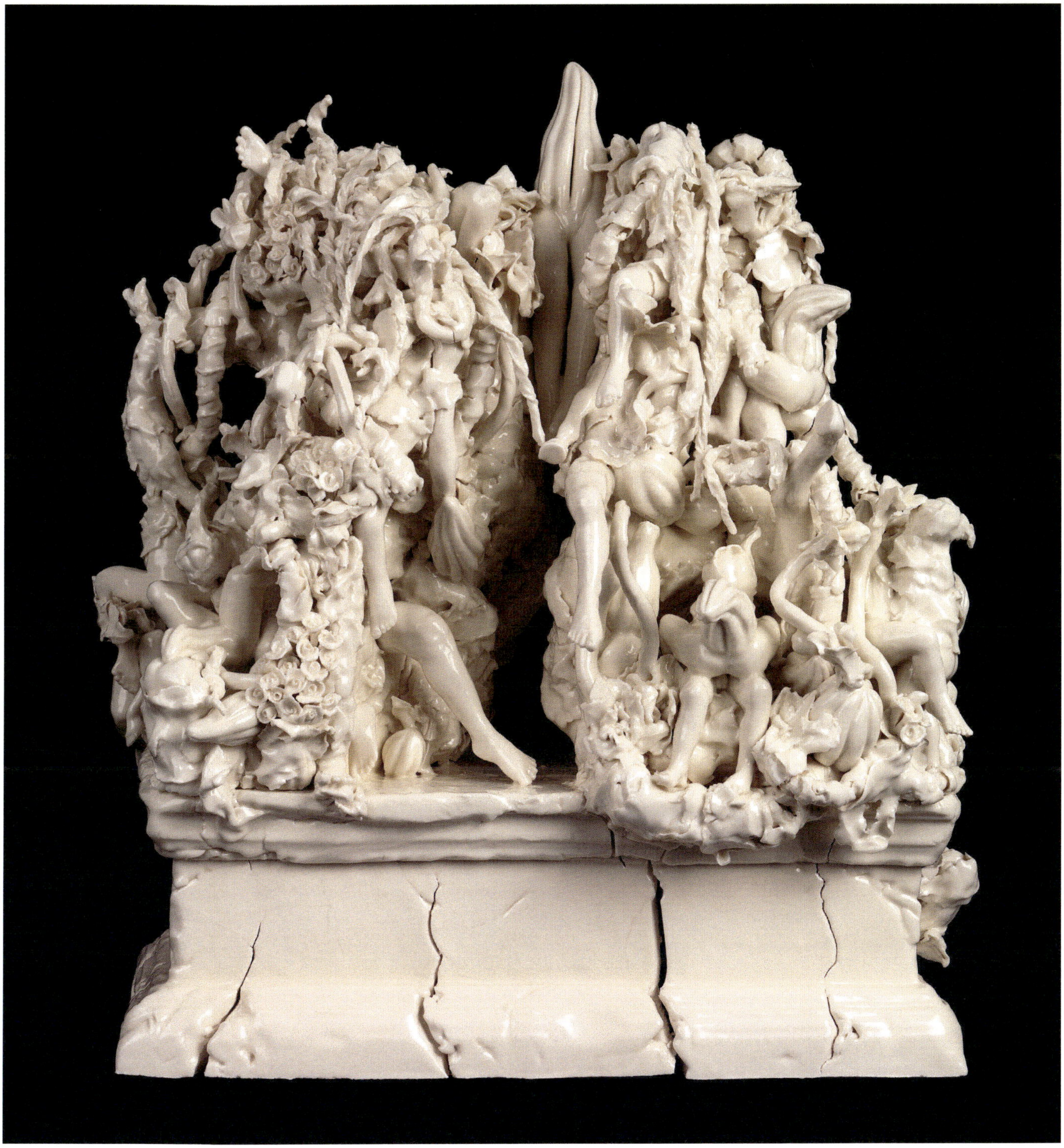

Rachel Kneebone
When I doubt I exist again, 2009
Porcelain
52.7 × 30.5 × 47.6 cm
Photo: Stephen White
© Rachel Kneebone
Courtesy of the artist and White Cube

Kamrooz Aram
Unstable Paintings for Anxious Interiors

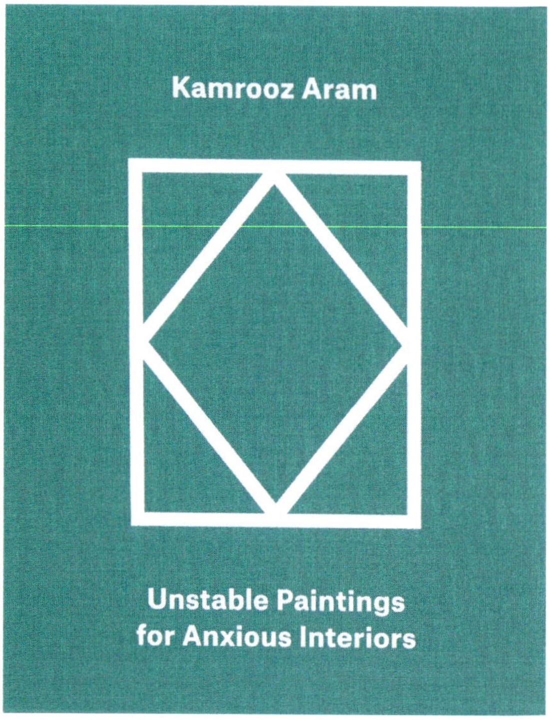

Contributors:
Eva Díaz
Media Farzin
Murtaza Vali
Kamrooz Aram

80pp
Hardback
318 × 248 mm
c. 50 colour and b/w images
ISBN: 978-0-9576936-6-1
RRP: £30
UK Release: 1 May 2014
Edited by Yasmin Atassi
Designed by Joe Gilmore
Printed by Die Keure, Bruges
Co-published by Green Art Gallery, Dubai and
Anomie Publishing, London

This monograph on Iranian-born, Brooklyn-based painter Kamrooz Aram (b. 1978) presents the *Palimpsest* series, in part inspired by the painting-over of graffiti on the streets of New York by the authorities. The ongoing cycle of painting, covering-up and repainting connects with Aram's longstanding fascination with modernism and the legacies of abstract painting. Also running through the series is a floral motif that Aram appropriated from a Persian carpet in a Manhattan shop – a motif that submerges and re-emerges within the layers of accumulated and erased marks on his canvases.

For many years, Aram's work has engaged the complex role that ornament has played in modern painting. The *Palimpsest* series expands on this project, raising questions about the possibilities of contemporary abstract painting, exploring whether the process of image-making can become central to the meaning of a painting. As the title *Unstable Paintings for Anxious Interiors* suggests, the paintings evoke the unstable dynamics of today.

Aram's interest in 'painting as palimpsest' evolved over years of observing and photographing walls in cities across the world, from Brooklyn to Beirut and Istanbul. The worn walls of Beirut still bear the scars of the civil war, while in Brooklyn, years of graffiti and its covering-up reveal the history of New York City. The phenomenon takes on a different meaning in a city such as Istanbul, where much graffiti is the result of public demonstrations related to the Gezi Park protests.

Kamrooz Aram graduated from Columbia University, New York, in 2003. Since then his work has been widely exhibited internationally and featured in publications such as *The New York Times*, *Artforum.com*, *ArtAsiaPacific*, and *Bidoun*. Aram was a recipient of the Abraaj Group Art Prize 2014.

The publication features texts by Eva Díaz, Professor of Contemporary Art at Pratt Institute in New York; art historian and critic Media Farzin and an interview with the artist by art historian and critic Murtaza Vali. A photo essay and text have also been contributed by the artist. The monograph, which has been edited by Yasmin Atassi, accompanied an exhibition of Aram's work at Green Art Gallery, Dubai, from 17 March to 3 May 2014.

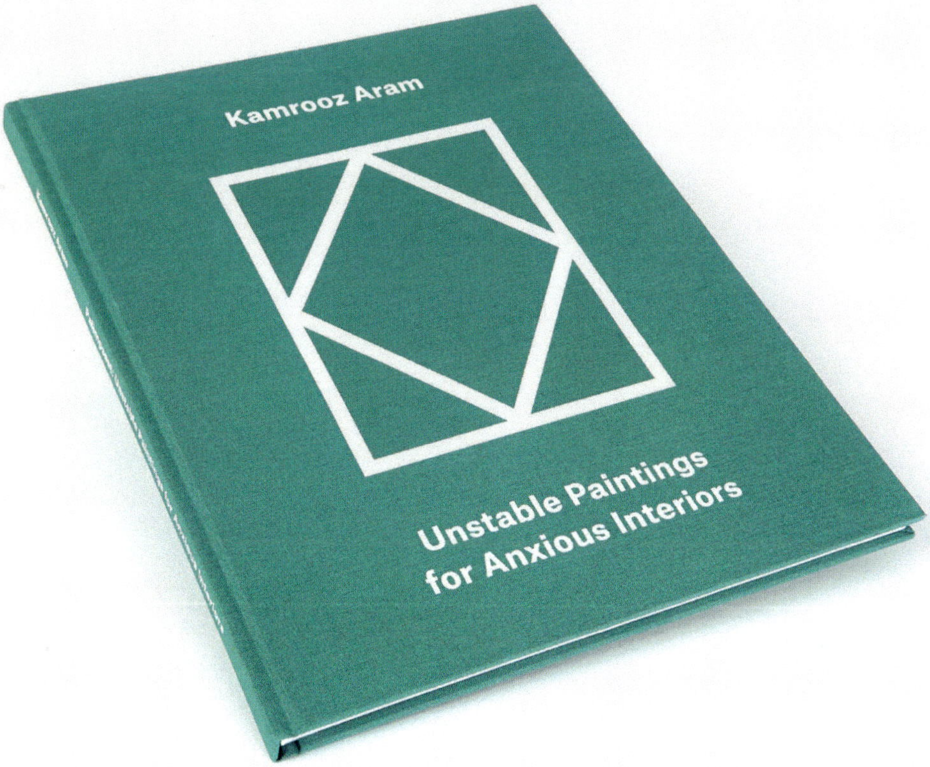
Kamrooz Aram
Unstable Paintings
for Anxious Interiors

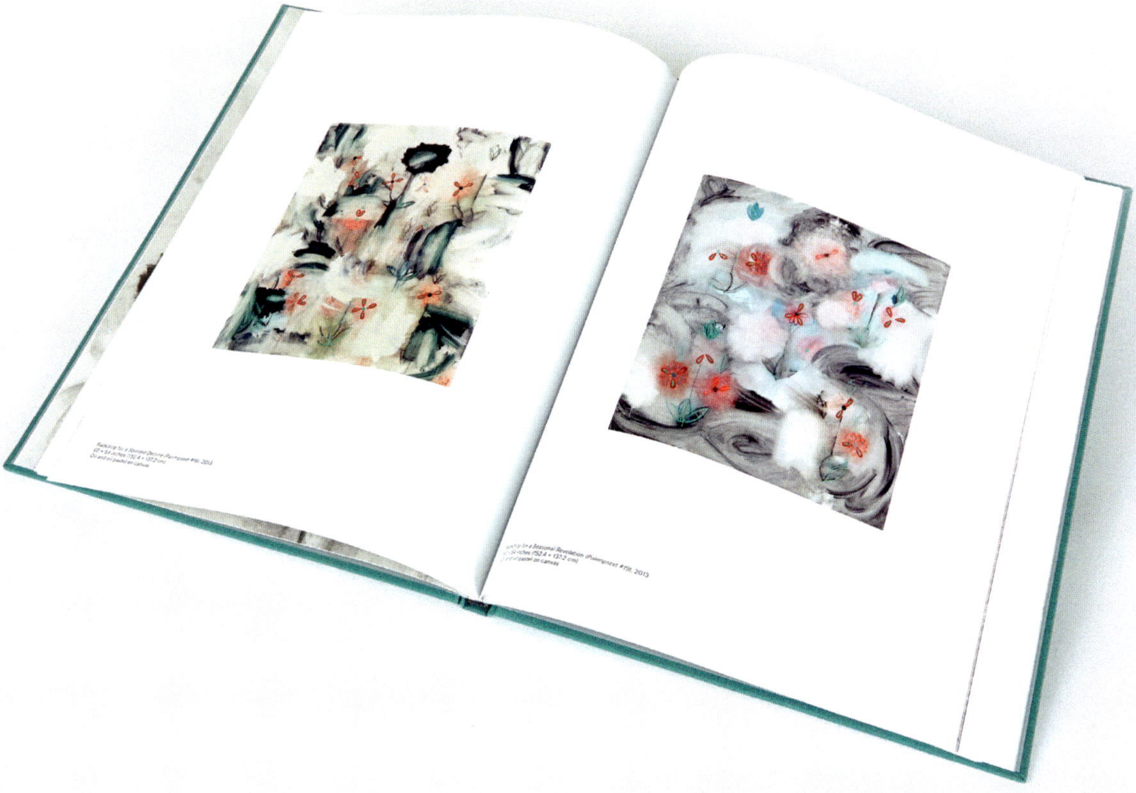

Meekyoung Shin

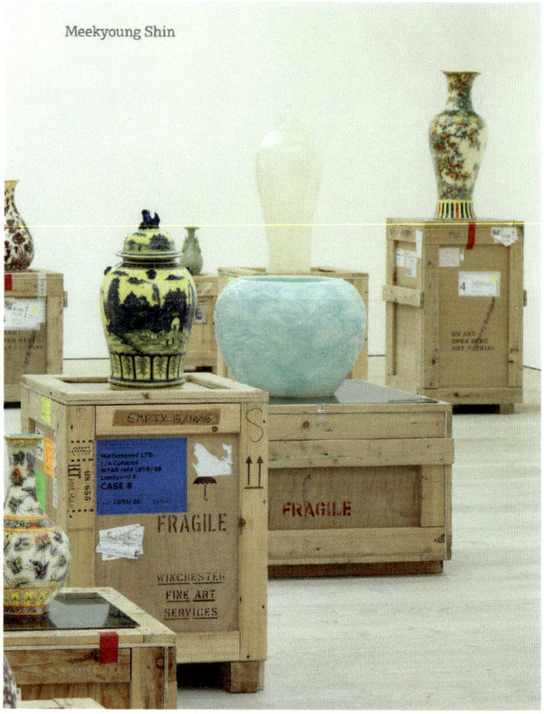

Contributors:
Jonathan Watkins
Ben Tufnell
Kyung An
Jade Keunhye Lim

108pp
Softback
280 × 220 mm
c. 50 colour and b/w images
ISBN: 978-0-9576936-5-4
RRP: £18
UK Release: 5 December 2013
Edited by Anne Blood, Co-ordinated by Kyung An
Designed by Matt Watkins
Published by Anomie Publishing, London, in collaboration with the Korean Cultural Centre UK, London

The London and Seoul-based Korean artist Meekyoung Shin (b. 1967) is internationally renowned for her sculptures that probe the mis- and re-translations that often emerge when cultural objects are uprooted from their original context. Made from soap, her works replicate artefacts and canonical works of art, from Asian porcelain vases to Greek and Roman sculptures, translating between continents, cultures and centuries.

In this new monograph, Jonathan Watkins sets the scene for Shin's solo exhibition at the Korean Cultural Centre UK in London in autumn 2013, a stone's throw from Nelson's Column and the *Fourth Plinth* commission of Trafalgar Square. Watkins eloquently introduces Shin's major bodies of work, capturing the cultural complexity, exquisite craftsmanship, conceptual elegance and natural wit embodied within them.

An essay by Ben Tufnell explores the cultural and historical references in Shin's work over the past fifteen years. Taking Shin's solo exhibition at Haunch of Venison in London in 2011 as his point of departure, he opens up questions of what is exhibited where and when, by and for whom. His incisive analysis of *Crouching Aphrodite* (2002) – a life-size sculpture of the artist's own body in the pose of the classical *Venus of Vienne* from the Louvre – raises issues of Eastern and Western culture, of originality and copying: 'Being neither fully Asian nor fully Roman it inhabits a cultural limbo space.' Tufnell explains: 'Shin's works are not simply replicas or reproductions but strange twins, uncanny avatars of their precursors.'

Curator and art historian Kyung An's text offers an illuminating account of Shin's *Written in Soap: A Plinth Project* (2012-ongoing), which takes the form of a public art project in which the artist recreates – out of soap – a large equestrian military statue of Prince William Augustus, the Duke of Cumberland, that once stood in Cavendish Square, London. Having exhibited her work on its empty London plinth, Shin then created subsequent versions for display in Seoul and Taipei. As An asks: 'What becomes of the monument when it is transplanted to a national museum dedicated to modern and contemporary art five thousand miles away?'

Jade Keunhye Lim's essay unpicks the various strands of Shin's *Translation* series, from the classical Greek sculptures through to *Toilet Project* (2004-ongoing) – in which portrait busts made of soap are placed in the washrooms of galleries and museums for visitors to use when washing their hands. Via cultural imperialism and the tastes of the affluent classes of the West, Keunhye Lim questions the value systems of objects and the logic of their accession into museums. How is beauty, cultural significance and value constructed, and how does this translate across cultures and time?

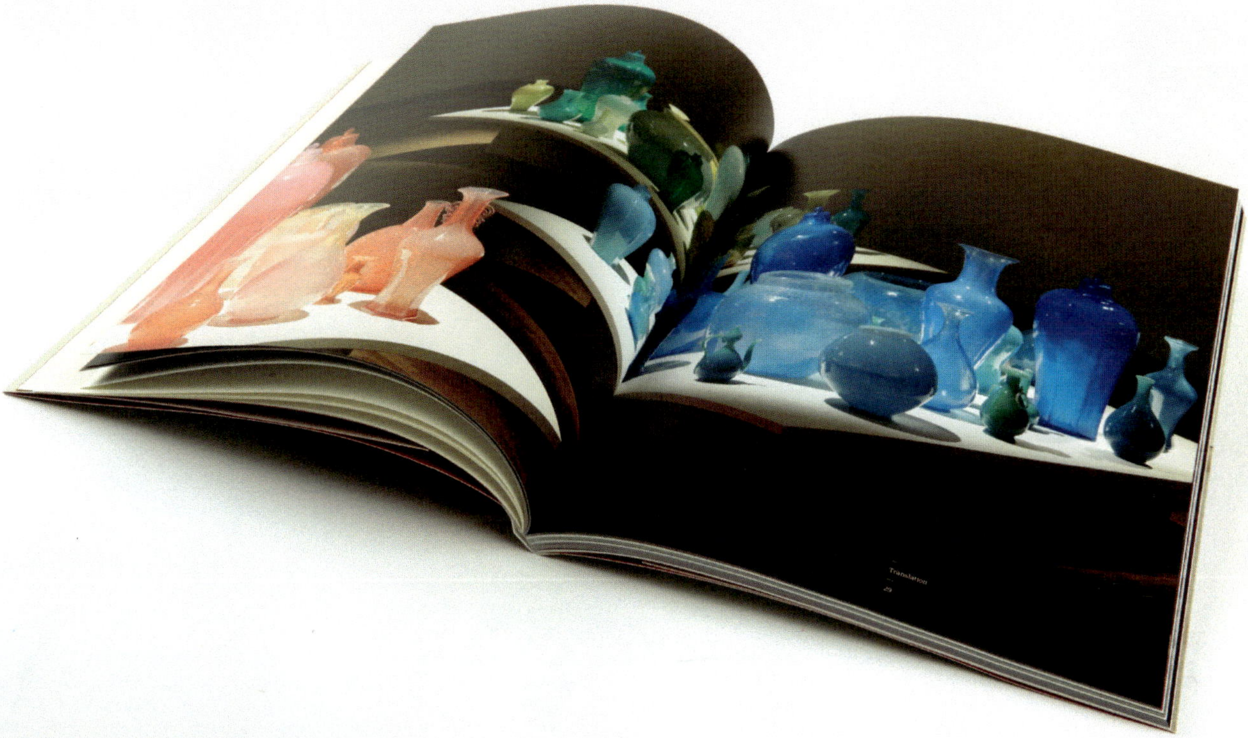
Translation
29

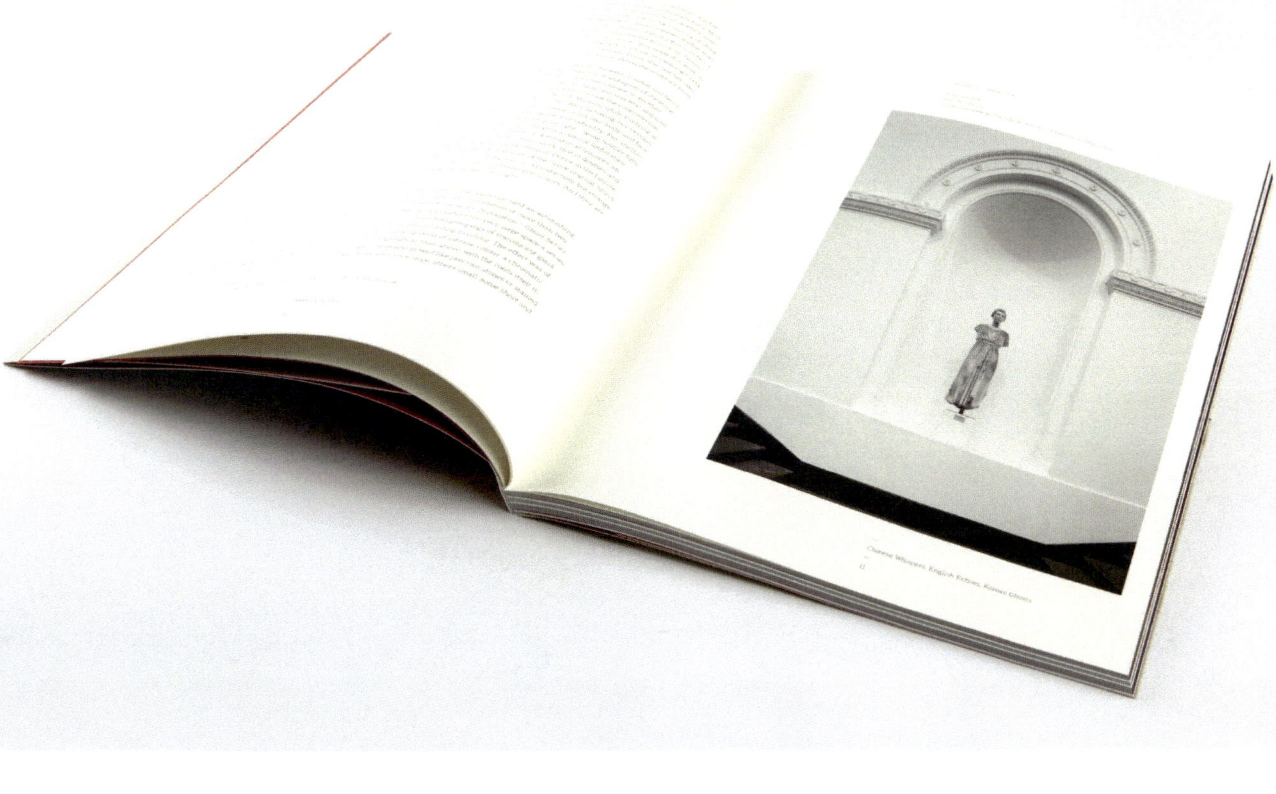
Chinese Whispers, English Echoes, Korean Ghosts
12

Robert Fry

Contributors:
Mamuka Bliadze
Dr. Anthony Fry
Jane Neal

88pp
Hardback
280 × 220 mm
c. 60 colour and b/w images
ISBN: 978-0-9576936-4-7
RRP: £30
Designed by Joanna Deans, Identity
Co-published by Anomie Publishing, London, and Galerie Kornfeld, Berlin

The paintings and etchings of Robert Fry confront viewers with an engaging exploration of the human form that asks profound questions about people's physical presence in the universe and the psychological, emotional, and spiritual engagement we have with the world through our bodies. With a deep sense of civilisations past, from the prehistoric to the ancient Egyptian, Medieval and Renaissance to the Enlightenment and beyond, Fry navigates a complex visual language that bridges the figurative and the abstract in a way that is evocative of body and mind, matter and spirit, life and death. Fry's search for universal truths leads into dark territory, into our subconscious minds and neuroses, our deepest fears, anxieties and insecurities. Both sacred and profane, Fry's work masterfully employs colour, mark, line, shape and form to bring us face to face with our inner and outer selves, with our humanity and, ultimately, with our own mortality.

This beautifully produced publication features around sixty selected works by the artist over the course of more than fifteen years, from very early works to 2013. Following an introduction to the artist's work by Mamuka Bliadze is an essay by the artist's father, distinguished consultant psychiatrist Anthony Fry, which investigates the themes of masculinity and maleness in his son's paintings, and in particular a series of works that refers to the Fry family, including a portrait of both Anthony and Robert Fry that seeks to unravel the complexities of the father-son relationship. A wider consideration of Fry's practice is pursued in an essay by critic and curator Jane Neal that addresses topics ranging from Saussurean signification to automatic writing, pagan fertility symbols to archetypal human forms, twentieth-century British painting to body builders.

The monograph was published in partnership with Galerie Kornfeld, Berlin and coincided with an exhibition there by the artist in autumn 2013.

Robert Fry (b. 1980, London) has had solo exhibitions in London, Berlin and Los Angeles, and has featured in group exhibitions including *Newspeak – British Art Now* at The State Hermitage, St. Petersburg and *The Curator's Egg* at Anthony Reynolds Gallery, London.

Robert Fry
Double Figure Study of Lord Frederick Leighton, 2013
Dry point etching on zinc plate
45.2 × 29.4 cm
Photo: Gerhard Haug
© Robert Fry
Courtesy of the artist and Galerie Kornfeld, Berlin

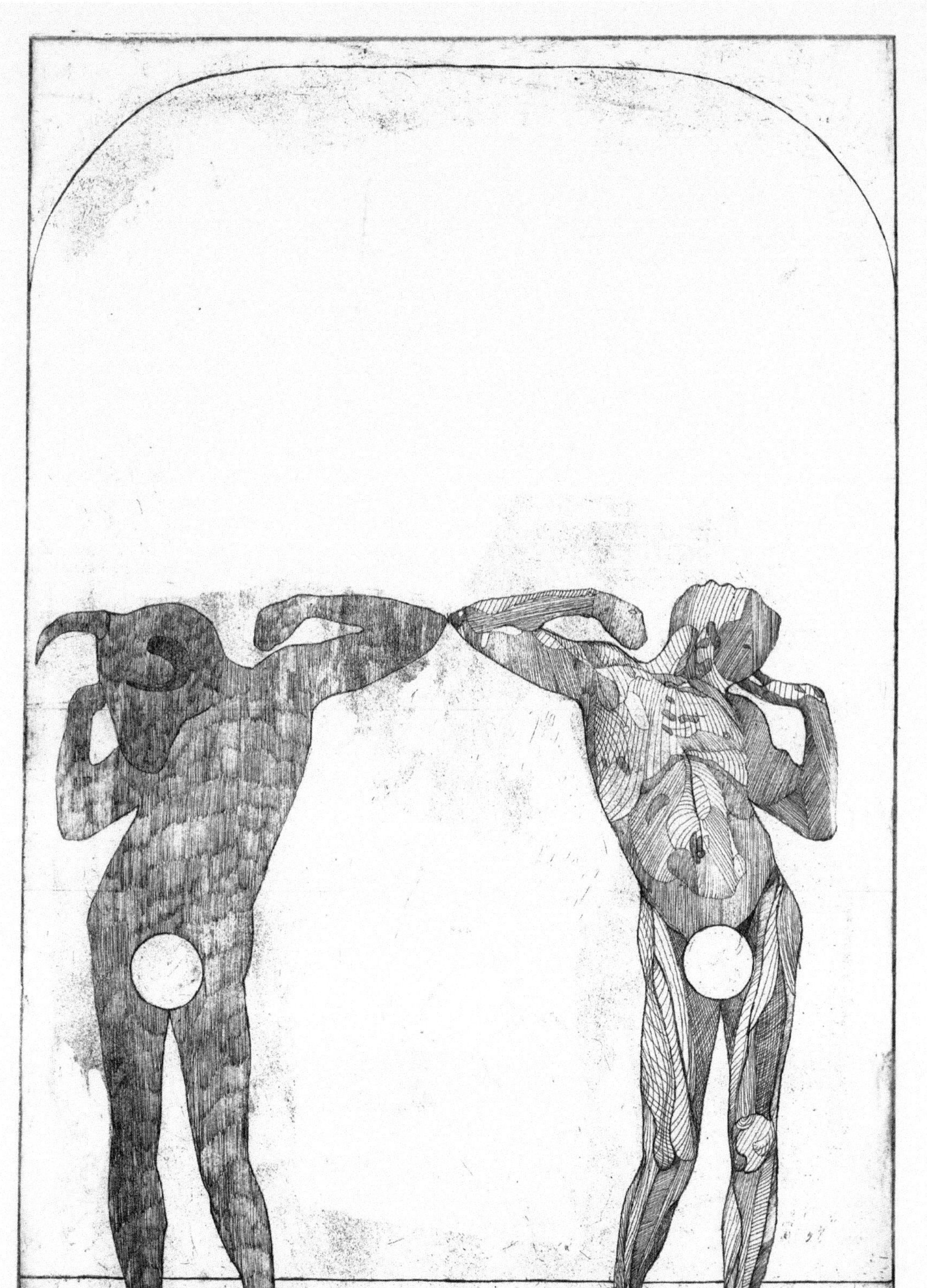
1/5 + 2 AP

Caroline Walker
In Every Dream Home

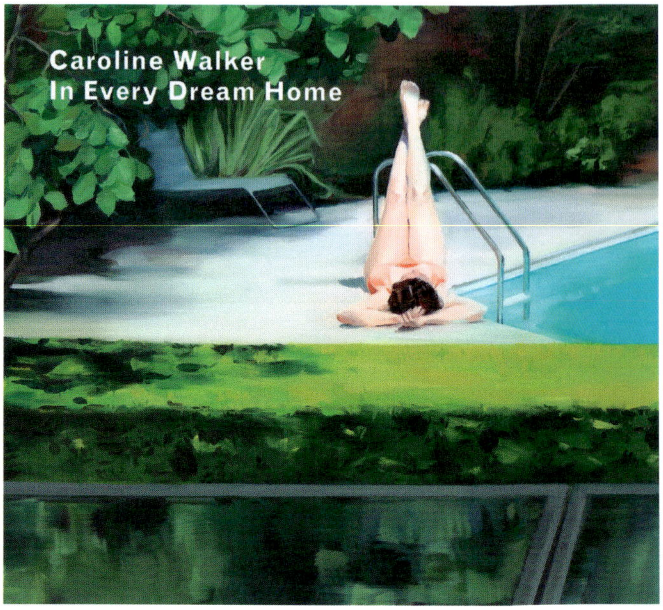

Contributors:
Marco Livingstone
Jane Neal
Matt Price

80pp
Hardback
190 × 220mm
c. 50 colour and b/w images
ISBN: 978-0-9576936-0-9
RRP: £20
Designed by Joe Gilmore
Published by Anomie Publishing, London

Caroline Walker (b. 1982, Dunfermline) has established herself as one of the UK's most exciting figurative painters of her generation working internationally today. By means of a seductive yet forthright use of paint, Walker makes paintings that explore ideas of femininity in relation to architecture, addressing people's physical, psychological, emotional and social relationships with the buildings in which they spend time. While the paintings are often charming and appealing, there is regularly something odd or unexpected underlying them –
occasionally verging on the threatening or dangerous. Sometimes dream homes can be anything but... Full of references and influences, Walker's work is an engaging journey into the modern female condition and the 'female gaze'.

Walker studied at Glasgow School of Art prior to an MA in Painting at the Royal College of Art from which she graduated in 2009. Within two years of graduating she had staged solo commercial exhibitions in London, Bucharest and New York, and in spring 2013 she showed with Project B Gallery, Milan. She has featured in group exhibitions including *John Moores 24* at Liverpool Art Gallery; *Jerwood Contemporary Painters* at the Jerwood Space, London; *Some Domestic Incidents: New Painting from Britain* at the Prague Biennale 5 and *Nightfall: New Tendencies in Figurative Painting* at MODEM, Hungary, and the Rudolfinum, Prague. Her work is represented in a number of private and public collections including the Saatchi Collection, the Franks-Suss Collection and the Jimenez-Colon Collection, Puerto Rico.

In Every Dream Home – the first monograph of Walker's work – features around fifty key paintings, oil sketches and ink drawings alongside an introductory text by art historian, critic and curator Marco Livingstone, an essay by independent critic and curator Jane Neal, and an interview with the artist by editor Matt Price.

The launch of Anomie's first publication was scheduled to coincide with the opening of an exhibition by the artist at Pitzhanger Manor in Ealing, West London – her first solo show in a public institution.

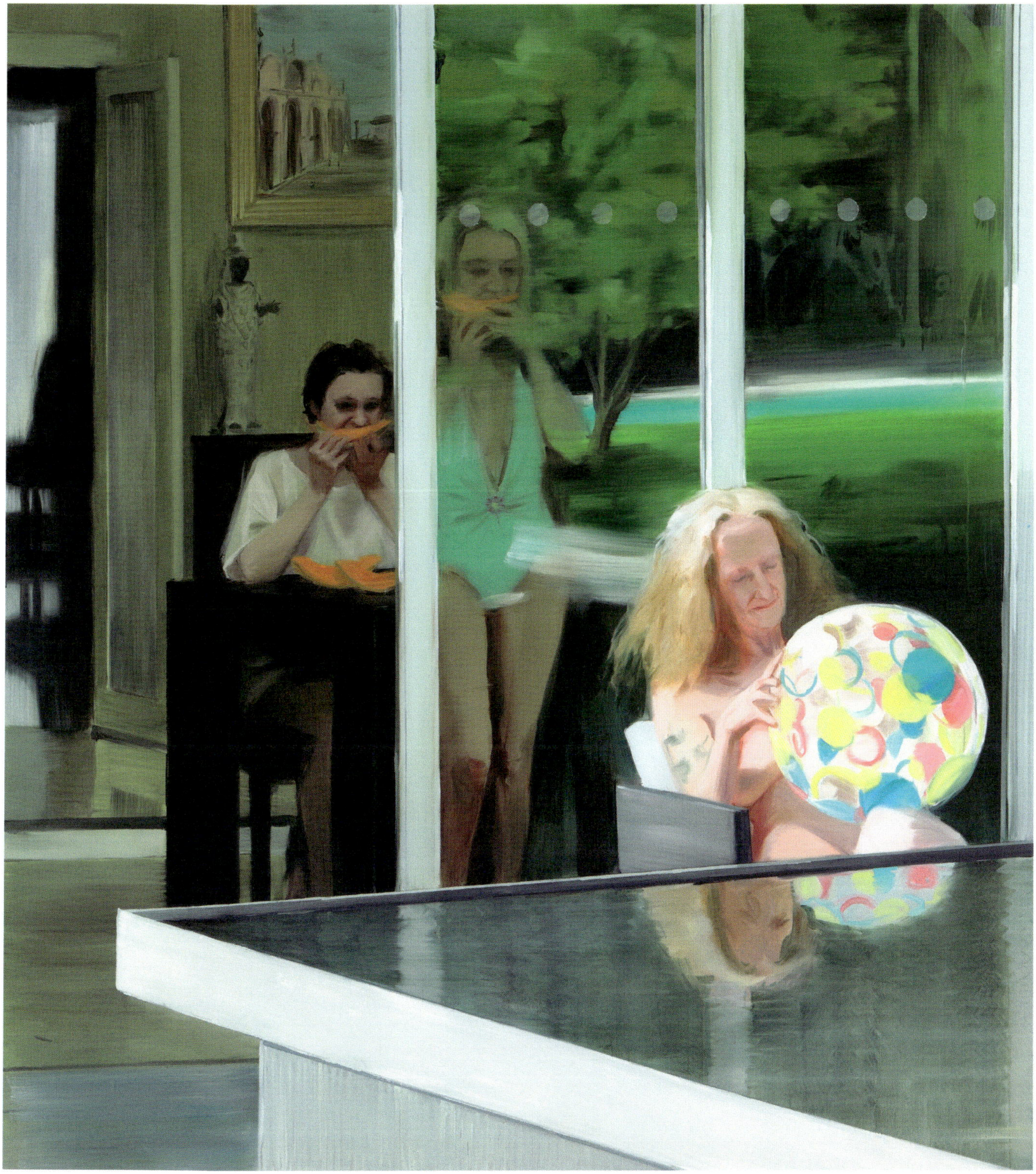

Caroline Walker
Consulting the Oracle, 2013
Oil on linen
193 × 175 cm

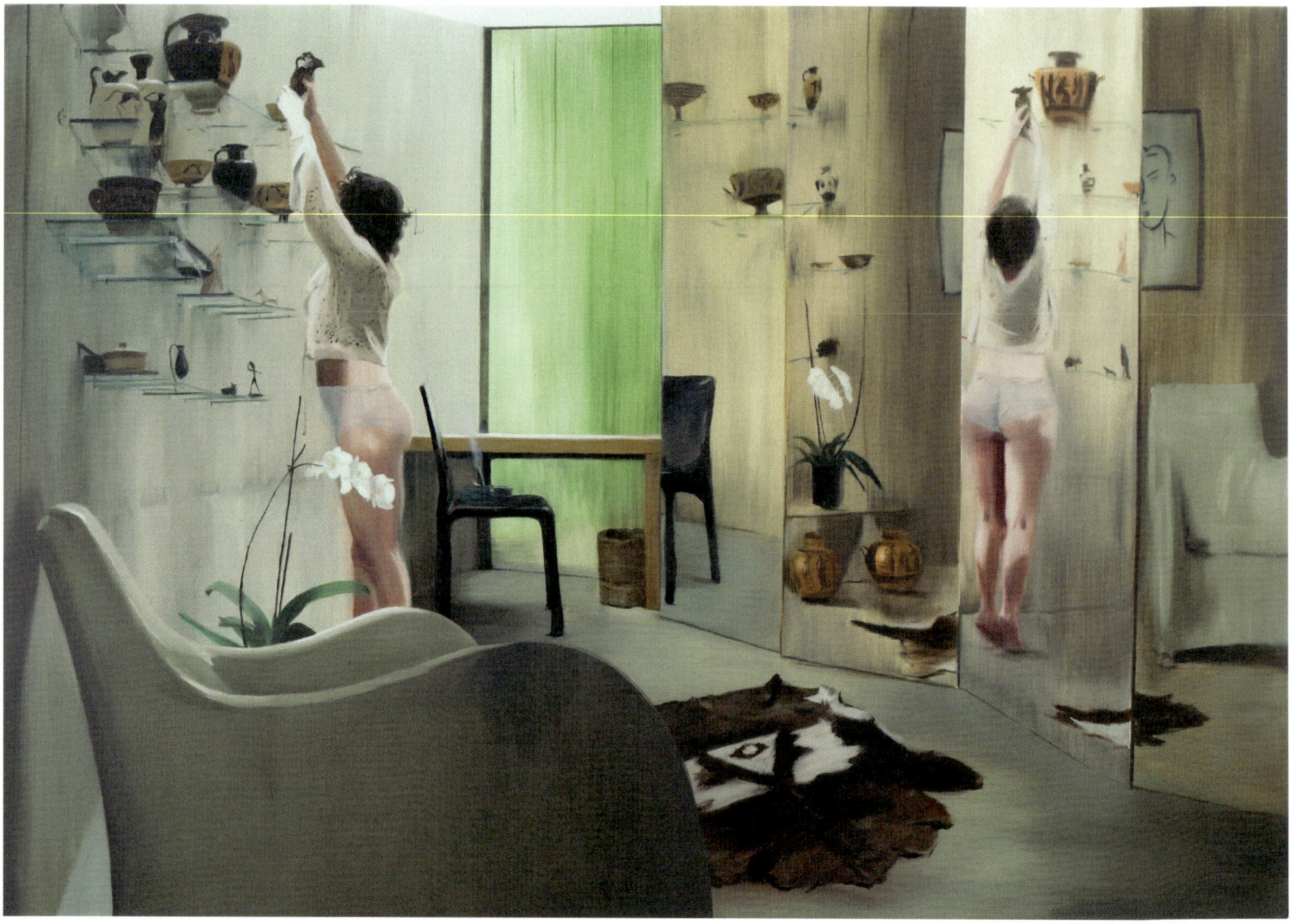

Caroline Walker
Conservation, 2010
Oil on canvas
200 × 290 cm

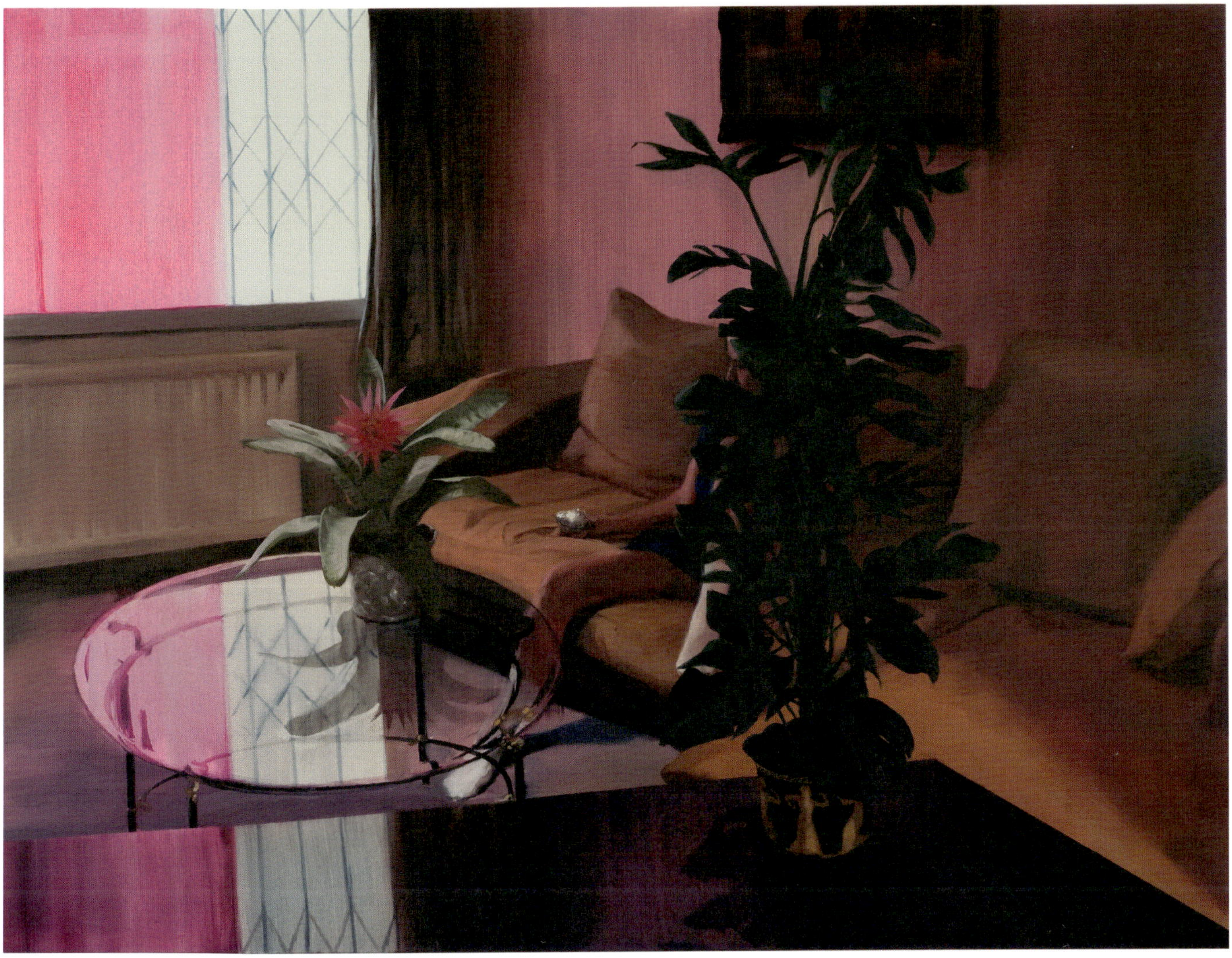

Caroline Walker
The Violet Hour, 2010
Oil on canvas
180 × 240 cm

All © and courtesy of Caroline Walker
Photos: Gustavo Valdes

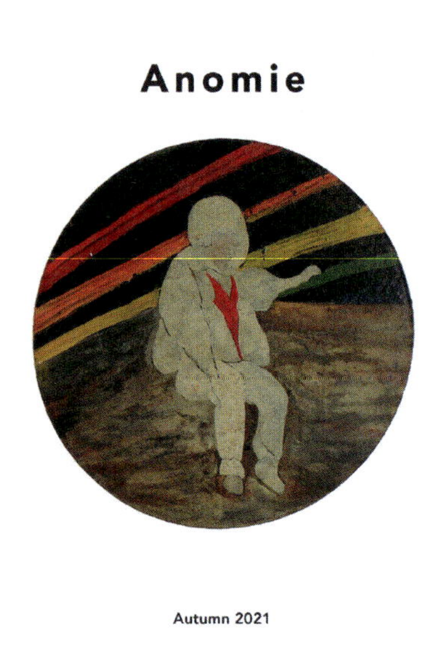
Anomie
Autumn 2021

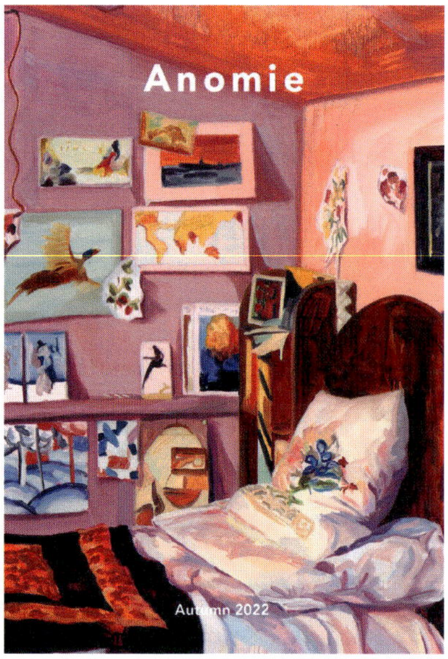
Anomie
Autumn 2022

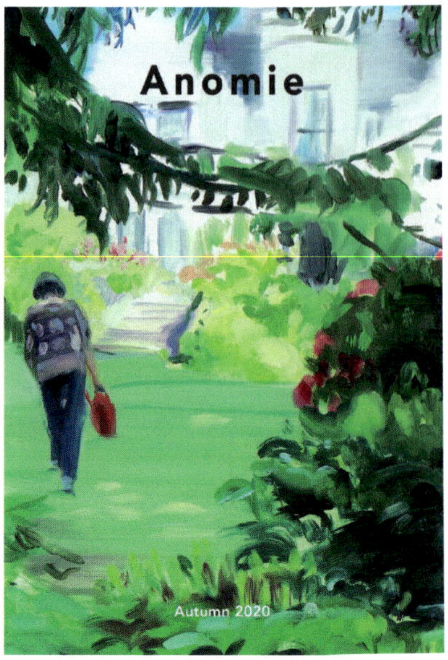
Anomie
Autumn 2020

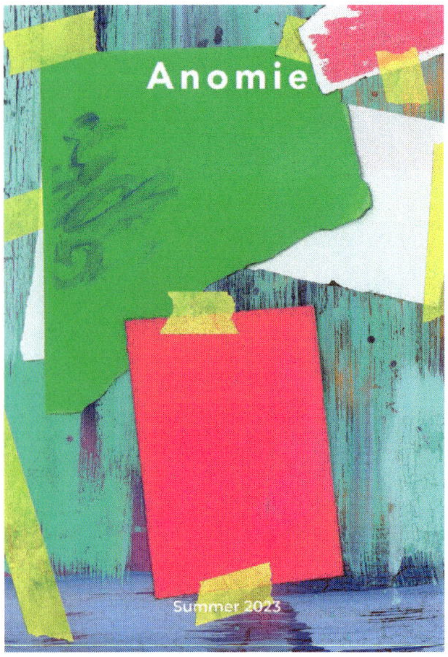
Anomie
Summer 2023

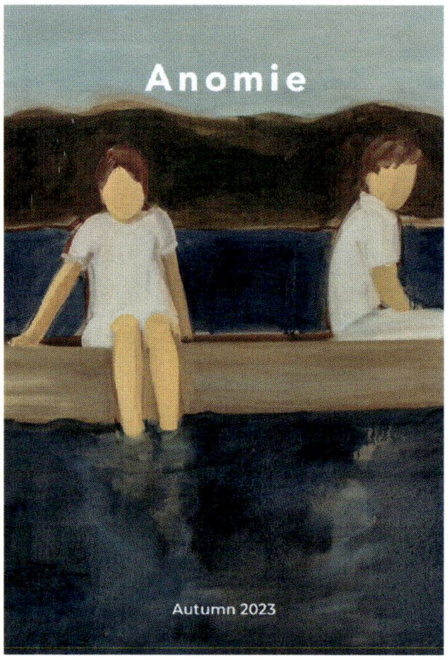
Anomie
Autumn 2023

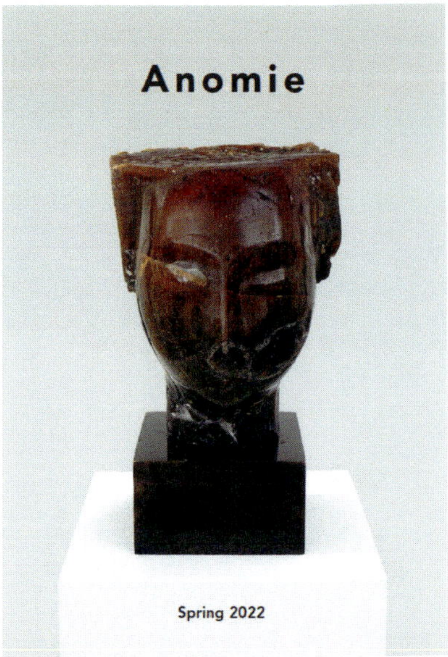
Anomie
Spring 2022

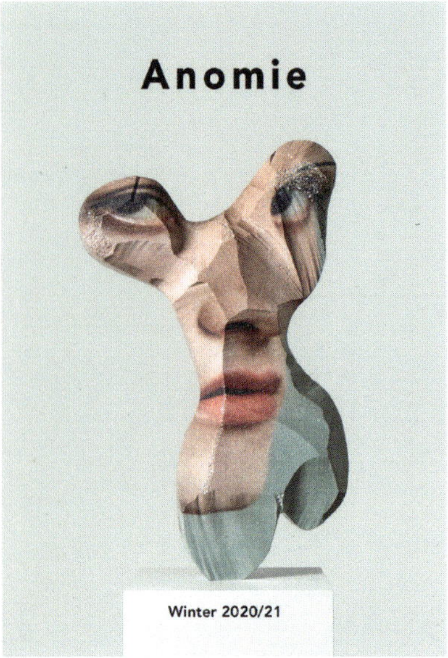
Anomie
Winter 2020/21

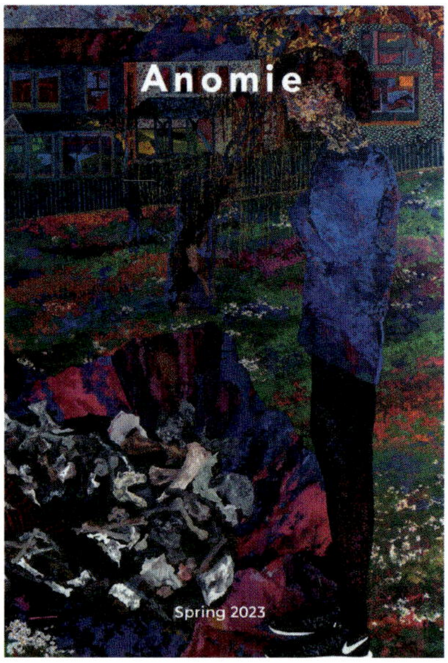
Anomie
Spring 2023

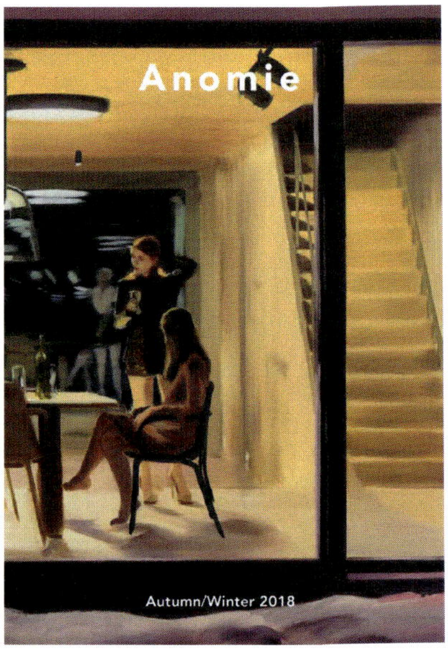
Anomie
Autumn/Winter 2018

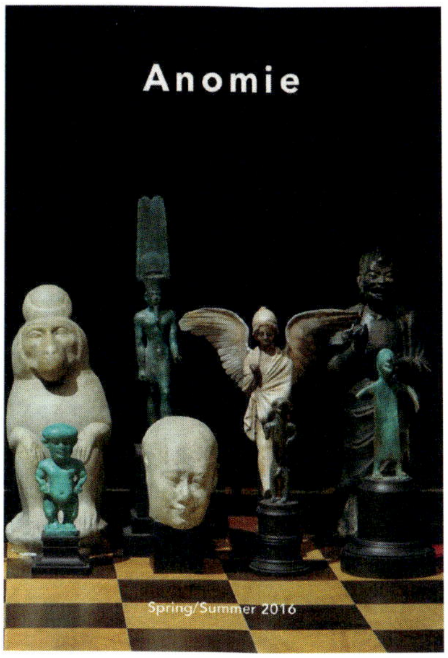
Anomie
Spring/Summer 2016

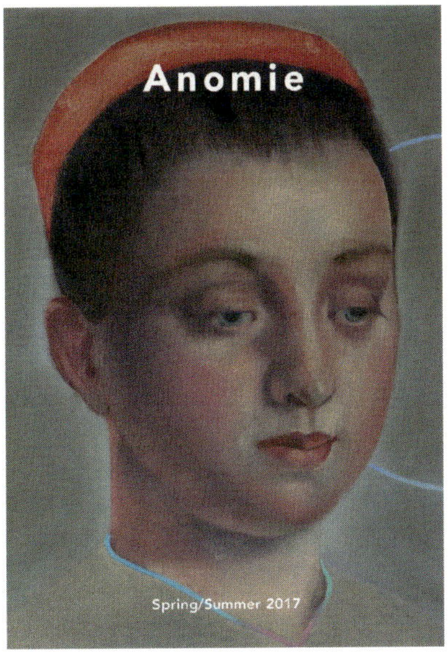
Anomie
Spring/Summer 2017

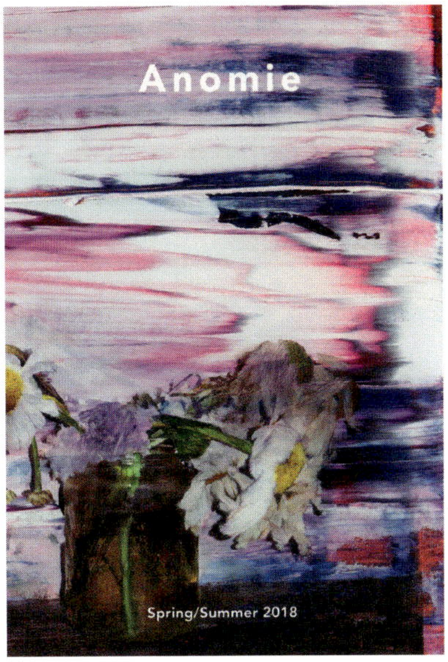
Anomie
Spring/Summer 2018

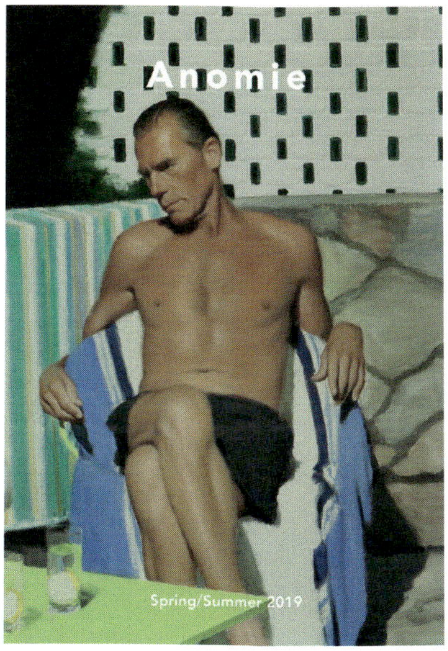
Anomie
Spring/Summer 2019

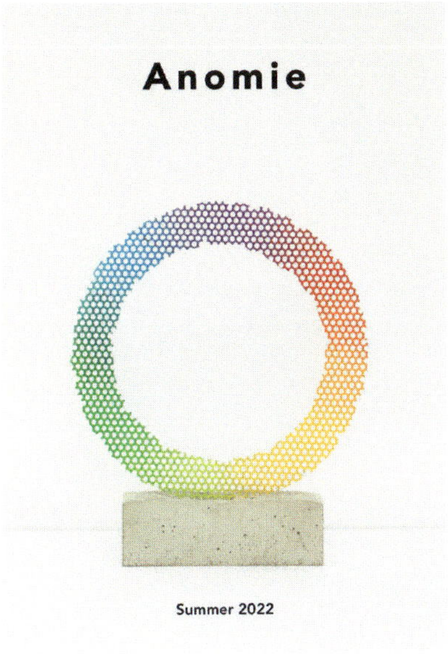
Anomie
Summer 2022

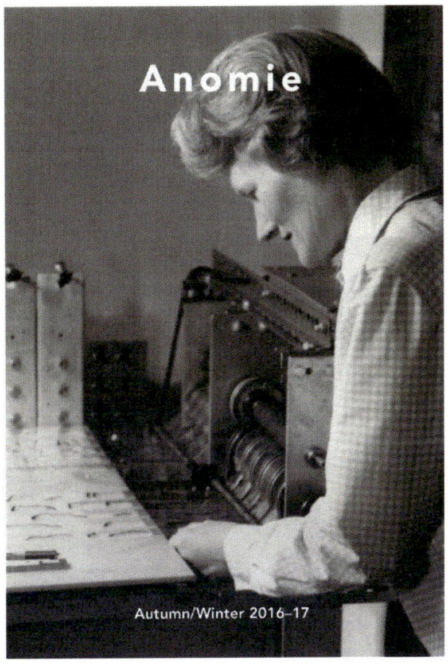
Anomie
Autumn/Winter 2016–17

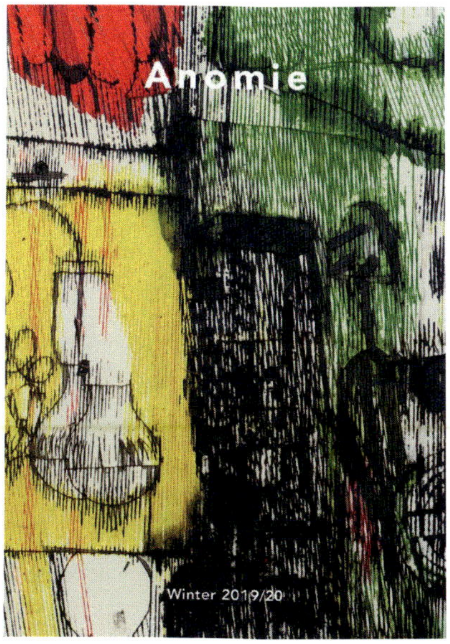
Anomie
Winter 2019/20

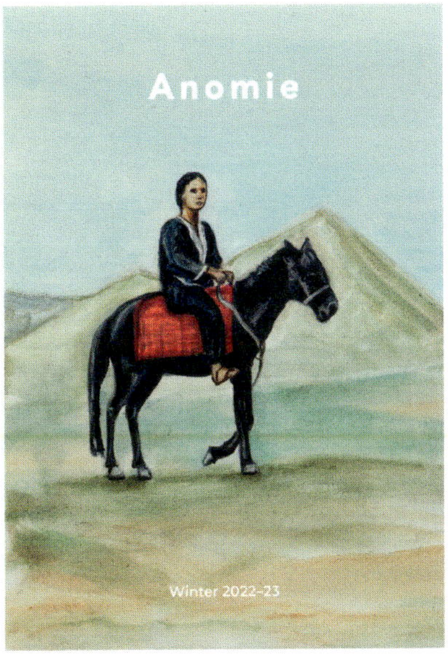
Anomie
Winter 2022–23

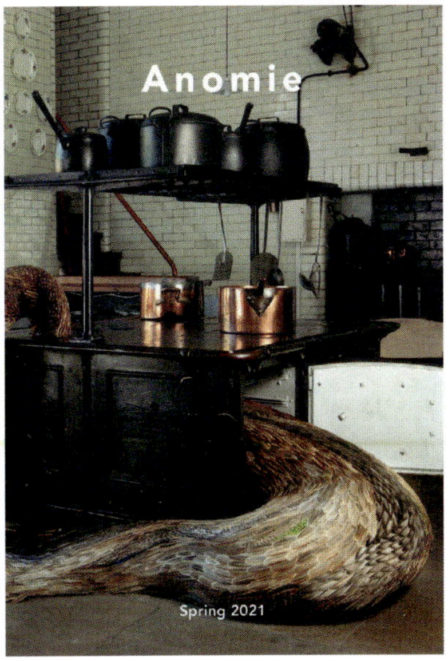
Anomie
Spring 2021

Colophon

Anomie
Ten Years of Independent Arts Publishing

Edited by Anna McNay
Designed by Anomie Studio with Joe Gilmore
Proofreading by William Lambie
Production by Hurtwood
Printed and bound in the UK

Q&A portrait photography © Peter Mallet

Published in 2023 by Anomie Publishing, London
www.anomie-publishing.com

© Anomie Publishing, 2023
Artwork © the respective artists

All rights reserved. No part of this publication may be stored, shared, reproduced or transmitted in any form or by any means without prior permission in writing from the publishers.

A catalogue record for this book is available from the British Library

ISBN: 978-1-910221-55-6

Cover image:
Justin Mortimer
Hoax 5, 2017
Oil and acrylic on canvas
51 × 51 cm
Courtesy of the artist and Parafin, London

Acknowledgements:

Matt Price would like to take this opportunity to thank all of the amazing artists, galleries, arts organisations, supporters, writers, editors, photographers, designers, reprographers, production managers, printers, binders, handlers, distributors, sales reps, shippers, wholesalers and retailers who have helped to make, publish, distribute and sell our books.

A particular thanks to Anomie's regular collaborators: Joe Gilmore, William Lambie, Anneka French, Anna McNay; Elisa Rosolin, Jean-Marc Evans and Girard Kratz; Francis Atterbury, Jo Hilton, Eliza Scott and Roger Jones; Richard Deal, Dan Kosta, Adam Penney and Dave Steggle; Jonathan Bortolazzi; Roy Killen; Demi Eve; Matt Appleton; Jo Deans; Herman Lelie and Stefania Bonelli; Peter B. Willberg; Richard and Florence Ingleby; Mark Sanders.

Personal thanks to my wife Coco Price, to Richard Price, Catherine, Philip and Lucy Haines, Bruce and Beverley Hayter, Vicky Desando and Giovanni Gallo.

Anomie Publishing